KASHMIR

D1474800

A project of the International Peace Academy

KASHMIR

New Voices,
New Approaches

edited by
Waheguru Pal Singh Sidhu
Bushra Asif
Cyrus Samii

LYNNE
RIENNER
PUBLISHERS

BOULDER
LONDON

oclc 62089911

Published in the United States of America in 2006 by
Lynne Rienner Publishers, Inc.
1800 30th Street, Boulder, Colorado 80301
www.rienner.com

and in the United Kingdom by
Lynne Rienner Publishers, Inc.
3 Henrietta Street, Covent Garden, London WC2E 8LU

Library of Congress Cataloging-in-Publication Data
Kashmir : new voices, new approaches / edited by Waheguru Pal Singh Sidhu,
Bushra Asif, and Cyrus Samii.
        p. cm.
    "A project of the International Peace Academy."
    Includes bibliographical references and index.
    ISBN-13: 978-1-58826-432-9 (hardcover : alk. paper)
    ISBN-10: 1-58826-432-7 (hardcover : alk. paper)
    ISBN-13: 978-1-58826-408-4 (pbk. : alk. paper)
    ISBN-10: 1-58826-408-4 (pbk. : alk. paper)
    1. Jammu and Kashmir (India)—Politics and government—21st century. 2. Azad
Kashmir—Politics and government—21st century. 3. Insurgency—India—Jammu and
Kashmir. 4. National security—South Asia. I. Sidhu, Waheguru Pal Singh. II. Bushra
Asif. III. Samii, Cyrus. IV. International Peace Academy. V. Title.
DS485.K27K3185 2006
954'.6053—dc22

                                                                    2005029706

British Cataloguing in Publication Data
A Cataloguing in Publication record for this book
is available from the British Library.

Printed and bound in the United States of America

The paper used in this publication meets the requirements
of the American National Standard for Permanence of
Paper for Printed Library Materials Z39.48-1992.

5 4 3 2 1

Contents

Foreword

Terje Rød-Larsen
President, International Peace Academy

The International Peace Academy (IPA) presents this volume, *Kashmir: New Voices, New Approaches*, at a hopeful time for this long-standing dispute. Old assumptions are being challenged about whether the rivalry between India and Pakistan is truly ingrained in each country's identity and whether notions of sovereignty can be modified to create space for forging peace in Jammu and Kashmir. Surely these issues are now open for the people of South Asia to decide. In recent years, voices in official circles, in civil society, and among experts in South Asia seem to indicate that the time for confrontation and standoff has passed. But of course, even if the best of intentions prevail, progress toward peace—as this volume argues—is never short or easy.

This volume is the product of an IPA project that sought to build the capacity of new voices, identify ways to move the agenda forward, and critically examine the role, if any, of international actors. The project and the volume were launched at a workshop in January 2005 hosted by the Institute of Defence and Strategic Studies (IDSS) in Singapore, which brought together a remarkable group of South Asia specialists and officials. The editors of the volume—Waheguru Pal Singh Sidhu, Bushra Asif, and Cyrus Samii—have drawn upon their rich combined experience in the region and on their work on separate, but in many ways related, issues of development, peace processes in other parts of the world, and international institutions.

We are deeply grateful to the International Development Research Centre in Canada for their support of this project. We are also indebted to our core donors—the governments of Denmark, Norway, Sweden, and Switzerland; the Ford Foundation; the William and Flora Hewlett Foundation; and the Rockefeller Foundation—whose generous contributions enable projects such as this one.

As peacemakers, the international community in general and the United Nations in particular have long been cast out to the margins of the Kashmir conflict, the occasional crisis mediation by a superpower notwithstanding. This is not to say that the international community is not self-conscious about this. Quite controversially, in December 2004, the chairman of the United Nations Secretary-General's High Level Panel on Threats, Challenges and Change, Anand Panyarachun, singled out the Kashmir issue along with the issues of Palestine and the Korean peninsula. In his transmittal letter of the panel's report to the Secretary-General, he emphasized that "no amount of systemic changes" to UN institutions would bring about significant progress toward realizing the ambitions of the UN Charter if "efforts are not redoubled" to resolve these three issues, "which continue to fester and to feed the new threats that we now face." At the same time, there is little doubt that it will have to be up to the people of South Asia to provide the major push for a resolution of the Kashmir issue. The international community cannot be passive, but must think creatively in identifying a constructive role.

In this volume, Jammu and Kashmir, on both the Indian and the Pakistani sides of the Line of Control, is presented as a complex political and social scene, rather than the passive subject of an international dispute. In my own experience as a mediator and envoy in the Middle East, I can say with conviction that such a mental map of these internal push and pull factors is absolutely necessary; without it, you will likely get nowhere in peacemaking. By opening up this possible line of thought, as well as others, it is our hope that this volume will contribute to a deeper understanding of the challenges and opportunities at hand for making and sustaining peace in Jammu and Kashmir.

Acknowledgments

This volume would not have been possible without the commitment and hard work of many dear colleagues and friends. Our foremost thanks go to the contributors for their dedication and good humor through the editorial processes. Of course, editorial norms and styles are not entirely consistent around the globe, and it has been an illuminating experience for us all to craft a work intended for audiences both within South Asia and in the broader international community.

A number of others have also contributed to the project, although their work could not be included in the volume. These include Mehraj Hajini, Rashid Ahmad Khan, and Arjimand Hussein Talib, to whom we are grateful for the important viewpoints that they offered. The anonymous reviewers provided insightful and detailed comments, for which we are also grateful. We also give our deepest thanks to Lynne Rienner for recognizing the value of a new, forward-looking contribution on Kashmir at this time of historic change in South Asia, and to Lesli Brooks Athanasoulis for her invaluable support in manifesting this vision.

The IPA's project "Kashmir: New Voices, New Approaches" served as our institutional home as we prepared this volume. We are very grateful to former IPA president David M. Malone and vice president Neclâ Tschirgi for their inspiration and leadership in developing the project. Our thanks go to the IPA's current president, Terje Rød-Larsen, and vice president, Elizabeth Cousens, for their strong support. Our very deep appreciation goes to Clara Lee for ushering us through the publication process, and to Vanessa Hawkins for her support and work on the program at the IPA. Many others at the IPA have been essential to the project and volume, both intellectually and operationally, and to them we are also grateful.

We had the pleasure of cohosting a workshop in January 2005 with the Institute of Defence and Strategic Studies (IDSS) in Singapore, and we want to thank IDSS director Barry Desker and the formidable academic and administrative team he has assembled there. The project would not have been possible without the generous backing of the International Development Research Centre (IDRC) in Canada, and we are especially grateful to Navsharan Singh and Pamela Scholey at IDRC for both their intellectual and institutional support. We also thank IPA's core funders—the governments of Denmark, Norway, Sweden, and Switzerland; the Ford Foundation; the William and Flora Hewlett Foundation; and the Rockefeller Foundation—whose support enabled this project. We have had numerous very fruitful exchanges with other scholars, journalists, and officials involved in complementary efforts in South Asia, North America, and Europe, and we thank them greatly for their input.

—*Waheguru Pal Singh Sidhu,*
Bushra Asif,
Cyrus Samii

Jammu and Kashmir

1

Introduction

Waheguru Pal Singh Sidhu

Kashmir, along with Palestine and the Korean peninsula, remains one of the three most intractable challenges that have defied solution, despite the various efforts of the international community over the past half-century.[1] These three crucial regional problems, which emerged soon after the end of World War II, continued to fester during and after the Cold War and pose a serious threat to international peace and security.[2] In fact, the post–Cold War period has seen a dramatic escalation of tensions and violence in all three regions. The three also exemplify the concept of regional conflict complexes.[3] In Kashmir (as in the Israeli-Palestinian conflict), these complexes are further complicated by their linkages to transnational terrorist networks and the nuclearization of the region.

Wedged between the two new nuclear-armed states of India and Pakistan, Kashmir has been described as "the most dangerous place on earth."[4] The region not only has witnessed the most sustained level of violence anywhere in the world since the end of the Cold War but is recognized as a crisis-prone nuclear flashpoint. Kashmir is also symptomatic of the challenge posed by transnational terrorist groups both to states and to indigenous liberation movements. Although accurate figures for casualties in Kashmir are difficult to come by, estimates of the total number of fatalities since the start of the latest *tahrik* (movement) in 1989 range from at least 30,000 to as many as 60,000.[5] Since the mid-1990s, the violence in Kashmir has accounted for an average of over 2,700 lives annually—equivalent to one September 11 episode and well above the death toll in the Middle East—every year.[6] Yet the efforts of the international community in addressing this lasting conflict have remained in general sporadic or, as in the case of the ongoing UN efforts in particular, painfully ineffective.[7] This contrast is very evident when compared to the sustained and, sometimes, effective attention paid to the Middle East by the international community as well as other key actors, such as the United States and the European Union.

Although the devastating Kashmir earthquake of 8 October 2005 caused nearly 90,000 deaths (more than the total estimated casualties in the ongoing conflict) and did see greater involvement on the part of the international community, including the North Atlantic Treaty Organization forces operating in neighboring Afghanistan, primarily in terms of relief operations, it has not facilitated a resolution of the crisis.[8] Indeed, the natural tragedy did not lead to a greater international engagement with the parties to the conflict, nor did it particularly improve relations between Islamabad and New Delhi. In fact, several factors ensured that the status quo of the conflict was sustained. This is in contrast to the Aceh experience, when the tsunami of 26 December 2004 proved to be a turning point for hammering out a peace agreement between Indonesia and the Acehnese and moving that enduring conflict further along the path toward peace.

Moreover, even when these international actors do pay attention to the South Asian region, it is invariably confined to interactions at the interstate level with Islamabad and New Delhi. While relations at the interstate level remain central to an ultimate resolution in Kashmir, it is important to recognize that the Kashmir issue exists on at least four interrelated levels: international, interstate, intrastate, and nonstate. All these dimensions will have to be addressed if a long-term resolution to Kashmir is to be sought.[9]

The Four Dimensions of the Kashmir Conflict

Since the emergence of India and Pakistan as independent states in 1947, the Kashmir issue has dominated the adversarial relations between New Delhi and Islamabad. The accession to India by Maharaja Hari Singh, the ruler of Jammu and Kashmir (J&K), in October 1947 was followed by a war over control of the territory. The Indian government appealed to the United Nations Security Council (UNSC), which in 1948 mandated a mission to secure a cease-fire, complete a troop withdrawal, and hold a plebiscite to determine J&K's final status. The mandate was never fully realized, although a cease-fire line drawn when the fighting stopped in 1949 was formally recognized as the Line of Control—the LoC—between the two countries in the 1972 Simla Agreement, and to this day the mandate remains a key point of contention in the conflict. In effect, the LoC divided the erstwhile princely state of J&K into two parts: *Azad* (Independent) Jammu and Kashmir (AJK), which is territory administered by Pakistan since 1947, and Indian-administered Jammu and Kashmir (IJK), which is territory administered by India since 1947.[10]

Since 1948, India and Pakistan have fought at least four conventional wars, and three of them were in, and over the issue of, Kashmir. Yet none of them led to the successful resolution of the Kashmir crisis, primarily because neither side has the necessary conventional military superiority to ensure an outcome in its favor.[11] While both sides increasingly recognize the futility of the military option, in the absence of a collective desire to pursue other, nonmilitary approaches, they have inevitably fallen back on this dangerous alternative. Following their reciprocal nuclear tests and pre-sentiments of the overt presence of nuclear weapons on both sides, pursuing the military option has become even more perilous. It is this recognition that has led both New Delhi and Islamabad to heed the persistent plea of the international community to seek to normalize relations.

However, bilateral diplomatic attempts at normalizing India-Pakistan relations have been frustrating and have generally ended in failure. They have fluctuated from the promise of the Lahore Declaration (February 1999) to the denouncement of the Agra summit (July 2001) to the hope of the Delhi summit (April 2005). Against this backdrop and despite the general sense of optimism, there is, predictably, some pessimism about the prospects of the latest cycle of resumed dialogue. Although the round of the comprehensive dialogue revived in January 2004 was described as "irreversible" by the principal interlocutors, it remains to be seen whether the dialogue will sustain.[12] The challenge, however, remains not only in sustaining this dialogue but also in ensuring that it is insulated from the day-to-day setbacks (in the form of terrorist attacks, for instance) that have often derailed the process in the past.

In addition to the interstate relationship between Islamabad and New Delhi, the crucial intrastate relationship between New Delhi and Srinagar on the one hand and Islamabad and Muzaffarabad on the other has to be taken into account in effectively developing a process to deal with the Kashmir issue. These intranational relations have always been significant, but they have become even more complex and multifaceted in the post-1989 period. For instance, in IJK before 1989, the National Conference and the Congress Party dominated relations between Srinagar and New Delhi respectively. Two additional types of political actors emerged in 1990: first, political parties, like the People's Democratic Party (PDP), who opposed the National Conference but were willing to work within the Indian constitution; second, coinciding with the start of the *tahrik*, a host of militant groups and political parties, including the Jammu and Kashmir Liberation Front, which advocated the overthrow of Indian rule in Kashmir. In 1993 the All Parties Hurriyat Conference (APHC)—a coalition of over twenty-six anti-India political parties as well as the Jammu and Kashmir Democratic Freedom Party, led by Shabir Shah—became key political actors. Finally, the formation of the PDP-Congress coalition government following the

2002 state elections (which the APHC boycotted) marked a new era as a non–National Conference government took power in Srinagar. Simultaneously, the APHC, which refused to join the political process, emerged as the leading political opposition to both New Delhi and the PDP-Congress combine. This forced the Bharatiya Janata Party–led coalition in New Delhi to deal not only with a new type of elected government in Srinagar but also with the unelected APHC through an interlocutor. The split in the ranks of the APHC in late 2003 has made the relationship between the center and the state even more complicated. This has also become evident in the differing attitudes toward Pakistan among these constituents of the APHC as well as their different attitudes toward making the Srinagar-Muzaffarabad bus journey.

These developments in IJK indicate a dramatic change and further complication of the political landscape. Although AJK, the Pakistan-administered part of the region, has not witnessed a similar upheaval, its political map has also undergone some changes; the Muslim Conference, led by Sardar Abdul Qayyum Khan, which dominated its politics for nearly half a century, finally lost its sway in 1990. Along with these political changes, Kashmir has also witnessed the emergence of an active civil society, which has begun to articulate governance and development issues. How New Delhi, Islamabad, and the political parties on both sides of the LoC in Kashmir manage this relationship will also affect the eventual resolution of the Kashmir issue.

Although the Kashmiri diaspora and other nonstate actors have always had a role in the tortured history of Kashmir, there has been a noticeable ascendancy in their involvement in the post–Cold War period, which also coincided with the commencement of the latest *tahrik*. Many of them, such as the Kashmiri American Council, mainly comprising Americans of Kashmiri origin, are politically active and have close ties to the APHC, which they consider to be the "authentic and legitimate voice of the majority of the people of Kashmir."[13] Most of these organizations also support dialogue among India, Pakistan, and the APHC.

In contrast there are armed groups of nonstate actors of practically every hue and calling who do not seek a peaceful solution or dialogue among the key parties. Instead, they seek to effect a change in the status purely through the barrel of the gun. As many of these transnational groups fought and emerged from Afghanistan, they are also battle-hardy and have few stakes in maintaining *kashmiriyat* (the cultural traditions of Kashmir, including the tolerance of other religions). Some of these actors are also linked to international terrorist groups, such as Al-Qaida, and see Afghanistan under Taliban rule as a model for Kashmir. Given their access to specialized military training and sophisticated weapons, these groups of foreign mercenaries have the ability to complicate the situation even further both at the interstate and at the intrastate level, especially as the national or the subnational actors' control over them has become tenuous.

There has been a series of impressive initiatives to deal with the Kashmir issue in the recent past by international, national, subnational, and even nonstate actors. The last category includes a number of non-governmental organizations and think tanks based in the West (primarily the United States and the United Kingdom), staffed principally by Western scholars, academics, and activists who have some interaction or consultations with leaders, scholars, and activists in India, Pakistan, and Kashmir. However, given their preoccupation with the prospect that the Kashmir crisis could lead to a nuclear war, most of these initiatives, whether indigenous or external, have tended to concentrate on the interstate level where the nuclear arsenals are located. Moreover they have also, understandably, tended to focus on the immediate rather than the medium to long term. One notable exception is the Kashmir Study Group (KSG), which has produced, perhaps, the only serious set of long-term proposals for the resolution of Kashmir.[14] However, the absence of voices from South Asia in this study makes it difficult to accept as anything but a noble effort by non–South Asians to deal with a problem that is, clearly, external to them.

Given the multifaceted challenges posed by Kashmir, it is clear that any attempt to develop a process to tackle them will have to address the international, regional, national, and subnational levels, in the short-, medium- and long-term timeframe. This calls for an innovative and multidimensional approach. This volume is an effort in that direction.

Outline of the Volume

The first section of the volume includes chapters on the subnational and national dimensions of the Kashmir conflict. The volume begins with chapters by Inpreet Kaur and Bushra Asif on IJK and AJK, respectively. Kaur documents the political, economic, and religious transformations that have taken place in IJK since the outbreak of militancy in 1989 and describes the ongoing turf battles that continue to undermine the resolution process. Based on this background, Kaur stresses that Kashmiri ownership of measures to improve their security and economic circumstances is essential to bring about the change in attitudes necessary as a foundation for peace. Asif documents Pakistan's heavy-handedness in governing political and economic affairs within AJK, suggesting that nonetheless, given Pakistan's more open attitude toward international engagement, the international community may be able to play a more prominent role in AJK with development and humanitarian assistance. In addition, promotion of political, economic, and social relations across the Line of Control dividing the two Kashmirs would bring a major sense of relief to both communities.

The next two chapters, by Suba Chandran and Rizwan Zeb, address militancy in the conflict, examining the approaches by governments in New Delhi and Islamabad to deal with this phenomenon. They conclude that both India and Pakistan still lack coherent and effective policies, which severely impedes the peace process.

Kavita Suri and Shaheen Akhtar examine women's experiences in IJK and AJK and how their societal roles have been affected by the conflict. Suri and Akhtar use extensive surveys of attitudes of women toward the conflict and programs by and for women in both sides of Kashmir to detail how women have been both victims of and participants in the perpetuation of violence in Kashmir. They also observe that the role of women is evolving into that of agents keen on resolving the conflict.

P. R. Chari and Hasan-Askari Rizvi examine the interstate dimension of the conflict, providing perspectives from New Delhi and Islamabad, respectively. Chari and Rizvi each explain how Kashmir features centrally in India and Pakistan's bilateral relationship. The authors also identify the principal actors and sources of the national Kashmir policy in India and Pakistan and suggest that working around the existing status quo might offer the best options for a viable solution. This is in line with the "soft border" idea promoted at the highest levels by both India and Pakistan beginning in 2005.

The second section of the volume examines the broader international dimensions of the conflict. Amitav Acharya and Arabinda Acharya lead off this section with a chapter that applies international relations theories to the Kashmir dispute. They conclude that regional processes of norm development and institution building are promising ways to ease tension between India and Pakistan and thus create space for peacemaking in the Kashmir conflict. Waheguru Pal Singh Sidhu follows with a chapter identifying a set of evolving post–Cold War norms that compel the world community to remain attentive to the Kashmir issue. However, he argues that despite this compulsion, international community engagement at the political and security levels is likely to remain episodic, sporadic, and generally ineffective. The third chapter in the section is by John Thomson, who explores the ways that India and Pakistan's overt acquisition of nuclear weapons affects the Kashmir conflict, and also how the Kashmir conflict affects nuclear risks in South Asia. Thomson concludes that "nuclearization" in itself has not yet made a perceptible difference in India's and Pakistan's attitudes toward Kashmir, but that the stakes have escalated dramatically. Eventually, India and Pakistan should find it in their interest to settle the Kashmir issue, but external nudging, perhaps by the United States, is called for.

The final section of the volume examines processes toward the settlement of the conflict. The chapter by Iffat Idris focuses on the "internal" peace process, which would involve resolving the armed conflict in IJK and addressing the grievances of Kashmiris in IJK and AJK. Idris argues that the "potential for resolution of internal issues in AJK and IJK definitely exists, but its realization is by no means certain." Nonetheless, Idris contends that the logic of the situation compels the actors to address the internal dimension as a precursor to any final status settlement at the Indo-Pak level. In the concluding chapter, Cyrus Samii discusses some specific sources of the conflict's intractability and suggests ways in which they can be addressed in the peace process. Samii argues that an effective peace process will require Kashmiris to put their political house in order and will compel New Delhi and Islamabad to demonstrate that they have come to terms with the legitimacy of Kashmiri grievances. New institutional arrangements and third-party support, in the form of either monitoring or economic assistance packages, could help to promote the peace process.

Conclusion

The Kashmir crisis poses a unique challenge to the international community. It is a twentieth-century problem born out of the process of decolonization, bred by the dominant concept of the nation-state and sovereignty as well as the right to self-determination and the sanctity of borders, and sought to be resolved through military means. Kashmir has now evolved into a twenty-first–century conflict, with characteristics of a regional conflict formation, with a distinct and dangerous nuclear dimension, and with militancy evidencing growing links to global terror networks; and a potentially rising state, coupled with a state at risk. Thus, resolution of the Kashmir deadlock now requires a twenty-first–century solution based not on Westphalian approaches but on innovative approaches to sovereignty, such as soft borders and subnational-, national-, and regional-level engagement. This volume seeks to offer some possible new approaches in this direction. The challenge, of course, remains in achieving consensus and operationalizing these new approaches.

Notes

1. See *A More Secure World: Our Shared Responsibility,* report of the United Nations High-Level Panel on Threats, Challenges and Change, 2004, p. xi, http://www.un.org/secureworld/.
2. There is no single, comprehensive study that deals with all three regions simultaneously. However, there is a vast literature dealing with each of these regions separately. For the most recent scholarly analysis of the Kashmir crisis, see Sumantra Bose, *Kashmir: Roots of Conflict, Paths to Peace* (Cambridge, MA:

Harvard University Press, 2003); Victoria Schofield, *Kashmir in Conflict: India, Pakistan and the Unending War* (New Delhi: Viva, 2003); and *New Priorities in South Asia,* Independent Task Force Report, Council on Foreign Relations (30 October 2003).

3. Regional conflict complexes, which have emerged as a major subject of study among international relations scholars in the post–Cold War period, have been defined as "sets of transnational conflicts that form mutually reinforcing linkages with each other throughout a region, making for more protracted and obdurate conflicts." See Charles K. Cater, *The Regionalization of Conflict and Intervention,* Report of the International Peace Academy New York Seminar, West Point (5–9 May 2003), pp. 3–4.

4. US President Bill Clinton used this description just before his visit to India and Pakistan in March 2000. See Jonathan Karp and Glenn Burkins, "Clinton to Face Diplomatic Challenge During His Visit to India: Pakistan Relations, Arms Control Rank High on His List," *Wall Street Journal,* 17 March 2000, p. 1.

5. See International Crisis Group, *Kashmir: The View from Srinagar* (ICG Asia Report No. 41), Brussels and Islamabad, 21 November 2002, for a brief history of the current *tahrik.* For figures of fatalities see p. 2 of the same report. See also Government of India, Ministry of Home Affairs, *Annual Report 2004–2005;* data collected by South Asia Intelligence Review (SAIR) (www.satp.org/satporgtp/sair/) and Rashed Uz Zaman, "WMD Terrorism in South Asia: Trends and Implications," *Journal of International Affairs* 7, no. 3 (September–November 2002). Zaman argues that "the number of annual fatalities in terrorist-related violence in South Asia far exceeds the death toll in the Middle East, the traditional cradle of terrorism." See also Praveen Swami, *Quickstep or Kadam Taal? The Elusive Search for Peace in Jammu and Kashmir,* United States Institute for Peace Special Report 133.

6. See Government of India, Ministry of Home Affairs, *Annual Report 2004–2005,* p. 19, and Annexure-II, p. 164.

7. For instance, the United Nations Monitoring Group in India and Pakistan (UNMOGIP) has acquired the dubious distinction of being the longest-running but still ineffective operation of its kind. Similarly, efforts by UN Secretary General Kofi Annan to use his good offices in 2002 to ease tensions between India and Pakistan were also thwarted by New Delhi.

8. See US Geological Survey, "Significant Earthquakes of the World for 2005," at http://neic.usgs.gov/neis/eqlists/sig_2005.html for geological details; for NATO's "Pakistan Earthquake Relief Operation," see http://www.nato.int/issues/Pakistan_earthquake/.

9. While all four dimensions are now recognized by scholars, there are still no book-length studies that address the international, interstate, intrastate, and non-state aspects of the Kashmir conflict. However, a series of reports put out by the International Crisis Group does cover these dimensions.

10. Throughout this volume "AJK" refers to the Pakistan-administered and "IJK" to the Indian-administered part of Jammu and Kashmir. "Jammu and Kashmir," abbreviated as "J&K," refers to the whole of the pre-1947 princely state. "Kashmir" is an abbreviated way of saying "Jammu and Kashmir," and also focuses attention on the area where much of the fighting has taken place.

11. Although on paper the Indian military is certainly bigger than the Pakistani military, the terrain of Kashmir imposes severe restrictions on deploying this larger force. This became apparent in the Kargil conflict of 1999 when a small Pakistani force was able to effectively pin down a much larger Indian force. While the larger Indian force was able to *prevent* further intrusions by Pakistan in Kashmir, it was

unable to *dislodge* the Pakistani troops from *all* the positions occupied. Thus it is unlikely that India will ever be able to mobilize enough troops to occupy parts of Kashmir presently under Pakistani control.

12. See Joint Statement, India-Pakistan, 18 April 2005, New Delhi, http://meaindia.nic.in/speech/2005/04/18js01.htm, and Amit Baruah, "India-Pakistan Peace Process 'Irreversible,'" *The Hindu,* 19 April 2005.

13. See the Kashmiri American Council website for details: http://www.kashmiri.com/.

14. The group is led by a prominent Kashmiri-American, Farooq Kathwari, and includes American academics, think-tankers, congressional representatives, retired diplomats, and others knowledgeable about South Asia. The KSG also includes a handful of British, Canadian, and German members, but it is primarily an American organization. Their study emphasizes a territorial rather than a political solution and calls for the creation of a "sovereign entity (but one without an international personality)" in Kashmir. For details of these proposals see Kashmir Study Group, "Kashmir: A Way Forward," February 2005, http://www.kashmirstudygroup.net/.

PART 1

Subnational and National Dimensions

2

Warring over Peace in Kashmir

Inpreet Kaur

In a statement read upon the conclusion of their 16–18 April 2005 summit, Prime Minister Manmohan Singh of India and President Pervez Musharraf of Pakistan declared the peace process between India and Pakistan to be "irreversible." At the heart of the peace process, initiated in January 2004, is the commitment of the governments of India and Pakistan to work toward a final settlement to the Kashmir conflict.

Such a final settlement would seek to extinguish an evolving struggle that has continued over, and in, the erstwhile princely state of Jammu and Kashmir (J&K) since partition in 1947. At that time, the Hindu ruler of the Muslim-majority state, Maharaja Hari Singh, gave up his goal of independence and signed an instrument of accession to India to secure Indian military support against an invasion of irregulars from Pakistan. The instrument held that India could govern only the state's external affairs, defense, and communications. Later, in 1950, Article 370 of the Indian constitution provisionally secured these special provisions as well as the state's right to its own constitution. Internally, both Indian rule and Pakistani rule over their respective portions of J&K have been marked by democratic subversion, political manipulation, and corruption.[1] Governments in New Delhi, in collusion with pliant state governments in Indian-administered Jammu and Kashmir (IJK), have eroded most of the autonomy provisions ostensibly intended to be secured by Article 370. Many Kashmiris in IJK lost faith in their political leaders as champions of their interests after a number of opportunistic deals with New Delhi governments. These include the 1974–1975 accord between Kashmiri leader Sheikh Mohammad Abdullah and Indira Gandhi, and the connivances of the sheikh's son Farooq with Rajiv Gandhi's government to rig the 1987 IJK state assembly elections.

13

This political background inspired separatist activists in the Kashmir Valley to resort to the gun in 1989, fighting variously for a plebiscite, outright independence, or accession to Pakistan.

Since the 1989 outbreak of the armed struggle in IJK, Kashmiris (Muslims as well as the minority Hindu Pandits) have suffered devastating losses. They have faced abuses at the hands of security forces and bureaucrats, as well as from the militants supposedly fighting on their behalf. Official Indian Ministry for Home Affairs figures suggest that by mid-2005, at least 40,000 people have been killed since 1989. Equal numbers of people have been arrested and booked under the charges of either participating in or supporting the militancy. Thus, at least 80,000 families in Kashmir have suffered directly, and the indirect effects spread far and wide in this tightly knit society. Many in the Kashmir Valley would estimate that the number killed and arrested is at least double the official tally.

The Singh-Musharraf summit came on the heels of the 7 April 2005 reinstatement of a bus service linking the capital of the Kashmir Valley, Srinagar, to Muzaffarabad, the capital of Pakistan-administered Azad Jammu and Kashmir (AJK). For the people of J&K, the resumption of bus service has come as perhaps the biggest single achievement in the fifty-eight years of bitterness between India and Pakistan over the region. The excitement has resonated. In India and Pakistan, it has become fashionable to talk about the peace process, track two diplomacy, and Indian delegations visiting Pakistan or vice versa in the name of "people-to-people" contact.

However, there is less excitement and little sense of success among the local populace in IJK. Nearly everyone in the predominantly Muslim Kashmir Valley and the Muslim-majority areas in Jammu continues to witness violence and the presence of militants, although there is no trouble in the plains of Hindu-majority Jammu and in Buddhist-majority Ladakh. Spoilers within IJK are waiting for the peace process to stumble. People continue to fear the specter of the gun, and Kashmiri ownership of the peace process is missing. The ground feeling is that the Kashmiri masses once again have been ignored. According to the street gossip in the Kashmir Valley, the script for the solution on J&K was written by the Americans and is being implemented by Indian and Pakistani officials to suit US interests in South Asia.

From the vantage point of IJK, what are the prospects for the renewed peace process for resolving the Kashmir conflict? What can be done to strengthen the process? The answer requires a realistic assessment of the situation that prevails in IJK and dynamics among the key political actors.

A Thin Veneer of Normalcy

On the surface, it may appear that normalcy is fast returning to the Kashmir Valley, the political heart of the freedom struggle in IJK. Tourists are returning, and in Srinagar, vendors are doing good business. Several banks and institutes are reopening, two wine shops and bars have reopened, and two movie theaters are functioning.

Nevertheless, the deeper reality is something else. No day passes when the people of the Kashmir Valley or the hilly Muslim-majority areas in Jammu do not bury half a dozen of their loved ones who have perished in the continuing violence. No day passes when at least one member of the Indian security forces is not shot dead in a gun battle. Sand bunkers on the streets continue to mark Srinagar and its surroundings. The Disturbed Areas Act (1990) and Armed Forces Special Powers Act (1990) continue, granting the Indian security forces a free hand.

Since the outbreak of militancy in 1989, Kashmiris have been living by the gun or under the shadow of the gun. The youth between 15 and 30 years of age are searching for a safe future. The middle-aged population, from 31 to 45 years, have spent their youth in cages of fear, stalling their progress and engendering a type of middle-age syndrome in IJK. This below-45 age group comprises half of the population in IJK—those whose lives have been shaped by the death, humiliation, and fear that have come with the Kashmiri struggle for *azadi* (freedom). Their memories are fresh. They have lost their loved ones and suffered economically and socially. Mothers continue to wait in side roads if their children do not return after sunset. No one wants to go outside their homes in the late hours.

Witnessing deaths every day and coerced by both the militants and the security forces, Kashmiri locals have adopted a distant and removed demeanor. Audiences are large for television channels like Al Jazeera, Pakistan TV, and other channels through which Muslims worldwide are portrayed (rightly or wrongly) as fighting for Islam.

No Bridges of Trust

The feeling among people in much of the Kashmir Valley and militancy-struck districts in IJK is that "outsiders" are ruling them. Indian army and paramilitary forces are active in counterinsurgency operations, and nearly all of these forces hail from outside IJK. The Kashmir police and local administration, some 95 percent of which are locals, have as most of their top officers individuals from outside IJK. These top officers belong to the Indian Police Service and Indian Administrative Services. The local police have not been very active in counterinsurgency operations, and there is a complete divide between the local officers and the officers from the outside.

Officers in the Indian forces have little attachment to IJK, and state laws prohibiting outsiders' acquisition of property or attendance at professional colleges institutionalize that separation.[2] Local police and administrative officers in the Kashmir Valley and other Muslim-majority areas in IJK feel that their place has been taken over by outsiders who do not understand the cultural values of the people.

The bridges of trust have long collapsed between the state and federal administrations and Indian forces on the one hand and the local population on the other. Security forces suspect the youth of aiding the separatists. Searches of young people on the streets of Srinagar are a common sight. In the rural areas, heavy-handed and incompetent treatment of civilians by the Indian security forces continues in the name of curbing militancy. If there is a high-profile visit by a political leader or any other such political activity in a locality, the whole of the locality is searched and cordoned, leading to hardship for the local population. Of course, any civilized innocent person arrested will feel harassed and humiliated and will likely think of revenge. The "gun culture" in Kashmir, fostered by the militants, provides a platform for humiliated youth to take that revenge, by either joining or indirectly supporting the militancy.

This situation gives extremists new life, while liberal and progressive forces are marginalized. The Indian forces' bad record of torture and custodial deaths leads to alienation as the IJK state government fails to hold the forces accountable. Democracy and freedom become meaningless without justice and rule of law. The public waits for some result from pending inquiries to serve as examples that New Delhi is serious in the dialogue process.

In the Kashmir Valley, any provocation by the Indian security forces leads to protests by the local populace. In the first six months of 2005, such incidents as an alleged rape of a mother and daughter in Handwara district by an army officer, killings in search and cordon operations, and alleged custodial killings led to instant street protests in many hamlets.[3] Whenever there is a killing of a militant, members of the militant groups and their sympathizers call upon the people to raise slogans. The instructions come through loudspeakers from the mosques. Locals in a procession take militants (including foreign-born) killed in an encounter to the graveyard amid Islamic and pro-freedom slogans.

These scenes usually play out in the rural areas. Even those less inclined to join the protest have no alternative but to be on the streets, lest they be taken to be informers for the Indian security forces or pro-government militias.

Steady Transformation of Muslim Society

After fifteen years of violence and the growth of Islamic fundamentalist militant groups, there is still hope that secularism, Sufism, and the syncretistic Kashmir Valley–based ethic of *kashmiriyat* (cultural traditions that include the tolerance of other religions) will prevail if peace is restored in IJK. The majority of Muslims in IJK still follow rigorously the local Sufi tradition of Islam in Kashmir. Political pundits in IJK are confident that a political solution to the Kashmir conflict could easily keep the missionaries of hard-line Islamic rule at bay.

But the lack of serious dialogue, people-friendly political leadership, and involvement of the Kashmiri people in the peace process has provided Islamic fundamentalist groups fertile ground to proliferate in IJK. Their support remains limited at the grassroots level, but resentment toward the Indian and pro-government forces contributes to the growth in support of the Islamists. With long-term goals that are always religious, the Islamist groups prey on local resentment against the government, sometimes spending money to resolve grievances and thus gain popularity.

Support from Pakistan has allowed the Islamic groups to increasingly solidify their position in parts of the Kashmir Valley and Muslim-majority areas in Jammu. Such Islamic outfits have completely taken over the insurgent role, leaving the most popular pro-Kashmiri and pro-independence outfits with little control over the security situation. All of the active militant groups, including Jaish-e-Mohammad, Lashkar-e-Taiba, and their dozens of front groups, seek to introduce Islamic rule in IJK. Support from locals may not be forthcoming, but the Islamic groups effectively manipulate violence and fear.

The Islamist infrastructure is increasingly visible in IJK, with the proliferation of mosques, *darasgahs* (Islamic schools), Islamic hostels, and even Islamic syllabi in schools. In the absence of recreational and sports clubs in Muslim-majority areas of IJK, the increasing number of mosques is a major concern. One estimate is that since 1990, at least 2,500 to 3,000 new mosques have been built across the state.[4] The new mosques are built in West Asian and Saudi-influenced style, with minarets and domes, unlike old mosques in Kashmir, which have stupa-type ceilings. Religious literature from Saudi Arabia is easily available and distributed for free. The mosques help militants, who sometimes use them as hideouts or to disseminate their thoughts and exchange information. The new mosques provide employment in the name of religion. Lastly, the new mosques have no link with Sufi institutions in Kashmir, such as the Auqaf trust, which manages most of the Sufi shrines in Kashmir.

This trend could only be reversed if secular leaders were able to achieve genuine political, economic, and humanitarian gains. If so, the chances are that the majority of Kashmiris, who continue to believe in Sufism and worship in Sufi shrines, would fall into line with the secular leaders. But for this to happen, the secular leaders would first have to iron out the differences among themselves.

Political Economy of the Conflict

A huge amount of money is being invested in Jammu and Kashmir in the name of reconstruction and development. These include a massive rail project slated for development and a special Rs 1,200 crore package announced by Indian prime minister Singh in early 2005. Official announcements suggest that about Rs 7,300 crore in new development assistance had been pledged in 2005, shifting the focus of the state government from fundraising to fund spending.[5] One would hope that all such monies would help the locals directly, but it is difficult to be optimistic given the level of corruption in IJK.[6] In the Kashmir Valley, there are hardly any visible developments after six years of democratic rule by the National Conference and the three-year rule of the People's Democratic Party–Congress coalition. The Vigilance Department of the state police has booked a number of government offices for corruption cases, but hardly a case has been decided, making a farce of accountability.

The amounts of development money announced by New Delhi and state politicians are not reflected in infrastructure growth. The roads are bad, telephone systems looks like relics, and electricity and water are rationed. No infrastructure exists for exporters and importers. For example, there is a lack of cold storage for IJK's most profitable industry, horticulture. No design school exists for promoting Kashmiri arts and carpet industries. Without adequate infrastructure, employment expansion programs can hardly be considered. Several suggested free trade projects between IJK and AJK are yet to be initiated; even if they were, discussions with some of the local people suggest that the contracts for the railways, roads, and other construction usually go to kith and kin of the ruling elite, or even to active and former militants.[7]

Nonetheless, locals profit out of the conflict. Real estate values in the Kashmir Valley continue to rocket up. In Lal Chowk, the main hub of commercial activities in Srinagar, a shop that in 1988–1989 would have sold for Rs 7 lakh today could bring 70 to 80 lakh. A June 2005 newspaper advertisement for Jammu and Kashmir Bank Ltd. boasted that it was the fastest-growing bank in India, with business turnover growth of 679 percent from Rs 4,529 crore of March 1996 to Rs 33,162 crore as of 31 March 2005.[8]

Despite the boom, income tax and other state tax revenues in IJK have been low, resulting in the need for the Indian Union government to grant budgets of thousands of crore to the IJK state government. The imbalance is truly puzzling. Statisticians say that the savings accounts in the post offices and fixed deposits in IJK banks are among the highest per capita in India.[9]

Significant cash flows reach the Kashmir Valley from different sources. Militants and separatist leaders receive money from Pakistan and several other Islamic institutions in the Islamic world, while "turncoats" receive similar favors from the Indian intelligence agencies. Huge amounts of resources are spent maintaining the security forces in Kashmir, and much of this flows into the local economy.

Thousands of Kashmiri Muslims in the last fifteen years of violence have left the Kashmir Valley and headed toward greener pastures in West Asia. My own informal survey would suggest that more than one hundred thousand Kashmiri Muslims are today working in Saudi Arabia, Dubai, Kuwait, Abu Dhabi, Masqat, Malaysia, and other West Asian Muslim countries as well as in Europe. The bank records in IJK show that annual remittances from overseas through the banking system are nearly Rs 50 crore. But how much is truly reaching Kashmir unaccounted is anybody's guess. Several *hawala* dealers were arrested, both in New Delhi and Kashmir.[10] The tragedy is that the money spent in the Kashmir Valley cycles in limited circles and hardly trickles down to the needy and poor.

Dynamics in IJK

In the wake of the April 2005 Singh-Musharraf summit, one could see very few actors in IJK and AJK who mattered in the peacemaking arena. In IJK, these include members of the ruling People's Democratic Party (PDP) and Indian National Congress coalition. But other players who matter in IJK have been slow to give open support to the peace process. Mainstream regional parties like Farooq Abdullah's National Conference, the Bharatiya Janata Party, and the Communist Party of India (Marxist) in IJK have been cautious in their endorsement. On the Pakistani side, other than President Pervez Musharraf and his coterie, no strong statements of support have been issued by such political outfits as the Pakistan People's Party and Muslim League. Militants and hard-liners have rejected the peace process.

Within IJK, a number of actors are caught up in the attempt to transform the theater of the Kashmir conflict into a peace zone. These actors can be divided into three main categories: mainstream political leaders; separatist leaders, both moderates and hard-liners; and the militants. An additional, often forgotten, set of actors in IJK includes the civil society organizations. All these parties to the dispute have been showing some willingness to bring change to the situation. But in doing so, they have hardly coordinated their actions to bring about this change. One leader in Kashmir very rightly defined the situation as a "peace war" rather than "peace process."[11]

Mainstream Parties

Having been formed in the political ferment of the 1930s by Kashmiri leader Sheikh Mohammad Abdullah, the Jammu and Kashmir National Conference (NC) is one of the oldest political parties in IJK and continues to have strong grassroots ties across Jammu and Kashmir. Following the October 2002 Jammu and Kashmir state legislative assembly elections, the NC secured the largest group of 28 seats for their legislative candidates. Nevertheless, the NC was forced into the opposition by the formation of an alliance government consisting of legislators from the Indian National Congress (20 seats) and the newly formed People's Democratic Party (PDP) (16 seats).[12]

Since the election, the NC has been buffeted by this new array of political forces in IJK. Nearly all leaders of the mainstream political parties, including the NC, Congress, and PDP, are targets of the militants and thus have to live under the protection of the Indian and state security forces. However, leaders and workers of the NC party in IJK suffer from two directions: They are targets of the militants for being supporters of the pro-India political system, while the PDP-Congress-led government declines to guarantee security for all NC leaders. Aboveground workers associated with militant groups blackmail NC supporters to provide hideouts to the militants or face death or injury. There is little or no security at all for the second-line leadership of the National Conference in rural areas, not to mention for local party workers. National Conference leaders accuse the PDP of not playing a fair game, arguing that PDP is bent upon destabilizing NC's grassroots strength in IJK by leaving them open to militant intimidation on the one hand and political machinations on the other.

The case of Uri, a district along the Line of Control (LoC), is instructive of these new "mainstream" political dynamics in IJK. The district has long been represented by Mohammad Shafi Uri, a senior NC party leader and former finance and education minister in the state. Shafi sought to retain his seat in the 2002 assembly elections, but lost by a slight margin to Congress candidate Taj Mohi-u-Din. If one were to visit the area of Uri and talk to locals in the market, one would find Shafi is still considered as the leader of Uri, despite the fact that he hardly visits the area, spending most of his time in the winter capital of IJK, Jammu. If one were to visit him in Jammu, he could explain the practical details of a type of politics that in thirty years of his political career in IJK he had never witnessed. For him, the influence of the Indian security forces in the mountains secured his defeat. His anger is not directed toward those who voted against him, but he worries that innocent people of Uri in remote border villages are nourished on false hope and propaganda enhancing the profile of local leaders only temporarily. He fears that by the time these innocent villagers realize that they were cheated, it will be too late to repair the damage.[13]

Despite bordering the LoC, Uri town, the heart of the district, has never been home to a large presence of militants or militant-related activity. Despite the exodus of Hindus (mostly the Pandits) from the rest of the Kashmir Valley following the outbreak of hostilities in 1990, the Hindus in Uri stayed back. But even with the absence of militancy and sustained Hindu presence, some from Uri, including Shafi, feel that the new politics in IJK is intensifying ethnic divisions. There is concern that Uri's Hindus were overly exposed in the media during the course of the April 2005 reopening of the Srinagar-Muzaffarabad bus service. In their appeals, government leaders have tried to gain political leverage by dividing the Punjabi-speaking people of Uri into *Paharis, Gujjars*, and *Bakerwals*. The fear is of a dangerous drift in which those caught in rivalries resort to ethnic divisions and intimidation to settle scores. These dynamics are both the partial result of and cause for the NC being dislodged from its grassroots base.[14]

The PDP leadership is quick to call these allegations rubbish, but they do not shy away from making their own accusations that some of the NC leadership is in league with the militant groups with the aim of destabilizing the state government. The PDP party president and daughter of the chief minister, Mehbooba Mufti, has several times stated that "the NC without power is frustrated and can go to any extent."[15] On 22 May 2005 an NC party leader and former legislator, Gul Rafiqi, was arrested for helping a top militant of Hizbul Mujahidin to cross over to Pakistan by giving him a ride in his official car to Punjab.

Pandits, members of the Hindu minority hailing from the Kashmir Valley, have also been forced to contend with the new dynamics.[16] Pandit leaders, especially those in the association of All India Kashmiri Samaj (AIKS), have very rightly criticized the PDP government for creating security zones for the Pandits returning to the Kashmir Valley. The Pandits have said that they will only return to their original dwellings in Kashmir and live in neighborhoods with Muslims. They feel that if they shift to the selected "secured" areas, they will needlessly be tagged with a separate identity and thus become sitting ducks for the militants.

Individual politicians may be able to score some points, but in the long run it is the Islamist groups who seek to spread their radical fundamentalism in IJK that take advantage of this scenario. Internecine fighting provides a perfect platform for those advocating religious solutions among Muslims in IJK, while confusion, lack of leadership, and intergroup rivalry create the ideal context for such radical Islamist organizations. They advocate their theory of progress either through the gun or through religious discourse. Their discourse attempts to comfort the defeated, angry, and vengeful, proposing that their suffering comes because they are Muslims living in an area where "the rule of Allah" has yet to descend. The division among the Kashmiri leadership further allows the Islamist groups to play a major role. There may be more than a hundred Kashmiri political leaders, but on a scale of one to ten, the popularity rating of each leader stands below three. If this scenario continues, then religion will soon dominate the politics of Kashmir.

Hard-Liners and Moderate Separatists

Of equal importance to the mainstream parties in shaping the political scene in IJK are the separatists, who strive together for an end to Indian rule over IJK but are divided in their desires for either J&K's independence or accession to Pakistan. The separatists in IJK are given voice chiefly (though not exclusively) by the All Parties Hurriyat Conference (APHC). The APHC was formed on 9 March 1993 as an alliance of thirty separatist organizations. During the early 1990s, deadly internecine fights among militant separatist outfits led to confusion in the militant ranks and among the Kashmiri people about the purpose and trajectory of the uprising. The APHC was thus formed to overcome this confusion and advance Kashmiri separatism. It was openly supported and promoted by Pakistan in the latter's quest to sustain support within IJK for keeping up the fight to pry the region from India.

As the dominant political group espousing separatist interests, the APHC cannot be ignored. But the APHC's representativeness is problematic. In the early years, there was no representation in the APHC from Jammu or Ladakh, and this has changed only slightly. Since its formation, the APHC's leadership has yet to be tested through elections or the implementation of any tangible policies aimed at improving the lives of people outside the organization. While most people in the Kashmir Valley do support the ideology of separatism to some extent, this does not necessarily translate into ready acceptance of APHC leadership.

The APHC also suffers from internal fissures. Since September 2003 the APHC has been divided into two factions: one led by Mirwaiz Umar Farooq, the heir to the hereditary title of "Mirwaiz" (head priest) of the Jamia Masjid in Srinagar, one of Kashmir's most important religious seats; and another by Syed Ali Shah Geelani, a former Amir of Jamaat-e-Islami in IJK who has a stronghold of support in Sopore in the northern Kashmir Valley. The Mirwaiz-led group, usually referred to as the "moderate" faction, came into existence on 7 September 2003, when four of the executive members of the APHC (Mirwaiz Farooq, Professor Abdul Gani Bhat, Maulana Abbas Ansari, and Bilal Lone) announced the election of Maulana Ansari as the new APHC chairman. At the time, Geelani, another executive member, stopped attending the executive meetings, demanding an explanation from Lone's People's Conference party for indirectly fielding candidates in the October 2002 state assembly elections. Although Lone vehemently denied the allegation, Geelani took to forming his own APHC faction and also his own party, the Tahrik-e-Hurriyat Jammu and Kashmir. In October 2004 Geelani was unanimously declared chairman of his APHC faction. Geelani's group is regularly labeled "hard-line" and "pro-Islamic."

The split has created additional problems for sustaining the unity of the separatists. Take for example the IJK-based faction of the pro-independence Jammu and Kashmir Liberation Front (JKLF).[17] The JKLF has tried to remain neutral between the APHC factions. JKLF (IJK) leader Yasin Malik worked with another pro-independence leader, Shabir Shah of the People's Democratic Front, the Kashmir Bar Association, and the Jammu and Kashmir Ahl-e-Hadith religious group to push for the APHC's reunification. But the reunification effort failed. Since then, the JKLF has maintained a separate political identity; the same is true of Shah's group, the Bar Association, and Ahl-e-Hadith.

Given the complexity of separatist politics, a number of misperceptions prevail. For example, a common perception, both within and outside IJK, is that there are simply two types of separatist leaders. Those who support accession to Pakistan are commonly considered also to be "hard-liners," while those who are fighting for independence are commonly dubbed "moderates." However, this perception is clearly false. Several pro-Pakistan leaders are more moderate than some of the pro-independence leaders.[18] All of these political leaders are executive members of the Syed Ali Shah Geelani faction of the APHC. But they are in this group more because of the splits in their respective parties than because of hardline ideology. Even Geelani is seen by his supporters not as a hawk, but simply as a pro-Pakistan ideologue. Moderate leaders of all political persuasions (pro-Pakistan or independence-minded) should be segregated from the hardliners and invited to participate in the peace process.

Involving only a section of moderates in the peace process would simply alienate other leaders in Kashmir, who could become either more or less rigid, depending on how they were treated. But so far, at least in the manner of New Delhi's attempts, these finer distinctions have been ignored.

Many also believe that the hardliners have been marginalized in IJK, but up to the present this theory has not been tested. The fear of the gun continues to rule in IJK. Scattered violent incidents punctuate the otherwise normal life in the streets of Srinagar and surrounding areas. The fact that hard-liners, and the militants with whom they are associated, "lie low" with respect to the peace process does not necessarily mean that they have become defunct in IJK. As with the Liberation Tigers of Tamil Eelam in the peace process in Sri Lanka, chances are equal that they are gaining breathing space and waiting for some political change before they become more aggressive. Such a course of action would be even more likely if the hard-liners and militants were to be insulted and marginalized.

Yet another misperception is that militants are all similarly intransigent with respect to the peace process. However, one should take the lessons from the July 2000 cease-fire between Hizbul Mujahidin (Majid Dar group) and New Delhi. A lack of results after the cease-fire led to the killing of four out of five commanders, including Majid Dar, who had participated in talks with the New Delhi authorities. The fifth commander, Zaffar, escaped death twice. There are different shades of moderation among the militants; however, any show of moderation is an extremely risky proposition for a militant leader. In engaging with the compromise-minded among the militants, New Delhi should extend security to all separatist leaders participating in the peace process.

The mainstream parties have been playing games of one-upmanship with the separatists. Some are boasting of soon achieving autonomy for Kashmir—indeed, the National Conference has called it their initiative. The ruling People's Democratic Party (PDP), in an IJK state governing coalition with the Indian National Congress, has sought to achieve a number of goals that were once the agenda of the separatist parties. These goals include redress for the atrocities committed by Indian forces in IJK. The PDP has also claimed the credit of opening the Uri-Muzaffarabad road and the consequent reinstatement of regular bus service between Srinagar and Muzaffarabad on 7 April 2005.

New Delhi and the IJK state government have been promising that there would be no discrimination against the separatist parties, and that the separatists are to be pulled in for any final peace settlement in Kashmir. Indeed, the ideal would be for the peace process to be woven in such a way that the separatist parties are asked to select their teams by whatever method they prefer, and to be engaged in a settlement process to develop settlement terms agreeable with the governments in IJK, New Delhi, and Islamabad. But in reality, the mainstream parties in IJK deliberately attempt to keep the separatists out of talks. The result is the disaffection of those separatist actors who were fighting for their rights in Kashmir and with whom the talks were *supposed* to have been held.

If New Delhi enters into a dialogue with the separatist and militant leaders, then over what political package could they bargain? What would be left if autonomy and porous borders had already been credited to the mainstream political parties in IJK, and if New Delhi continued to insist that boundaries could not be changed? A sense of no achievement by the separatist leaders could lead to desperation and rigidity. As it stands now in the Kashmir Valley, a sense of humiliation seems to be setting in, and separatists are left to sustain vociferous demands for independence or the implementation of United Nations resolutions.

Ego clashes between leaders of different groups contribute to an overflow of chaos and confusion. The result may be more perils rather than solutions. It would be dangerous to jump to the conclusions that the Kashmir Valley is returning to normalcy and that fatigue in the local populace has brought an end to separatist demands or tendencies toward violence.

After returning from an unprecedented visit to AJK and Pakistan proper in June 2005, APHC faction leader Mirwaiz Farooq and JKLF leader Malik have been asking for a chair at the dialogue table. During the visit, the top militant leadership in Pakistan, including Hizbul Mujahidin chief Syed Salahuddin, refused to meet the APHC leadership. On their return from Muzaffarabad in AJK, according to comments in the media at the time, the visiting delegation was to bring about a cease-fire from the militants' side. If this was an objective, given the surge in violence that came about in the following months, the APHC certainly failed.

Militants

The militant groups presently active in Kashmir are hardcore Islamic militants who have their headquarters and top commanders based in Pakistan or AJK.[19] After training in different camps, militants wait in the launching camps until they get the call from their commanders from the field to join them. Their numbers are somewhat difficult to gauge, although they likely number in the low thousands. The IJK state police, for example, estimate the militancy to consist of little more than 1,500 militants, believing these to be pan-Islamic and focused solely on defending Islam in Kashmir.[20] The Indian security forces battling armed militants in the valley say that the number of the militants might be lower but that they are more dangerous and dedicated, and they carry more weapons on them than ever.[21] The IJK State Ministry of Home Affairs, however, has stated that in 2003 and 2004 a total of 2,470 militants were killed.[22]

The fact remains that in Kashmir, no one has the exact figures of how many militants are active. The official figures are calculated from interrogation reports of the captured militants as well as from intercepted messages. In 2001, in an interview with a militant, I was told that they "don't require more than 2,000 militants at a time to keep the Indian security forces engaged." The militant also claimed that as some are killed, the vacuum is easily filled with new recruits, as there is "a long waiting list" of those who want to join and fight Indian troops.

The militants live in the mountains in the summer and mingle with the local population in winter months to avoid snow and cold in the mountains. Indian officers will attest that the militants fight till the death and hardly ever surrender. Such dedication gains the militants respect among the local population, particularly in the rural areas, where the militants often receive food and shelter.

Levels of violence have remained high despite developments in the peace process over the course of 2004–2005. The generally warmly received April 2005 resumption of Srinagar-Muzaffarabad bus service was followed by a spate of killings across IJK. In addition, the trends of the attacks by the militants suggested that the urban militancy is being reintroduced in the Kashmir Valley. In April 2005, officials reported that 144 persons were killed, including 111 militants and their commanders, 21 civilians, and 12 security force personnel. In the same period in the previous year, 130 were killed, including 54 militants, 41 civilians, and 35 security force personnel. In the past, it has been observed that whenever a top militant is killed, in retaliation there is an assassination, a suicidal militant attack, or a major blast in Kashmir. Militants have set off reprisal blasts in public places, such as banks and schools.[23] Victims of such blasts have almost as often been innocent bystanders, including children, as security forces or civilians thought to be cooperating with security forces or official intelligence services, or even participating in local governing bodies. Targets have included central government departments such as passport offices, income tax department offices, and paramilitary camps.

All militant organizations presently active in IJK and AJK have rejected the peace process. Some of the outfits have asked their cadres to increase the attacks on the security forces. In an interview published in the newspaper *Greater Kashmir* in late April 2005, Syed Salahuddin, chief of the militant outfit Hizbul Mujahidin and the pro-Pakistan and AJK-based militant umbrella organization United Jihad Council, asked his cadres to increase such attacks in Kashmir. Earlier that year he officially rejected an invitation to meet the visiting Hurriyat leaders in Pakistan.

Civil Society

In a complex political system such as exists in IJK, where several different political parties (mainstream and separatist) claim to be leaders of the masses, a peace process requires the involvement of civil society organizations. In IJK, such organizations include the Bar Association, the Chamber of Commerce and Industries, the Kashmir Hotel and Restaurant Association, the Jammu and Kashmir Traders Federation, labor associations, the Fruit Growers Association, the University Teachers Association, student associations, the transport association, and the government employees association.

Civil society institutions have survived amid the gun culture and militancy that have overtaken life in IJK since 1989. They have been remarkably successful in maintaining high ethical standards and in sustaining electoral processes for selecting their leaders.[24] Minority group organizations have also held elections, including the hassle-free election of managers for Sikh Gurdwaras (temples).[25] This is in contrast to the IJK state assembly and the other political elections in IJK, which are attacked by the separatists and the militants. Political parties and organizations that have not participated in the state elections are also conducting internal party elections.[26]

These civil society leaders and their organizations are the soul of the Kashmiri population, who matter in opinion building and need to be roped into the peace process even if the confusion among the political parties continues. The election process in the majority of civil society keeps hope alive that the infrastructure for the democratic process still continues and is well accepted by people in IJK, including in the politically charged and militancy-wracked Kashmir Valley. But over the course of attempts to resolve the conflict, civil society leaders who matter in Kashmir have been ignored. So far, not a single known and elected civil society leader has been taken into confidence in the peace process. They have neither prepared to participate in the process nor been invited. In addition, there are many "nonactors" who are engaged just for their personal vested interest. These include some self-styled militant groups; NGOs functioning in either IJK, AJK, New Delhi, Islamabad, or even foreign countries; single persons or small political parties with no genuine followings; and other paper tigers who exist only in the realm of press statements. These nonactors thrive only insofar as the gap between the people of IJK and the leaders engaged in the peace process continues to exist. A weeding out can only happen when the main separatist political outfits are able to confidently play their role in the process.

Conclusion

Confidence-building measures (CBMs) are required to catalyze public support for and leadership interest in the peace process in IJK. On the basis of the discussion above, such CBMs should include support for improving accountability among the police and bureaucracies, invitations to civil society leaders into the peace process, efforts to ensure fair play in elections, and infrastructural development programs, among other measures. But the implementation of such CBMs should abide by a few considerations. Given the complex dynamics at work in IJK, daily monitoring throughout the peace process is necessary. One has to analyze the gains and failures on a day-to-day basis, to document the public mood, and to generate advice and direction on the basis of these observations. Every step of implementation needs to build upon previous steps, like perfect masonry work; close scrutiny is required before taking the next step. The people should be allowed to decide whether the CBM is helping them or not. Sensitivity should be sustained to the ways in which CBMs do or do not have multiplier effects among the masses. The steps so far, such as the reinstatement of the Srinagar-Muzaffarabad bus service, have brought relief for only a few individuals.[27] One should not look vainly for results from a misguided measure, and no matter how costly such a measure may have been, it should be retracted or revised immediately. It should be assumed that spoilers are waiting for such missteps to enter the fray and stir up suspicions among locals. In addition, long quiet periods between CBMs should be avoided, although less national media attention is necessary than has been the case. Back in New Delhi, a national consensus and a single policy on the Kashmir issue are obligatory.

Another consideration: If the New Delhi government is going to give credit exclusively to the mainstream political parties ruling the state for CBM achievements like the Srinagar-Muzaffarabad bus service, then how are the people on the streets and the separatist leaders to be satisfied? What achievements could be awarded to those separatists who are ready to participate in the dialogue process?

The peace process may face bumps in the road, or may even crash, if the sense of achievement is not perceptible among major parties to the Kashmir conflict. This is especially so for separatist groups like the IJK branch of the JKLF, which had once advocated violence but relinquished it and turned instead to politics to achieve its goals in Kashmir. Some in IJK suggest that CBM achievements should be designated as victories for separatist parties accepted by the masses and with no serious cases against them. This would allow these leaders to satisfy their egos while giving Kashmiris a sense that their struggle and losses were not a waste. If the separatist parties are simply sidelined or shown as defeated, then the Islamic fundamentalists will have yet another basis for disseminating their agenda among the defeated families in coming years.

A widely held view is that ultimate custody of the peace process should be given as a gift to the Kashmiri people, who should have some reason to celebrate after living through fifteen years of horrific violence. It is possible that a critical mass in the Kashmir Valley would be ready for something less than independence or implementation of UN resolutions calling for a plebiscite if the respectability of the local masses were visibly restored. This sentiment was captured well by Sajjad Lone, chairman of the People's Conference, commenting on the reopening of the Uri-Muzaffarabad road: "If inauguration of the bus journey from Uri to Muzaffarabad on 7 April 2005 had been allowed to happen by the people of Kashmir, not the security forces and the ruling political class, the euphoria among the people would have been different. Thousands would have been on the streets dancing and celebrating the achievement."[28]

Of course, such CBMs are only a temporary relief. For the permanent resolution of the Kashmir conflict, several important separatist leaders, those who matter or enjoy support of the masses, should be roped into the settlement process. Encouragement should go to building a local model solution by involving the intelligentsia of the Kashmir Valley in devising a settlement. Solutions imported from outside Jammu and Kashmir can only trigger resentment and anger and leave people with little ownership of the model. If locals can script steps for a solution, they will be able to garner prestige and spread the hope that can bring grassroots changes. Presently, people in the Kashmir Valley feel that they have no representation and no voice with the imperfectly elected state government.

In the context of the peace process, the quality of *leadership* should not be compromised. In the last fifteen years, hundreds of leaders with no individual capabilities have come and gone in IJK; the result has been no results. Today, no one is a leader among the Kashmiris. Through actions by New Delhi and within the state, Kashmiris have been divided and their potential suppressed. Leaders in New Delhi and in IJK have been working without a strategy, and today we are at a loss as to how to move forward. The state, and India beyond, are now suffering, as no one knows whom to trust. Let us all learn from the mistakes.

Notes

1. Political developments in Pakistan-administered Azad Jammu and Kashmir are described in Bushra Asif's chapter in this volume.

2. Children of Indian central government officials are allowed to have schooling in IJK, but for admission to IJK professional colleges, it is a criterion that the student holds state subject status in IJK.

3. A few incidents that epitomize the phenomenon include the following: On 26 March 2005, a local militant of South Kashmir, Ashiq Hussain Shah, a district commander of the banned Hizbul Mujahidin militant organization, was killed in an encounter. His funeral attracted a massive gathering of thousands of pro-freedom and pro-Islamic slogan-shouting locals and was reported in nearly all local newspapers in Kashmir. On 22 July 2005 in Pulwama, forty kilometers south of Srinagar, the *Indian Express* and several other local newspapers reported massive protests after the alleged murder of Pervez Dar, a sixteen-year-old student and resident of Pulwama, who went out with his father to water their paddy fields. Patrolling Indian security troops (members of the 55 Rashtriya Rifles) mistook him for a militant and shot him dead. The police and security forces' version was that the boy was killed in crossfire, while protesting villagers alleged that he was killed without any provocation. Police had to use tear gas shells to disperse the angry crowd. The Commissioner of Pulwama ordered an inquiry.

On 24 July 2005, protests were held after three students were killed in a mistaken identity situation at Bagargund, a village in Kupwara, ninety kilometers north of Srinagar, on the night of 23 July. A massive rally against the security forces and India surfaced across the Kupwara district. Police used tear gas shells to disperse the protestors. Local administration announced a night curfew, and the local administration and army called for an inquiry. The IJK chief minister called for an emergency meeting of the Unified Headquarters to discuss the situation.

4. An independent survey conducted in two phases in 2000–2001 and 2002–2003 by a few journalists and media school students (including this author) physically surveyed two districts of Srinagar and Baramulla. Several interviews were conducted, including with officials of the security forces, local police, students, teachers, passengers in bus stands coming from remote villages (where the team could not have access), religious leaders, civil administration members, and others. The team in Srinagar district visited selected areas of Srinagar town, Kangan, Ganderbal, Hazratbal, Zadibal, Iddgaha, Khanyar, Amirakadal, Sonwar, Batmallo, and other spots. In addition, the Baramulla district team visited selected areas of Bandipore, Sumbal, Safapora, Sopore, Pattan, Rafiabad, Baramulla town, Uri, Tangmarg, Gulmarg, and Sangrama. It was found that more than 630 new mosques were constructed in the last fifteen years in the two districts (rural and urban areas). This was used to estimate the growth in the number of mosques statewide, based on the fact that there are fourteen districts in J&K, and out of these fourteen, Muslims predominate in nine districts. One can multiply 300 mosques for each of the nine districts and add the few hundred known to exist in the five Hindu-dominated districts where there are also sizable Muslim populations. To be safe, our study took a lower estimate, coming to the conclusion that some 2,500 to 3,000 mosques are newly built in Kashmir. In a 2001 interview by the author, the former police chief of IJK, A. K. Suri, said, "one of the concerns in J&K is the increased number of mosques in Kashmir, which are in the hundreds since the rise of insurgency in the state."

5. The economic advisor to the IJK state government, Haseeb Drabu, in an interview with the *Daily Excelsior* newspaper (15 June 2005) described a Japanese Bank of Industrial Cooperation grant of Rs 3,600 crore (US$820 million), an Asian Development Bank grant of Rs 1,700 crore (US$390 million), as well as a World Health Organization grant of Rs 2,000 crore (US$450 million).

6. A 2005 study found that IJK state ranked only behind Bihar as the most corrupt state in India. See Transparency International India and the Centre for Media Studies, *Indian Corruption Study 2005 to Improve Governance*, New Delhi, 30 June 2005.

7. In Shopian and Pulwama in the south Kashmir Valley, personal observation suggests that most of the construction contracts have gone to families who have direct or indirect links with the militants.

8. *Greater Kashmir* newspaper (Srinagar), 8 June 2005.

9. Author's interview with the Border Security Force intelligence chief in Srinagar, Deputy Inspector General K. Srinivasan, December 2004.

10. *Hawala* refers to informal, often illegal, person-to-person money transfer networks.

11. Sajjad Lone, chairman, People's Conference (a moderate separatist political organization in IJK), May 2005.

12. On 2 May 2005 a top NC leader, a former minister and Shia leader, Maulvi Iftikhar Ansari, defected to PDP, adding another seat to the ruling PDP-Congress bloc.

13. Mohammad Shafi Uri, interview by author, 10 May 2005.

14. The Muslim-majority district of Doda, which is in the Hindu-majority Jammu region, has witnessed similar dynamics. NC party leader Khalid Najeeb Soharwardy, former home minister of the state, was dislodged by independent candidate Abdul Majid in the 2002 Assembly elections. As an engineer and Mirwaiz (head priest) of Doda, Soharwardy retains a large following in his area. But having luckily survived three major bomb blasts at public meetings, Soharwardy has limited his movement. He has expressed his feeling that there is a deliberate joint attempt by politicians and militants to dislodge NC from grassroots politics. Interview by author, 11 May 2005.

15. As reported numerous times in *Greater Kashmir*, Mehbooba Mufti has reiterated this point in public meetings in IJK since the 2002 election.

16. The minority Hindu Pandits have traditionally occupied places of privilege in the Kashmir Valley. Nonetheless, their cohabitation with Muslims and Sikhs there is an expression of Kashmir Valley inhabitants' mutual accommodation and syncretism, embodied in the principle of Kashmiriyat.

17. The JKLF is also divided between the IJK-based faction led by Malik and a faction in AJK led by Amanullah Khan. The split came with Malik's renunciation of violence in 1994. During a landmark June 2005 visit to Pakistan and AJK, Malik met with Amanullah. The two released a joint press release about reunifying the JKLF and formed a committee to work through the details. To the date of writing, however, no new developments have been visible.

18. Examples of such moderate pro-Pakistan leaders include Nayeem Khan, chairman of the National Front; Ghulam Nabi Sumbji, president of the Muslim Conference; Aga Syed Hassan, a popular religious Shia Muslim leader from Budgam district; and Ghulam Mohammad Hubi, chairman of the People's Conference. Sumbji, for example, had contested elections in 1987 and won in South Kashmir.

19. For more details on the militants in IJK and their links to Pakistan and beyond, see chapters in this volume by D. Suba Chandran and Rizwan Zeb.

20. Shesh Paul Vaid, inspector general of police, Jammu division, interview by author, May 2005.

21. An officer of the Rashtriya Rifles, the Indian counterinsurgency security force in South Kashmir, who did not want to be named; interview by author, May 2005.

22. In the state legislative assembly on 12 March 2005, IJK State Home Minister A. R. Veeri gave the following figures for the years 2003 and 2004: A total of 2,470 militants were killed in various encounters with security forces in Jammu and Kashmir; of these, 1,494 were killed in 2003 and 976 in 2004. Also, 714 security personnel lost their lives while fighting terrorism in the state during the last two years: 384 were killed in 2003, while 330 lost their lives in 2004. The information was furnished in a written reply to a question from assembly member S. D. Shariq.

23. In spring/summer 2005, after a string of school bombings and burnings in the Kashmir Valley, as well as Doda, Poonch, and Rajouri, newspapers in IJK reported that militants were targeting schools supported by Indian army or border security forces.

24. The Kashmir Bar Association has held elections every year, and the contests have been very interesting. The elections are observed with much interest from people who matter, as lawyers in Kashmiri society enjoy great respect. Some six hundred lawyers participate and vote. The Kashmir Bar Association is one of the top intellectual organizations in Kashmir, and most politicians in Kashmir are former lawyers. This includes the chief minister, tourism minister, finance minister, educa-

tion minister, and others. The Chamber of Commerce and Industries is another example—a prestigious organization of the business leaders in IJK. Elections are held every year, and members of the Chamber of Commerce and Industries choose their president and other officeholders. They even advertise their elections in local newspapers. The Kashmir Hotel and Restaurant Association, members of which are directly involved in the tourism industry, also have elections every year for the president and secretary.

25. Sikh Gurdwara management organization elections took place in all the districts of Jammu and Kashmir in September 2003, according to the regular schedule of elections every five years. In the Kashmir Valley, there are no more than forty to fifty thousand Sikhs, living in scattered districts of Srinagar, Pulwama, Anantnag, Baramulla, and Kupwara.

26. This includes Jamaat-e-Islami, which is seen in Kashmir as a fundamentalist outfit.

They hold elections and select their working bodies, called the *Rukans*. These Rukans then elect the *Majlis-e-Numaindgaha* (Assembly), which then elect their leader, called the *Amir* (Chief). Syed Nazir Ahmad Kashani was elected Jamaat-e-Islami Amir in 2003. Similarly, another fundamentalist religious outfit, Ahl-e-Hadith, also holds elections to select their chief. Maulvi Shawkat is their elected chief.

27. One may note that the 16 June 2005 bus trip from Srinagar to Muzaffarabad carried only one passenger.

28. Sajjad Lone, interview by author, May 2005. Lone had a similar quote during a television discussion program on NDTV in the second week of April 2005.

3

How Independent Is Azad Jammu and Kashmir?

Bushra Asif

Azad Jammu and Kashmir (AJK) is the part of Kashmir under Pakistani administration. It comprises the Mirpur district of Jammu, the bulk of Poonch, and a portion of the northwestern Kashmir province (excluding Gilgit and Baltistan, which form Pakistan's "Northern Areas") of the Jammu and Kashmir state, as it existed prior to 1947.[1] Currently these areas constitute AJK's administrative districts of Muzaffarabad (also AJK's capital), Bagh, Poonch, Sudhnoti, Kotli, Mirpur, and Bhimber.[2]

Given the obvious regional and international focus on the Indo-Pak conflict over the disputed state of Jammu and Kashmir, internal political and social development in AJK and the nature of its relations with Islamabad have not received much academic or policy attention.[3] AJK has all the trappings of an autonomous state. Its constitution—the Interim Constitution Act of 1974—provides for a parliamentary form of government with a president as the constitutional head, a prime minister as the chief executive, and a forty-eight-member legislative assembly. AJK also has its own Supreme and High Courts, an election commission, and even its own national anthem and flag. For all practical purposes, however, AJK's administration has traditionally been regulated by Islamabad through its Ministry of Kashmir Affairs and Northern Areas (KANA) and, since 1974, also by the Azad Jammu and Kashmir Council. Pakistan has tried to maintain the post-1948 status quo in AJK based on its claim that the entire Kashmir region (including the areas under its administration) is a "disputed territory" whose fate can only be decided through a plebiscite in accordance with United Nations resolutions of 1948 and 1949.[4] Integrating AJK into the Pakistani state would therefore adversely affect its claim to the Indian-held parts of Kashmir. Both the critical importance of the interstate territorial conflict to Pakistan and AJK's vague legal status have allowed Pakistan to intervene actively in AJK's administrative and political life and to shape its interaction with Indian-administered Jammu and Kashmir (IJK).

This chapter analyzes the political and economic dimensions of the relationship between Islamabad and Muzaffarabad. Given the intrinsic connection of AJK-Pakistan relations with the Kashmir conflict, it also highlights the importance of addressing AJK's internal problems and improving external linkages between Muzaffarabad and Srinagar for a sustainable resolution of the conflict. The first section of the chapter briefly traces the evolution of AJK-Pakistan relations and discusses the formal and informal mechanisms through which Pakistan has gradually expanded its influence over AJK's political and administrative life. The second section examines AJK's politics and Islamabad's role in shaping the nature and course of its political process. Within this context, the role of Pakistan's military is discussed. Next, the chapter reviews economic development in AJK, briefly analyzes the status and role of its civil society, and evaluates the contested status and politics of the Northern Areas. Placing AJK-Pakistan relations within the broader context of the Kashmir conflict, the next section throws light on the nature, prospects, and importance of political, economic, and civil society linkages between Muzaffarabad and Srinagar. Finally, charting a way forward, the conclusion offers policy recommendations for addressing key problems highlighted in the preceding sections.

Throughout the chapter, I argue that Islamabad's relationship with Muzaffarabad is one based on control rather than autonomy, with negative consequences for AJK's political and economic development. Although the patron-client nature of the relationship has structured political competition in AJK so as to encourage and reward political compliance from local political actors, AJK-Pakistan relations are far from frictionless. The status quo continues to generate resentment toward Islamabad and can be an impediment in peace initiatives between India and Pakistan.

Historical Background

AJK, like the Kashmir conflict itself, is a product of the events surrounding the partition of the Indian subcontinent in 1947 and the division of some 562 princely states between India and Pakistan.[5] The first Indo-Pak war over the princely state of Jammu and Kashmir (1947–1948) culminated in the division of the state into two entities, with the bulk of the Vale of Kashmir and Jammu, Ladakh, and a portion of Poonch coming under Indian control, and the Northern Areas (Gilgit and Baltistan) and Azad Kashmir falling under Pakistani administration.[6]

The United Nations Commission on India and Pakistan (UNCIP), which oversaw the cease-fire, defined AJK as a "local authority with responsibility over the area assigned to it under the ceasefire agreement."[7] Although the exact functions of this "local authority" were left vague, the Karachi Agreement of 1949 concluded between the government of Pakistan and AJK's provisional Muslim Conference[8] government allotted control of defense, foreign policy, negotiations with UNCIP, and the affairs of the Northern Areas to the former, while local administration and economic development were assigned to the latter.[9] This defined the broad parameters within which the AJK government could exercise its political powers. Subsequently, the Rules of Business of the Azad Kashmir Government, a 1950 ordinance, vested executive and legislative powers in the Supreme Head of State (a position exercised by the Supreme Head of the Azad Kashmir Movement, i.e., the Muslim Conference). The president of AJK was elected by and held office "at the pleasure" of the working committee of the Muslim Conference.[10] Real power, however, resided elsewhere.

Set up in 1948, Pakistan's Ministry of Kashmir Affairs and Northern Areas "probably had the best claim to being the real head of the AJK government" until the early 1970s.[11] Headed by a civil servant of the rank of joint secretary, KANA was to serve as a coordinating link between the government of Pakistan and AJK. From 1948 to the early 1970s, KANA's jurisdiction extended far beyond coordination. The joint secretary, as chief advisor to the AJK government, exercised de facto control over AJK's politics and administration. The working committee of the Muslim Conference also operated under his supervision.

By the late 1950s, Pakistan's interference in AJK's political, economic, and administrative affairs began to incite severe criticism from various leaders of the Muslim Conference who saw KANA as "pursuing a policy of colonialism in AJK."[12] Their opposition centered on demands for greater autonomy and the right to adult franchise. This resentment continued over the next decade until the Pakistani government of General Yahya Khan granted AJK the right to adult franchise in 1970 under the Azad Jammu and Kashmir Government Act. The 1970 act introduced a presidential form of government with an elected legislative assembly "with broad legislative powers except in the fields of defence, currency and UNCIP resolutions i.e. relations with India."[13] By 1970 a formally democratic system was in place, but real decisionmaking power still resided with Pakistan, not with AJK's president or legislative assembly.

Under Pakistan's first elected government of Prime Minister Zulfiqar Ali Bhutto, AJK's presidential system was scrapped in favor of a parliamentary one through the Azad Jammu and Kashmir Interim Constitution Act of 1974 (hereafter referred to as the 1974 Act). The 1974 Act has remained the law of the land, with minor amendments, up to the present. The formal introduction of a parliamentary system, however, did little to alter the balance of political power in favor of Muzaffarabad. The 1974 Act preserved Islamabad's jurisdiction over AJK's defense, foreign affairs (including foreign aid and trade), and currency[14] and clearly laid down that "the executive authority of the government shall be so exercised as not to impede or prejudice the responsibilities of the government of Pakistan."[15] More significantly, the constitution set up an Azad Jammu and Kashmir Council to serve as a "coordinating link" between Pakistan and AJK. Comprising thirteen members, with the chief executive of Pakistan as its chairman and the AJK president as its vice chairman,[16] it was given exclusive executive and legislative powers over fifty-two functions (including key areas such as taxation and communications).[17] The legislative authority of AJK's assembly was thus restricted to residual matters not covered by the council.[18] Council decisions were also kept outside the purview of AJK's Supreme Court so as to shield them from potential challenges from within AJK. Though the formation of the AJK Council gradually diluted the influence of KANA over the affairs of AJK, KANA continued to exercise primary responsibility for "policy administration" in the Northern Areas.[19]

In addition to these formal mechanisms of coordination, Pakistan appoints federally recruited civil servants to top administrative positions (the chief secretary, the finance secretary, the inspector general police, and the accountant general) in AJK. Finally, the Pakistani military's interventionist role, discussed below, in the politics and administration of AJK is another defining feature of Islamabad-Muzaffarabad relations.

Parties and Politics in AJK

The Muslim Conference exclusively dominated AJK's political landscape from 1948 to the late 1960s. Despite the party's overt pro-Pakistan stance, its leaders frequently voiced dissatisfaction over the lack of democratic institutions and demanded greater autonomy for AJK's administrative and political affairs.[20] But for all practical purposes, the party acted as a rump of the pro-establishment Pakistan Muslim League (PML). This was evident not just in its general acquiescence in Pakistan's political control over AJK but also in the instrumental role of its working committee in "bringing Pakistan's man" to the office of the president.[21] AJK's other main political party, the Pakistan People's Party (PPP-AJK), entered the political scene in 1970 and subsequently won the first legislative elections of 1975 held under the 1974 Act. Since then, formal political power in AJK has alternated between the PPP-AJK and the Muslim Conference.

Other pro-Pakistan parties, such as the Jamaat-e-Islami and the Jammu Kashmir People's Party,[22] operate on the political margins, but pro-independence parties such as the Jammu and Kashmir Liberation Front (JKLF)[23] are practically barred from the political process. The 1974 Act clearly lays down that "no person or party in AJK shall be permitted to propagate against, or take part in activities prejudicial or detrimental to, the ideology of the State's accession to Pakistan."[24] Individuals desirous of contesting elections are required to sign a declaration reaffirming their commitment to Kashmir's accession to Pakistan. In 2001, thirty-two JKLF leaders were barred from contesting the polls for refusing to sign the declaration and were arrested while holding a protest rally.[25] Political repression and harassment by government authorities have further fueled the demands of JKLF and other pro-independence parties for an independent Kashmir.

While political parties remain the dominant form of political identification in AJK, divisive *baradari* (kin-based) loyalties are also significant.[26] It can be reasonably argued that the continued political salience of these kin-based loyalties, exacerbated further by Islamabad's manipulation of the political process, have undermined political parties and weakened partisan affiliations.

Playing Politics

Pakistan's national security imperatives, centered on its perceived threat from India, define the boundaries of political participation and representation in AJK. Security concerns notwithstanding, the fear of pro-independence sentiments serving as a rallying point for Kashmiri demands contrary to Pakistan's official policy also drives Islamabad's desire to limit and direct AJK politics.

Islamabad has frequently been accused of manipulating the electoral process in AJK.[27] According to a former AJK prime minister, elections have been managed by Islamabad to ensure that "the party affiliate of the ruling party in Islamabad comes to power in AJK."[28] This strategy of control has reduced the autonomy of the prime minister and created a widespread perception that AJK governments are proxies of Islamabad. The patron-client nature of this relationship is also evident in the consequences of political change in Pakistan on the political processes and outcomes in AJK. After displacing Pakistan's elected PPP government in a coup in 1977, for instance, General Zia-ul-Haq dissolved the AJK legislative assembly, replaced the parliamentary system with a presidential system (as in Pakistan), and appointed a serving army brigadier as the AJK chief executive. Parliamentary elections were eventually held in 1985, but election rules were amended to sideline opposition political parties (notably the PPP-AJK).[29] Similar political engineering continued under Pakistan's elected civilian governments in the late 1980s and 1990s.

AJK's most recent elections, held in July 2001, were also notable for the role of Musharraf's military regime in stacking the rules of the electoral game against the incumbent PPP-AJK.[30] The unsurprising result was the election of Sardar Sikander Hayat, a pro-Pakistan stalwart from the Muslim Conference, as prime minister. Sardar Mohammad Anwar, a major general in the Pakistan army, was hurriedly retired from his post a few days before the elections and elected president with the backing of the Muslim Conference.[31] While manipulating the electoral process helped the military install a favorable government, it deepened factional rifts within the Muslim Conference between Hayat and a dissident group led by Sardar Abdul Qayyum and his son, Sardar Attiq.[32] In November 2004, Prime Minister Hayat moved to resolve the infighting by expanding his cabinet to include members of the pro-Qayyum group, reportedly under pressure from the Pakistan military.[33]

Pakistan's control over AJK's politics is not complete, however. Local political leaders are anything but passive subjects kowtowing to Islamabad. The Muslim Conference and the PPP-AJK have capitalized on their utility to Pakistan's interest in maintaining the political status quo in AJK by demanding and acquiring political space and material assistance for consolidating their hold over their political constituencies. Despite espousing pro-Pakistan rhetoric and sentiments, AJK politicians have also frequently expressed their frustration with the lack of political freedoms and the continuing restrictions on political rights and participation. However, their military and economic dependence on Pakistan and the highly unequal nature of the relationship set the constraints and opportunities within which local political actors operate.

Military Machinations

The Pakistan military is the most important political actor in the politics and administration of AJK, a consequence mainly of its dominance over the politics of Pakistan. The centrality of the Kashmir conflict in Pakistan's external security calculus and the state of perpetual hostility with India that flows from it have allowed the military to primarily, if not always exclusively, determine and control Pakistan's Kashmir policy. It has also provided the military the basis of legitimacy for its political role both in Pakistan and in AJK.

For Islamabad, control over AJK is deemed critical, since it provides it with much-needed strategic depth against India (in the case of a conventional attack from across the border) and also serves as a site for launching militant incursions into the Kashmir Valley. AJK's military dependence on Pakistan has its roots in the 1949 Karachi Agreement, which categorically placed AJK's defense and foreign affairs under Pakistan's control. The 1974

Act too vested these powers in Pakistan, reaffirming the military's central role in the affairs of AJK.

In the early 1960s, General Ayub Khan actively encouraged sabotage activities across the Line of Control (LoC) through the Kashmir Public Committee, which was authorized to provide "all out support for guerrillas to be inducted into Kashmir."[34] Around seven thousand guerillas led by special units of the Pakistan army were infiltrated into IJK with the aim of encouraging revolt in the valley.[35] The revolt never materialized and the misguided operation culminated in the second India-Pakistan war over Kashmir in 1965. The advent of an indigenous Kashmiri uprising against Indian rule in the Kashmir Valley in 1989 provided the Pakistan military with another opportunity for "liberating" Kashmir. Groups like JKLF received weapons and training from the military's Inter-Services Intelligence (ISI) agency to launch attacks across the LoC. By 1993 the "independentist JKLF" was sidelined in favor of the Hizbul-Mujahidin, a pro-Pakistan Islamist guerrilla group linked to the Jamaat-e-Islami.[36] As Pakistan gradually expanded the scope of its cross-border militant operations by supporting a variety of jihadi outfits, AJK became a springboard for a low-intensity conflict between India and Pakistan.[37] Pakistan's alleged role in cross-border terrorism has been a major irritant in tension reduction efforts between the two countries.[38]

There is evidence to suggest that the scope and scale of the military's interference in AJK's political affairs increase during direct military rule in Pakistan. In 1960, General Ayub introduced his Basic Democracy system in AJK. Basic Democrats were to serve as the electoral college of the AJK president and council of ministers. Similarly, in 1977 General Zia replaced AJK's parliamentary system with a presidential one. The October 1999 coup has been different only in form. According to Sardar Qayyum, "since AJK is a politico-defense unit of Pakistan, the military takeover in Pakistan has also had a spillover effect in AJK."[39] Local human rights groups claim that "military intelligence agencies are heavily involved and influential in AJK" and routinely interfere in its politics and governance.[40] The Pakistan military has actively sought to direct and control AJK politics through the office of General Officer Commanding (GOC) twelve division stationed in the city of Murree (district of Rawalpindi). Seen by political observers as "the linchpin for AJK and the defense of Pakistan,"[41] the GOC Murree is believed to have been instrumental in shaping the outcome of AJK's 2001 legislative assembly elections. For instance, suitable candidates for the posts of president and prime minister and for the cabinet were allegedly approved by the GOC.[42] This direct manipulation of AJK's political affairs only highlights AJK's parliamentary façade, and according to Sardar Khalid Ibrahim, a former AJK legislator, "is damaging not just for AJK but also for Pakistan's stand on Kashmir."[43]

Economics of Control

The Kashmir conflict has had a deleterious impact on economic development on both sides of the LoC (for an analysis of IJK's economy see Kaur in this volume). However, the conflict is only one explanation for AJK's economic plight.

At the time of partition, AJK consisted of some of the poorest areas in the Dogra principality, with the exception of Muzaffarabad and Mirpur.[44] However, it boasted significant natural resources, especially for hydroelectric power generation. Except for the Mangla Dam, AJK's potential for energy generation has remained underutilized.[45] Even in that case it has been denied royalties of approximately Rs 1 billion ($16.75 million) annually, despite Islamabad's promise of "preferential treatment to AJK in the power tariff" at the time of the construction of the dam in 1967.[46] While the dam caused severe socioeconomic disruption, especially in the Mirpur district, "the benefits of Mangla's electricity were felt in Lahore, and even in Karachi, long before power lines began to be installed in rural Mirpur."[47] Similarly, other potential sources of revenue generation, such as mining of precious stones and tourism, have been neglected. Lack of public and private investment and productive economic opportunities has resulted in substantial migration overseas in search of jobs.[48] But in the absence of a sound investment environment, the potential economic benefits from expatriate remittances have remained untapped.

As a result, AJK continues to be dependent on Islamabad for its developmental and nondevelopmental budgetary needs. Over the years Islamabad has plugged AJK's budget deficits with direct injections of grants, but the level of expenditure on socioeconomic development has fallen short of the territory's development needs.[49] Allocation shortages are compounded by the underutilization of available funds due to the government's limited administrative capacity and poor infrastructure.[50] AJK's economic dependence goes beyond financial resources, though. Its annual budget is prepared by a centrally appointed finance secretary, and broad economic priorities are determined by Islamabad through the AJK council and the chief secretary. According to a former AJK prime minister, "There is debate and discussion in the assembly, but at the end of the day it's the finance secretary who makes the budget, not us."[51] Simply put, Pakistan holds the purse strings.

Over the years, AJK's economy has been gradually integrated into Pakistan's economy, but this integration has occurred within the context of dependent development, with adverse consequences for AJK's political and economic development. Cross-LoC trade can help ameliorate some of AJK's economic problems. However, in the absence of economic autonomy, the benefits of such trade are likely to be limited.

The devastating 8 October 2005 earthquake has wreaked havoc on AJK's civil infrastructure and destroyed sources of livelihood and commerce.[52] Given the enormous scale of the damage, physical reconstruction and rehabilitation of displaced Kashmiris are likely to be a long-term process. Although it is too early to predict the impact of economic devastation on the political and economic relations between AJK and Pakistan, one can reasonably speculate that it is likely to exacerbate AJK's traditional economic dependence on Pakistan.

Civil Society in AJK

Economic and political underdevelopment, weak political institutions, and legal restrictions on freedom of association have undermined the development of civil society in AJK and hampered the ability of civil society actors to articulate public interests and demands. Islamabad has frequently used the sensitive nature of AJK to limit the space for democratic forms of contention. For instance, the Maintenance of Public Order Ordinance, which prohibits "activities prejudicial to public safety," is often employed to deter and suppress opposition and dissent. Similarly, press freedoms are severely curtailed. Journalists frequently complain of harassment and intimidation at the hands of intelligence agencies and accuse the government of "using advertisements as an instrument to subdue a hostile press when it criticizes its policies."[53] As a consequence, independent information about politics and government in AJK is conspicuous by its absence.

In an environment where the rights of participation and association are circumscribed, civil society organizations operate in the sanctioned, nonpolitical areas of service delivery, community welfare, and rural development.[54] Islamabad has not been averse to allowing international donor agencies to partner with local organizations for improving health and education facilities, sanitation, rural development, microcredit schemes for women, environmental conservation, refugee resettlement, and related initiatives.[55] Though these efforts have helped address social-sector development deficits within AJK, they have been restricted to projects and programs approved by Pakistan. Hence local ownership remains low.

While some civil society groups, such as student and bar associations, have occasionally tried to mobilize public opinion through protests and demonstrations,[56] many others derive benefits from the state by espousing pro-Pakistan rhetoric and validating Pakistan's traditional stance on Kashmir. These pro-Pakistan organizations and activists usually represent AJK civil society at both domestic and international forums.

AJK has been a major source of migration to the United Kingdom, the United States, and Canada. Members of the diaspora community have maintained strong social, economic, and political ties with their homeland. Their remittances have been a valuable source of foreign exchange reserves for Pakistan. AJK's legislative assembly has a reserved seat for members of its diaspora community. All major AJK political parties also maintain chapters abroad, which raise funds, rally political support, and try to engage the diaspora community in political developments at home.

More importantly, the diaspora is "the main site of Kashmiri-ness outside the supervision of India and Pakistan and its agents."[57] Protected from the restrictions imposed by Islamabad and New Delhi, members of the Kashmiri diaspora have sought active engagement in the politics of their adopted country while staying connected with political developments in Kashmir. Though political identities and affiliations vary along pro-Pakistan/India/independence lines and some members of the diaspora have frequently been accused of "extending political and financial support to the political movement in IJK,"[58] there is evidence to suggest that their shared displacement, at the hands of India and Pakistan, has created a sense of a collective Kashmiri identity among diaspora communities from both sides of the LoC.[59] This is evident from various diaspora-initiated efforts aimed at conflict resolution, such as the US-based Kashmir Study Group. Such organizations as the Kashmiri American Council and the British-based Kashmiri National Identity Campaign have sought to bring the two sides closer by providing a common platform for discussion and debate on Kashmir. These diaspora groups have frequently engaged the United Nations, European Union (EU), and other international actors in bringing attention to human rights abuses, economic neglect, and denial of political freedoms in Kashmir. Prominent individuals of the diaspora community, such as AJK's Nazir Ahmed, a member of the British House of Lords, have also publicly advocated a peaceful resolution of the conflict and have used their public positions to highlight the issue in international forums.

And the Northern Areas

While Pakistan has been careful to maintain the separate political status of AJK, the Northern Areas (which form the northern sector between Kashmir and China) have been gradually integrated into the Pakistani federation. Successive AJK governments have challenged this incorporation, maintaining that the Northern Areas are a part of Kashmir and should therefore be administered by them. In 1992 the AJK High Court passed a verdict against the denial of political rights in the region and directed the AJK government to assume administrative charge of the region. Pakistan challenged this verdict in the AJK Supreme Court, which declared the Northern Areas as part of the Jammu and Kashmir state, not "Azad Kashmir." As a result of that decision, the responsibility of the administration of the Northern Areas continues to reside with Pakistan.[60]

The Northern Areas are administered by KANA, which has had an intrusive role in its affairs. Party politics was banned in the Northern Areas until 1994. The first party-based elections were held in October of that year; subsequently, the twenty-six–member Northern Areas Executive Council was formed. Following a 1999 Supreme Court decision to grant the Northern Areas a defined constitutional status and representation in the national legislature,[61] Pakistan replaced the executive council with a legislative council, the Northern Areas Legislative Council (NALC). The NALC was granted powers to legislate on local matters and impose local taxes. However, the overall control of KANA in the policy administration of the Northern Areas remained intact, rendering the NALC virtually powerless, with nominal financial and legislative powers.[62] Following General Musharraf's October 2004 "comprehensive package for empowerment of the Northern Areas,"[63] an appellate court was established in May 2005. However, its administration resides with KANA, which raises serious questions about its autonomy.

Sporadic reform efforts by Islamabad have not created meaningful avenues of political participation or addressed the economic neglect of the Northern Areas. Coupled with sectarian Sunni threats to the majority Shias of the area,[64] they have further fueled local demands for greater autonomy, as well as more radical separatist ones for self-determination.[65]

Muzaffarabad-Srinagar Relations

The Kashmir conflict continues to shape political and economic development in AJK and its relations with Pakistan. The importance of addressing AJK's internal problems as part of a broader peace process between India and Pakistan cannot be overemphasized. Internal dimensions on both sides of the LoC fuel the conflict and need to be addressed simultaneously with the external dimension (see Idris in this volume). An interrelated and equally important aspect in conflict resolution is Muzaffarabad-Srinagar relations.

Communication links between AJK and IJK were severed after the first war between India and Pakistan over Kashmir. Although covert cross-border movements of militants have been frequent, open contacts between political leaders and civil society actors from both sides have been neither encouraged nor allowed. Strict security checks on travel and arbitrary denial of visas have prevented even ordinary Kashmiris from interacting with one another. In December 2004, political leaders from the two sides met at a conference organized in Kathmandu by Pugwash.[66] Similarly, a delegation of the All Parties Hurriyat Conference (APHC) was allowed to travel to AJK and Pakistan in June 2005 and January 2006. Though potentially significant, such occasions for contact and debate have been rare.

Reestablishing and strengthening intra-Kashmir contacts are important for a sustainable resolution of the Kashmir conflict. Cross-border linkages between Muzaffarabad and Srinagar will address the humanitarian and economic costs incurred by Kashmiris on both sides of the LoC by years of forced separation. These include the division of families and the disruption of centuries-old trade routes. Although the issue of divided families generates much political debate in Pakistan and AJK, there is evidence to suggest that many "refugees" seem to have either migrated overseas or assimilated in Pakistan. However, displacement caused by the conflict remains an important symbolic problem plaguing Srinagar-Muzaffarabad relations.[67]

India and Pakistan's decision to initiate a bus service between Muzaffarabad and Srinagar in April 2005 is an important first step toward that end. Though vulnerable to disruption, it serves as a positive symbolic gesture in bringing the two sides closer, if not in addressing the underlying causes of the conflict. In the aftermath of the October earthquake, India and Pakistan also agreed to open four additional crossings along the LoC to provide aid to quake victims and facilitate meetings of divided families. It is important that such linkages be extended to other parts of Kashmir. Once such links are established they can be gradually expanded and institutionalized by establishing joint forums of parliamentary representatives and prominent political and civil society actors for addressing issues of common interest, such as trade and commerce, environmental protection, tourism, hydroelectric power, and cross-border transport, among others.[68] Enhancing such contacts will not only lead to benefits within Kashmir but offer the potential of increasing incentives for and creating powerful constituencies for peace on both sides of the LoC. However, enhanced interaction should also be accompanied by efforts to include Kashmiris in any dialogue process over the fate of the disputed territory.

What Lies Ahead?

As shown in the preceding analysis, the territorial conflict over Kashmir sets the boundaries and limits within which AJK politics, economics, and governance are structured. Pakistan has routinely interfered in the affairs of and circumscribed the autonomy of governments in AJK. Despite the marked absence of violence in relations between the two (in contrast to that characterizing Delhi's relations with Srinagar), restrictions on political freedoms and participatory rights, as well as lack of economic opportunities, continue to generate popular, if muted, resentment toward Islamabad.

In the absence of a meaningful resolution of the Kashmir conflict, the broad contours of Islamabad-Muzaffarabad relations are likely to remain the same. However, Pakistan can take steps to address issues of political and economic development within AJK by curtailing the overbearing role of KANA and the Kashmir Council, allowing for free and fair elections open to pro-independence parties, reducing the role of intelligence agencies and security forces, and increasing the powers of the Northern Areas Legislative Council.

Greater involvement of the international community in supporting economic and civil society initiatives can also provide opportunities for improving the lives of the Kashmiris. External donors such as the EU and the UN can design and fund targeted development schemes for enhancing access to health facilities; improving education; providing microcredit initiatives, especially for women; and addressing environmental conservation within AJK and the Northern Areas. Aid agencies can also share technical resources and skills to strengthen and build the capacity of AJK's civil society. More urgently, humanitarian aid for internally displaced people and refugees needs to be expanded. Such efforts should be complemented by greater emphasis in external policy and aid programs for expansion of democratic participation and association in AJK. The international community can also provide resources and facilitate civil society and people-to-people contacts across the LoC. Other efforts could include funding joint initiatives between AJK and IJK for promotion of tourism, environmental conservation, and infrastructure development.

If taken in tandem with a broader bilateral peace process between India and Pakistan, these steps can help address AJK's internal problems, ameliorate the fissures in AJK-Pakistan relations, and also improve the prospects of a durable resolution of the Kashmir conflict.

Notes

1. Alastair Lamb, *Kashmir: A Disputed Legacy 1846–1990* (Karachi: Oxford University Press, 1991), p. 188.
2. See http://www.ajk.gov.pk.
3. Notable contributions include Leo Rose, "The Politics of Azad Kashmir," in Raju G. C. Thomas, ed., *Perspectives on Kashmir: The Roots of Conflict in South Asia* (Boulder: Westview Press, 1992) and Rifaat Hussain, "Pakistan's Relations with Azad Kashmir," in Henry Rowen and Rafiq Dossani, eds., *Peace and Security in South Asia* (Stanford: Stanford University Press, 2005).
4. United Nations resolutions, http://www.un.org/documents/scres.htm.
5. Lamb, *Kashmir*, p. 4.
6. The cease-fire line separating the two parts of Kashmir, later renamed the Line of Control (LoC) under the 1972 Simla Agreement, is to this day the de facto border between India and Pakistan. See Rose, "The Politics of Azad Kashmir," p. 236.

7. United Nations resolutions, ibid. UNCIP Resolution, 13 August 1948, clause A-3.

8. Set up in 1932, the All Jammu and Kashmir Muslim Conference was the state's first political party. By 1941, it had split up into the All Jammu and Kashmir National Congress and the Muslim Conference. Headed by Sheikh Abdullah, the National Conference drew its support from Muslims in the Kashmir Valley and had strong links with the Indian National Congress. The Muslim Conference was popular with Muslims from Jammu, Poonch, and Mirpur (areas that were to later constitute Azad Kashmir) and was allied with the Muslim League. Its members included G. M. Sadiq, Mirwaiz Yusuf Shah, and Sardar Abdul Qayyum. See Lamb, *Kashmir*, pp. 85–98.

9. For a full text of the Karachi Agreement, see Hussain, "Pakistan's Relations with Azad Kashmir," pp. 111–155.

10. Rose, "The Politics of Azad Kashmir," p. 238.

11. Ibid.

12. Josef Korbel, *Danger in Kashmir* (Princeton: Princeton University Press, 1966), p. 201.

13. Rose, "The Politics of Azad Kashmir," p. 240.

14. The Azad Jammu and Kashmir Interim Constitution Act, 1974 (as modified, May 1994), article 31 (3).

15. Ibid., article 19 (2-A).

16. Six members of the council are elected from the AJK legislative assembly, and five nonvoting members are nominated by the chairman of the council from among federal ministers and members of the Pakistan National Assembly. The Federal Minister of KANA serves as an ex-officio member of the council.

17. The 1974 Act, articles 21 and 31 (2).

18. The 1974 Act, articles 22 and 31. AJK's legislative assembly consists of 48 members, 40 elected and 8 nominated. Out of the 8, 5 seats are reserved for women, 1 for *Ulema* (religious scholars), 1 for Kashmiri diaspora, and 1 for technocrats.

19. See http://www.pakistan.gov.pk/kashmiraffairs-ministry/aboutministry/overview.jsp.

20. Sardar Ibrahim, AJK's first president, had demanded the right of adult franchise as early as 1954.

21. Anonymous source, author's confidential interview, Islamabad, August 2004.

22. Distinct from the PPP-AJK, the Jammu and Kashmir People's Party is headed by Sardar Khalid Ibrahim, son of the late Sardar Ibrahim Khan.

23. JKLF was formed in the mid-1960s. Led by Amanullah Khan and Yasin Malik, it emerged as the vanguard of the Kashmir struggle for an independent state in 1989–1990.

24. The 1974 Act, article 7 (2).

25. http://web.amnesty.org/library/index/engasa330142001.

26. Rose, "The Politics of Azad Kashmir," p. 244.

27. International Crisis Group, *India/Pakistan Relations: Steps Toward Peace*, Islamabad, Brussels (ICG Asia Report No. 79), 24 June 2004, p. 8.

28. A former AJK prime minister, interview by author, Muzaffarabad, August 2004.

29. Two amendments were promulgated in the 1984 Political Parties' Ordinance and the 1970 Assembly Elections Ordinance to ban "nonregistered" parties such as the PPP from contesting the elections. See Rose, "The Politics of Azad Kashmir," pp. 241–242.

30. This observation is based on author's confidential interviews conducted in August 2004.

31. This was done in violation of government rules that civil and military officials have to wait a mandatory two-year period after retirement or resignation before entering politics. See Sadaqat Jan, "The POK Puppet Show," *Frontline* 18, no. 16, 4–17 August 2001.

32. The current supreme head of the Muslim Conference, Sardar Qayyum, is a former president and prime minister of AJK.

33. "11 More Inducted into AJK Cabinet," *Dawn* (Karachi), 14 November 2004.

34. General K. M. Arif, *Khaki Shadows: Pakistan 1947–1997* (Karachi: Oxford University Press, 2001), p. 47.

35. Sher Khan Mazari, *A Journey to Disillusionment* (Karachi: Oxford University Press, 1999), p. 129.

36. For an analysis of Pakistan's involvement in cross-border militancy see Bose, *Kashmir,* pp. 102–126.

37. Militant groups like Lashkar-i-Taiba, Hizbul Mujahidin, Al Badar Mujahidin, and Harkat-ul-Ansar have received weapons and training to launch attacks across the LoC. Though exact figures are not available, Indian and foreign media reports put the number of training camps along the Pakistani side of the LoC during the 1990s at ninety-one. See Hussain, "Pakistan's Relations with AJK."

38. Anwar Iqbal, "No Exception in Terrorism, India Tells U.S," *Washington Times,* 21 September 2004.

39. Sardar Abdul Qayyum, interview by author, Islamabad, August 2004.

40. M. Imran, "Intelligence Agencies Interfering in AJK Affairs, Says HRCP," *Daily Times* (Lahore), 20 July 2004.

41. Sardar Abdul Qayyum, interview by author, Islamabad, August 2004.

42. Ahmed Hassan, "Power Game in AJK Begins," *Dawn,* 13 July 2001.

43. Sardar Khalid Ibrahim, interview by author, Islamabad, August 2004.

44. Muzaffarabad was on the main route into the Kashmir Valley until 1947, and Mirpur was the homeland of the *Sandans* (Muslim *Rajputs*), who served in large numbers in the Indian army. See Rose, "The Politics of Azad Kashmir," p. 237.

45. Built on AJK territory in 1967, the Mangla Dam serves as the principal water storage reservoir for the canal system of West Punjab.

46. Rauf Kalsra, "AJK PM Seeks Islamabad's Help in Settling Power Tariff Row with WAPDA," *News* (Islamabad), 19 May 2003.

47. Roger Ballard, "Kashmir Crisis: View from Mirpur," in Gull Mohd Wani, *Kashmir: Need for Sub-continental Political Initiative* (New Delhi: Ashish Publishing House, 1995), p. 33.

48. Ibid., pp. 28–35.

49. Editorial, "The AJK Budget," *Dawn,* 21 June 2005.

50. "Half of AJK Development Allocation Remains Unutilized," *Dawn,* 29 April 2004.

51. A former AJK prime minister, interview by author, Muzaffarabad, August 2004.

52. See Syed Talat Hussain, "Anatomy of a Disaster," *Newsline* (Karachi), November 2005.

53. Human Rights Commission of Pakistan, "State of Human Rights in Azad Jammu and Kashmir: Report of HRCP Fact-finding Mission," July 2004, p. 11.

54. These include government-funded organizations such as the National Rural Support Program (NRSP), locally funded welfare organizations, Pakistan-based non-governmental organizations (NGOs), and externally financed programs and projects.

55. "NGOs Sign MoU to Boost AJK's Poor Households," *News*, 16 February 2003.

56. Sultan Shahin, "Across the Divide: The Pakistani Model of Freedom," *Asia Times,* 17 December 2004.

57. Nasreen Ali, "Diaspora and Nation: Displacement and the Politics of Kashmiri Identity in Britain," *Contemporary South Asia* 12, no. 4 (December 2003), p. 476.

58. Hasan-Askari Rizvi, this volume.

59. Ali, "Diaspora and Nation," p. 477.

60. Iffat Malik, *Kashmir: Ethnic Conflict, International Dispute* (Karachi: Oxford University Press, 2002), p. 219.

61. Afzal A. Shigri, "Status of Northern Areas," *News*, 30 August 2004.

62. Navnita Chadha Behera, *State, Identity and Violence: Jammu, Kashmir and Ladakh* (New Delhi: Manohar, 2000), pp. 195–196.

63. "NALC Expanded, New District Created," *Dawn*, 12 October 2004.

64. Followers of the Shia sect constitute the majority in the Northern Areas (the Shias are a minority in Sunni-dominated Pakistan). Their demands have included revision of the school curriculum in favor of the Shia majority. See "Gilgit Shias to Resume Syllabus Reform Protests from October 01," *Daily Times,* 29 September 2003.

65. Prominent among these is the Balwaristan National Front (BNF), which has gained many adherents since 1999. See Victoria Schofield, "Pakistan's Northern Areas Dilemma," at http://news.bbc.co.uk/1/hi/world/south_asia/1491179.st.

66. Details of the conference can be found at http://www.pugwash.org.

67. See Patricia Ellis and Zafar Khan, "Kashmiri Refugees: The Impact on Kashmiriyat," *Contemporary South Asia* 12, no. 4, pp. 523–538.

68. Bose, *Kashmir,* pp. 263–264.

4

India and Armed Nonstate Actors in the Kashmir Conflict

D. Suba Chandran

India and Pakistan believe that they are the only parties to the Kashmir conflict, and Kashmiris on both sides of the Line of Control (LoC) consider themselves to be the third party. But there is yet another distinct entity—armed nonstate actors (NSAs)—who cannot be ignored in resolving the Kashmir conflict. India considers them as trained and armed by Pakistan, while the latter considers them an indigenous phenomenon.

Armed NSAs assume importance for many reasons. Their objectives are different from those of India, Pakistan, and the Kashmiris. An understanding reached among these three parties may not be accepted by the armed NSAs. For one thing, the latter do not form a monolithic block and are divided on objectives, strategies, and local support. Furthermore, in the post–September 11 era, some of them are clearly at odds with their host and patron, Pakistan. Attacks inside Pakistan since 2003, including the assassination attempts on President General Pervez Musharraf, reveal that the state's control over them is weak and uncertain. Finally, the armed NSAs are significant simply because they are armed. They may not possess the firepower to overwhelm the Indian security forces, but they have the potential to undermine any peace process. A single major attack inside or outside Jammu and Kashmir could derail the peace process between India and Pakistan, leading them into a military confrontation.

This chapter looks into the reasons behind the rise of armed nonstate actors, along with their various differences. It analyzes the various militant, jihadi, *ikhwan*, and renegade groups; their support base; strategies; and objectives. Finally the chapter also critiques the recent efforts by the government of India and lists possible courses of action for the future.

Proliferation of Militant Groups in the Kashmir Conflict

Many reasons could be identified for the proliferation of armed NSAs in the Kashmir conflict. The frustration among a section of the younger generation, especially after the 1987 elections, has been attributed as the primary cause. These frustrations had been building steadily as a result of cynical misgovernance and the failure of successive governments in Srinagar and New Delhi to reach a permanent understanding on autonomy. The rigged 1987 elections created a total mistrust in electoral politics among the Kashmiri population, especially in the Kashmir Valley.[1] A significant number in this younger generation took up arms in 1989 believing that only Kashmir's independence could address their problems. This first group, mainly belonging to urban areas and educated in Srinagar and other cities in IJK, also believed in a democratic and secular independent Kashmir.[2] A powerful section in Pakistan, led by its army and its Inter-Services Intelligence (ISI), soon sought to exploit the anti-India feelings and political frustration among the Kashmiris through arming and sustaining armed militants.[3]

New groups emerged or were created when the strategies of previous armed NSAs underwent a change. For example, when the Jammu and Kashmir Liberation Front (JKLF) gave up armed struggle, violence was sustained by the Hizbul Mujahidin.[4] While Pakistan had less to do with the emergence of the JKLF, it then created the Hizbul Mujahidin.[5] In the late 1990s, Lashkar-e-Taiba (LeT) and Jaish-e-Mohammad (JeM) were created with different sets of objectives when the HM started declining after 1995. While the recruits of the JKLF and HM were primarily from the Kashmir Valley, the LeT and JeM cadres are primarily from Pakistan. Some of the Afghan mujahidin groups, for example Hekmatyar's faction of the Hizb-e-Islami, also spared their fighters.[6] The availability of cadres willing for various reasons to engage in violence adds further sustenance to the armed struggle.

Easy availability of weapons and recruits, mainly due to regional instability elsewhere, also contributed to the proliferation of armed groups. It is no coincidence that the armed struggle in Kashmir emerged and violence rose after the end of the anti-Soviet jihad in Afghanistan. Many who participated in jihad against the Soviet Union shifted their attention in the early 1990s to Kashmir.[7] Instability in Southeast Asia was also a factor, in terms of transferring weapons into South Asia; for example, the militant groups in Kashmir "accessed AK-47s" from that region.[8]

Finally, any prolonged armed struggle has a tendency to generate an element of local criminalization. As a result, new armed militant groups may emerge with short-term financial motivations and few or no political objectives. It has happened elsewhere in India; for example, the United Liberation Front of Assam (ULFA) and the naxalite movement in Central and South India are engaged in extortion.[9] As discussed below, in Kashmir a similar phenomenon has also occurred.

Mapping the Militants

Armed groups operating in Kashmir do not constitute a monolith. They have different objectives, orientations, beliefs, and support bases—both internal and external. There is a major divide between the militants and counterinsurgents, as well as between Kashmiri and non-Kashmiri militants. Even within the groups there are internal divisions. Four classifications could be made: militants, jihadis, *ikhwans* (countermilitants), and renegades. As discussed below, these groups have sometimes had contentious relations, and their sources of sustenance and recruits have varied.

The Militants

The foremost armed militants are led by the Hizbul Mujahidin (HM), which is widely considered indigenous.[10] Its objectives are political, not religious. There are two strands of opinions about what it wants. A section inside Kashmir believes that the HM fights for an independent Kashmir; others, both inside and outside Kashmir, believe that it wishes to merge Kashmir with Pakistan. Though the HM leadership, based in Muzaffarabad, has never clarified its political orientation, its actions have served the limited objective of "freeing" Kashmir from "Indian occupation."[11] Such has been evident from its willingness to enter into a political dialogue with the government of India, which it did in July 2000.[12] Though HM has used religion for its purposes, it is not promoting Islam like the LeT or the JeM. HM rarely indulged in communal killings or carried out many *fidayin* (suicidal) attacks, unlike LeT or JeM. HM may be associated with the Jamaat-e-Islami; some of its cadres are also members of the latter, but in terms of religious objectives, the Hizbul remains political. HM has mainly targeted Indian security forces, and it has rarely attacked the police in IJK, with the exception being attacks on the Special Operations Group (SOG).[13]

Jihadis

LeT and JeM are most prominent among the jihadi groups. Unlike HM, these organizations have explicit pan-Islamic objectives. Kashmir is the means to achieve their broader objective of spreading Islam within the subcontinent and beyond.[14] While HM's activities have been Kashmir-focused, LeT and JeM have operated at the national level, apparently with the hope of destabilizing India by subversive activities and exploiting Hindu/Muslim fault lines. These militants have worked closely with Dawood Ibrahim and his underground mafia and with other Islamic right-wing organizations beyond Kashmir, for example, the Students' Islamic Movement of India (SIMI).[15]

LeT and JeM differ from HM in terms of their composition, being largely staffed by Pakistani and Afghan militants.[16] Most Kashmiris in the valley are against these groups and their grand objectives;[17] however, they are supported by other pan-Islamic groups within IJK.[18] Asiya Andrabi, the chairperson of Dukhtaran-e-Millat, and other minor groups, including Lashkar-e-Jabbar and Al-Badr, have been supporting these pan-Islamic militants against the HM,[19] though well-known Kashmiri leaders like Amanullah Khan, Abdul Ghani Lone, and Sardar Abdul Qayyum Khan have condemned them.[20]

Some jihadi groups have also tried to impose a Taliban-type Islam in IJK. In 2001, Lashkar-e-Jabbar (LeJ), widely suspected to be an LeT front,[21] threatened to attack women for not wearing the *burqa*.[22] Later that year, LeJ announced that there should be segregation of the sexes in public transport[23] and asked Hindu women to wear a *bindi* on their forehead, and Sikh women to wear saffron *dupattas* to differentiate them from Muslim women.[24] Kashmiri women have resisted this dress code; Mehbooba Mufti, a prominent Kashmiri politician and daughter of IJK chief minister Mufti Mohammed Sayeed, led the counterattack along with others.[25]

Jihadi groups mainly target the Indian military and paramilitary forces. Like HM, these groups have declared they would not attack the police forces, apart from the SOG.[26] However, they have targeted minority communities. Most communal killings have been carried out by these organizations, apparently to widen religious fault lines in IJK and elsewhere. Massacres in Chittisingpora and Nadimarg appeared to be calculated attacks against the minority Sikh and Hindu communities.[27] The objective of such attacks, according to one prominent analyst, has been to start a "Hindu migration to areas south of the Chenab," leading to Hindu communal mobilization elsewhere and resulting in "Muslim consolidation north of the Chenab."[28] Hindu communal elements have fallen into this trap in Jammu, leading to communal coloration being given even to secular events.[29]

Ikhwans

The third group of armed militants includes the *ikhwans*—the countermilitants who mobilized and were sustained by the Indian security forces in the mid-1990s for "ending the Hizbul Mujahidin's reign of terror."[30] Though the exact numbers are not known, most *ikhwans* are former militants belonging to various groups that surrendered to the Indian security forces at various times. They are not monolithic; they have been led by such diverse Kashmiris as Mohammad Kukka Parrey, Liaqat Khan, Javed Shah, and Ghulam Azad. The state and union governments have lacked a coherent policy toward *ikhwans,*[31] and failure to rehabilitate them or formally integrate them into the state security sector has generated resentment among them toward the government.[32] There are also numerous allegations against the *ikhwans* of extortion; illegal trade, especially in timber; and human rights violations. Their funding sources have been controversially linked to state (IJK) bureaucrats and the union government.[33]

Renegades

Since the early 1990s, prolonged militancy has also led to increasing levels of criminalization in IJK. Continuous splits within groups and the mushrooming of the number of minor groups were the main reasons for such criminalization. Inclusion of foreign militants, especially mercenaries, added to the problem. Some separatist leaders, on both sides of the LoC, have condemned profiteering by foreign militants.[34] Some of the *ikhwans* have also exploited their alliance with the Indian security forces to extort money from the local population.[35] There have been a few instances of individuals masquerading as politically or religiously inspired militants to indulge in looting, extortion, rape, and murder.[36]

Relations Among Militant Groups

Relations have sometimes been contentious among the militant groups fighting in IJK. The United Jihad Council (UJC), ostensibly an alliance including HM, LeT, and JeM, among others, does not exercise effective control over all of its members. Each group is independent on operational issues, plans, and objectives. Militant groups' relations have been tense due to conflicts between their objectives and those of their patrons in Pakistan.[37] Divisions among HM, LeT, and JeM have increased in the post–September 11 period, particularly after the United States' attack upon the Taliban in Afghanistan. In the wake of these developments, Pakistan stopped supporting the Taliban fighting in Afghanistan and its supporters inside its own territory. Several mercenaries and jihadis entered the part of Jammu and Kashmir under Pakistani administration, and open street fighting between the HM and LeT cadres was reported on both sides of the LoC.[38] Within the groups themselves, leadership struggles have sometimes led to violent infighting. HM cadres, for example, have engaged in such cross-LoC fighting with each other as well.[39]

Support Bases

A conventional official line from New Delhi is that there is little or no support for militancy inside IJK and violence is sponsored by foreigners as part of Pakistan's proxy war. Militants themselves and Islamabad tend to convey that Kashmiri society is against "Indian occupation" and supports militancy as part of an indigenous freedom movement. Both these perceptions are debatable. A majority of people in the Kashmir Valley are against the Indian establishment and the presence of the Indian security force, but most of them do not support the militants or Pakistan. Thus, only a minor segment in IJK, which despises the Indian establishment and security forces, provides moral and logistical support to the militants and serves as a recruitment base. Among this local support base, however, the LeT and JeM are seen as foreigners and "guests," and local support to them is limited. Indeed, mainstream separatist leaders and even HM militants have spoken out against foreign elements.[40]

Other support has come through coercion and crime. Some in IJK unwillingly support the militants out of fear, given that refusal to support them or yield to their requests has resulted in killings and the destruction of their properties.[41] Coupled with this is other criminal activity, including looting of banks. Such incidents underwent an increase in the post–September 11 period, when most of their accounts (for example those of LeT and JeM) were frozen, and when Pakistani President General Musharraf began distancing Pakistan from these groups. (See Table 4.1.) The looting of banks in IJK also increased as a result of deployment of Indian troops along the border in 2002, thereby reducing the cross-LoC supply of arms and cash.[42] Besides looting, there are reports of the militants taking up narcotic smuggling to mobilize funds for their operations.[43]

Enormous support for the militancy comes from outside IJK. Pakistan has been the main single source of this external support in terms of provid-

Table 4.1   Militant Looting in IJK

Year	Amount Looted (rupees)	Year	Amount Looted (rupees)
1990	22,691,200	1996	3,000,000
1991	6,230,768	1997	1,478,970
1992	6,485,563	1998	1,091,060
1993	8,357,626	1999	2,409,200
1994	13,919,288	2000	1,005,061
1995	15,000,071	2001	4,383,893

Source: South Asia Terrorism Portal, available online at www.satp.org/satporgtp/countries/india/states/jandk/data_sheets/amount_looted.htm.

ing weapons, training, and funds. Some sections in the state and society in Pakistan support these groups. However, according to one 2002 report, only 10 to 25 percent of the total finances necessary to sustain militancy and the political movement was coming from Pakistan, with the rest coming from elsewhere.[44] Evidence suggests that the militant groups have also received support from the Middle East and the Kashmiri diaspora, particularly from the UK and through Ayub Thakur's World Kashmir Freedom Movement.[45] According to another report, an estimated Rs 400–500 crore ($80–100 million) reaches IJK annually to support militant-related activities, mainly arriving through *hawala* (indigenous illegal money transfer) channels.[46]

Recruitment

The Indian government and the security forces often hold that there are no indigenous militants in IJK, except for a few misguided youths led by foreign mercenaries. The Pakistani government, on the other hand, tends to emphasize that those fighting in IJK are freedom fighters. Both perceptions are grossly exaggerated. The militants fall into two groups—Kashmiri and non-Kashmiri. Indian army statistics put the ratio at approximately 40 Kashmiris to 60 non-Kashmiris on the basis of militants killed or captured, while other open sources suggest that Kashmiris may make up between 40 and 60 percent.[47] Among the militants from Kashmir, the rural and urban divide is also significant. Kashmiri militants mostly come from the rural border districts of Rajouri, Poonch, and Baramulla. Anecdotal evidence suggests that during the early years of the insurgency, more recruits came from the urban areas. But by the mid-1990s, seemingly as urban youth began to realize the futility of armed struggle for their goals, recruits from rural areas began to outnumber urban recruits. In the period following the 1999 Kargil conflict, there was significant exfiltration from IJK across the LoC.[48] In 2001 alone, 1,500–2,000 young men in their mid-twenties, largely from Kupwara and Baramulla districts, crossed over the LoC for doctrinal and guerrilla training in facilities in AJK.[49] In 2003, approximately 400 people from Rajouri and Poonch districts were reported to have crossed the LoC to receive training.[50] (See Table 4.2.)

Individual motivations among young men in IJK for joining the armed struggle have ranged from the ideological to the banal. For some in IJK, there is the genuine interest in an independent Kashmir, the total alienation from India, and the belief that the gun is the only option available for achieving these nationalist goals. Others are provoked by harassment by security forces and other human rights violations. According to Ashok Bhan, inspector general of police, J&K, "It's the urge to join the jehad for some, and a better life and money for others. I believe that religious indoc-

Table 4.2   Militants Killed in J&K Since 1990

Year	Total Militants Killed	Foreign Militants Killed	Year	Total Militants Killed	Foreign Militants Killed
1990	550	0	1997	1,075	267
1991	844	2	1998	999	406
1992	819	6	1999	1,082	548
1993	1,310	79	2000	1,520	870
1994	1,596	77	2001	2,020	1,198
1995	1,332	77	2002	1,707	1,063
1996	1,209	219	2003	1,447	1,004
			2004 (to Oct.)	660	349

Source: Indian Army, available online at www.armyinkashmir.org/v2/statistical_facts/ft_actual_data.shtml.

trination is the main thing but unemployment too plays an important role."[51] According to a deputy inspector general of the Border Security Force (BSF), "apart from religious indoctrination and the motivation for jehad, money and gun [sic] as a status symbol also play an important role."[52] Some believe that "boys became militants to impress their girlfriends or a youth to win a girl who would otherwise turn down his advances," although such factors may be somewhat exaggerated.[53]

The non-Kashmiri militants largely come from Pakistan and Afghanistan, mostly as part of LeT and JeM. Pakistanis constitute the majority of the foreign militants, and somewhat surprisingly, most come not from *madrassas* (religious schools), but rather from state-run schools and colleges.[54] Most Pakistani militants come from Punjab, followed by Sindh and the North-West Frontier Province (NWFP).[55] The non-Pakistani, non-Kashmiri militants are mostly mercenaries from Afghanistan. There are reports of Al-Qaida members entering the Kashmir Valley with other organizations, especially after the US action against the Taliban in Afghanistan.[56] However, Kashmiri leaders have refuted the claim that Osama bin Laden's men have entered Kashmir.[57] Militants also come to fight in IJK from other parts of the world, especially from the Middle East and the UK. According to a *Sunday Times* (UK) report, nine hundred UK Muslims are trained every year to fight in J&K, and "about 10 per cent of those stay and fight, the rest take their political and religious indoctrination and bring it back to their communities, mostly for fund raising and recruitment."[58] Most foreign militants, especially from Pakistan, are motivated by jihad. Persons with a criminal background from Pakistan also seem to have been sent to Kashmir with a promise of charges against them being dropped, but this factor need not be exaggerated.[59]

Dealing with Armed Militancy in IJK: Approaches Since 1999

The successive governments in J&K and in New Delhi have not pursued a uniform policy, which remains the main problem in dealing with the violence. Primarily it was seen as a law and order issue, with occasional alternative approaches; for example, the cease-fire with HM and the Ramzan cease-fire in 2001. Violence was largely seen as a part of cross-border terrorism and proxy war.

The Bharatiya Janata Party (BJP) government in India pursued a series of ad hoc policies from 1999 to 2004. The BJP in its political rhetoric continuously emphasized pursuing a proactive policy against terrorism in IJK. In practice, however, its cease-fire politics and proactive rhetoric, including surgical strikes, preemptive strikes, hot pursuit, and limited war, failed to convince either the moderates or the militants. Thus, once in power, the BJP government could not pursue military action against militancy, as there was no political will. This was demonstrated during the 2002–2003 military confrontation with Pakistan, during which plans to destroy militant camps across the LoC were not implemented.

As Table 4.3 shows, militant activities spurted from 2000 to 2002, leading to increased casualties. It took three years for the security forces to bring the violence back to the pre-2000 level. In addition, the communal divide widened in IJK; this was apparent after the Nadimarg and Chittisingpora massacres, which only helped the militants, as they exploited the state's inability to provide security. The widening communal divide also politicized the military campaign against the militants for short-term gains, losing out on any long-term objectives.[60] The BJP-led government's most consequential blunder was in agreeing to release Maulana Masood Azhar, Mushtaq Ahmed Zargar, and Omar Saeed Sheikh during the Indian Airlines flight IC 814 hijacking in December 1999. This yielding to the hijackers' demands provided the militancy with new vigor, demoralized the security forces, and highlighted the weakness of the BJP government. (See Table 4.3.)

A major peace initiative was launched in 2000 in the aftermath of the failed cease-fire with the HM. Abdul Majid Dar, one of HM's leaders, declared a cease-fire in 2000, which was reciprocated by the state. The July 2000 cease-fire announced by the HM failed because Pakistan and the All Parties Hurriyat Conference (APHC), after initially agreeing, later realized they were being marginalized. In addition, the union government and the HM were unprepared for the fast-unfolding events leading to the cease-fire collapsing.[61] K. C. Pant was appointed as the chief interlocutor to hold discussions with the various Kashmiri groups and individuals, but he failed to make any substantial progress; Kashmiri leaders and the local population

Table 4.3   Annual Casualties in Terrorist Violence, 1988–2004

Year	Terrorists	Civilians	Security Force Personnel	Total
1988	1	29	1	31
1989	0	79	13	92
1990	183	862	132	1,177
1991	614	594	185	1,393
1992	873	859	177	1,909
1993	1,328	1,023	216	2,567
1994	1,651	1,012	236	2,899
1995	1,338	1,161	297	2,796
1996	1,194	1,333	376	2,903
1997	1,177	840	355	2,372
1998	1,045	877	339	2,261
1999	1,184	799	555	2,538
2000	1,808	842	638	3,288
2001	2,850	1,067	590	4,507
2002	1,714	839	469	3,022
2003	1,546	658	338	2,542
2004	951	534	325	1,810

Source: South Asia Terrorism Portal, available online at www.satp.org/satporgtp/countries/india/states/jandk/data_sheets/annual_casualties.htm.

perceived this development as without any objective. The militant attack on the Indian parliament in December 2001, however, sealed the fate of any political dialogue with the nonstate actors.

The Congress-led United Progressive Alliance government, which came to power in India in 2004, has withdrawn some troops from IJK, indicating that it could withdraw more troops if the ground situation improves. Since the political process with Pakistan became intense, the Congress government's priority in Kashmir seems to be based on engaging Pakistan rather than the nonstate actors or the political groups in IJK. The bus service between the two Kashmirs and the opposition to it from the armed NSAs, along with a section among the separatist group led by Syed Ali Shah Geelani, have further caused the Congress government not to focus on any political approach vis-à-vis the armed groups.

Conclusions: Lessons and Approaches

The state government of Jammu and Kashmir and the union government of India need to pursue a long-term policy toward tackling the armed nonstate actors. Segments of both governments believe only in a military approach, convinced that militancy can be militarily defeated, while others prefer a political and military approach, so that the militants would be pressured and ultimately coopted into the political mainstream. A policy based on the second approach would prove to be productive in the long term.

Different policies need to be pursued toward the various armed militants in Kashmir. Militant groups like the HM, if willing to support a peace process—whether bilateral or trilateral—can be engaged politically, as was the case in the 2000 cease-fire. The jihadi groups, including LeT and JeM, have objectives extending beyond IJK and are against any Indo-Pak rapprochement on Kashmir.[62] Unilaterally, India can only deal with these organizations militarily. Bilaterally with Pakistan, India could pressure but also help Pakistan to take effective action against the jihadi groups. India could help Pakistan in achieving these objectives by sharing intelligence, and also by considering the merits of joint patrolling to monitor the LoC.[63]

Countering militancy in IJK should be seen in the context of counterinsurgency elsewhere and at other times in India. For example, the government of India could take positive lessons from its experience in dealing with Khalistani separatist insurgents in Punjab. Empowering the local police and making them the primary force in opposing militancy would prove to be productive.

Winning the minds of the local population was yet another major factor that weakened local support and sympathy toward the insurgents in Punjab. The government of India and the state government in IJK should devise long-term policies for surrendered insurgents and *ikhwans* by rehabilitating and integrating them into society. Using them for short-term gains backfires over the long term. Unless a successful policy is framed and implemented, it would be difficult for the state to encourage more surrenders in the future.

At the operational level, countermilitancy operations need to be made more humane. Elements among the local population, as mentioned above, support militancy due to the collateral damage caused during countermilitancy operations. While some excesses may be unavoidable in these operations, this collateral damage to the civilian population needs to be minimized. What could be done is to give more teeth to the State Human Rights Commission and the National Human Rights Commission. This would make the security forces more accountable.

Notes

1. See Sumantra Bose, *Kashmir: Roots of Conflict, Paths to Peace* (Cambridge, MA: Harvard University Press, 2003), pp. 47–53.

2. For example, the Jammu and Kashmir Liberation Front. See Sumit Ganguly, *The Crisis in Kashmir: Portents of War, Hopes of Peace* (Cambridge: Cambridge University Press, 1997), Appendix 5, p. 170.

3. See Manoj Joshi, *The Lost Rebellion: Kashmir in the Nineties* (New Delhi:

Penguin Books, 1999); Sati Sahni, *Kashmir Underground* (New Delhi: Har-Anand, 1999).

4. The JKLF finally renounced armed violence in May 1994. See Manoj Joshi, *The Lost Rebellion,* pp. 288–289.

5. Amir Rana, a Pakistani journalist, catalogues these differences among organizations in AJK. He quotes a JKLF leader as stating, "Actually the ISI had given Hizbul Mujahidin the task of liquidating JKLF altogether from Occupied Kashmir. This is because JKLF demanded an autonomous Kashmir, and it was the largest organization." See Amir Rana, *Gateways to Terrorism* (London: New Millennium, 2003), p. 34.

6. Manoj Joshi, *The Lost Rebellion,* p. 179.

7. Tara Kartha, *Tools of Terror* (New Delhi: Knowledge World, 1999), pp. 205 and 214.

8. Tara Kartha, *Tools of Terror,* p. 237.

9. See "Assam Tea Gardens: No Escaping from Extortion," *Business Line,* 17 June 2004; "Ulfa Extortion Net Foxes Army," *Telegraph,* 16 September 2004; "Rebels Serve Extortion Notices on Assam Tea Estates," *Deccan Herald,* 20 June 2004; "Extortion by Naxalites on the Rise," *Hindu,* 29 December 2004.

10. Abdul Majid Dar stated in an interview in 2000 that the strength was in the thousands and less than 5 percent are non-Kashmiris. See "We Will Support Any Serious Initiative to Resolve Kashmir Issue," http://www.rediff.com/news/2001/apr/06inter.htm. According to independent reports, the figure is around 1,500. See "Hizbul Mujahideen," http://www.satp.org/satporgtp/countries/india/states/jandk/terrorist_outfits/hizbul_mujahideen.htm.

11. See the interviews given by Syed Salahuddin. "We Will Continue Our Struggle to Liberate Kashmir," http://www.newsline.com.pk/NewsJune2003/cover4june2003.htm; elsewhere he has commented, "Pakistan is not Pakistan without Kashmir." See "For Dialogue and Armed Struggle, Together," *Frontline* 20, no. 11, 24 May–6 June 2003.

12. See "Hizbul Announces 'Ceasefire,'" *Hindu,* 25 July 2000; Praful Bidwai, "The Hizbul Ceasefire Offer," *Frontline,* 18 August 2000, pp. 101–102; Praveen Swami, "Terror Unlimited," *Frontline,* 1 September 2000, pp. 4–18.

13. The SOG is the state's (IJK's) counterinsurgency force, formed in 1994. See "Hizb Condemns Killing of Cops," *Pioneer,* 1 January 2003.

14. Mohammad Hafiz Saeed, Amir of the LeT, stated in an interview: "There is only one jihad and that is jihad for Allah. All other forms of jihad are also for Allah. Jihad is only for Allah." See "In Defense of Jihad," *Frontline,* 9 May 2003, p. 43. A poster pasted up by the Al-Badr on the Hasiyot Mosque in Rajouri read: "Beloved brothers of Hasiyot: We have left our country to fight for your freedom. But still you people feel no sense of gratitude. We urge you to stop helping the *Kafirs* (unbelievers). After this, no one who does so will be spared. He who helps a Kafir is also a Kafir. If you still do not pay heed, Allah has given his soldiers enough strength to finish you as well as the Kafirs." Quoted in Praveen Swami, "Cloaks and Daggers," *Frontline,* 17 January 2003, p. 22.

15. See Praveen Swami, "Kashmir After Kandahar," *Frontline,* 4 February 2000, pp. 4–8; Praveen Swami, "A Widening Network," *Frontline,* 3 January 2003, pp. 33–37; Anupama Katakam, "Terror in Mumbai," *Frontline,* 11 April 2003, pp. 44–45. For a note on SIMI, see "Students Islamic Movement of India," *South Asian Terrorism Portal,* available at http://www.satp.org/satporgtp/countries/india/terroristoutfits/simi.htm.

16. See "Lashkar-e-Taiba," http://www.satp.org/satporgtp/countries/india/

states/jandk/terrorist_outfits/lashkar_e_toiba.htm; B. Raman, "The Lashkar-e-Taiba," http://www.saag.org/papers4/paper374.html; "Jaish-e-Mohammad," http://www.satp.org/satporgtp/countries/india/states/jandk/terrorist_outfits/jaish_e_mohammad_mujahideen_e_tanzeem.htm.

17. See text of poster in note 14; see Praveen Swami, "Cloaks and Daggers," p. 22.

18. See "Pan-Islamic Outfits Bid to Create Communal Trouble," *Daily Excelsior*, 23 February 2001; Praveen Swami, "The Nadimarg Outrage," *Frontline*, 25 April 2003, pp. 38–40.

19. Dukhtaran-e-Millat is supposedly a militant organization with women cadres, but its role is limited to the organization by its chairperson, Asiya Andrabi, of periodic press interviews. She is a known supporter of Syed Geelani, Lashkar-e-Taiba, and Jaish-e-Mohammad. See "Hurriyat, HM Have Sold Themselves: Andrabi," *Daily Excelsior,* 5 January 2001, and "Hizbul Role Doubtful, Lone an Indian Agent: Asiya," *Greater Kashmir,* 5 January 2001.

20. "PoK Leader Flays Foreign Militants," *Daily Excelsior,* 2 January 2002; "JKLF Chief Attacks Harkat, Lashkar," *Asian Age,* 9 July 2000.

21. "Is Jabbar a Front for Lashkar?" *Hindustan Times*, 4 September 2001.

22. "Burqas Make a Comeback at Gun Point," *Indian Express*, 18 August 2001. Also see Praveen Swami, "Cloaks and Daggers," pp. 22–25.

23. "Burqa Order Is Followed by One on Buses," *Times of India*, 6 September 2001.

24. "Now, a 'Diktat' to Non-Muslim Women," *Hindu*, 9 September 2001.

25. Mehbooba stated, "There is no guarantee that these people who are today asking womenfolk to observe purdah will tomorrow ask women not to come out of their homes. They can even tell girls not to join the medical colleges because males also study there. The campaign is not going to lead us anywhere." See "Kashmiri Women Raise Their Voice Against Dress Code Terrorism," *Kashmir Times*, 1 September 2001; "Kashmiri Women Don't Need Morality Lessons," *Indian Express*, 7 September 2001.

26. According to a statement made by a spokesman of LeT, "Kashmiri police personnel are our brothers and as such we owe no grudge and enmity against them." See "We Won't Attack Kashmir Police: LeT," *Greater Kashmir*, 15 February 2001.

27. See "Pan-Islamic Outfits Bid to Create Communal Trouble," *Daily Excelsior*, 23 February 2001; Praveen Swami, "The Nadimarg Outrage," pp. 38–40. LeT is seen to be behind these attacks. See "Planner of Nadimarg Massacre Arrested," *Daily Excelsior,* 11 April 2003; "'LeT Behind Nadimarg Massacre,'" *Hindu,* 11 April 2003.

28. Praveen Swami, "Massacres and Cold Facts," *Frontline*, 13 August 1999, p. 26. Also Praveen Swami, "Traumatic Transition," *Frontline*, 13 October 2000, pp. 66–71.

29. Praveen Swami, "'Pro-Active' After Pokhran: A Perspective on Terrorism in J&K," *Faultlines* 1, no. 1 (May 1999), pp. 87–112.

30. Praveen Swami, "A Beleaguered Force," *Frontline*, 12 February 1999, p. 41.

31. For example, Lieutenant General Kishan Pal stated in March 1999 that the army would fund the groups led by Kukka Parrey and Liaqat Khan, while ignoring those led by Javed Shah and Ghulam Azad. See Praveen Swami, "Funding, Covert and Overt," *Frontline*, 21 May 1999, p. 41.

32. Abdul Rahman, an Ikhwan, has stated, "Maybe I should have just stayed on with the Hizbul Mujahideen. I would have been dead, but my family would have

been richer by now, and we would have been living on our land. And I wouldn't have had the welfare of a wife and a daughter to worry about." Praveen Swami, "Funding, Covert and Overt," p. 41.

33. According to Praveen Swami, "Covert funding by the Ministry of Home Affairs (MHA) for all militia organizations was traditionally routed through two top State bureaucrats. Over time, there were complaints that the militia leaders were appropriating the funds without sharing them. Alternate proposals to route funds through the State Director General of Police were made, but they fell through for a variety of reasons." See Praveen Swami, "Funding, Covert and Overt," p. 41.

34. Sardar Abdul Qayyum Khan, former president of AJK, accused the foreign militants of damaging the Kashmir cause by making money in the name of jihad. See "PoK Leader Flays Foreign Militants."

35. The case of an illiterate barber in Budgam who surrendered to the security forces after becoming a militant is illustrative. Mohammad Hajam, alias Jabba Nayyid, used to identify local people as "militants" and extort between Rs 5,000 and 20,000 for releasing them. See "Barber Takes BSF for a Barbarous Ride," *Daily Excelsior*, 15 December 2001.

36. See "Two Fake Terrorists Nabbed in Poonch, Ultra Killed," *Daily Excelsior*, 23 June 2002.

37. See Amir Rana, *Gateways to Terrorism*, p. 34.

38. See "Kashmiris Struggle in PoK; LeT Let Loose a Reign of Terror," *Daily Excelsior*, 4 February 2002; "Foreigners Attack Locals to Gain Control of Marwah Belt; 7 Terrorists Killed in HM-LeT Clash," *Daily Excelsior*, 13 June 2002. M. L. Kak, "It's Hizb vs Lashkar in Valley," *Tribune*, 18 June 2002.

39. The divide within the HM came to the fore with Abdul Majid Dar distancing himself from Syed Salahuddin. Ultimately Dar and his supporters, including Zaffar Abul Fatah and Yazdani, were expelled; Dar was killed by the Salahuddin group in 2003. See "Hizb Holds Meet to End Rift," *Hindu*, 24 November 2001; "Hizb Expels Majeed Dar, Zaffar, Yazdani," *Daily Excelsior*, 5 May 2002; "Hizb Infighting in PoK, 3 Killed," *Hindustan Times*, 25 March 2003.

40. See "Foreign Militants in Kashmir Detrimental to It: Qayyum," *Daily Excelsior*, 27 June 2002; "Mirwaiz Terms Pak Militant Groups as 'Virtual Thieves,'" *Daily Excelsior*, 26 April 2002; "Hizb Rules out Role for Foreign Militants," *Hindu*, 21 November 2001.

41. See, for example, "Refused Shelter, Ultras Torch Houses in Rajouri," *Daily Excelsior*, 21 May 2001.

42. See "Cash Starved Militants Start Looting Banks in South Kashmir," *Daily Excelsior*, 21 March 2002.

43. See "Are Ultras Smuggling Narcotics?" *Tribune*, 3 January 2003; "Narcotics Seizure from Ex-militants," *Daily Excelsior*, 11 January 2003.

44. "30 Top Kashmiri Businessmen Spared After Warnings," *Kashmir Times*, 6 April 2002.

45. On diaspora support, see "UK Deports Pak Cleric for His 'Lashkar Fundraising,'" *Indian Express*, 12 October 2001; "Militants Being Funded by Muslims in Britain," *Daily Excelsior*, 10 June 2002; "Geelani Arrested Under POTA, Shifted to Ranchi Jail," *Daily Excelsior*, 10 June 2002.

46. "30 Top Kashmiri Businessmen Spared After Warnings," *Kashmir Times*, 6 April 2002; "Hawala Money for Ultras Seized, 1 Held," *Tribune,* 27 July 2002; "Hawala Transactions Have Terrorist Linkages in J&K," *Daily Excelsior*, 5 March 2002; "Racket Funding Militants in J&K Busted," *Daily Excelsior*, 29 June 2002.

47. Personal interactions of author with officials and civilians in IJK. Also see

"Row over Killing of 'Militants,'" *Hindu*, 10 November 2001. Caution is necessary in analyzing state figures on foreign militancy. Militants killed and identified as "foreigners" have sometimes turned out to be from IJK. State authorities have explained that at times, when the bodies are not identified or claimed, they are presumed to be foreigners.

48. Muzamil Jaleel, "Valley's Troubled Teens Drop Satchel, Sling Gun," *Indian Express*, 13 August 2001.

49. "1,500 Boys Went to PoK for Training," *Times of India*, 7 December 2001.

50. "Lure of Money Makes 400 Cross over to Pak," *Times of India*, 12 January 2003.

51. Muzamil Jaleel, "Valley's Troubled Teens Drop Satchel, Sling Gun."

52. Ibid.

53. N. S. Jamwal, "Terrorists' Modus Operandi in Jammu and Kashmir," *Strategic Analysis* 27, no. 3, July–September 2003, p. 385.

54. According to Amir Rana, "The list of martyrs from six jihadi organizations indicates that student martyrs from schools and colleges outnumbered those from madrasas by five times." See Amir Rana, *Gateways to Terrorism*, p. 32.

55. According to Amir Rana, "Punjab province is the nerve centre of the jihadi organizations. They derive 50 per cent of their human resource from here. . . . The desire to join jihadi organizations is more intense among the youth of Multan, Bahawalpur and Dera Ghazi Khan districts." Amir Rana, *Gateways to Terrorism*, p. 57.

56. See "Al Qaeda Men Sneak into Valley, Operating with Jaish Cadres," *Daily Excelsior*, 9 May 2002; B. L. Kak, "Are Al Qaeda Terrorists in J&K?," *Daily Excelsior*, 25 July 2002; "Two Al Qaeda Groups Sneak into Kashmir," *Daily Excelsior*, 13 June 2002.

57. For example, Abdul Qayyum Khan stated, "Kashmir is very difficult terrain and it is not possible for Arabs to operate there especially when they don't know the area and the language. . . . I discouraged them and luckily they listened to me." See "Osama's Men Not in Kashmir: Qayyum," *Daily Excelsior*, 12 May 2002.

58. "900 UK Muslims Trained Every Year to Fight in Kashmir: report," *Daily Excelsior*, 22 January 2001.

59. N. S. Jamwal, "Terrorists' Modus Operandi," p. 385.

60. See Praveen Swami, "From Kargil to Sarp Vinash: The Continuing Story of the Use and Abuse of the Indian Army by the NDA Government," *Frontline*, 18 July 2003, pp. 20–23.

61. See Praveen Swami, "Terror Unlimited," pp. 4–18.

62. Hafiz Mohammad Saeed, chief of LeT, had warned that General Musharraf "would have to pay the price for his friendship with Vajpayee." See "LeT, Harkat Warn Musharraf Against Getting Close to India," *Daily Excelsior*, 9 June 2001.

63. For details on joint monitoring and its positive implications, see Suba Chandran, "Monitoring an Active Border: A Case for Neutral Observers," *Swords and Ploughshares* 25, no. 3 (Winter 2003–2004), pp. 3–5.

5

Pakistan and Jihadi Groups in the Kashmir Conflict

Rizwan Zeb

The mercenaries and auxiliaries are useless and dangerous, and if any one supports his state by the arms of mercenaries, he will never stand firm or sure, as they are disunited, ambitious, without discipline, faithless, bold among friends, cowardly among enemies, they have no fear of God, and keep no faith with man. Ruin is only deferred as long as the assault is postponed, in peace you are despoiled by them and in war by the enemy.[1]

—Machiavelli

Contrary to popular belief, the phenomenon of armed nonstate actors is not new. One can find mention of such groups as early as the writings of Herodotus.[2] Yet no precise definition of an armed group is available. They are described as freedom fighters, guerrillas, warlords, militants, terrorists, etc.[3] This lack of consensus on a definition implies that the debate over whether such groups are terrorists or freedom fighters remains unresolved. Or, in other words, "one person's terrorist is another person's freedom fighter" continues to be the case.

The world has witnessed the emergence of many such groups in the last century. Kashmir, the site of a protracted conflict between India and Pakistan, is one such region, where a number of armed militants or jihadis, as they are popularly known, are involved. A problem with protracted conflicts is that over a period of time, a number of new factors and actors get involved and make the conflict more obdurate. The conflict over Kashmir is one such conflict, which today involves a number of actors as well as factors that were not there at the time of the partition of the subcontinent.

In primarily a territorial dispute between India and Pakistan as recognized by the United Nations, today a third faction, Kashmiris, constitute a party to the conflict. Pandits of the valley, Dogras of the Jammu region, an armed freedom struggle, and freedom fighters—these are all additions to this conflict, making the resolution even more difficult. Most of them, over time, have turned out to be part of the problem instead of part of the solution. Prime among these are the jihadi groups. Their involvement and presence have made any possible settlement of the Kashmir conflict far more complex. Any attempt toward the settlement of the conflict will now require acknowledging their existence and addressing and perhaps also including their perspectives. Of the estimated fifteen or so jihadi groups active in Kashmir,[4] this chapter will focus on Hizbul Mujahidin (HM), Harkat-ul-Mujahidin (HuM), Al Badr, Lashkar-e-Taiba (LeT), and Jaish-e-Mohammad (JeM), because in the author's understanding these are the major groups that are significant for, or might also have a role (if not positive, then that of a spoiler) to play in, any peace process between India and Pakistan.

There are a number of reasons these groups cannot be ignored. They are armed, skilled, and motivated, as well as prepared to fight to achieve what they feel is right. Over the years this has added a new dimension to the Kashmir conflict. These groups have their own views on how to resolve the Kashmir conflict that may or may not coincide with what India and/or Pakistan, or even the local population, thinks or wants. Any attempt to resolve the conflict needs to acknowledge their existence and include them in the process. Otherwise they might play a spoiler's role. These groups have lately been considered a threat to peace and stability in the region. At least on one occasion they almost caused a war between the two countries.[5] Internationally, many who fail to differentiate between a freedom struggle and terrorism have begun to view this as an issue of terrorism. According to one observer, such elements were raised and nourished by the military establishment to fill the conventional military gap with India, with the realization that the Pakistani military cannot push India to a solution regarding Kashmir. In such circumstances, these groups were a "cost-effective option."[6] However, since President Musharraf came to power, the realization that this is a liability arose, and President Musharraf's administration started taking action against these groups prior to September 11. Since September 11, these jihadi groups and the government of Pakistan are also at loggerheads, as is evident by the ban imposed on the groups and the deadly and almost successful assassination attempts on the military and civilian leadership of the country. The jihadi groups view the ongoing peace process between India and Pakistan, initiated in April 2003, as a threat to their existence as well as a betrayal of the ideological foundations of Pakistan and Islam. This makes it all the more relevant to study the phenomenon of these jihadi groups.

Unfortunately there is a dearth of written scholarly work on armed militants in Kashmir, and the available literature is often sensationalist. This chapter mainly draws on the work of Amir Rana (2004)[7] and Amir Mir (2004).[8] The limitation of this chapter is that the author has relied on secondary sources, mainly the above-mentioned works. However, the chapter aims at contributing to the discussion of the role of the armed militants in light of the peace process initiated by India and Pakistan in January 2004.

The chapter begins with a discussion of the composition of jihadi groups, followed by their sources of financial and human support, their links with Pakistan, their reaction to recent developments in South Asia, and their role in the peace process.

Composition of Jihadi Groups

In 1989 the Kashmiri freedom struggle took an altogether new direction.[9] At that time the Kashmiris decided to take up arms and fight for their freedom, mainly due to repeated and increasing human rights violations by the Indian forces, ongoing Indian mishandling of Kashmir, and continued rigging of polls. In fact, the rigging of polls turned out to be the immediate trigger of this uprising. Most observers agree that the armed struggle was indigenous.[10] However, after being initiated mainly by the Jammu and Kashmir Liberation Front (JKLF), it was taken over by the more religiously oriented nationalist organization, HM, and later Harkat-ul-Ansar (renamed Harkat-ul-Mujahidin). Amanullah Khan, founder of JKLF, once complained, "After two or three years, our movement was hijacked by religious extremists, many of them veterans of the Afghan war."[11]

Most of the armed militants active in Kashmir from the late 1990s onward could be called jihadi groups, as their raison d'être is ostensibly to fight wherever Muslims are oppressed. "South Asia's Islamist political movements trace their inspiration back to Sheikh Ahmed Sirhandi's challenge in the sixteenth century to the ecumenism of Mughal emperor Akbar," writes Husain Haqqani.[12] The first jihadi group of the subcontinent was the Tahrik-ul-Mujahidin, led by Sayyid Ahmed of Bareili, who was deeply influenced by the ideas of Muhammad Ibn-Abdul Wahhab. Husain further states that "Sayyid Ahmed's revival of the ideology of jihad became the prototype for the subsequent Islamic militant movements in South and Central Asia." He classifies existing jihadi groups into three categories: groups centered on the Jamaat-e-Islami, Deobandi groups, and Wahhabi groups.[13]

Syed Abul A'la Maududi, founder of the Jamaat, has produced a literature that divides the world into Islamic and un-Islamic sections. He has also "laid out a stage-by-stage strategy for Islamic revolution in his many speeches and writings."[14] His book *Al-Jihad-fil-Islam* (Jihad in Islam) remains a comprehensive text on the subject. The Deobandi school has always emphasized the importance of jihad. "In recent years, Deobandi Ulema have articulated jihad as a sacred right and obligation, encouraging their followers to go to any country to wage jihad to protect the Muslims of that country."[15] LeT justifies its ideology on the basis of the quranic verse: "You are obligated to fight even though it is something you do not like" (2:216). In a publication titled *Hum Jihad Kyun Kar Rahe Hain?* (Why Are We Waging Jihad?), an LeT ideologue has given reasons to justify their struggle.[16]

There are exceptions, however, to the classification of militant groups as jihadi. In the author's view, for example, HM would not qualify as a jihadi group, as its aims are more nationalistic, although with a clear Islamic leaning (see Table 5.1).

These jihadi groups have similar sources of financing, but what is notable is that many of these sources are private and at least somewhat independent of Pakistan government policy. Primary among these private channels have been charity contributions from common Muslims, who do this because they consider it a religious duty and not because they favor such groups; sales of skins of sacrificial animals; funds from Pakistanis of Kashmiri origin living abroad; and donations from sheikhs of various Gulf States.[17]

Amir Rana points out that these groups used to send their representatives to different countries for collection of funds. He notes that HuM in particular used to collect through its representatives, who were on the move for this purpose throughout the year.[18] Funds were also raised from within Pakistan, including through donation boxes in ordinary shops and jihad funds collected from mosques during Friday prayers. Another source for HuM was the agricultural land given to it by the Taliban authority in Afghanistan,[19] but since the fall of Taliban this source has dried up. JeM also used to earn money through charity organizations such as the Al-Rashid Trust and the Al-Akhtar Trust International.[20] The ideologues of LeT argue that in the absence of a true Islamic state, LeT has the right to collect *zakat* (alms); however, how successful they actually have been in doing so remains unclear. LeT has also been innovative in using the Internet to raise funds.[21]

No reliable sources are available on the amount spent by these groups for their activities in IJK. According to Indian sources, US$70–80 million is spent annually in Kashmir.[22] This observation, according to the commandant of the Indian Border Security Force, N. S. Jamwal, is made on the basis "that even a large . . . outfit like Hizb-ul-Mujahedeen needs no more than US $6 to 8 million annually. There are no more than 10–15 such outfits in the valley."[23] However, there are no independent reports or sources available to verify this claim.

It has been alleged by the Indians that these groups have been actively involved in criminal activities, such as kidnapping for ransom and bank rob-

Table 5.1   Militant Groups Active in Kashmir

Group	History
Hizbul Mujahidin (HM)	The Hizbul Mujahidin was formally established in November 1989 as the armed wing of the Jamaat-e-Islami in IJK. Its constitution was put in place on 10 June 1999. HM is one of the oldest jihadi groups active in Kashmir and comprising Kashmiris. Its first chief was Master Ahsan Dar. In September 1991 the supreme advisory council of HM elected Syed Salahuddin as its supreme commander. Syed Salahuddin is also the chairman of the Muttahida Jihad Council (United Jihad Council), an umbrella organization of more than seventeen jihadi groups. On 19 September 1996, the Indian government, under the J&K Criminal Law Amendment Act of 1983, declared HM an unlawful organization. Reportedly, intense rivalry also surfaced between two groups within HM, the Salahuddin loyalists and the Masood Sarfraz (famously known as the Lion of Pir Panjal) group. In July 2000, HM declared a three-month ceasefire against the Indian forces but was unable to sustain it due to a number of factors. Majid Dar and his followers were of the view that the armed struggle has played a significant role in bringing the Kashmir issue to the world's attention, yet it cannot ensure the final solution; therefore other options should also be explored, and this cease-fire was one of them. However, after the failed cease-fire attempt, the differences between the two groups intensified. In a meeting held on 2 May 2002 Sayed Salahuddin decided to sack Majid Dar. As the high command of HM differed strongly on this decision, it further divided the group. Dar was killed in Sopore in March 2003.
Harkat-ul-Mujahidin (HuM)	HuM was formed by the merger of Harkat-ul-Jihad al-Islami and Harkat-ul-Mujahidin and was led by Maulana Saadatullah Khan. Originally known as Harkat-ul-Ansar (HkA), it was renamed HuM in 1998 when it was declared a terrorist organization by the US. Under the leadership of Sajjad Shahid, HkA started its activities in 1991. Soon its network of operation expanded to Baramulla, Poonch, and Anantnag, and it emerged as a strong jihadi group in Kashmir. HkA made its first attempt to rescue Masood Azhar and Sajjad Afghani by kidnapping foreign tourists from the valley. This was carried out by two of its commanders, Mohammad Sikandar and Abdul Hameed, under the name of Al-Faran. They demanded the release of Masood Azhar and Sajjad Afghani in exchange for the kidnapped tourists. This move proved to be a fatal blow to the organization, as the act was highly condemned internationally. Subsequently, both Harkat-ul-Ansar and Al-Faran were declared terrorist organizations by the US state department. The Harkat leadership denies any involvement in the kidnapping or knowledge about Al-Faran to date. However, the American decision compelled the leadership of Harkat-ul-Ansar to rename itself Harkat-ul-Mujahidin.
Al-Badar	Al-Badar Mujahidin was a comparatively smaller but effective jihadi group under the leadership of Bakht Zameen. Its members believe in Jamaat-e-Islami (JI)'s ideology and claim that Al-Badar is the continuation of a pro–United Pakistani organization of the same name that operated in East Pakistan with the Pakistan army during the 1971 war. According to the organization's literature, when jihad began in Indian-administered Kashmir, young men who were with the JI decided to create an organization of their own to take part in the struggle. This *(continues)*

Table 5.1   continued

Group	History
	organization was called Al-Badar. In October 1990 Al-Badar's leadership announced its merger with Hizbul-Mujahidin. After a long association, however, Al-Badar decided to retain its separate identity. According to sources and insiders, the reasons for this split were personality clashes and finances. According to Al-Badar sources, HM and JI were betraying the cause of jihad. Another factor leading to the separation was the alleged strict control of JI on HM matters.
Lashkar-e-Taiba (LeT)	Formed in 1990 in the Kunar province of Afghanistan, LeT was the military wing of Markaz-ud-Dawa-wal-Irshad, an Islamic fundamentalist organization of the Ahl-e-Hadith sect in Pakistan. The Markaz was based in Muridke near Lahore, Pakistan, and headed by Hafiz Muhammad Saeed. Its first presence in J&K was recorded in 1993. According to one source, the first operation of LeT was conducted under the leadership of Abu Khalid Aftab Ahmed; according to another, the first major operation of LeT was a raid on the headquarters of the Eleventh Jammu and Kashmir Light Infantry. By 1997, LeT broadened its activities and started to attack Indian installations, offices, and forces in the Jammu region and gained prominence for its *fidayin* (suicide) attacks. The most important of these included an attack on the Indian army barracks at Badami Bagh, on the Red Fort, and on Srinagar airport. The founders of the Markaz and LeT, Hafiz Saeed and Zafar Iqbal, are now at odds with each other. Zafar Iqbal's camp accuses Hafiz Saeed of diverting the party from its original objectives, misusing funds, and giving away important posts to his relatives belonging to the Gujjar caste. It has created a splinter organization called "Khairun Naas" (People's Welfare) and includes Zafar Ibqal, LeT chief Zaki-ur-Rehman Lakhvi, Abu Shoaib, Abu Naser Javed, and Maulana Abdul Salam Bhatvi.
Jaish-e-Mohammad (JeM)	JeM was launched on 31 January 2000 by Maulana Masood Azhar after he was released from an Indian jail following the hijacking of Indian Airlines flight IC 814. Masood Azhar was the general secretary of Harkat-ul-Ansar in 1994 and, according to sources, was on a special mission in J&K when he was arrested on 11 February. The creation of JeM adversely affected other jihadi groups, especially HuM, as most of its cadres joined JeM, including a number of leading figures such as Maulana Abdul Jabbar, Sajid Usman, Qari Sadiq, Qari Zarar (also known as Qasai), Ghulam Murtaza, Abdullah Shah Mazhar, and others. This led to a dispute between the two organizations over property that each claimed as its own. HuM sources claimed that JeM took over HuM property worth Rs 30 million. According to insider reports, Osama bin Laden was finally able to resolve the matter, though the differences remained. JeM also suffered a split in its own circles when Abdullah Shah Mazhar and Abdul Jabbar, along with a dozen members, left JeM to launch their own organization. Abdullah Shah Mazhar later accused Masood Azhar of betraying the cause of jihad.

Sources: Amir Mir, *The True Face of Jihadis;* Muhammad Amir Rana, *A to Z of the Jihadi Organizations in Pakistan;* Praveen Swami, "Terrorism in Jammu and Kashmir in Theory and Practice," in Sumit Ganguly, ed., *The Kashmir Question: Retrospect and Prospect,* pp. 55–88; jihadi literature, mainly monthly magazines of LeT, JeM, HM, and HuM.

beries, and have contacts with transnational criminal networks. They especially point out the alleged links between such groups and the Dubai-based Dawood Ibrahim.[24] However, there is little if any independent proof to verify such claims.

Within Pakistan, all major jihadi groups have their own areas of influence from which to recruit.[25] Mostly these recruitments have taken place in rural, economically underdeveloped, and backward areas where economic opportunities are limited and people can hardly make ends meet.[26] JeM was also successful in attracting volunteers from Sipa-e-Sahaba and student organizations like Jamiat-e-Tulba-e-Islam.[27] Most of these recruits, or *mujahids*, include Urdu–medium school dropouts, *madrassa* students, as well as members of the unskilled and jobless sections of the population.[28] Many young Pakistanis from European countries have reportedly also joined such organizations.[29] LeT also recruits former criminals and drug addicts as part of a rehabilitation process in which they commit to become practicing Muslims.

Training courses are more or less the same for all of these groups, even though the courses are given names, such as *Dura Ama* and *Khasa, Jund-Ullah*.[30] A basic training course typically runs for twenty-one days and includes basic arms handling. An advanced training course runs for three months and offers weapons handling, raiding and ambush, and survival techniques.[31] The life in the training camps is much as in any other guerrilla training camp. Regarding ideological indoctrination, LeT lately started a small course after the twenty-one–day *Dura Ama* in which the new recruits were trained in *Dawa* (preaching) techniques, Islamic teachings, and indoctrination based on Ahl-e-Hadith literature. Those who successfully pass this are then sent to the advanced training: *Dura Khasa*.

The reasons boys and young men join jihadi groups are many, involving psychological, ideological, political, socioeconomic, and cultural factors. The most important reason is a reaction to human rights violations and killings of Kashmiris by the Indian forces. Reports of such killings are used as propaganda by the jihadi groups to instruct potential recruits that by joining, they will be protecting the honor of their sisters and mothers.[32] Ideological reasons derive from the literature produced by such Islamist scholars as Syed Maududi, Syed Qutab, and Abdullah Azam, which builds the case that the primary duty of a Muslim is to establish the rule of Allah on this earth. Some parents in Pakistan have expressed the notion that since one can't escape death, it is a good thing if their sons become martyrs.[33] Along these lines, some express the need to avenge the atrocities committed against Muslims the world over, including beyond Kashmir: in Palestine, Bosnia, Chechnya. *Madrassa* education in Pakistan also teaches students that they are the saviors of Islam and it is their duty to spread God's message and eliminate *kufar* (infidelity). However, *madrassas* do not provide military training, nor do they send their graduates or students to join these groups. Socioeconomically, most of the volunteers come from areas of extreme poverty with poor educational facilities.[34]

On a few occasions, European Pakistanis and Pakistanis from well-to-do backgrounds join these groups. Their motivation comes from the realization, due to their exposure to world events, that Muslims the world over are victims of discrimination and injustice. Drug addicts and ex-criminals have also been known to join these groups to "relive" their lives in the dignity that is seen as coming with waging jihad.

Pakistan and Armed Militancy in Kashmir

When the Afghan jihad against the former USSR started, Pakistan supported it mainly because Zia thought that this would eliminate the threat of Pashtun nationalism and also the chances of further advance of the Red Army. "Moreover the concept of Pakistan's need for strategic depth that military strategists argued a friendly Afghanistan could provide Pakistan against India, created an alluring dogma. The country's lack of depth in space, they argued, prevented Pakistan from fighting a prolonged war with India and a friendly Kabul could rectify this strategic shortfall."[35]

Eqbal Ahmed pointed out that from the beginning of the twentieth century the idea of jihad was hardly present in Muslim minds, until the United States revived the idea of what he described as "Jihad International, Inc." to fight the Soviet occupation in Afghanistan.[36] Thousands of Muslim volunteers from various countries were trained, armed, and sent to fight the Soviets in Afghanistan.[37] From 1979 until 1989, Pakistan was thus a frontline state in the war against the Soviet Union. Pakistan's costs for this involvement included at least three million Afghan refugees and the emergence of a large illegal arms market through which light weapons were easily available.[38] After the withdrawal of the Soviet troops from Afghanistan in 1989, a number of jihadis turned their attention to the indigenous uprising that had just begun in Kashmir. Their involvement soon transformed the uprising from an indigenous secular nationalist movement into a transnational Islamist resistance movement. Indians viewed this as a Pakistani plan to bleed India.[39]

It is difficult to find hard data to prove that Pakistan's intelligence service was supporting all of the jihadi groups that became involved in the Kashmiri struggle,[40] yet it is widely believed that these groups were supported by some sections of religious parties, intelligence officials, etc. Some argued that while the Pakistan army could not win a war decisively, the mujahidin were fighting the Indians effectively in IJK without much cost to Pakistan's national exchequer.[41] As Ayesha Siddiqa has put it,

One of the explanations for Islamabad's supposed negligence of the threat posed by non-state actors or the large number of militants present within its boundaries is that such elements were raised and nourished by the military establishment to fill the conventional military gap vis-à-vis India. While not being able to force a military solution of Kashmir on Delhi, the militants were viewed as a cost-effective option.[42]

Soon after assuming power in a bloodless coup of 1999, President Musharraf started taking measures toward elimination of these groups and their support bases. As early as February 2001, Interior Minister Moinuddin Haider announced that the government had decided to prohibit the militant groups from fundraising in the name of jihad (anywhere in the world), from showing banners, and from displaying arms.[43] Haider also assigned the National Crisis Management Cell (NCMC) to compile data on jihadi activities, fundraising, and funding sources of all such organizations. President Musharraf has also on a number of different occasions presented and projected the true and humane spirit of Islam. The president's address to the gathering of religious scholars/leaders on the occasion of the Seerat Conference is a case in point.

The attacks of September 11, 2001, helped to propel already existing moves by the Pakistani government regarding these groups.[44] Having ended its diplomatic support for the Taliban and joined the US coalition in its "war on terror," the Pakistani government intensified its actions against these groups by officially banning all their activities and offices inside Pakistan (see Table 5.2). The tension in the relations between the jihadi groups and the government of Pakistan was clearly indicated in the (almost successful) assassination attempts on the president of Pakistan in December 2003, allegedly by a splinter JeM cell; on the prime minister and then the finance minister in July 2004; and on the corps commanders in Karachi in June 2004, allegedly by a group called Junad Allah (Allah's Army).

The Post-2004 Indo-Pak
Peace Process and the Jihadi Groups

For all of the jihadi groups active in the Kashmir conflict, the solution could only come through an end to Indian "occupation," although at least a few of them, including JeM and LeT, would also like to use gains in IJK as a platform to fight against mainland India.[45] For these groups, progress in an India-Pakistan dialogue on terms acceptable to India would effectively mean that Islamabad was surrendering Kashmir to India. Indeed, after the January 2004 Islamabad declaration, Syed Salahuddin, supreme commander of HM and the chairman of the AJK-based United Jihad Council, wrote,

Table 5.2   Militant Groups and the Post-2004 Peace Process

Properties	Characteristics of Group
Name	Hizbul Mujahidin (HM)
Splinter group	Hizb-e-Islami, Al-Badar
Views on Kashmir	End of Indian occupation
Current status	Active
Role in peace process	Potential partner
Name	Harkat-ul-Mujahidin (HuM)
Splinter group	Jaish-e-Mohammad (JeM)
Views on Kashmir	With Pakistan, but an Islamic Kashmir. Fazlur Rehamn Khalil in one of his interviews said that HuM has no objection to an independent Kashmir and that it only wants the ouster of the Indian army from Kashmir. However, this is not the view shared by the rest of the HuM leadership.
Current status	Inactive. Banned since 29 September 2001. The renamed organization, Jamaat-ul-Ansar, was also banned on 20 November 2003.
Role in peace process	Potential spoiler
Name	Lashkar-e-Taiba (LeT)
Splinter group	Khairun Naas
Views on Kashmir	Kashmir is the beginning of a long war against the infidels. Kashmir is perceived as a gateway to India.
Current status	Inactive. Banned since 5 January 2002.
Role in peace process	Potential spoiler
Name	Jasih-e-Mohammad (JeM)
Splinter group	Tehrik-ul-Furqa
Views on Kashmir	Kashmir is the gateway to India, where a larger jihad for the liberation of the Indian Muslims is to be fought.
Current status	Inactive. Banned since January 2002. The renamed organization Khudam-ul-Islam was also banned since 15 November 2003.
Role in peace process	Potential spoiler
Name	Al-Badar
Splinter group	Unknown
Views on Kashmir	Not clear, but most reports suggest that it has no objectives beyond the liberation of Kashmir from Indian occupation.
Current status	Inactive
Role in peace process	Unknown

Source: Criminal Investigation Department Headquarters, Jammu and Kashmir (IJK) Police, Srinagar.

"Since 9/11, Pakistan has totally changed its policy on Kashmir. It has backtracked on the issue of UN resolutions and plebiscite. It is also not supporting the freedom struggle in Kashmir and repeatedly has said that it will not allow cross-LoC infiltration."[46]

Salahuddin also reacted harshly to the proposals made by President Musharraf in October 2004 on a possible resolution of the Kashmir problem.[47] LeT's response to the developments in the post-2004 peace process was simply to assert that they had enough arms and ammunition in the valley to fight the Indian troops for at least the next six months.[48] According to the jihadi leadership, the Indians could not be trusted, and the peace process would eventually fail like all earlier attempts.[49]

Every peace process has spoilers, especially those who believe that if a negotiated settlement is reached between the parties, their power and worldview will be threatened. Such spoilers use violence to undermine the process.[50] Stedman has categorized the spoilers into different types. Will the jihadi groups act as spoilers in the Indo-Pak peace process? Or can they reconcile with the fact that the time has changed? A look at Table 5.2 reveals that only HM has been identified as a potential partner in the peace process, whereas LeT and JeM have been identified as potential spoilers. However, in this author's view these two groups will not be in a position to harm the peace process in a major way. The attack on the Srinagar bus terminal on 6 April 2005, though not claimed by either of them, just a day before the first bus service between the two Kashmirs, is a case in point; it failed to achieve the desired outcome. In the changed regional environment, Pakistan has initiated large-scale operations against these groups, expressed and acted on commitments of not letting its territory be used for any terrorist activity, and engaged in confidence building measures (CBMs) with India. Kashmiris from both sides have been interacting and strengthening a constituency for peace in both countries. Thus, the chance of these groups causing any serious damage is remote, though it cannot be ruled out entirely. With a continued peace process showing visible developments on the ground, change in the situation in the valley and elsewhere will result in gradual elimination of any spoilers.

HM, as an indigenous Kashmiri group fighting primarily for the right of self-determination and not for any larger agenda, is an obvious partner in the peace process. Their track record is also a proof of this fact. The sooner the Indian side includes them in the peace process, the better.

Former Pakistani Interior Minister Moinuddin Haider has suggested a number of measures India and Pakistan can take, including:

- A policy of noninterference in each other's affairs
- Introducing meaningful reforms to eradicate a sense of deprivation in various sections of society
- Intelligence sharing and coordination
- Implementation of the South Asian Association for Regional Cooperation charter on combating terrorism
- Stopping propaganda against each other and harboring and supporting terrorism
- Institutional measures to check terrorism by using technology and other means

- Positive role of media in South Asia to check terrorism
- Exposing and neutralizing various terrorist groups by denying them support or encouragement by state authorities
- Better utilization of resources mobilized to deal with the challenge of terrorism[51]

Conclusion

In the strategic circumstances prevailing in the post–September 11 era, the Pakistani leadership has been struggling to rid itself of a menace created under Zia's rule by the advocates of strategic depth. President Musharraf has likened the magnitude of the challenge to that which Pakistan faced three decades ago, calling it a "1971-like situation."[52] It seems that the leadership has drawn a number of important conclusions about the current situation.[53]

According to one view, the jihadi groups have also weakened the Pakistani case on Kashmir. If the struggle had remained with JKLF or HM, the situation would be much different today, because these are truly Kashmiri groups. The Indians could not have claimed that there were any foreign terrorists, or even if they had, they would not have found such an eager audience. The involvement of jihadi organizations such as HuM, LeT, and JeM has weakened the Kashmiri cause in the sense that a large majority started to view it as an issue of terrorism instead of a rightful struggle of Kashmiris for their right of self-determination. As Javed Ashraf Qazi, former director general of Inter-Services Intelligence (ISI) and the education minister under Musharraf, has pointed out, "We must not be afraid of admitting that Jaish-e-Mohammad was involved in the deaths of thousands of innocent Kashmiris, in the bombing of the Indian parliament, in Daniel Pearl's murder and in attempts on General Pervez Musharraf's life and that both Jaish [JeM] and Lashkar [LeT] have harmed the Kashmiri struggle the most."[54]

Another view is that the end to militancy might in fact prove to be a good thing for Islamabad and the Kashmiris. The Indian government, instead of relying on Pakistan as a scapegoat, will have to deal with the hardcore realities in Kashmir. However, when a visiting Kashmiri leader was recently asked about the future of the movement, he said that the Kashmiris are in their houses only because there are Indian troops in the valley. The moment they go or are redeployed, the Kashmiris will take to the streets in larger, much larger, numbers than in January 1990.[55] This is something the Indians realize very well. The dilemma for the Kashmiris at the moment is that so long as militancy remains, they will suffer the Indian atrocities, whereas the moment the militancy ends, the Indians will claim that there is no Kashmir problem.

In a televised address on 12 January 2002, President Pervez Musharraf "assured India of effectively curbing cross-border militancy. Pakistan asked India to better the situation in its controlled parts of Jammu and Kashmir by preventing severe human rights violations."[56] Recent reports indicate that he has fulfilled his promise.[57]

India not only has to have faith and trust in Pakistan's actions against these groups, but it also has to show patience. While Pakistan continues to do its best against these jihadi groups, India must improve the human rights situation in IJK; it must eventually decrease the number of troops and initiate a meaningful dialogue with the political leadership of Kashmir, as well as with groups like HM. The commitment to peace by both sides in the post-2004 period has been encouraging. Vajpayee very appropriately said, "A country cannot change its neighbor."[58] Both India and Pakistan seem to have accepted this fact in continuing toward peace in the region.

Notes

1. Machiavelli, *The Prince* (Chicago: GBF, 1964) pp. 40–41; also see Khaled Ahmed, "Foreword," in Amir Mir, *The True Face of Jehadis* (Lahore: Mashal, 2004).

2. Pablo Policzer, *Neither Terrorists nor Freedom Fighters*, paper presented at the American Political Science Association Conference, Chicago, IL, 2–5 September 2004, http://www.armedgroups.org/images/pdfs/policzer%20neither%20terrorist%20nor%20freedom%20fighters.pdf (accessed 9 December 2004).

3. Pablo Policzer, *Neither Terrorists nor Freedom Fighters*.

4. Amir Mir, "Cap the Camps: US," *Weekly Independent* (Lahore) 1, no. 18, 25–31 October 2001.

5. The attack on the Indian parliament in October 2002 led to a yearlong military standoff between the two nuclear armed adversaries. The Indians alleged that JeM and LeT were the ones who did it.

6. Ayesha S. Agha, "Pakistan's Security Perspective: Problems of Linearity," in P. R. Kumaraswamy, ed., *Security Beyond Survival* (New Delhi: Sage, 2004), p. 170.

7. Muhammad Amir Rana, *A to Z of Jehadi Organizations in Pakistan*, translated by Saba Ansari (Lahore: Mashal, 2004).

8. Amir Mir, *The True Face of Jehadis*.

9. The Kashmir resistance movement has continued since 1947, mostly political but violent at times as well. In the mid-1960s, Maqbool Butt and Amanullah Khan created the Jammu and Kashmir Liberation Front (JKLF). When Maqbool Butt went to the valley to establish the operational base of his organization, he was arrested and sentenced to death; however, he managed to escape and went to Pakistan. In the 1970s, Al-Fatah, a small group under the leadership of Gulam Rasool Zehangir, appeared on the scene but faded out without making any impact. Maqbool Butt again emerged in 1976 when he returned to the valley, but he was soon arrested by the Indian authorities. Amanullah Khan moved to the United Kingdom.

10. On the indigenous roots of the freedom struggle see Jessica Stern, *Terror in the Name of God* (New York: Ecco, 2004), pp. 116–117.

11. Ibid.

12. Husain Haqqani, "The Ideologies of South Asian Jihadi Groups," http://www.carnegieendowment.org/files/idelogies.pdf (accessed on 14 June 2005).

13. Ibid.

14. Ibid.

15. Ibid. According to Husain Haqqani, books by Masood Azhar best explain the Deobandi jihadi ideology. These are *Ma'arka* (The Struggle), *Faza'il Jihad* (The Virtue of Jihad), and *Tuhfa-e-Saadat* (The Gift of Virtue) (Karachi: Idara Al-Khair, 2001, all in Urdu).

16. Ibid., fn. 12 (pdf file).

17. For details see Amir Rana, *A to Z of Jehadi Organizations*.

18. Ibid., p. 254.

19. For details regarding the nature of the land and use of the proceeds from the sale of the products of this land, see Amir Rana, ibid.

20. Amir Mir, "Matters of Trust," *Herald*, November 2003, pp. 43–48.

21. Jessica Stern, *Terror*, p. 207; also see Amir Mir, *The True Face of Jehadis*, p. 112.

22. N. S. Jamwal, "Terrorist Financing and Support Structures in Jammu and Kashmir," *Strategic Analysis* 26, no. 1 (January–March 2002).

23. Ibid., p. 141, quoting Indian senior government and security officials.

24. For details about the Indian viewpoint on this issue, see D. Suba Chandran's chapter in this volume.

25. This discussion of the recruitment patterns and areas from which these recruitments are made draws heavily on Amir Rana's work *A to Z of Jehadi Organizations*.

26. Amir Rana, *A to Z of Jehadi Organizations*, p. 251.

27. Jamiat-e-Tulba-e-Islam is the student wing of Jamiat Ulema-e-Islam. People from this organization join JeM because they share their views on almost all religious issues. Another factor has been Masood Azhar's personality.

28. A review of the jihadi literature containing biographies of the martyrs clearly illustrates this point.

29. Amir Rana, *A to Z of Jehadi Organizations*, p. 100.

30. Ibid., pp. 115–116.

31. Ibid.

32. This is the most strongly emphasized fact in the jihadi literature.

33. In jihadi literature such as LeT's *Al-Dawa*, stories used to come in every month illustrating that when parents heard the news that their son was martyred in jihad, they would readily send their other sons to volunteer.

34. A closer look at the areas from which these groups get most of their recruits proves this point. Following the biographies of the martyrs in jihadi magazines, one realizes that most of them were jobless, day laborers, school dropouts, etc.

35. Rizwan Zeb, "War Against Terror and Lessons for Pakistan," *Journal of South Asian and Middle Eastern Studies* 25, no. 3 (Spring 2002), p. 56.

36. Eqbal Ahmed, "Jehad International Inc.," *Dawn*, 4 February 1998, as quoted in Jessica Stern, *Terror*, p. 117.

37. For a comprehensive and detailed account of the war and how it was fought, see Mohammad Yousaf and Mark Adkin, *The Bear Trap: Afghanistan's Untold Story* (Lahore: Jang Publishers, 1992).

38. For details see Rizwan Zeb, "War Against Terror."

39. Ajay Darshan Behera, "The Supporting Structures for Pakistan's Proxy War in Jammu & Kashmir," *Strategic Analysis* 25, no. 3 (June 2001).

40. Amelie Blom, "The 'Multi-Vocal State': The Policy of Pakistan on Kashmir," in Christophe Jaffrelot, ed., *Pakistan Nationalism Without a Nation?* (New Delhi: Manohar, 2002), p. 301.

41. Ibid.

42. Ayesha S. Agha, "Pakistan's Security Perspective," p. 170.

43. Amir Mir, "Jihadis Plan to Frustrate Government Ban on Fund Raising," *Friday Times*, 23 February–1 March 2001.

44. Ibid.

45. Hafiz Saeed has on a number of different occasions stated that the whole of India belongs to the Muslims of the subcontinent and they will get it back; they will raise the flag on the Red Fort. He specifically mentions Junagarh, Hyderabad, etc.

46. Syed Salahuddin, "Hum Kahan Sey Kahan Pohunch Gey" (in Urdu), *Daily Ausaf*, Islamabad, 7 December 2004.

47. Ibid.

48. Point raised and discussed by Pakistani journalists who visited Indian Kashmir in a meeting with a select audience of scholars at the Institute of Strategic Studies, Islamabad, 28 October 2004.

49. Syed Salahuddin, "Hum Kahan Sey Kahan Pohunch Gey."

50. Stephen John Stedman, "Spoiler Problems in Peace Processes," *International Security* 22, no. 2 (Fall 1997), p. 5.

51. Lt. General (retired) Moinuddin Haider, "Global Terrorism: Its Genesis, Implications, Remedial and Counter Measures," paper prepared for Institute of Regional Studies seminar, August 2005.

52. Rizwan Zeb, "War Against Terror," p. 70.

53. Refer to Rizvi's chapter in this volume for the economic, political, and diplomatic lessons that have affected Pakistani foreign policy in general and vis-à-vis India in particular since 2001.

54. Amir Mir, *The True Face of Jehadis*, p. 70. Also see "Jaish Behind Attempts on Musharraf's Life: Asharaf Qazi Says Jaish and Lashkar-e-Taiba Harmed Kashmir," *Daily Times*, 6 March 2004; Editorial, "Former DG-ISI's Admission," *Daily Times*, 7 March 2004.

55. The remarks were made by Barrister Abdul Majid Tramboo in a meeting held at the Institute of Regional Studies, Islamabad, 9 June 2005.

56. Lt. General (retired) Moinuddin Haider, "Global Terrorism."

57. See footnote 10 in Cyrus Samii's chapter in this volume. See also "Infiltration Down, Says Indian Army," *News*, 24 November 2003; "Infiltration Has Stopped: Report," *Dawn*, 22 December 2003; "Islamabad Has Taken Steps to Curb Infiltration: Fernandes," *News*, 12 February 2004; Praveen Swami, *Quickstep or Kadam Taal? The Elusive Search for Peace in Jammu and Kashmir*, United States Institute of Peace Special Report no. 133, March 2005, electronic edition.

58. Rizwan Zeb, "War Against Terror," p. 73.

6

Women in the Valley:
From Victims to Agents of Change

Kavita Suri

As millions of innocent people have been caught in the Kashmir conflict, the women of IJK, like every group, class, and community there, have had to face an abnormal situation with many implications. Years of strife have taken a toll on the lives of women, who have suffered as "soft targets" of violence from security forces and who have faced damage to well-being in psychological, emotional, economical, and educational terms. This chapter catalogues how women have been affected by the conflict in IJK and critically examines the ways in which the problems faced by women have affected their notions of war, peacebuilding, and reconstruction. In addition, as winds of change are blowing across the entire subcontinent and as both India and Pakistan are inching toward peace, this chapter will discuss the role of Kashmiri women in supporting the peacebuilding process.

The general perception among people about Kashmiri women is that they have remained mute victims in the years of turmoil since the outbreak of hostilities in 1989. In addition, few efforts have been targeted at mitigating their suffering. As discussed below, the few studies that have been conducted on the impact of militancy on the lives of women and children in IJK have shown women as among the worst sufferers of the turmoil. But in much of the existing literature on Kashmir, women remain invisible. Little explicit attention is paid to the fact that women have never been direct beneficiaries of the democratic processes in IJK and that they have remained the most marginalized actors in the politics of IJK—be it the "mainstream" state politics or the separatist politics.

The chapter thus addresses a very important problem of marginalization that has, more or less, remained unaddressed except in journalistic and impressionistic forms. Despite a plethora of work on Kashmir, especially in the context of militancy during the last fifteen years, there is not much research reflecting nontraditional security perspectives that includes issues such as women's experiences in conflict. Examining the conflict from a gender perspective contributes to an understanding of the security situation from the perspective of the people. In this context, this chapter examines a number of issues relating to women's responses to the conflict situation, in an attempt to break down stereotypes of women as passive recipients of conflict, and rather to see them as having an active role. Indeed, many women have acted with courage amid the conflict, deserving praise but going unnoticed even in the eyes of their own people.

The chapter includes two sections. The first section elaborates on the impact of the conflict and the political situation on women in IJK. The second section deals with Kashmiri women's active roles in the conflict and politics in IJK, and their potential roles in resolving the conflict and improving the political situation.

Women in IJK and the Uprising

Both Muslim and Hindu women's roles in political and public life in Kashmir have historically been limited. In traditional Kashmiri society, women's lives were mostly confined to their family household, and their outside social roles were minimal. However, the condition of Kashmiri women was much better in comparison with women in the rest of India. The women in Kashmir were not suppressed like the women in the rest of the country.[1] Kashmiri women from aristocratic families had a good lifestyle; they did not work in the fields like those women who belonged to middle and lower classes; they ate good food, lived in good houses, and were mostly confined to their homes.[2] Rural Kashmiri women participated in domestic and agricultural chores along with their men, including working in the fields and harvesting the paddies.[3] But even this active economic role did not give them economic independence and social status. Kashmir has been predominantly a patriarchal society. It might be noted, however, that common Kashmiri Muslim women, except for those belonging to Khawaja or Peer or Syed (higher classes) clans among Kashmiri Muslims, did not adhere to purdah (the practice of veiling or seclusion from public observation). Hindu women never used a veil.[4]

In the 1930s, the position of Kashmiri women started changing along with the political changes in Kashmir during the rule of Maharaja Hari Singh. Kashmiri women participated in the National Conference's political movement for self-rule initiated by Sheikh Abdullah in 1931. They supported the Kashmiri leader Sheikh Abdullah in his "Quit Kashmir movement" against the autocratic rule of the maharaja of Kashmir.[5] Abdullah's movement at that time was progressive in calling for equal participation of women in public life.[6] After India's independence in 1947, women in IJK got a further boost through the local reforms implemented in various areas, notably including education.[7] After 1947, women entered jobs in various fields and began to enjoy economic independence by earning their own salaries, and thus their status outside and within their families improved.

Despite these improvements in economic opportunities, political activism by women in IJK had hardly been visible in IJK up until recently. Few women's organizations focused on women's issues. Women were underrepresented and denied access to political life; according to Jammu-based scholar Hari Om, "The only reason is the extremely conservative Muslim society, which was in no way different from the Muslim societies in the rest of contemporary India."[8]

Women became more visible in politics, however, in the initial phase of militancy in IJK (1989–1994).[9] During this period of mass uprising, Kashmiri Muslim women throughout Kashmir were often seen leading mass protests and agitations against Indian rule. Women acted as couriers or messengers, sometimes putting their own lives at great risk. They also allowed themselves to be used by the separatists' propaganda machinery. They supported their husbands, brothers, and sons in seeking arms training to participate in the jihad and, at least in the early years, voluntarily provided food and shelter to the "mujahidin"[10] in their armed struggle against the Indian security forces. Kashmiri women kept up the household when their men were away, allowing the men to participate in the uprising. Women would sing traditional Kashmiri songs, welcoming the gun-wielding militants and even showering them with flowers and candies.

A new phenomenon emerged in Kashmiri society as militancy was glorified in the early 1990s such that Muslim Kashmiri girls were drawn toward the gun-toting young men, seeing them as heroes in the struggle for *azadi* (independence). Parents sometimes even married off their daughters to the Che Guevera–style militants. One example is the story of Riffat Kar, considered one of the most beautiful girls of Baramulla town (in the Kashmir Valley) and belonging to a locally respected family of attorneys. After Kar married a militant, many more girls followed, creating a trend of girls marrying militants.[11]

By the mid-1990s, however, the *tahrik* (movement) came to be seen as increasingly corrupted as people used militancy for their own benefit—to grab land or even the leftover properties of Kashmiri Pandits, to settle scores with someone, or to marry someone forcibly, at gunpoint, etc.[12] The attitude of women to the militancy and the militants underwent a substantial change. Women began to shut their doors to militants, sometimes informing the security forces about the presence of militants in the areas.[13] As militants were killed, the euphoria died down, and the wives of militants and these wives' parents came to recognize the pitfalls of such marriages.

Despite resistance, women were forced into such marriages against their will. By 1999, in Mahore Tehsil, situated in the Pir Panjal range in Jammu, there were sixty-five forced marriages among a population of 2,000.[14] Parents tried to cope by marrying off their daughters very young or sending their daughters away from Kashmir. Hundreds of girls and women kidnapped by the militants simply disappeared.[15] Many became pregnant and were abandoned by their kidnappers.[16]

Either as a consequence or as a cause of this change in attitudes, attacks against women increased through the 1990s, especially in the hill districts of the Jammu division.[17] The attacks themselves may be largely attributed to women's rejection of militancy and the end of support to militants.[18] This increase in attacks may also have come about because of war-weariness and growing indiscipline within the militant ranks. (See Table 6.1.)

Economic, Emotional, and Societal Effects of the Conflict on Women in IJK

Since the outbreak of hostilities in 1989, IJK has experienced a significant rise in cases of psychological disorders, including depression; recurrent, intrusive, and distressing recollection of the events; irritability and outbursts of anger; difficulty in concentrating; insomnia; persistent sadness; and disinterest in social activities.[19] In the Government Hospital for Psychiatric Diseases in Srinagar, the number of outpatient cases has gone up from 20 per day in 1989 to 125 in 2002.[20] In the 1980s, 8 to 10 patients per year would on average come to this hospital for the treatment of mental depression, but the number rose to 18,000 in 1994 and 48,000 in 2003.[21] While 775 patients visited the same hospital in 1985, this number reached 48,654 in 2002. (Interestingly, the state government has since 2002 banned journalists from visiting this hospital. A board at the entrance of the hospital clearly reads "Journalists are not allowed.") A fear psychosis was created as a result of the routine deaths, hostile encounters, crossfire, grenade blasts, and search-and-cordon operations.[22] Doctors also believe that only about 10 percent of those in need of psychiatric care are actually approaching the hospital because of the social stigma associated with psychological disorders.

The tremendous increase in psychological trauma has ripped apart the social fabric in the valley, resulting in an increased number of suicides in Kashmir. Prior to the 1990s, the suicide rate was low (three to four cases per year, according to Professor Bashir Dabla), but now it has gone up. Rough estimates suggest a tenfold increase in suicides during the last ten years. Suicides among newly married men because of impotence (which doctors attribute to mental trauma from shock) and among teenage girls who fail in examinations or don't meet the expectations of their parents are on the rise

Table 6.1 Violence and Violations Against Women for Jammu and Kashmir (IJK), January 1990–31 August 2005

Nature of Incidents	1990	1991	1992	1993	1994	1995	1996	1997	1998	1999	2000	2001	2002	2003	2004	Aug. 31 2005	Total
Women killed by militants	18	28	27	36	30	74	80	28	82	90	43	103	123	94	82	33	971
Women kidnapped/hanged to death	—	—	2	—	3	1	—	2	2	—	1	1	1	—	1	1	15
Women abducted and killed other than by hanging	2	1	7	6	10	12	5	3	3	2	5	16	10	11	9	2	104
Women abducted, raped, and killed	—	—	—	1	4	2	1	—	—	1	—	—	—	—	—	—	09
Women abducted, shot, and injured	1	—	—	1	—	1	—	—	—	—	—	—	—	—	1	—	4
Women abducted	8	8	13	26	20	31	20	19	10	16	15	19	13	19	20	4	261

in Kashmir.[23] Dr. Ghulam Nabi Yatoo, associate professor at Sher-e-Kashmir Institute of Medical Sciences, Srinagar, says at least three to five new suicide or para-suicide cases are registered each week in the hospital's Accident and Emergency Department. An unpublished survey conducted by Dr. G. M. Malik, professor in the Department of Medicine, Shri Maharaja Hari Singh Hospital, Srinagar, reveals that in a random sample of 164 para-suicide cases, 114 were females (69.51 percent) and 50 (30.49 percent) were males. Another study, in 2002, revealed that among the 1,000,000 psychiatric patients, 100,000 cases are more severe, with suicidal tendencies.[24] At least 20 percent of the depressed group attempt suicide in the Kashmir Valley. Women are more sensitive, and therefore the incidence of suicides among them is much higher than among men.

Sexual abuse is also another offshoot of fifteen years of violence in Kashmir. Foreign terrorists who treat women very badly have added a new dimension to the sexual exploitation of women. Women who do not help the militants as couriers are sexually exploited and disfigured—their ears, nose, or tongue cut—and then, in many cases, even killed. Kashmiri women have also suffered on account of their sexuality, as militants banned sterilization and abortion in the initial years, terming these "anti-Islamic," resulting in Kashmiri women in big numbers thronging to Jammu to get rid of unwanted pregnancies.[25] During normal conditions, such things as the flesh trade, prostitution, and trafficking of women were unknown to Kashmiri society; nobody had heard of or indulged in such practices. Not any longer. Though sociologists had been discussing these things in hushed tones during the past couple of years, a bold statement comes from renowned sociologist Professor Dabla, who terms it a "degenerative inferno" that is likely to engulf Kashmiri society. However, Professor Rekha Chowdhary of the Department of Political Science at the University of Jammu considers it "a bold expression of Kashmiri women's sexuality."[26] While Dabla believes that the flesh trade and prostitution in Kashmir are directly linked to the forced imposition of Islamic dress codes by the militant groups in Kashmir, Chowdhary argues that Kashmiri women are also trying to break the stereotypes related to their expression of sexuality in these changing times. The sociologists argue that one of the main reasons for the flesh trade in Kashmir is the forced imposition of religious codes. In a way, it is a kind of protest, which has led to the moral degradation of Kashmiri society. Besides, as widows live in abject poverty in various parts of Kashmir and have no source of income, they are forced to enter prostitution to sustain their families.

The turmoil in Kashmir has resulted in an army of widows who have lost their husbands to the mindless violence. There are those women too who have come to be known as "half-widows," as their husbands have been missing or have simply disappeared. Though no authentic data are available in Kashmir[27] as to how many women have become widows and how many children have been orphaned, rough estimates suggest that over 25,000 women have become widows in Kashmir and that there are 40,000 orphan children in the valley.[28] Dardpora, a village in Kupwara, has come to be known as the village of widows, as most of the women of this small hamlet have lost their husbands, most of whom were militants.[29]

Widows have suffered on various accounts. Most of them were thrown out of the houses of their in-laws, who kept the ex gratia relief (a sum of Rs 100,000/US$2,200 given to the next of kin in cases of accidental killing). The wives of killed militants did not get this money. The majority of them either are now living separately or have even moved in with their parents. Supporting three to six children on average, they are unemployed and are sustained by relatives, parents, in-laws, neighbors, NGOs, meager government relief, Sadka-e-Fitr (donations during the religious festival Eid), *zakat,* their children, part-time business, handicrafts, their husband's remaining money or pension, and agriculture activities. A few women, like those from Dardpora, have even resorted to begging. Suffering from various psychological ailments after the death of their husbands (emotional stress, loneliness, depression, etc.), these widows, over the years, have developed a high tendency to commit suicide.[30] Professor A. G. Madhosh, an educationist in Kashmir who has conducted a study, "Women and Children Under Armed Conflict in Kashmir," reports that 80 percent of the widows have very high suicidal tendencies after their husbands' death and the breakup of the family. The widows' moving between parental and in-law homes has also resulted in a sudden break in normal family life. There is a deterioration of family environment and declining social control over children, resulting in a negative impact on their personality growth.[31] Though Islam has a provision for remarriage, most of the Kashmiri widows do not want to remarry to ensure the social security of their children. While widows reconcile to the deaths of their husbands, the "half-widows" of Kashmir lead more miserable lives than the widows as they run from pillar to post to get some information about the 10,000 missing husbands.

Violence has resulted in a dearth of marriageable men in the valley. Professor Dabla says that a major crisis surfaced in Kashmir's marriage market in these years, as parents did not find eligible and qualified grooms for their daughters. The situation forced many boys to leave Kashmir for their studies or for better future prospects, and at the same time hundreds of young boys were also killed. Those who secured good jobs wanted highly qualified wives from an affluent background. The shortage of boys in the marriage market caused an increase in the marriage age for girls. In many cases, highly educated girls had to marry less well educated boys. Professor Dabla notes that, before the rise of militancy, women in Kashmir traditionally married in their early or middle twenties, but now many girls are unmarried. Delayed marriages have resulted in increased stress and a rise in congenital disorders, particularly Down syndrome, which is associated with the higher age of the mother at childbirth.[32] "Multi Dimensional Problems of Women in Kashmir," a study sponsored by the Indian Planning Commission, suggests that late marriages, an increasing reality in Kashmir, affect the general health of couples and their children.

The Association of Parents of Disappeared Persons (APDP) says that since the conflict started in IJK, about eight to ten thousand Kashmiris have been subjected to enforced or involuntary disappearances. However, the state minister of parliamentary affairs says that only 3,931 people have gone missing in Kashmir. The state officials say they have joined militant outfits, a claim disputed by many families. Out of this total, about 1 percent have been declared dead by the government.

As the popular uprising in Kashmir acquired a fundamentalist coloration, the Kashmiri woman's identity also was Islamized to some extent. A little over four years ago, Dukhtaran-e-Millat (Daughters of the Faith), an all-woman organization headed by Asiya Andrabi, supported a new group named Lashkar-e-Jabbar (LeJ). This outfit had come into the fore after its activists reportedly threw acid on two women in Srinagar on the grounds that they were not dressed in "Islamic style." However, the Kashmiri women rejected this campaign, which was for the "beginning of a comprehensive social reform movement based on true Islamic thought."[33] Women who had tasted economic independence and knew well the importance of their economic freedom also rejected the outfit's diktat to stay away from government jobs. Interestingly, no one in Kashmiri society—both its male and female members who had been interacting openly within homes and outside too— adhered to another diktat proclaiming that bus operators were to segregate men and women on their vehicles. Though the burqa threat forced a few women to wear the veil, yet again, burqas of all designs, colors, and prices flooded the markets. There was a competition to wear the latest designer- wear burqas and it again became a fashion trend. And the shopkeepers made a lot of money out of it. As Islamic militants failed to enforce conservative standards, in some cases, it also helped girls to continue meeting their male friends, for nobody could recognize them behind the disguise of the veil. Thus, Kashmir women used the burqa for their own benefit also.

Women in the Peacebuilding Process

Women, Peace, and Elections

In Kashmir, women always remained underrepresented in political and deci- sionmaking positions; hence there could not be a perpetuation of policies and practices that could serve the needs of women. As Professor Hari Om puts it,

> The only visible face in Kashmir politics has been that of Begun Sheikh Abdullah, wife of Sheikh Abdullah, who remained a member of parliament twice, that too by virtue of being the sheikh's wife. And now Mehbooba Mufti, MP, president of People's Democratic Party and the daughter of Jammu and Kashmir chief minister Mufti Sayeed. But these women have been able to carve some political space only due to their political family background.[34]

Women's equal participation in political life, as voters, candidates, and members of electoral committees, could play a crucial role in the advancement of women, the reconstruction of a violence-ridden society, and also formal or informal peace processes.

Though women haven't come forward in the political sphere in any real sense, for the first time in the twenty-seven years of the troubled history of the state, the local bodies' (civic) elections were held in Jammu and Kashmir in February–March 2005. This was the first time in the history of Jammu and Kashmir that women came forward and participated in the elections, held after such a long gap, even, in the troubled valley, taking part as the contestants.

What actually ensured the participation of women candidates in big numbers was the quota the government had allotted to these women. In 2001 the Jammu and Kashmir government introduced a bill in the state legislative assembly that was first passed by the assembly and then sent to the upper house (the state legislative council), which passed it after a debate. Thus the bill became a law under which women of Jammu and Kashmir, for the first time, got a 33 percent reservation of seats in *panchayats* (elected village councils) and other local bodies' elections. The opposition National Conference, which was in power at that time, actually led the campaign in favor of the law, along with other opposition parties and individuals. Quotas have been one of the most successful mechanisms for guaranteeing a minimum percentage of women in some elected positions, as witnessed in Kashmir recently. In these elections, which were held in conditions of extremely cold weather, a total of 934 women ran for office, a significant number keeping in mind the fact that women, until now, never tried to break the stereotypes and enter politics. Of these, 270 women ultimately made it to the municipal council and committees throughout the state.[35]

What surprised the entire world was the fact that, despite facing strong barriers in the elections due to coercion by male relatives and threats or intimidation by militant groups, Kashmiri women contested and won. In the civil elections for Jammu municipal corporations, 161 women ran for election; the number in Srinagar was 61; in Kupwara, 27; in Baramulla, 75; in

Anantnag, 51; in Pulwama, 9; in Kathua, 108; in Budgam, 22; in Udhampur, 89; in Doda, 66; in Poonch, 19; and in Rajouri, 36.[36] At last, for the first time in the history of the state, Kashmir women ultimately got some say in decisionmaking through these civil elections, which could pave the way for their inclusion in peace processes. "Real progress toward gender equality will be seen when women have more say in the decisions that affect their lives. Even though it could be termed as a beginning, these elections can give an opportunity to Kashmiri women to express newly found political impact," says Professor Chowdhary of the University of Jammu.[37]

Until now, local women saw politics as synonymous with fear and violence; but when some efforts were made by the government to give them opportunities to strengthen democracy at the grassroots level, Kashmiri women came forward enthusiastically to contest the polls. And now the confidence of the elected women corporators could well inspire other local women into political activism.

Women Picking Up the Gun Against Violence

For the past decade and a half of terrorism, Kashmiri women faced the brunt of terrorism and remained its worst victims. But now the yearning for peace and the desire to lead peaceful lives without terrorist violence have forced the women of the border district of Poonch-Rajouri to pick up guns against terrorists.[38] This is an outcome of their strong desire for peace, and thus they are protecting themselves from the militants and saving their honor and dignity.

An all-women brigade—the first women's Village Defense Committee (VDC)—has been set up in the twin villages of Marah and Kulali in the Poonch district.[39] Peace for the women here means life without any sexual assault, torture, rape, or the killing of their menfolk. Thus, the women of the area who had been "mute sufferers of terrorism" made up their mind to fight against the terrorists. They showed their willingness to get weapons and training from the security forces to protect themselves and their children from the militants' excesses. These women's VDCs are part of the security grid to fight terrorism in the villages situated close to the Line of Control, which experiences infiltration and movement of terrorists from across the border. S. D. Singh Jamwal, senior superintendent of police (SSP) in Poonch, says that all of the VDC members, including the only women VDC, are volunteers who are "trained, assisted and armed" by the district police and also by the local army units.[40] However, they do not have any political affiliations. These women's desire for peace is so strong that they even repulsed militant attacks on their houses twice when their men were away in the fields. On both the occasions when terrorists knocked at their doors for food and shelter, they fired at them, injuring them and forcing them to flee.[41]

Women Waging Peace

Parveena Ahengar, a simple housewife who never thought of coming out of her house and bringing together the mothers of Kashmir grieving over sons gone missing in the violence, today has become synonymous with the Association of Parents of Disappeared Persons, an organization she formed with human rights activist Parvez Imroze in 1994. Since then, she and other grieving mothers of Kashmir who want to know the whereabouts of their sons have been visiting security officials, police stations, politicians, courts, and prisons throughout India with photographs of sons, brothers, fathers, and husbands, trying to settle the uncertainty surrounding the disappearances. These women have been doing this at the risk of their lives,[42] despite the fear of being dubbed *mukbhir* (informers) by the militants.[43] But undeterred, they go from one place to another, holding placards, yearning for the restoration of peace in their lives, when their sons will return and there will be no further violation of human rights. Peace, they say, should return to Kashmir so that in the future no mother will suffer as they have suffered.

Other women in Kashmir are trying, like Parveena, to change the lives of Kashmiri women and children by bringing some peace into their lives through their efforts. Nighat Shafi Pandit and Dilafroz Qazi are two such women. Pandit, age fifty-four, who is actively involved in the promotion of peace and harmony in Kashmir, chairs the Human Effort for Love and Peace (HELP) foundation, an NGO working for the welfare of orphans and the rehabilitation of widows. Qazi, who is forty-three, heads an engineering college in Pattan and is also running several primary schools in which many orphans of the conflict receive free education. Incidentally, recently these three Kashmiri women—Parveena Ahengar, Nighat Shafi Pandit, and Dilafroz Qazi—were nominated for the 2005 Nobel Peace Prize for their contribution to peace and human dignity by an organization called 1,000 Women, which is supported by the Swiss government, UNIFEM (United Nations Development Fund for Women), and UNDP (United Nations Development Program).[44] They were among 92 Indians in a list of 1,000 women worldwide who had been nominated, albeit unsuccessfully, for the 2005 Nobel Peace Prize.

In a similar endeavor, WISCOMP (Women in Security, Conflict Management, and Peace), a New Delhi–based initiative of His Holiness the Dalai Lama, is also working in Kashmir. Ashima Kaul Bhatia, a nonresident Kashmiri, has taken an initiative under WISCOMP, which she has named

Athwaas, a Kashmiri word meaning "the handshake." Its goal has been to find a common language born of pain and grief among Kashmiri Pandit (Hindu), Muslim, and Sikh women, to begin a dialogue reaching beyond the blaming syndrome toward empathetic mutual understanding. Their effort, to allow women to forge a coalition on the basis of crosscutting identities beyond their common identity as victims, has been widely appreciated as these women have the potential to mobilize as a constituency for peace, says Bhatia. Women in this forum learn to listen empathetically, to talk to each other across the conflict divide, and to move beyond victimhood to recognizing the need and value of mobilizing together for peace. Kashmir University professor Hameeda Bano, Sikh educator Gurmeet Kour, grass-roots women workers, and renowned Hindi writer Dr. Khema Koul are some of its members.

Conclusion

When women talk about peace, they talk not from the vantage point of having won wars but from the pain that wars inflict. The women who supported militancy now fervently hope that peace on the borders will extend within their villages, towns, and homes. By *Aman*, or "peace," they mean not just the absence of physical violence, but a system based on social security, equal opportunities, access to resources, distribution, economic rights, and accountability; a welfare state, a literate, developed, and child-welfare-oriented society; and a society where there is social justice, progress, and development for all groups. For most of them, peace begins from their immediate family and goes on to cover the whole region, the country, and the world. This is "positive peace," which encompasses a vision of what society should be. It requires not only that all types of violence are minimal or nonexistent, but also that the major potential causes of future conflict are removed. In other words, the root causes and major conflicts of interest, as well as their violent manifestation, need to be resolved. The resolution of the vexed Kashmir dispute itself could go a long way toward minimizing all these problems.

   Peacebuilding attempts, in order to promote sustainable peace, need to address not only the distribution of resources, but also the opportunities shaped by social and political institutions and relationships. In this process, principles of democratic participation, human rights, and gender equality are crucial elements. A three-tier effort is needed, including individuals, society, and the state. All of them need to coordinate, organize, and implement relevant programs for the betterment of women and children. The IJK government initiated a major step toward the betterment of women's lives by promoting their participation in the electoral process through the reservation of seats in the February–March 2005 civic bodies elections, but policymakers and governments need to take many more steps to support women's participation in peacebuilding by strengthening women's representation in local, national, and international bodies for the regulation of conflicts. More could be done in shaping economic opportunities in the rehabilitation of the thousands of widows and orphaned children across IJK. NGOs also need to work more and take serious initiatives in this regard.

Though the 8 October 1005 earthquake has not changed much for the women of urban Kashmir, for the hundreds of thousands of Kashmiri women living in the villages along the Line of Control in the Baramulla and Poonch districts of IJK, things have changed as many of them have lost their houses. (However, the effect of the earthquake overall on the Indian side of Kashmir is not great.) Perhaps this is the appropriate time for the NGOs that have started working in the quake-affected areas to focus on these women. Involvement of grassroots functionaries and nongovernmental organizations would help shape a community approach to tackle all of the problems mentioned above.

Notes

1. Bashir A. Dabla, Sandeep Nayak, Khurshid-ul-Islam, *Gender Discrimination in the Kashmir Valley* (New Delhi: Gyan Publishing House, 2000), pp. 30, 33, 35.

2. Ibid.

3. Ibid.

4. Professor Bashir A. Dabla, interview by author, Kashmir University, 29 October 2004.

5. Sheikh Mohammad Abdullah, *Flames of the Chinar: An Autobiography,* abridged, translated from Urdu, introduced by Khushwant Singh (New Delhi: Penguin India, 1995).

6. Dr. Farooq Abdullah, interview by author, 20 May 2005. Also see Sheikh Mohammad Abdullah, opening address to Constituent Assembly, 5 November 1951, http://jammukashmir.nic.in/profile/cntit2.htm.

7. Dr. Farooq Abdullah, interview by author, 20 May 2005. Reforms in postpartition Kashmir were part of the implementation of Sheikh Abdullah's vision of a new, modern, developed "Naya Kashmir."

8. Hari Om, head of the Department of History, Jammu University, and member of the Indian Council for Historical Research (ICHR), interview by author, Jammu, 16 February 2005.

9. Sudha Ramachandran, "Women Lift the Veil on Kashmir Struggle," *Asia Times Online,* 7 March 2002, http://www.atimes.com/ind-pak/DC07Df01.html.

10. Up to the present, most Kashmiris call both local and foreign militants *mujahidin,* meaning "freedom fighters." Recently a slight change has begun, with very few Kashmiris referring to them as terrorists or militants.

11. Shahzada Yusuf (whom I interviewed in Kashmir on 4 November 2004 at separatist leader Hashim Qureshi's office) had married a JKLF top commander,

Idress Khan, knowing well that he was a mujahid. He died in 1995. She now lives with her three children in Malbagh Mohalla, Hazratbal, Srinagar. Similarly, Sharifa married an HM militant, Abdul Qayoom Shah, of Padshahi Bag. After his murder, she now lives with her parents. There are hundreds of such cases in Kashmir.

12. Suresh Dugger, "Vicious Ultras Ravage Women in J&K," http://www.hvk.org/articles/0197/0005.html.

13. Rita Manchanda, "Kashmir's Worse-Off Half: Women Are the Silent Sufferers in the War over Kashmir," *Himal* 12, no. 4 (May 1999).

14. "Parents Marrying Off Their Daughters Early in Kashmir," *The Statesman*, 19 November 2000.

15. Suresh Dugger, "Vicious Ultras."

16. Ibid.

17. Kavita Suri, "Scarred for Life," *The Statesman*, 14 December 2004.

18. Rita Manchanda, "Kashmir's Worse-Off Half."

19. Mushtaq Margoob, psychiatrist, interview by author, Srinagar, January 2004.

20. Ibid.

21. Aasia Jeelani, "Turmoil and Trauma," *Voices Unheard: A Newsletter of Kashmiri Women's Initiative for Peace and Disarmament*, 2002.

22. Bashir A. Dabla, *Impact of Conflict Situation on Women and Children in Kashmir*, Save the Children Fund North West India, June 1999; "Rise in Stress-induced Ailments," *Tribune*, 18 January 1999; Rashid Jehangir, "Militancy Increases Psychological Disorders in Valley," *Kashmir Times*, 18 August 2004.

23. M. L. Kak, "More Women Choose Death in J&K," *Tribune,* 27 September 2000.

24. Bashir Dabla, "Suicides in the Kashmir Valley," *New Hope Journal,* March–April 2001.

25. Information gathered on the basis of frequent interactions with Professor Rita Jitendra, eminent social worker of Jammu and member of SWC (J&K State Commission for Women), and Dr. Santosh Khajuria, gynecologist.

26. Rekha Chowdhary, interview by author, 16 January 2005.

27. The J&K government had asked all of its fourteen District Development Commissioners to make a complete list of the widowed women and orphaned children in the state. Even after a lapse of two years, nothing has come out. So one has to rely on the secondary data available.

28. "20,000 Orphans, Widows in Kashmir," *Tribune*, 9 May 2000.

29. Kavita Suri, "Bleak Widows," *The Statesman*, 6 June 2005.

30. Arshad Me'raj, "80% War Widows Have Suicidal Tendencies," *Greater Kashmir*, 6 November 2004.

31. "Widows: Jehad for Survival: Battling It Out in Embattled Land," Women Feature Service, October 2004.

32. Fayaz Bukhari, "Dying Day by Day," *Himal*, November 2002.

33. Ashima Koul Bhatia, "Give J&K Women Economic *Azadi*," Women Feature Service, 2004.

34. Professor Hari Om, University of Jammu, interview by author, Jammu, 26 March 2005.

35. Data from the office of the chief electoral officer, Jammu and Kashmir [IJK] state government.

36. Ibid.

37. Professor Rekha Chowdhary, Department of Political Science, University of Jammu, interview by author, Jammu, 16 January 2005.

38. Kavita Suri, "Village Defence Committee of Kashmiri Women," http://www.sawf.org/newedit/edit02212005/kashmir.asp.

39. Ibid.

40. Senior superintendent of police, interview by author, Poonch, 10 July 2005.

41. Ibid.

42. Rita Manchanda, "Kashmir's Worse-Off Half," pp. 30–33.

43. Asha Hans, "Women Across Borders in Kashmir: The Continuum of Violence," *Canadian Women's Studies* 19, no. 4 (Winter 2000), pp. 77–87.

44. "Three Kashmiri Women Among 1,000 Nobel Prize Nominees," *Daily Excelsior,* 2 July 2005.

7

Women and Peacebuilding in Azad Jammu and Kashmir

Shaheen Akhtar

Given that there is no insurgency active within Azad Jammu and Kashmir (AJK), women there do not directly participate in the violent conflict as combatants or facilitators. However, women in AJK are directly and indirectly affected by the continuing Kashmir crisis. Broadly speaking, they are affected in three ways. First, they are affected indirectly as part of divided families, facing various difficulties in procuring visas and in traveling to Indian-administered Jammu and Kashmir (IJK) to meet their relatives living across the Line of Control (LoC). Second, at times of escalation in Indo-Pak tension, they are affected directly by the intermittent shelling along the LoC, which not only damages their homes and hearths but also endangers their lives and displaces them internally. Third, as a result of active conflict in IJK since 1989–1990, women from IJK across the LoC have been forced to cross into AJK, where they endure various kinds of hardship in the refugee camps[1] set up by the AJK government or face the hard consequences of life outside the camps.

The main argument in this chapter is that although women in AJK are not actively involved in the Kashmir conflict, their lives are deeply affected by it, and hence they should be involved in conflict resolution and peacebuilding in Kashmir. A small sample survey conducted in AJK (discussed further below) shows that women in AJK in general—and the three groups categorized above in particular—interpret the causes of the Kashmir conflict more or less along the same lines as the men who tend to dominate discourse in AJK. However, the women strongly feel that the problem of Kashmir should be resolved peacefully and that aspirations of the Kashmiris should be given foremost importance in the final settlement of the issue. It should be underscored that despite the societal constraints, AJK women, with a relatively very high literacy rate,[2] have great potential to play a more prominent, important role in conflict resolution and peacemaking in Kashmir.

This chapter looks into Azad Kashmiri women's notions of peace and security and explores the possibilities of bringing women's agency into conflict resolution in Kashmir.[3] The focus is on the impact of the Kashmir crisis on the lives of women belonging to the three groups identified above and how AJK women in general, and these women in particular, can be involved in the informal or formal peace processes in Kashmir. A survey consisting of a group of 150 women, 50 in each category, was conducted from December 2004 through March 2005 to assess the hardships faced by them in consequence of the Kashmir conflict, their perspectives on the resolution of the Kashmir crisis, and their possible role in peacebuilding.[4] The targeted groups of women included different stakeholders, such as students, teachers, professionals, housewives, maids, women activists, and politicians, and their ages ranged between 19 and 45. The survey was carried out both in the camps and outside the camps. In addition, an attempt has been made to suggest ways and means to bring them and women's agency in AJK into the peace process. The study tries to fill the gap in the literature on the impact of the Kashmir conflict on women in AJK and the role of women in building peace in Kashmir.

Historical Background

AJK is a traditional and conservative society. Traditional patriarchal values and attitudes determine the role and status of women in the socioeconomic and political affairs of AJK. Since this study deals with women's perspectives on the Kashmir conflict and conflict resolution, the concepts of "patriarchy" and "gender" need explanation. Patriarchy is used here as defined by feminist theory, which emphasizes the "vast inequalities of power that exist in most societies today based, not on biological differences per se, but on the social and cultural differences that patriarchy enforces."[5] Similarly, gender in the study refers to the "socially constructed roles ascribed to women and men, as opposed to biological and physical characteristics. Gender roles vary according to socio-economic, political and cultural contexts, and are affected by other factors, including age, race, class and ethnicity. Gender roles are learned and are changeable."[6]

Women in AJK are in relatively weak social, economic, and political positions compared to men. While their condition has improved over the last three decades due to improved access to healthcare, education, and skills, their social position remains largely unchanged, and discrimination on the basis of social and cultural traditions remains common.[7] It is quite evident that the domination of patriarchal values continues to keep them as a disadvantaged group in society. But the spread of patriarchy is not even, and the nature and degree of women's subordination vary across classes, districts, and the rural/urban divide. The women belonging to the upper and middle classes in rural and urban areas have relatively greater access to education and employment opportunities, and the disparity is particularly pronounced in comparison to the situation of women living in rural areas. In poor households with meager resources, gender discrimination is more pronounced.

Most women in AJK do not enjoy economic empowerment, which is very important in bringing women's agency in peacebuilding. Their presence in the public sector is minimal, though they play a crucial role in the agricultural economy. Education and skill development facilities for women offer few options; therefore, employment opportunities for them are limited to the health and education sectors. Women are also engaged in home-based professions, such as handicrafts, sewing and stitching, etc.

The political history of AJK is dominated by male decisionmakers, who have played the leading role in the question of war and peace in Kashmir. As a result the role of women in the political and public life of AJK has been limited, and women's narrative on the issues of peace and security is either invisible or overshadowed by male discourse. Generally, as for men, the division of Kashmir is felt by most of the women, whether living in villages or towns, or whether well or poorly educated. They react strongly to the situation in Kashmir and express anger over the human rights violations in IJK. They are often resentful that the international community is not doing enough for the resolution of the Kashmir dispute. They want to see the reunification of Kashmir and the organization of a plebiscite. However, in case of reunification, Indian control is out of the question.[8]

Although women are not politically very active, they have been participating in the politics of AJK and have been represented in the cabinet since 1985. There are five women's seats reserved in AJK's legislative assembly of forty-eight members. These reserved seats are normally filled by the nominees of the major political parties. As a corollary, they do not take independent stances on the Kashmir conflict and its resolution but follow the traditional positions taken by the political parties they represent.[9]

Women's Notions of Peace and Security in AJK

The position of women in AJK in the Kashmir conflict affects their notions of war and peacebuilding. It also determines their role in conflict resolution and in bringing women's agency into the peace process in Kashmir.

Women in AJK are uniquely positioned in the Kashmir conflict as they are not located in the conflict zone or directly involved in the combat operations. Nor does it seem that they enable militancy by providing shelter or logistical support or through encouraging their children to go to war. But women do extend their political and moral support to the freedom struggle. They also express their solidarity with the women directly affected by the Kashmir crisis in IJK. In this context, the sociocultural and politicoeconomic milieu greatly shapes their perspectives on the Kashmir conflict and peacebuilding in Kashmir. Women have regularly articulated their views and raised their voices during rallies to express solidarity with the struggle in IJK. The views expressed tend to be consistent with the male-dominated discourse on peace and security in the region. Such women's expression and participation have taken place in the midst of the 1948, 1965, and 1971 Indo-Pak wars on Kashmir, the ongoing uprising in IJK since 1989, and the Kargil crisis in 1999.

Efforts to boost women's participation in AJK politics are quite weak at both the societal and the governmental level. As a corollary, not much has been done at the civil society level to bring women into conflict resolution processes in Kashmir. However, by virtue of a relatively high literacy rate of 40.46 percent[10] and a demographic strength of 49.70 percent in a total estimated population of 3.21 million (1998 census),[11] women in AJK constitute a vibrant group that can be turned into a critical mass for peacemaking. They can be actively involved in the informal and formal peace processes in Kashmir.

Impact of the Kashmir Conflict on Women in AJK

In today's warfare, according to a study by the humanitarian nongovernmental organization Oxfam, approximately 80 percent of civilian casualties are women. In addition, the United Nations High Commissioner for Refugees estimates that 80 percent of all refugees and internally displaced people worldwide are women and children.[12] The report from the UN's landmark 1995 Beijing conference on women emphasized that the specific experience of women in armed conflict is deeply linked "to their status in societies and their sex."[13] Women's experiences of the Kashmir conflict have indeed reflected this linkage. These experiences can be divided into the three distinct types mentioned above: women of divided families, women affected by shelling along the LoC, and women IDPs (internally displaced persons) from IJK who have taken refuge in AJK since 1990. These distinct experiences are analyzed below.

The Kashmir Conflict and Women of Divided Families

The division of Kashmir since 1947 has separated thousands of Kashmiri families who are living on both sides of the LoC. The continuous conflict has badly affected the free movement of the divided families across the LoC, with the greatest effect on the women who are married across, or have relatives on either side of, the LoC. According to AJK official sources, 150,000 Muslim Kashmiris crossed into Pakistan and AJK in 1947–1948 when the conflict began.[14] Similarly, Hindu Kashmiris moved out of AJK and settled in IJK or India. Historically speaking, 3,000 non-Muslim families migrated to Jammu from AJK, and today non-Muslim refugees to IJK total just over 100,000.[15] The 1965 and 1971 wars resulted in another wave of 50,000 Kashmiri IDPs crossing into AJK.[16] The stream of IDPs flowing into AJK and Pakistan has never stopped. The uprising in IJK since 1989 has generated a fresh wave of IDPs crossing into AJK. There are about 24,574 registered and 35,000 nonregistered IDPs living in the camps and outside camps respectively.[17]

The situation of women of divided families is quite tragic, as they are separated for decades from their near and dear ones living across the LoC. Mothers have been separated from their children and sisters from their brothers. For many divided families there is a distance of only a few miles between them, but they have not been allowed to meet each other for the last fifty-eight years. Their trauma can be gauged from the story of just three women, one living in IJK and two in AJK.

Seventy-two-year-old Bibi Jaan was married in Adisa village in IJK before 1947, and her maternal village happens to be just two kilometers away, on the other side of the LoC. "For the last 56 years, she has not seen her two brothers and their families. Her parents have since died. With tears, she says, 'We are separated by two kilometers, but to reach my maternal village is my lifetime dream. I could not see my ailing parents before they died.'"[18] It should be noted that every resident in Adisa has at least one family member on the AJK side of the LoC.

The travails of another woman, Fatima, living in Chilina village along the AJK side of the LoC, are equally moving. She got a chance to see her brother on the other side of the LoC. "Weeping and wailing, Fatima waved frantically to her brother standing just 20 meters away on the opposite bank of the Neelum river that divides this part of Kashmir between India and Pakistan."[19]

The third woman, Zarina Bibi, who had a chance to see her parents across the LoC, lost control. Holding her small baby, she slipped into the river in excitement when she saw her parents waving at her. "She kept crying as people pulled her out from the freezing water. 'Oh my God they are alive,' she shouted hysterically, 'I can't believe they are standing right there.'"[20]

These women were among thousands of Kashmiris, separated for decades by the conflict, who in February 2004 lined up along the Neelum River for hours in rain and cold weather, looking for their family members.

This was the first time in more than twenty years that they were allowed to come so close, to exchange greetings and throw letters weighted with stones across the river to their relatives and friends. No permission was granted, but authorities made no move to stop the gathering. Similar scenes were repeated when the BBC organized satellite video conferencing facilities for the meeting of the divided families in June 2004.[21]

For most Kashmiri women, separation from their loved ones is an issue close to their hearts. They face many obstacles to travel, while other means of communication, such as telephone contacts and mail service, have remained suspended since the 1990 crisis. The distance between Muzaffarabad and Srinagar is only 75 miles (130 km), but women of divided Kashmiri families, like the men, have to face tremendous problems in getting visas and traveling via New Delhi and Lahore to reach their destination in Srinagar or Muzaffarabad. This journey sometimes takes months, and in many cases years, as they have to wait for visas in both Islamabad and New Delhi.[22] AJK nationals are not given Indian visas for IJK, as they are considered noncitizens by India. In fact, most of the "first generation of separated families has already passed away, its dreams to reunite left unfulfilled."[23] There is no NGO providing any relief to the women of the divided families.

The survey of seventy-five women respondents conducted by the author, as explained at the beginning, revealed the utter lack of communication between the women belonging to the divided families on both sides of the LoC, with 98.6 percent responding that they have not been able to visit their relatives at all during the last two decades, some even three decades, due to problems in getting visas. (Survey results are presented in Table 7.1 at the end of this section.) The 1.4 percent lucky enough to get visas visited just once in twenty or thirty years. A great majority of the respondents (97.3 percent) complained about the long and costly traveling, which they cannot afford.

Mail service and telephone contact are also almost nonexistent or are at a minimum. The Indian authorities suspended satellite links between IJK and AJK in 1990, so receiving any phone calls from their relatives in IJK is impossible. This has added to the miseries of the divided families. Survey respondents also complained that there is a lot of disruption in lines when they make calls from Pakistan. About 93 percent of the respondents stated that they did not have any telephone contact with their relatives. Only 7 percent were able to maintain such contact from Pakistan or other countries. Some used e-mail to keep in touch. Most of them maintained contact through relatives living in foreign countries or through other people from the villages of their relatives visiting AJK or Pakistan.

Before 1947, there were options for the free movement of people between various parts of Kashmir, including bus services between Srinagar and Rawalpindi passing through Muzaffarabad and Sialkot and Jammu. The bus services were halted in 1947 when the territory was divided. However, between 1949 and 1956, local deputy commissioners issued permits for individuals to cross over to the other side on foot.

The proposal of reopening Srinagar-Muzaffarabad bus service in October 2003 brightened the hopes of reunion for many Kashmiri families. But the talks were deadlocked by a disagreement over India's insistence that passports be used as travel documents, which Pakistan felt would have compromised the disputed status of Kashmir. The two sides finally agreed in early 2005 to use entry permits in place of passports once identities of the travelers are verified. The first two buses departed on 7 April 2005. Altogether, 49 passengers, 30 from Muzaffarabad to Srinagar and 19 the other way, made this historic journey. Divided families were given priority on the bus service, which initially ran every two weeks and will later be converted into a weekly service.

The divided families strongly supported the cease-fire on the LoC begun in November 2003 and the opening of the Srinagar-Muzaffarabad bus service in April 2005 as it would enable people from both sides of the state to see each other and unite. It would cut the travel time from two to four days to barely two hours and would also cut the cost of the journey via the international border. A large number of female respondents belonging to the divided families and constituting 98.6 percent were in support of a cease-fire on the LoC and 92 percent were in favor of the bus service, though they do not see it as the solution to the Kashmir problem. However, about 8 percent opposed it, as they felt that it was an attempt to put the main issue of Kashmir on the back burner.

In expressing perspectives on a solution to the Kashmir conflict, the women of the divided families have overwhelmingly supported the right of self-determination for the Kashmiris. They voiced a desire for a peaceful and political solution to the Kashmir problem, satisfying the aspirations of the Kashmiris. A vast majority of women respondents, 76 percent, stated that they wanted a complete end of Indian control over Kashmir and that they favored a UN-sponsored plebiscite in Kashmir. A group of 11 percent desired a unified independent Kashmir, while 13 percent desired partition of IJK. We may infer, then, that the majority was expressing an interest in acceding to Pakistan. Women of the divided families wanted an early resolution of the conflict. One respondent said it is "a political issue between India and Pakistan and we innocent people are just suffering."[24] Another, who was married to a relative across the LoC and returned to AJK with her family after the beginning of the uprising in 1989, stressed an "urgent solution as women cannot survive there due to atmosphere of stress, fear and threat of abuse and death."[25]

Kashmiris of the divided families are also concerned about the identity

Table 7.1   The Kashmir Conflict: Impact on Women of Divided Families in AJK and Their Preferred Solutions

Area of Question and Response	Yes (%)	No (%)
Impact experienced		
Visa restrictions	98.6	1.4
Travel	97.3	2.7
Telephonic/mail/Internet contact	7	93
Cease-fire on the LoC	98.6	1.4
Srinagar-Muzaffarabad bus service	92	8
Preferred solutions		
UN resolutions	76	24
Independence	11	89
Partition of IJK	13	87

Source: Survey conducted in AJK by the author from December 2004 to March 2005.
Note: Number of respondents = 75.

and political status of their future generations and fear that in the absence of any mechanism to preserve their numerical strength, they will lose the right to play a role in the future dispensation of Kashmir.[26] This would certainly hurt the interest of Kashmir women of the divided families.

The Kashmir Conflict and Women
Affected by Shelling Along the LoC

The next directly affected group includes women who are part of the population living along the LoC, especially women of the Neelum Valley area (see Table 7.2 at the end of this section). These women have been directly and physically exposed to the intermittent firing on the LoC, threatening their lives, killing, injuring, and displacing many of them as well as members of their communities. It has disrupted their everyday lives, causing socioeconomic hardship and psychological stress.

AJK is very vulnerable to feeling the brunt of the conflict situation between India and Pakistan, as five of its seven districts are located along the LoC. Only the Mirpur and Bhimber districts do not share a border with the LoC. According to the AJK government's official reports, during 1990–2002, a large number of the 199,188 people living along the LoC were forced to leave their homes due to shelling from the Indian side. They belonged to the districts of Muzaffarabad (21,686), Bagh (25,231), Poonch (28,192), Kotli (13,793), and Bhimber (110,286). Casualties included 1,314 reportedly killed and 4,705 injured.[27]

This group includes a large number of women and girls who were forced to leave their homes along with their families to take shelter in safer areas, either with their relatives or in the camps set up by the AJK government. The shelling has also destroyed and damaged their property, worth millions of rupees, and smashed infrastructure, especially roads, electric lines, educational institutions, and health facilities located close to the LoC.[28]

The repeated disruption has made the region unviable for conventional livelihoods like tourism. The survey of these women found that constant shelling has had drastic effects on livelihood. A huge majority, 94 percent of respondents, pointed to economic hardship resulting from the disruption and dislocation of their families. This has deprived the local population of opportunities for earning a living through price escalation, including transport charges, as well as through deforestation and through wariness on the part of potential investors. All this has contributed to severe levels of poverty in the communities along the LoC, adversely affecting the women there. A great majority, 92 percent, reported that they were facing problems in accessing even basic facilities such as clean water, healthcare, and education. The Neelum Valley, one of the poorest areas of AJK, has been the worst hit by the shelling during the conflict. This is an area generally neglected by NGOs and the government because of its inaccessibility, and healthcare facilities are virtually nonexistent. There are no "mother and child" healthcare facilities, and there is a shortage of female doctors.[29]

The shelling also has left a psychological impact on the female population of the affected areas. The constant threat to life, along with the problems of dislocation, have caused stress and anxiety disorders among the women. A substantive group of 56 percent of the women reported that they were facing stress-related disorders due to the security situation in the area. Most affected are the women who have lost someone in the family or who have had to take over the responsibility for their household.

The cease-fire on the LoC since 24 November 2003 has benefited the area most, as Indian machine-gun posts no longer fire at the vehicles and people traveling on the AJK side. A vast majority, 96 percent, of the respondents welcomed the cease-fire, but most of them have been unable to go back to their homes, as thousands of landmines—placed in the evacuated areas during the 2001–2002 standoff between the two armies—are still there. In addition, the reconstruction and rehabilitation work is not adequate to bring people back.

Relief work is also under way to alleviate the situation. Islamic Relief has initiated the Neelum Valley Disaster Preparedness Project (NVDPP) to help save lives and minimize casualties caused by firing along the LoC. The Neelum Valley Integrated Development Programme (NVIDP) has also been launched, aiming to improve access to basic healthcare for approximately 43,000 people in the Neelum Valley.[30] The Pakistan Red Crescent Society (PRCS) is providing some relief to displaced people in AJK. Provision of a mobile health unit with ambulance has been planned for selected disaster-prone districts to support first aid training activities at the subdistrict level on a regular basis.

In expressing perspectives on solutions to the Kashmir crisis, a vast majority of the women in this group welcomed the beginning of Muzaffarabad-Srinagar bus service, as a large number of the divided families are from the Poonch-Rajouri area, divided by the LoC. The LoC here has divided not only the territory but also villages and even individual houses. An overwhelming majority of the women, 96 percent, was in favor of the bus service and wanted the opening of more entry points at the LoC. But they made it clear that it should in no way put aside the solution of Kashmir. However, a group of 6 percent of the respondents was more apprehensive that it would be used to sideline the resolution of the problem.

On the question of a preferred solution to the Kashmir problem, women here strongly expressed their support to the right of self-determination for the Kashmiris and a UN-supervised plebiscite. A 76 percent majority supported this solution. A group of 10 percent stood for independence, while another group of 14 percent wanted the division of IJK on the basis of the religious ratios of their population. Again, we may infer that most were expressing an interest in accession to Pakistan.

The Kashmir Conflict and Women IDPs (post-1990) from IJK

All forms of armed conflict make women more susceptible to physical and sexual violence, expose them to various forms of deprivation, and impact their physical and psychological health both directly and indirectly. The third directly affected group of women consists of Kashmiri women IDPs, who started flowing into AJK with their families in 1990, due to the ongo-

Table 7.2   The Kashmir Conflict and Women Affected by Shelling Along the LoC

Area of Question and Response	Yes (%)	No (%)
Impact experienced		
Effects on livelihood	94	6
Social distortions	92	8
Psychological effects	56	44
Cease-fire on the LoC	96	4
Srinagar-Muzaffarabad bus service	94	6
Preferred solutions		
UN resolutions	76	24
Independence	10	90
Partition of IJK	14	86

Source: Survey conducted in AJK by the author from December 2004 to March 2005.
Note: Number of respondents = 50.

ing uprising in IJK. They are currently living along with their families in camps set up by the AJK government or with their local relatives.

Since 1990, there has been a continuous flow of Kashmiri IDPs, especially from the bordering areas of IJK, into AJK. At present about 25,000 of them are living in about 15 IDP camps throughout AJK. There are more than 14,000 in 9 camps in Muzaffarabad, 3,500 in 4 camps in Bagh district, about 5,000 in 2 camps and some with locals in Kotli district, more than 470 in Mirpur district, and about 100 in Rawalakot district.[31] There are also more than 35,000 nonregistered IDPs, most of them living either independently or with their relatives.[32] Many of these women have directly faced the brunt of the Kashmir conflict and were forced to cross into AJK for safety and survival. A large number of them belong to very poor families.

There is relatively little information and literature on the situation of these IDPs, especially women. As an exception, Khalid Rehman and Ershad Mahmud have described in depth the miseries women have faced in AJK and Pakistan. They observe that ordinary Kashmiri IDPs face countless problems in their social relations, their culture, education of their children, health, etc.[33]

The author's survey of the women IDPs (see Table 7.3 at the end of this section) revealed that most of them crossed into AJK due to routine operations of the Indian army against the civilian population (94 percent), especially along the LoC. Responding to the question about the impact of the Kashmir conflict, a vast majority of them observed that it has shattered their lives and families and that they had to leave their homes due to threats to life, including general "fear" or "attack on village" (98 percent), as well as psychological trauma (88 percent) resulting from "humiliation," molestation, harassment to become informers for the security forces, or "search operations" by the Indian army and other paramilitary forces. Only a few have left for other reasons, such as coming to Pakistan for studies, etc. One of the respondents said, "Routine firings, blasts and curfews were becoming a hurdle in the smooth running of my studies, and therefore my parents wanted me to leave Kashmir and take refuge in Pakistan."[34]

All of these women have come either with their family or with at least one male relative. Not all of them had relatives in AJK. Those who had relatives were staying with them, and those who could afford it were living independently. Many were living in the camps, but some of them have moved from them and are working, depending on their education and skills. The unskilled had started working as domestic servants. Some of them had moved into the Pakistani cities adjacent to AJK and taken up some work. A majority of them lost family members in the conflict. One respondent, who was working as a Lady Health Visitor,[35] said that she had "lost all [her] family members, except one son." Another said that she had lost five members of her family in the conflict. There were very few who had not lost any loved ones in the conflict. Women who had lost someone in the family suffered from acute emotional disorders, and those who had been raped were undergoing psychological trauma and had low esteem in the family. Many young women felt depressed and were suffering from anxiety.

Relief work is under way to help IDPs. Currently the AJK government has provided housing, drinking water, education, and medical facilities to the IJK IDPs living in the camps. The IDPs' families have been provided financial assistance, but it has been quite nominal. Apart from a onetime grant per family of Rs 600–2,000 on arrival, an Rs 750 subsistence allowance per head has been given per month.[36] The plight of Kashmiri IDP women has remained largely ignored in official rehabilitation policy. There has been no separate financial assistance provided to these women. The international community also has not provided any assistance to them, largely because their status—whether they are refugees or IDPs—is not clear. Pakistan has been reluctant to take any step that makes it appear as if it were accepting the current division of Kashmir.

The IDP families have made their tiny mud-brick villages in various parts of AJK with the help of the local administration and civil society. Some NGOs have been providing relief to them, especially the healthcare facilities. These include the Relief Organization for Kashmiri Muslims (ROKM), set up in 1990 and headed by Ghulam Nabi Nowsheri, which has carried out relief work for the affected families along the LoC and in the IDP camps in AJK. Its projects, such as providing medical facilities in the camps and women's vocational centers, directly benefit the women IDPs.[37] Kashmir Surgicals and the Al-Mustapha Society have set up medical centers, while the Human Foundation has set up dispensaries in the camps. ICNA Relief–Helping Hand, a division of the Islamic Circle of North America (ICNA), has also run projects for Kashmiri IDPs in the camps, including a skills training program, health relief projects, and an education program. All of these projects have helped women IDPs. However, no local or international NGOs have been involved in the rehabilitation of rape victims or those suffering from psychological disorders.

IDP women in the study expressed the following perspectives on solutions to the Kashmir crisis. A majority of women IDPs' families, especially those living in the camps, wanted to go back to their homes, provided security would be guaranteed to them on their return. A huge majority of them, 86 percent, expressed their desire to go back to their original homes in the valley or Jammu. However, 14 percent of the respondents, most of them living outside the camps, did not want to go back, as they either have found jobs or settled or are too afraid of the environment of fear and insecurity in IJK. A vast majority of women in this group (98 percent) welcomed the cease-fire on the LoC, and 88 percent of them appreciated the Srinagar-Muzaffarabad bus service but expressed reservations that it should not push the solution of Kashmir to the back burner. Kashmiri women IDPs greatly benefit from the decision to use the permit system, as most of them do not have any passport or travel documents.

The women IDPs called for an immediate end to the killings of men, women, children, and youth by the Indian troops. A 98 percent majority wanted a peaceful solution for Kashmir and favored *azadi* (freedom) from Indian rule. A great majority (68 percent) was for UN resolutions and a plebiscite, followed by the division of IJK (18 percent) in accordance with the ratio of the Muslim, Hindu, and Buddhist population. Another 14 percent were for the complete independence of Kashmir.

Constraints and Coping

The three groups of women discussed above have borne the costs of the Kashmir conflict in distinct ways. The coping mechanisms available to them are limited by the traditions of Kashmiri society and their resulting inability to become economically independent. The policies of the AJK government toward these affected women are largely gender-blind and there is no significant NGO, whether local or international, focusing specifically on the rehabilitation of the affected women. Within these parameters, relatives are the only source of succor, but most of them are not in a position to share their burden. More often than not, women are left to grapple with the loss of livelihood, dignity, and identity, living with hunger and disease, persecution and repression. They are coping with the day-to-day basic needs of their families and keeping them together. Here it should be noted that these affected women have largely displayed remarkable strength, endurance, and resourcefulness, which can contribute positively to peacebuilding in Kashmir.

Table 7.3   The Kashmir Conflict and Women IDPs (post-1990) from IJK

Area of Question and Response	Yes (%)	No (%)
Impact experienced		
Army operations	94	6
Threat to life	98	2
Psychological trauma	88	12
Cease-fire on the LoC	98	2
Srinagar-Muzaffarabad bus service	88	12
Preferred solutions		
Azadi	98	2
UN resolutions	68	32
Independence	14	86
Partition of IJK	18	82

Source: Survey conducted in AJK by the author from December 2004 to March 2005.
Note: Number of respondents = 50.

The October 2005 earthquake has heightened the need for peace in Kashmir, and especially for the women in AJK. Though the quake badly affected the AJK women in general and the three groups of women discussed in the study in particular, it has also opened new avenues for peacemaking in Kashmir. The opening of five points on the LoC in the wake of the disaster and the participation of several Pakistani and international NGOs in the relief, rehabilitation, and reconstruction efforts provide an opportunity for the AJK women, especially the affected women, to come out of their traditional mold and organize themselves for peacebuilding. How it actually works out will depend on how the local women's groups and the NGOs in the affected areas, as well as those from Pakistan, India, and abroad, come to their assistance and support their capacity for peacebuilding.

AJK's Women and Building Peace in Kashmir

How can women in AJK make a difference in the efforts to resolve the Kashmir conflict? What are the main strategies that can be employed by them in peacebuilding initiatives? What are the constraints on their role? How can their grievances be addressed in the process toward settlement?

No peace process can be sustained unless it has the support of the civil society. Women, being a vital part of civil society, can have a unique impact on peace processes. Involving women in peacebuilding in Kashmir would reinforce women's agency in this important exercise. Women in conflict zones around the world are working toward constructing new visions of peace and security that place human concerns at their center. They are doing it in all their varied roles as community leaders, social organizers, farmers, teachers, welfare workers, etc. Women in AJK can learn from and teach others about their experiences and build their capacity to participate actively in informal peace processes.

However, it should be underscored that if women are not participating in the decisionmaking structures of a society, they are unlikely to become involved in decisions that define the terms of the conflict or the peace process.[38] Indeed, women in AJK suffer from certain limitations that can hamper their active involvement in the informal or formal peace processes in Kashmir. First, the traditional setting of Kashmir, coupled with a consequent lack of political and economic empowerment, constrains their active participation in the peace movement. Second, although there are a number of NGOs operating in Kashmir and there is also an all-women's association, called the Society for Advancement of Women (SAW), working for gender mainstreaming in environmental protection, there is none focusing on bringing women into the peace process. The Kashmir Women's Forum (KWF), led by Shamim Shawl, an IDP from Baramulla (IJK), is largely a political outfit, but the group does highlight issues relating to Kashmiri women IDPs from IJK now living in AJK.[39] The Muzaffarabad-based Kashmir Institute of Internal Relations (KIIR) has made some effort to involve women in its peacebuilding efforts.[40]

To ensure that women's perspectives feature in peacebuilding, there is a need to build women's own peacebuilding capacity, especially for participating in the informal peace processes. This can be done through building a network of local coalitions focusing on building relationships with and between organizations involved in peacebuilding activities. This also requires an awareness-raising process to highlight concerns related to women's experiences in the conflict and their potential contributions to peacebuilding. The women identified in the three categories need to organize themselves and initiate a networking process focusing on building relationships with civil society networks in the AJK, especially those of women, such as SAW. The relatively high literacy rate among AJK women is an asset for raising awareness about peacebuilding and mobilizing for the peace process. The fact that women are heavily engaged in AJK's rural economy and have great "grassroots presence" could be utilized in forming women's caucuses for peacemaking. Women, especially those who are active in AJK politics, could become involved in the formal peace processes by targeting policymakers and practitioners in AJK and IJK and in India and Pakistan. It may sound idealistic, but peace activism is all about the advocacy of peacebuilding in civil society, and by way of that, creating pressure on governments to take peace initiatives at their level.

The peace process itself could be built, in part, through processes addressing the grievances discussed above. The reopening of the Srinagar-Muzaffarabad bus service has already served to reunite divided families after several decades. This not only has provided space for holding the long-awaited intra-Kashmir dialogue, but has elevated the hopes of the Kashmiris and provided them with a direct stake in the peace process between India and Pakistan. The women of the divided families would greatly benefit if India and Pakistan agreed to similar measures, including opening the three roads in the Jammu and Poonch region, namely the Suchetgarh-Sialkot road, the Mirpur-Bhimber-Rajouri, or Mughal, road, and the intra-Poonch route as maximum numbers of divided families belong to these areas. Other steps would also be of great value, including the construction of family reunion centers along the LoC under international observation and the provision of guarantees for the safety of civilians crossing the LoC. Women affected by LoC shelling would greatly benefit if the rehabilitation work in the affected areas were expedited and also supported by international NGOs and if women-specific facilities were given priority in reconstruction. The women IDPs from IJK would greatly benefit if both the governments of India and Pakistan and the administrations in AJK and IJK paid attention to their safe return and rehabilitation.

Conclusion

The analysis of AJK's women's perspectives on the Kashmir conflict reveals that women's lives are deeply affected by their closeness to the conflict zone of IJK, not only in terms of physical exposure to shelling but through the existence of thousands of divided families and the presence of women IDPs in the AJK region. However, the women's peace movement is very weak, and there is a great need to use the experiences of indigenous women at the grassroots level and to mobilize women's agency for peacebuilding. For that, women need to learn from the experiences of their sisters who are actively involved in peacemaking in other conflict zones. However, they will have to adapt them to their unique position, given the particularities of Kashmiri society and given that there is no insurgency situation within AJK.

Notes

1. The terms *refugees* and *internally displaced persons* (IDPs) have been used interchangeably in the literature on Kashmiri refugees. The Kashmiris regard themselves as IDPs, while the government of Pakistan does not recognize them as refugees and is according them dual citizenship, and the government of AJK has been issuing state subject certificates to them. This chapter uses the term *IDPs* for refugee women from IJK who have crossed the LoC into AJK since 1989–1990.

2. The female literacy rate in AJK is 40.46 percent. "Literacy Rate in Azad Kashmir Nearly 62 pc," *Pakistan Times,* http://www.pakistantimes.net/2004/09/27/kashmir5.htm.

3. There has been remarkable growth of feminist scholarship on conflict, and the gender-specific aspects of conflict, in South Asia in the last few years. This has added new dimensions to the way conflict is understood, perceived, interrogated, and resolved. Some of the pioneer work is produced by Suvir Kaul, *The Partitions of Memory* (Bloomington: University of Indiana Press, 2001); Ritu Menon and Kamila Bhasin, *Borders and Boundaries* (New Brunswick, NJ: Rutgers University Press, 1998); Urvashi Butalia, *The Other Side of the Silence* (Durham, NC: Duke University Press, 2000); Rita Manchanda, ed., *Women, War, and Peace in South Asia*, (New Delhi: Sage, 2001); Urvashi Butalia, *Speaking Peace: Women's Voices from Kashmir* (New Delhi: Kali for Women, 2002); and Rita Manchanda, Bandita Sijapati, and Rebecca Gang, *Women Making Peace* (Kathmandu: SAFHR, 2002). While the first three deal with the partition of the subcontinent in 1947 and emphasize its impact on the lives of ordinary people, including women, the last three focus on women's experiences in the current violent conflicts in the region, including the Kashmir conflict, but mainly analyze IJK women's perspectives on the Kashmir conflict. In addition, Sumona Das Gupta's *Breaking Silence: Women and Kashmir*

and Sudha Ramachandran and Sonia Jabbar's *The Shades of Violence: Women and Kashmir* (New Delhi: WISCOMP Perspectives 1, 2003) focus on women's experience of conflict in IJK. The dearth of literature on the perspective of AJK women on Kashmir conflict and peacebuilding is largely because there is no armed conflict in AJK. The fact remains that they are visibly affected by the Kashmir conflict and there is no worthwhile literature on the subject.

4. In terms of responses, the number of respondents for women from divided families shot up to 75, primarily due to an overlap with the women affected by the LoC shelling. Percentages for women from divided families come from this group of 75 women, while the other two categories numbered 50 women each.

5. See instructional1.calstatela.edu/tclim/gpe_glossary.htm.

6. United Nations, *Gender Mainstreaming: An Overview*, Office of the Special Advisor on Gender Issues and Advancement of Women (New York: United Nations, 2001), p. 1.

7. "Between Hope and Despair: Participatory Poverty Assessment," Azad Jammu and Kashmir Report (Islamabad: Government of Azad Jammu and Kashmir, 2003), p. 102.

8. Patricia Ellis and Zafar Khan, "Partition and Kashmir: Implications for the Region and the Diaspora," in Ian Talbot and Gurharpal Singh, eds., *Region and Partition: Bengal, Punjab and the Partition of the Subcontinent* (Karachi: Oxford University Press, 1999), pp. 292–293.

9. The major political parties operating in AJK are the Muslim Conference (MC), the People's Party (PPP-AJK), and Jamaat-e-Islami (JI-AJK). The MC feels that "militancy is a result of conflicts in Afghanistan and Central Asia, and non-Kashmiris in militant groups have damaged the true cause of Kashmiris." It supports the peaceful solution of the Kashmir issue within the framework of the UN resolutions and stresses "intra-Kashmiri dialogue" and the inclusion of Kashmiris in the dialogue process. The PPP-AJK, a branch of the Pakistan People's Party (PPP), "supports Kashmiri self-determination" and advocates "free movement" between the Kashmiri people "through safe and open borders," without prejudice to UN Security Council resolutions for a plebiscite. The AJK chapter of JI strongly supports the "just struggle" of the Kashmiris and a plebiscite in Kashmir based on UN resolutions. It has supported the peace process between Pakistan and India and welcomed the cease-fire along the LoC and the Srinagar-Muzaffarabad bus service, but it has called for a timeframe to settle the dispute. Human Rights Commission of Pakistan, *State of Human Rights in Azad Jammu & Kashmir: Report of HRCP Fact-finding Mission*, Islamabad, July 2004, www.hrcp-web.org; Ashraf Mumtaz, "PPP to Unite Kashmiris Across Borders: Bhutto," *News,* 9 December 2001; Raja Asghar, "Groups Differ on Kashmir Future," http://www.jammu-kashmir.com/archives/archives2004/kashmir20041127a.html, *Dawn,* 27 November 2004; Naveed Ahmed, "Qazi Assures Support to Kashmiris' Just Struggle," *News,* 30 March 2004.

10. "Literacy Rate in Azad Kashmir Nearly 62 pc." The male literacy rate is 70.52 percent.

11. Dr. Hamid-ur Rehman, "Azad Jammu & Kashmir Community Development Program (AJKCDP): Baseline Study, Socio-Engineering Consultants (SEC)," February 2004, p. 96.

12. As reported in "General Campaign Information: Why a Women Building Peace Campaign?" http://www.international-alert.org/women/wbp_campaign_overview.html.

13. Report of the Fourth Conference on Women, Beijing, 4–15 September 1995 (New York: United Nations Publication, Sales No. E.96.IV.13), Chapter 1, resolution 1, annex I and II.

14. Relief & Rehabilitation Department, AJK Government. Also see Ghulam Nabi Fai, "Kashmir: Past, Present and Future," *South Asian Journal*, January–March 2004, http://www.southasianmedia.net/Magazine/Journal/kashmir_pakindia.htm. Josef Korbel states that some 200,000 Kashmiri refugees crossed into AJK in 1947. Josef Korbel, *Danger in Kashmir* (Princeton: Princeton University Press, 1954, 1966), p. 199.

15. Ershad Mahmud, "The Trauma of Divided Kashmiri Families," *News*, 22 March 2004.

16. Relief & Rehabilitation Department, AJK Government. Kashmiri IDPs are spread all over the world. Some 400,000 live in Britain and about 250,000 are scattered in other parts of the world. Ghulam Nabi Fai, "Kashmir: Past, Present and Future."

17. Relief & Rehabilitation Department, AJK Government.

18. Statement on the reunion of Kashmiri families received by the Commission on Human Rights, press release, Asian Legal Resource Centre (ALRC), ALRC-PL-11-2004, 30 March 2004.

19. Zahid Hussain, "Bridge over Troubled Waters," *Newsline*, February 2004.

20. Ibid.

21. "How the BBC Helped Bring Kashmiris Together," BBC, 22 June 2004, http://www.jammu-kashmir.com/archives/archives2004/kashmir20040622c.html.

22. Syed Muzammil Hussain, "Srinagar-Muzaffarabad Bus Service . . . Why Not?" http://www.pakistantimes.net/2003/11/23/guest1.htm.

23. Asian Legal Resource Centre, http://www.alrc.net/mainfile.php/59written_item10/169/.

24. Observation made by a respondent in the author's survey.

25. Ibid.

26. Ershad Mahmud, "The Trauma of Divided Kashmiri Families."

27. Relief & Rehabilitation Department, AJK Government.

28. Ibid.

29. There are no healthcare facilities at all for 25,000 people living between Athmuqam and Dawarian. These people have been confined by the cross-border firing. See Neelum Valley Health Programme (NVHP), http://www.islamicrelief.com/projects/AJK/3.htm.

30. Neelum Valley Disaster Preparedness Project (NVDPP), http://www.islamic-relief.com/projects/AJK/2.htm.

31. "25,000 Refugees in AJK Camps," *News*, 30 November 2004.

32. Relief & Rehabilitation Department, AJK Government. Also see note 22.

33. Khalid Rehman and Ershad Mehmood, *Kashmiri Refugees: Facts, Problems and Ways Out,* in Urdu (Islamabad: Institute of Policy Studies, 2003).

34. Observation made by a respondent in the author's survey.

35. Lady Health Visitors (LHVs) are the midlevel healthcare providers who deliver healthcare to mothers and children under age five. They are high school graduates whose two-year training includes midwifery, which covers prenatal, delivery, postnatal, and newborn care.

36. Relief & Rehabilitation Department, AJK Government.

37. *Kashmir Mirror* 12, no. 3 (March 2005).

38. *Women, Peace and Security* (United Nations Publication, Sales No. E.03.IV.1, 2002), p. 2.

39. She is currently in London, and in her absence Khadija Tirabi is the acting president of the organization.

40. Since 2000, KIIR has been trying to create a dynamic of reconciliation and

transformation in all four regions of Kashmir. This dynamic would serve as a prelude to bringing representatives of the regions together in a series of bridge-building meetings in a neutral location, in order to begin rebuilding a sense of community across the LoC. The organization believes that the process will help lead directly or indirectly to a just peace accord.

8

Sources of New Delhi's Kashmir Policy

P. R. Chari

Kashmir is India's most important internal security problem. There is also little doubt that Pakistan is India's most important external security problem. This chapter will discuss New Delhi's perspectives on the Kashmir issue against the backdrop of Indo-Pak relations before suggesting possible steps for its resolution.

Conventional official thinking in India strenuously denies the centrality of Kashmir in its foreign policy, but it is easily demonstrated. Kashmir was the main cause and/or major operational theater in all previous Indo-Pak conflicts, as well as several bilateral crises, such as the spring 1990 crisis.[1] However, the traditional official belief in India holds that resolving the Kashmir issue will not mitigate Pakistan's animus toward India. This belief is at odds with Pakistan's perceptions, which have anointed Kashmir as the "core issue" bedevilling Indo-Pak relations, a belief shared by the population in Indian-administered Jammu and Kashmir (IJK) and Azad Jammu and Kashmir (AJK). Kashmir has, in fact, been designated a "nuclear flashpoint" by the United States[2] after India and Pakistan conducted their reciprocal nuclear tests in May 1998.

How does the present political dispensation, namely the Congress-dominated United Progressive Alliance (UPA) government, view these issues? Its Common Minimum Program (CMP) states:

> The UPA Government is pledged to respecting the letter and spirit of Article 370 of the Constitution that accords a special status to Jammu and Kashmir (J & K). Dialogue with all groups and with different shades of opinion in J & K will be pursued on a sustained basis, in consultation with the democratically elected State government. The healing touch policy pursued by the State government will be fully supported and an economic

and humanitarian thrust provided to it. The State will be given every assistance to rebuild its infrastructure quickly.[3]

On its approach to Pakistan, the CMP baldly notes, "Dialogue with
Pakistan on all issues will be pursued systematically and on a sustained
basis."[4] The Congress Election Manifesto of 2004 had elaborated, "It
[Congress] has always advocated formal and informal talks on the basis of
the historic Simla Agreement of 1972. At the same time, the Congress is
firm in its view that Pakistan's sponsorship of cross-border terrorism must
end completely."[5]

These expressions do not markedly differ from those made by the earlier National Democratic Alliance (NDA) government, except in their genu-
flection to the Simla Agreement negotiated by Indira Gandhi with Zulfiqar
Ali Bhutto. They reflect the broad consensus existing within India and IJK
that any solution to the Kashmir imbroglio must be sought through dialogue
with Pakistan but must require the latter to cease supporting cross-border
terrorism for an enabling atmosphere to be created.

The complexities of the obdurate Kashmir dispute, which has cardinal
significance for normalizing Indo-Pak relations, will be highlighted in this
chapter, with a focus on the intricacies of this long-standing issue to explain
its obduracy, while recognizing its significance for normalizing Indo-Pak
relations. The domestic forces prominent in seeking or opposing a resolution of the Kashmir problem and the policy of the current UPA government
in contrast to its predecessor, the NDA government, will then be discussed.
A review of the post-1971 efforts by India and Pakistan to seek a rapprochement, prominently the Simla and Lahore Agreements and the abortive Agra
summit meeting, will be followed by a description of the ongoing India-
Pakistan peace process and the dialogue between New Delhi and Srinagar.
The role of external powers, notably the United States, in defusing these
crises will be discussed, as well as the systemic factors that either mitigate
or aggravate Indo-Pak relations, with a focus on the Kashmir problem. The
concluding section will elaborate the contours of a possible solution to the
Kashmir dispute.

Complexities of the Kashmir
Issue Within Indo-Pak Relations

A half-century-old problem like Kashmir obviously cannot be settled
overnight; it requires a sustained effort to evolve its resolution. This has not
occurred. Past attempts to address the Kashmir issue were episodic. Three
intricacies underlying this dispute and complicating its resolution can be
noted.

First, a complex mix of geographical, strategic, historical, communal, ethnic, and international factors distinguishes the Kashmir dispute and makes the conflict intractable. How should its geographical limits be defined? Should a solution be restricted to the Kashmir Valley? This would be illogical. Or annex the entire Jammu and Kashmir state to India? Or include both IJK and AJK, reconstructing the erstwhile princely state? Several demographic groups with distinct religious and ethnic identities and contending aspirations inhabit these various subregions. There are deep chasms among Jammu (predominantly Hindu), the Kashmir Valley (predominantly Muslim), and Ladakh (Buddhist and Muslim). The difficulty of satisfying these conflicting interests highlights the need for compromise, but maximalist positions are being adopted by India and Pakistan for political advantage. Both India and Pakistan have laid claim to the territory of Kashmir that is in the adverse possession of the other. Similarly, the Kashmiris have argued in favor of *azadi* (independence), which has great emotional appeal, without specifying its contours or what exactly that term implies.

Second, Pakistan's insistence on holding a plebiscite in terms of the historical 1949 and 1953 United Nations Security Council Resolutions on Kashmir has been overtaken by the efflux of time.[6] Pakistan's President General Pervez Musharraf has expressed his willingness "to go beyond [the] U.N. resolutions and not press for plebiscite."[7] India has always insisted on the cessation of cross-border terrorism into IJK, while Pakistan has made an invidious distinction between freedom fighters and terrorists to justify its support to the former. However, the realization has now accrued that these maximalist positions are counterproductive. As noted by Pakistan's foreign minister, Khursheed Mahmud Kasuri: "It is very obvious that India and Pakistan are necessary parties to this [Kashmir] dispute. Pakistan can't solve this issue by ignoring India. Similarly, India should not think that it can solve the Kashmir issue by bypassing Pakistan. And both of us should not think that we can solve the issue by bypassing the people of Kashmir."[8]

This formulation is unexceptional, but it highlights the practical difficulties in structuring any dialogue on Kashmir. The possible permutations are New Delhi–Islamabad, New Delhi–Srinagar, Pakistan-Muzaffarabad, and Srinagar-Muzaffarabad. A plethora of dialogues confuses the situation, but excluding the various interests involved from the negotiations could prejudice them. Squaring this circle is the challenge before India and Pakistan. A further challenge arises in discovering who should be the dialogue partners between New Delhi and Srinagar, apart from the duly elected state government of IJK. How should the opposition parties, and the militant groups—including the separatists and supporters of Pakistan—be accommodated?

Third, the reciprocal nuclear tests conducted by the two countries in May 1998 consolidated a state of nuclear deterrence in South Asia. This, however, did not inhibit Pakistan from supporting militancy and cross-border terrorism in IJK, nor did it deter Pakistan from intruding across the Line of Control (LoC) into the Kargil sector leading to the Indo-Pak conflict of May–July 1999. Nuclear deterrence also did not inhibit India from precipitating the border confrontation crisis, from December 2001 to October 2002, between the two countries. Nuclear threats were frequently issued during these two crises, aggravating international beliefs that Kashmir is a "nuclear flashpoint" and precipitating external pressures on India and Pakistan to resolve the Kashmir issue.

Sources of India's Jammu and Kashmir Policies

What have been New Delhi's traditional policies toward Kashmir? How do they compare with those pursued by the UPA government and differ from those adopted by its predecessor, the NDA government? Broadly evaluated, the UPA was initially averse to negotiating the Kashmir issue with Pakistan, since this contradicted its constant reiteration that the princely state of Kashmir had legally acceded to India, hence there was nothing left to negotiate. However, it later reconsidered its position and continued the negotiations initiated by the NDA government, reflecting a bipartisan approach.[9] Elections have been successfully held in IJK; hence both the Indian and IJK governments have argued that the IJK population supports the state's accession to India. Undoubtedly, there are nuances in the policies pursued by the two governments. The NDA's approach to Pakistan and the militancy in Kashmir was more aggressive; it was in favor of, for instance, attacking militant training camps across the Line of Control (LoC).[10]

The NDA coalition, incidentally, was politically at odds with the Congress-dominated Progressive Democratic Party (PDP) government in Srinagar. This is no longer the case with the Congress-led UPA coming to power in New Delhi. The significance of this political development cannot be underestimated, since the governments in Srinagar and New Delhi are now in sync and better able to evolve common policies to negotiate with Pakistan and deal with the unrest in IJK. The need, moreover, for political posturing and scoring debating points has also diminished. However, the challenge before New Delhi arises from the need to accommodate the militant groups (including the secessionists and supporters of Pakistan), apart from the parties in power and opposition in Srinagar, within a dialogue. The modality adopted by the NDA and UPA governments has been to appoint interlocutors to negotiate with all those interested in reaching a solution to the Kashmir imbroglio. These efforts are continuing in a desultory manner

with regular replacements of interlocutors. For instance, the NDA government had appointed K. C. Pant and Arun Jaitley, political heavyweights, as
its interlocutors in 2002 to bring the alienated Kashmiri groups to the negotiating table. An eight-member Kashmir Committee, headed by former law
minister Ram Jethmalani, was also functioning since mid-2002, but was dissolved when retired bureaucrat N. N. Vohra was appointed in February 2003
as the NDA's interlocutor.[11] Vohra is continuing as the interlocutor of the
UPA government for the present. It is difficult to account for these whimsi-
cal changes in New Delhi's interlocutors, especially when they are believed
to have been provided with no clear negotiating mandate. But it is possible
to suggest that the desire for quick results with agreeable outcomes ani-
mates the central government, leading to early disillusionment with the
interlocutors. Little progress can be expected unless New Delhi provides the
interlocutors with a clear mandate on what demands can be conceded and
what is nonnegotiable.

A long-enduring dispute like Kashmir creates its own constituencies.
Several politicians in Srinagar and New Delhi have no real interest in
resolving the dispute, given that it has ensured not only their importance in
the political firmament but also access to the large development funds provided by the union government to Kashmir to appease the local population.
Much of this largesse is reputed to be misused by the administrative
machinery, which includes both the politicians and the concerned bureaucracies. The Indian military, however, unlike its counterparts in Pakistan,
has no desire to keep the Kashmir fire burning; indeed, the army leadership
dislikes being involved in counterinsurgency operations, preferring to
bestow attention on the defense of the borders. This cannot be said of the
concerned bureaucracies in Srinagar and New Delhi, especially the paramilitary and intelligence agencies, which have a stake in the Kashmir dispute
to acquire large budgets and retain their importance in the scheme of things.
Undoubtedly these are broad assertions, and there are many honorable
exceptions to these general observations. Unsurprisingly, the population in
IJK is most interested in a solution, as they suffer daily privations. Many
lives have been lost, and human rights violations have been committed
against them by the militants and the Indian security forces. Despite these
complexities, India and Pakistan have in the past reached several major
bilateral agreements, which are discussed below.

First, it would be useful to note the broad attitudes in civil society and
the media toward these issues, which differ from the obsessive concerns of
the decisionmaking elites in New Delhi with Pakistan and the Kashmir
problem. These general attitudes have three distinct aspects. First, public
opinion in Kashmir and, more broadly, in India is supportive of the peace
process in the hope that it will ultimately resolve the Kashmir problem.
Their enthusiasm has been palpable whenever Indian and Pakistani leaders

have met for negotiations and whenever New Delhi or Srinagar has engaged in dialogue. Second, popular perceptions are known to change with time and circumstances, and to shift during crisis situations in favor of pursuing a hard-line military approach. Third, large numbers of Indians outside IJK remain unaware of the complexities of the Kashmir issue and are not focused on them; their concerns are with such pressing issues as inflation, unemployment, maintenance of law and order, civic problems, and so on.

Earlier Indo-Pak Rapprochement Efforts

The Indus Waters Treaty (1960)

A substantive Indo-Pak confidence building measure (CBM) that has survived unscathed through recurrent wars and crises is the Indus Waters Treaty, mediated by the World Bank. The treaty in effect partitions the Indus basin between India and Pakistan, allowing each country the exclusive use of three of its six major rivers. A permanent Indus Waters Commission was established under the terms of the treaty, which meets annually to share hydrological data and resolve disputes.[12] Significantly, neither country has attacked the other's river valley projects during hostilities, nor, despite occasional hiccups, has either abrogated the treaty. Kashmiris on both sides are interested in the further development of the Indus river basin to use its waters for irrigation and power generation; they could also be used for navigation. For instance, the construction of a barrage on the Jhelum River, below Wullar Lake, would raise the water level in the river, permitting its use for river traffic. This would allow greater connectivity downstream of the barrage within IJK, and between India and Pakistan. Further exploitation of the Indus basin, based on spatial planning principles, could change the socioeconomic profile of this region while serving as a major political CBM.[13]

The Non-Attack Agreement (1988)

The Agreement on the Prohibition of Attack Against Nuclear Installations and Facilities enjoins India and Pakistan to "refrain from undertaking, encouraging or participating in, directly or indirectly, any action aimed at causing the destruction of, or damage to, any nuclear installation or facility in the other country."[14] Both parties need to inform each other of the coordinates of their nuclear installations and facilities every year. Significantly, the provisions of this agreement, categorized as a nuclear CBM, have been faithfully observed by both parties. India had suggested the extension of this Non-Attack Agreement to population and economic centers during an exchange of "non-papers" process in January 1994, but this was unacceptable to Pakistan at the time; it raised the issue of holding a plebiscite in Kashmir, which effectively stalled these negotiations.[15]

The Simla Agreement (1972)

This agreement exhorts both India and Pakistan to refrain from hostile propaganda, to take steps to resume communications, to promote travel facilities, to enhance trade and cooperation, and to facilitate scientific and cultural exchanges. As regards Kashmir, it envisaged a bilateral heads of government meeting, preceded by an earlier meeting of their representatives, to "discuss further the modalities and arrangements for . . . a final settlement of Jammu and Kashmir."[16] Several factors stalled the implementation of the Simla Agreement, notably a delay caused by differences in interpreting Article 4, dealing with the disengagement of forces, which did not specify whether the withdrawals from across the international border and delineation of the LoC would be simultaneous or independent operations. Moreover, some outposts in the Tangdhar Valley had changed hands after the cease-fire, and the Thako Chak segment lay partly athwart the international border and partly across the LoC. Both situations led to differences in interpreting the provisions of Article 4, requiring further negotiations and a political decision, compounding the delay in proceeding with delineating the LoC. Further delays occurred thereafter, occasioned by issues surrounding repatriating the prisoners of the 1971 war; explosion of a "peaceful nuclear device" by India in 1974; Pakistan's reverting to hostile statements and raising the Kashmir issue in international forums; and the Soviet invasion of Afghanistan, which altered the contours of South Asian security and politics.[17] Indira Gandhi and Zulfiqar Ali Bhutto, the Simla Agreement's architects, also encountered internal political difficulties in proceeding toward a "final settlement" by converting the LoC into an international border, as they had privately agreed in Simla.[18] Dialogue and negotiations between designated officials continued but came to nothing,[19] and Indo-Pak relations resumed their familiar pattern of polemics, tensions, instabilities, crises, and conflicts.

The Road to Lahore

India and Pakistan's reciprocal nuclear tests in May 1998 transformed Indo-Pak relations with profound implications for the Kashmir issue. International pressure to stabilize the nuclearized situation in South Asia persuaded Prime Minister Vajpayee to embark on his "bus diplomacy" to Pakistan in February 1999 and seek a modus vivendi. Vajpayee's visit was preceded by an intense diplomatic engagement between the foreign secretaries of the two countries, who met in October 1998 and defined their national positions in "non-papers"[20] so as to chart a roadmap for further negotiations. This included an agreement on advance notification of ballistic missile tests, cooperation in multilateral forums to promote nuclear disarmament, and improvement of existing CBMs, especially by providing multiple redundancy hotlines between different authorities. All of these found a place in the Memorandum of Understanding (MoU) accompanying the Lahore Declaration.[21] Several other proposals to emplace nuclear CBMs were included in the MoU, for example engaging in "bilateral consultations on security concepts and nuclear doctrines with a view to developing measures for confidence building in the nuclear and conventional fields"; notifying of any "accidental, unauthorized or unexplained incident"; and maintaining the "unilateral moratorium on conducting further nuclear test explosions."

The symbolism of two events during this visit is worth noting. The first was a resumption of road traffic, which had ceased after the Indo-Pak war of 1965, between the two countries through the Wagah checkpoint.[22] Second, Vajpayee's visit to the Minar-e-Pakistan (built to commemorate the Lahore Resolution of 1940 seeking the creation of Pakistan) was designed to demonstrate India's public acceptance of Pakistan's separate existence. Earlier, the Bharatiya Janata Party (BJP) promoted the *Akhand Bharat* (indivisible India) rhetoric highlighting its ambition to undo Pakistan.[23] The Lahore Declaration lost its sheen when the Kargil conflict (May–July 1999) intervened shortly thereafter.

The Agra Summit (2001)

Vajpayee's invitation issued to Musharraf on 25 May 2001 suggesting a summit meeting in Agra was wholly unexpected.[24] It ended in disaster, since it was not preceded by any consultations or even an agenda. A serendipitous hope existed in India that back-channel diplomacy would ensure the meeting's success, reinforced by the personal chemistry that Vajpayee would establish with Musharraf. Once the two leaders agreed to the broad outlines of an agreement, the bureaucrats could hammer out the details.[25] A joint declaration was drawn up but could not be announced. In the Pakistani perception this "did not happen because the hardline elements of BJP sabotaged that agreement."[26] In my view, "Pakistan's attempt to accord centrality to the Kashmir issue and smuggle in the plebiscite concept by urging the need to ascertain the will of the people and India's efforts to incorporate the need for moderating cross-border terrorism ensured the summit's failure to produce a joint statement."[27] The failure of the summit led to great disappointment in India. This bitterness increased after the terrorist attacks on the J&K legislative assembly building in October 2001 and the Parliament House in New Delhi in December 2001, leading to a year-long border confrontation between the two countries over 2001–2002.

The foregoing analysis makes clear that the history of India-Pakistan interactions has witnessed serious attempts to reconcile their differences. The record is mixed. The Indus Waters Treaty and the Non-Attack Agreement have endured. The Simla Agreement kept the peace for over one decade, and has continued relevance for the ongoing peace process. The Lahore Declaration fell by the wayside. One can speculate on the reasons for this checkered history. Personality factors, such as maturity and farsightedness in being able to compromise and moderate time-honored positions in the larger national interests, are critically important. It required the personal intercession of Jawaharlal Nehru and General Ayub Khan to ensure finalization of the Indus Waters Treaty, of Indira Gandhi and Zulfiqar Ali Bhutto to conclude the Simla Agreement, and of Rajiv Gandhi and Benazir Bhutto to settle the Non-Attack Agreement. Systemic factors were also operating. American pressure persuaded Vajpayee to undertake the bus journey to Lahore and invite Musharraf to Agra. That nothing came of these initiatives is indicative of Pakistan's intransigence; perhaps the time was not ripe. The promise of the Simla Agreement and the Lahore Declaration was wasted by subsequent adverse events. Unless both countries, therefore, feel convinced they are in a win-win situation, rapprochement efforts will only reveal an unpredictable record. These questions are relevant to the peace process currently proceeding between India and Pakistan since 6 January 2004, which is discussed below.

Post-2003 Peace Process

Prime Minister Vajpayee's offer of his "hand of friendship" to Pakistan on 18 April 2003, symbolically made in Srinagar, marked the genesis of the most recent and ongoing peace process.[28] Speaking later in Parliament, Vajpayee said, "We are committed to the improvement of relations with Pakistan, and are willing to grasp every opportunity for doing so. However, we have repeatedly expressed the need to create a conducive atmosphere for a sustained dialogue, which necessarily requires an end to cross border terrorism and the dismantling of its infrastructure."[29] Thereafter, India returned its high commissioner to Islamabad and restored civil aviation links (withdrawn and disrupted respectively during the 2001–2002 border confrontation crisis),[30] resumed the Delhi-Lahore bus service,[31] and offered to restore sports engagements, especially cricket.[32] Pakistan thereafter banned three militant groups, including the notorious Jaish-e-Mohammad (JeM), and offered a cease-fire along the LoC in Kashmir,[33] later extended to the Siachen glacier.[34] This cease-fire is holding up and constitutes the single most important military CBM after the Kargil conflict and the border confrontation crisis. India has since fenced the LoC to check cross-border infiltration, despite Pakistan's protests that this would imbue the "temporary" LoC with a semblance of permanency. Subsequently, the two countries also exchanged a series of CBM proposals.[35]

The peace process received a fillip with an agreement reached by the two leaderships in Islamabad (January 2004) to "commence the process of the composite dialogue in February 2004,"[36] which had been initiated in 1997 but later abandoned. The issues included in the composite dialogue are Kashmir, peace and security, Siachen, the Wullar Barrage and Tulbul navigation project, Sir Creek, terrorism and drug trafficking, economic and commercial cooperation, and the promotion of friendly exchanges in various fields.[37] The Baglihar hydroelectric project in J&K has since been added. Negotiations were held between the two foreign secretaries in February and June 2004,[38] and between different sets of officials in July–August 2004. The progress achieved was modest. Cautiously worded communiqués issued after these meetings, describing the talks as "friendly," "frank and candid," held in a "cordial and constructive atmosphere," and "in the spirit of goodwill and cooperation," indicate that no substantive progress was achieved. Settling these disputes requires a radical change in the mindsets of their establishments, but, more importantly, the exercise of political will to make the compromises necessary, to moderate obdurately held negotiating positions, and to reach a modus vivendi. This would serve the long-term interests of peace and security of both India and Pakistan.

Some seventy-one new CBMs were suggested thereafter for Pakistan's consideration by India during their foreign ministers' meeting in September 2004,[39] comprising a mixed bag of military CBMs, political measures, communication links, people-to-people contacts, and increased economic cooperation. They included an agreement on peace and tranquillity along the LoC, opening the Srinagar-Muzaffarabad and Jammu-Sialkot routes, and permitting cross-LoC trade and people-to-people contact through identified checkpoints. Separately considered, these CBMs may seem inconsequential, but their negotiation would induce a positive change in India-Pakistan relations.

The reopening of the Srinagar-Muzaffarabad road in April 2005 is the most significant CBM; this could be the precursor for establishing several more road links across the LoC in Kashmir. A road link between Lahore and Amritsar and a rail link between Munabao and Khokrapar have been established. The latter link is of special importance, since it shortens distances between Sind in Pakistan and Rajasthan, and Gujarat in India. A large proportion of families separated by the partition live in these states. The devastating earthquake that ravaged IJK and, more largely, AJK has united both countries and communities living on both sides of the LoC in joint efforts to provide relief to the affected population. Trainloads of relief material were sent by India to Pakistan, and the latter's troops were permitted to cross the LoC into IJK to conduct relief operations. Five border crossings were also opened as a humanitarian measure for permitting separated families to meet each other.[40] Further, the nuclear CBMs included in the MoU to the Lahore Declaration are under discussion to address the universal angst that Kashmir is a nuclear flashpoint. Some progress was achieved by establishing additional hotlines between the foreign secretaries of both countries and concluding a prenotification agreement on missile test flights. More agreements on conventional and nuclear CBMs would greatly augment strategic stability in South Asia.

The situation obtaining at the time of this writing is that two rounds of the composite dialogue have been held. Following a meeting of foreign ministers in September 2004, Pakistan's then finance minister, Shaukat Aziz, had stated, "The best CBM for Pakistan is to engage India in two things—dialogue on Kashmir and progress on the gas pipeline. I really believe in it. When you create a mutual dependency, you open many other doors."[41] Previously India linked the overland gas pipeline proposal to various demands on Pakistan, such as access by the land route to Afghanistan, which Pakistan was unwilling to concede until the Kashmir issue was resolved, and granting of Most Favored Nation (MFN) status.[42] These demands have since been withdrawn and, despite considerable pressure from the United States to halt these negotiations and isolate Iran, there is fair hope that the Iran-Pakistan-India pipeline project will fructify. By creating a desirable state of "mutual dependency," the pipeline would ensure energy security, but also erode the existing tensions in Indo-Pak relations.

These events might be evaluated alongside political developments in IJK. The most important was the formation of the Congress–People's Democratic Party (PDP) government after the October 2002 state elections. Since then, the state government has adopted an enlightened development program without resorting to the excuse made by the earlier National Conference (NC) government that no development was possible unless militancy and terrorism were stamped out.[43] However, improvement in the internal situation in IJK requires the central and state governments to work in unison for achieving development, reconciliation, and good governance. With the Congress-led UPA government coming to power in New Delhi, the milieu is propitious for proceeding in this direction. This was evident in the smooth change in the chief ministership of the state from the PDP to the Congress in terms of an earlier agreement to this effect reached in October 2002 by these two parties.

A counsel of wisdom offered by a Pakistani observer recommends that an enduring rapprochement between New Delhi and Srinagar requires India to get the genuine representatives of the Kashmiri people on board and engage them in the search for peace, to reduce its military presence in

Kashmir to match the end of jihad, and to give maximum autonomy to the people of Kashmir.[44] These are unexceptional suggestions. The ground situation reveals that most Kashmiris want *azadi* (independence), which means different things to different people—autonomy, relief from misgovernance, or freedom. New Delhi's policy has been to seek a dialogue with the concerned interests in IJK through interlocutors, given the fragmented nature of political parties in the state. Unfortunately, New Delhi has been impatient and unsteady in supporting its interlocutors, which is apparent from their rapid turnover[45] and muddies an already confused situation. The New Delhi–Srinagar dialogue remains consequently in a nascent state with equal chances of failure and success. Much depends on progress in the Indo-Pak dialogue; its success would isolate the hard-liners in both IJK and AJK.

External Influences on the Kashmir Imbroglio

It is well recognized that the United Kingdom had an extraordinary and, from India's perspective, pernicious involvement in the Indo-Pak dispute over Kashmir.[46] Not merely that, its influence over US policies toward South Asia was overwhelming in the early years when the Kashmir dispute crystallized. Attempts by the Duncan Sandys–Averell Harriman mission in 1963, for instance, to resolve the Kashmir issue by partitioning the Kashmir Valley were greatly resented by India.[47] This early experience explains India's resistance to external mediation and obsession with bilateralism in negotiations with Pakistan over Kashmir. The Simla Agreement specifically notes in its preamble that both countries "will not use force for the settlement of any differences between them and [will] settle their differences by peaceful means through bilateral negotiations." Could it accept US mediation in the future? In truth, India's reservations against external involvement seem overstated. It had accepted World Bank mediation to finalize the Indus Waters Treaty (1960) and mediation by the Soviet Union to negotiate the Tashkent Agreement (1966). Further, Article 51 of the Indian constitution enjoins the state to "encourage settlement of international disputes by arbitration," which encompasses external mediation to resolve India's disputes with its neighbors.[48]

Proceeding further, India's reservations about external intervention also derive from its unsatisfactory experience with taking the Kashmir issue to the UN Security Council in 1948. This question was subsequently enmeshed in Cold War dynamics and the compulsion of the UK and the United States to favor Pakistan in the hope of deterring a Soviet presence in Afghanistan. The Security Council, therefore, was reluctant to name Pakistan as the aggressor that had invaded Kashmir with its regular forces; instead it was more concerned with stopping the fighting and passed resolutions that required a withdrawal of Pakistani forces from Kashmir and the holding of a plebiscite by India to ascertain the wishes of the people. Neither of these events has occurred up to the present; hence the Security Council resolutions remain, in effect, a dead letter. This dismal history conditions India's responses to suggestions about external intervention in Kashmir.

Why, then, could it accept American mediation, provided under more euphemistic terms such as "facilitation" and "friendly advice"? In the first place, the international system has been radically transformed since the years when the UN was in its infancy. The Cold War has ended with the decisive victory of the United States over the Soviet Union, with whom India had a "core" relationship. After September 11 and the launching of its war against terrorism, the United States established military bases in Pakistan and Afghanistan, and thus it has a vested interest in stabilizing Indo-Pak relations that conflict around Kashmir. Indubitably, "Only New Delhi and Islamabad can resolve their rivalry and reach an accord over Kashmir,"[49] but there is little reason for India to shun external mediation. Apropos, it had accepted President Clinton's intercession to end the Kargil conflict,[50] and it yielded to US calls for restraint during the border confrontation crisis in 2001–2002.[51]

How does this play into India's larger foreign policy goals, which have considerably enlarged now to accommodate its growing economic and technological power? India believes it will compete with China in the future for power and influence in West Asia, Central Asia, and Southeast Asia. It would therefore need to balance its "strategic partnership" with the United States with a growing cooperative-competitive relationship with China. Within this vision, normalizing its relations with Pakistan and resolving the Kashmir issue in its internal dimensions are essential for India to strive for these larger aspirations, which include bidding for a permanent seat in the Security Council. Whether external powers would build on these larger Indian aspirations to encourage a serious resolution of the Kashmir problem seems unlikely; not as a trade-off, at least. No doubt, a certain angst obtains that the unresolved Kashmir dispute could trigger another Indo-Pak conflict, with its ever-present nuclear dangers. Enlarging the permanent membership of the Security Council, however, raises basic questions regarding the distribution of power within the international system, which impinges on the foreign policy interests of the five veto-wielding permanent members of the Security Council, who have no great interest, therefore, in enlarging their club, and no desire to share their veto power with others.

Conclusions: Elements of a Kashmir Solution

Over the past half-century India has considered virtually every conceivable solution for the Kashmir dispute, ranging from merger to trifurcation to maintaining the status quo to its repopulation. None of these propositions could gain acceptance and overcome the conflicting interests of the political parties in IJK. The latter are agreed, however, that no solution to the Kashmir problem is possible unless greater autonomy is conferred upon the state. This is resisted by New Delhi on the reasoning that according greater autonomy to IJK would lead to secessionist demands in other Indian states, raising major issues of devolution and the balance of administrative, legislative, and financial powers between the federal and state governments in India. These questions underlie the structure of the Indian constitution, explaining why this basic issue has always been skirted.

Coming to the larger issue of resolving the Kashmir dispute, the three main options available are its total merger with either India or Pakistan, granting independence, and maintaining the status quo. Neither India nor Pakistan would be agreeable to merge IJK or AJK currently in their possession with the other. Such a merger would try to restore the contours of the erstwhile princely state by passing either IJK to Pakistan or AJK to India. Both India and Pakistan have invested too much blood and treasure over the years to contemplate this arrangement. The valley Kashmiris would not favor merger as they would be reduced to a minority in the new state. The independence option leaves open the conundrum as to how the two parts of Kashmir would coalesce to form a single political entity, but survive in dependence on the goodwill of India and Pakistan. The larger issue embedded in this option is that the nonviability of the independent state would invite external intervention, leading to instability in South Asia and Central Asia. That leaves the status quo option: a conversion of the LoC into an international border, with some minor adjustments to promote its greater rationality. The present LoC does not follow any discernible territorial principle—division of the two parts of Kashmir along natural features like watersheds, rivers, and so on. A rationalization along some agreed principles would also ensure its greater defensibility. Significantly, the Clinton-Sharif statement of 5 July 1999 made repeated references to the LoC being "respected," and for its "restoration" and "sanctity," suggesting a US preference for the LoC's inviolability that embodies its conversion into a permanent boundary between India and Pakistan.[52]

The objections to this LoC solution cannot, of course, be disregarded. The rhetorical argument has been made in both India and Pakistan that the LoC, being the problem, cannot be the solution. Further, the partition of Kashmir would create a hiatus between the divided families on both sides of the LoC. Despite their number being small, the psychological impact of enabling them to socialize easily would be immense. It is arguable therefore that a de facto if not a de jure solution would be more viable. This could include opening more road links across the LoC, like the Jammu-Sialkot road and the Kargil-Skardu road; devising an easier visa regime; drawing down the level of armed forces; and partially demilitarizing IJK and AJK. In effect, such measures would soften the LoC and provide a bridge between the "merger'" and "LoC as international border" modalities. This solution should be acceptable to New Delhi as it would facilitate its dialogue with Srinagar and reduce the salience of the Kashmir dispute in Indo-Pak relations.

A complex four-point formula was suggested, incidentally, by General Musharraf involving, stage by stage, dialogue at the highest levels between India and Pakistan; agreement on the centrality of Kashmir as the main issue in contention; elimination of all formulas unacceptable to either party; and, finally, discussion on the actual solution.[53] An objection voiced against this four-point formula is that it excludes the plebiscite option, international mediation, and tripartite talks (India, Pakistan, and the Kashmiris) to reach a solution.[54] A more serious objection is that the elimination of all formulas unacceptable to either side might leave nothing for negotiation on the table. Musharraf has also suggested a new roadmap to "identify the region [within Kashmir], demilitarize it and change its status," before moving to the various possible options for a solution.[55] Identifying the Kashmir Valley, which is the bone of contention between India and Pakistan, and demilitarizing it would require similar steps being taken by Pakistan in AJK but would highlight the same basic options—merger, independence, and status quo or softening the LoC.

What are the factors outside of the control of the leaderships in New Delhi and Islamabad but nonetheless influencing the peace process? The process could be derailed by a spectacular act of terrorism, such as an attack on a national monument, or a sudden change in leadership in either country, especially if brought about by violent means. More recently, Musharraf has voiced the need for demilitarizing and enlarging the quantum of autonomy provided to both parts of Kashmir.[56] No details having been provided, these sudden proposals have strengthened beliefs in India that they are not seriously intended but are only designed to impress foreign audiences. Thereafter, concern evinced by India regarding the deteriorating internal situation within Baluchistan has predictably been resented by Pakistan and introduced a certain coolness into the bilateral dialogue, as of this writing.[57] The factors presaging a continuance of the peace process are more compelling. These include the globalization of security, implying that developments in South Asia have implications for the international nuclear regime and the global war against terror; making territorial revisions difficult to achieve; and the encrusting of the US presence in South Asia, which now has a vested interest in its stability. Pakistan and India have also realized the inner logic of their reciprocal nuclear tests that has established a state of nuclear deterrence between them. The Kargil conflict and 2001–2002 border confrontation crisis highlighted that interstate borders cannot be redrawn by military force. Pakistan has also realized that its dichotomous policy of waging war against terror on its western borders but promoting cross-border terrorism in the east is untenable. This assertion needs qualification in view of the situation developing after the devastating earthquake in AJK. Unable to provide relief measures expeditiously using its armed forces, Pakistan has unofficially permitted these duties to be performed by militant groups like the Lashkar-e-Taiba, which presages their continued official patronage. For India this includes the likelihood of continued cross-border terrorism into IJK and other parts of the country. The only redeeming feature here is that both countries have not permitted these issues to derail their ongoing bilateral negotiations and dialogue.

Finally, no ideological reasons constrain the UPA government from seeking a modus vivendi to end the Kashmir dispute and improve its relations with Pakistan. The factors noted above would, indeed, persuade the UPA government to accelerate its efforts to meet the aspirations of the people in India and within Kashmir. Fortunately, there are several internal and external compulsions operating on the leaderships of both India and Pakistan to encourage the hope that the current peace process would be pursued to a successful conclusion that includes a resolution of the Kashmir dispute.

Notes

1. P. R. Chari, Pervaiz Iqbal Cheema, and Stephen P. Cohen, *Perception, Politics and Security in South Asia: The Compound Crisis of 1990* (London: RoutledgeCurzon, 2003). The 1971 war is often dissociated from the Kashmir conflict, but during the course of the war a major Pakistani attack was launched in the Chamb sector, and India lost the strategic territory west of the Munawar Tawi. Fierce battles were also fought across the LoC, notably in the Kargil sector, where India was successful in enlarging the salient to protect its vital Srinagar-Leh highway.

2. The origins of this phrase remain obscure, but it has been used to identify a crisis that is prone to conflict and could acquire a nuclear dimension. Most references to "nuclear flashpoint" have been made in the United States and United Kingdom. They usually pertain to Kashmir and Indo-Pak relations, although the Middle East also finds mention in this context. Former Indian president Narayanan refuted these allegations during the Clinton visit to New Delhi in March 2000, saying, "It has been suggested that the Indian subcontinent is the most dangerous place in the world today, and Kashmir is a nuclear flashpoint. These alarmist descriptions will only encourage those who want to break the peace and indulge in terrorism and violence. The danger is not from us who have declared solemnly that we will not be the first to use nuclear weapons, but rather it is from those who refuse to make any such commitment." See "Remarks by President Clinton and President Narayanan in

an Exchange of Toasts," press release by Rashtrapati Bhawan, 21 March 2000, http://clinton4.nara.gov/WH/New/South Asia/speeches/20000321_2.html.

3. *Kashmir Times* (Jammu), 28 October 2002.

4. Full text may be seen in "UPA Government to Adhere to Six Basic Principles of Governance," *Hindu,* 28 May 2004.

5. Text may be seen in paragraph 3 of the Congress manifesto under "Defence, National Security and Foreign Policy," http://www.congress.org.in.

6. See page 145, especially note 16 of Chapter 9 by Hasan-Askari Rizvi in this volume.

7. "Willing to Go Beyond U.N. Resolutions: Kasuri," *Hindu,* 27 October 2004.

8. Khursheed Mahmud Kasuri, Foreign Minister of Pakistan, "If India Fears Infiltration, They Should Talk," interview by BBCHindi.com. See also Op-Ed, *Indian Express,* 26 April 2003.

9. The major steps taken by the UPA government to continue the peace process initiated by its predecessor, the NDA government, include honoring the cease-fire along the LoC; continuing the negotiations on the eight items under consideration within the Indo-Pak "composite dialogue"; starting technical-level talks on other issues, such as the Baglihar hydroelectric project and nuclear CBMs; and, finally, negotiations on the establishment of a whole series of road and rail communications.

10. George Ipye, "Advani Warns Troops to Strike Across LOC to Quell Proxy War in Kashmir," *Rediff Net,* 25 May 1998, http://www.rediff.com/news/1998/may/25geo.htm.

11. "Kashmir Committee Suspends J-K Peace Talks," *Indian Express,* 24 February 2003.

12. Jagat S. Mehta, "The Indus Waters Treaty: A Case Study in the Resolution of an International River Basin Conflict," *National Resource Forum* (United Nations) 12, no. 1 (February 1988), p. 73. A brief negotiating history of the treaty is available in Sisir Gupta, "The Indus Waters Treaty," *Foreign Affairs Reports* (New Delhi) 9, no. 12 (December 1960).

13. The text of the treaty may be seen in Michael Krepon and Amit Sevak, eds., *Crisis Prevention, Confidence Building, and Reconciliation in South Asia* (New Delhi: Manohar, 1996), pp. 245–250. A provision for future cooperation recognizes their "common interest in the optimum development of the Rivers, and, to that end, they declare their intention to co-operate, by mutual agreement, to the fullest possible extent."

14. The text of the agreement may be seen in Michael Krepon and Amit Sevak, eds., *Crisis Prevention,* pp. 254–255.

15. A factual account of this "non-papers" exchange process can be found in USIS Official Text, *Third Report to Congress: Update on Progress Towards Regional Non-Proliferation in South Asia,* 19 April 1994, pp. 8–10.

16. This formulation occurs in Article 6 of the Simla Agreement. For the text of this agreement see P. R. Chari and Pervaiz Iqbal Cheema, *The Simla Agreement 1972: Its Wasted Promise* (New Delhi: Manohar, 2001), pp. 204–206, also available at http://www.jammu-kashmir.com/documents/simla.html. A detailed discussion of the reasons why this clause was not implemented may be seen in the section "Élan Begins to Fade," pp. 73–78.

17. Ibid, pp. 63–65.

18. Ibid, pp. 70–73.

19. P. R. Chari, "Declaratory Statements and Confidence Building in South

Asia," in Michael Krepon, Jenny S. Denzin, and Michael Newbill, eds., *Declaratory Diplomacy: Rhetorical Initiatives and Confidence Building,* Report 27 (Washington, DC: The Henry L. Stimson Center, April 1999), pp. 118–130.

20. Chris Gagne, "Nuclear Risk Reduction in South Asia: Building on Common Ground," in Michael Krepon and Chris Gagne, *Nuclear Risk Reduction in South Asia* (New Delhi: Vision Books, 2003), pp. 64–65. According to the author, he was able to piece together these proposals on the basis of his interviews with anonymous officials in both countries.

21. The text of the Lahore Declaration of 21 February 1999 may be seen at http: www.ipcs.org/documents/1999/1-jan-mar-htm.

22. Wagah lies roughly midway on the highway connecting Amritsar in India with Lahore in Pakistan.

23. Amit Baruah, "Stable Pakistan in Indian's Interest," *Hindu,* 20 February 1999.

24. The text of the invitation letter may be seen in P. R. Chari, Mallika Joseph, and Suba Chandran, eds., *India and Pakistan: The Agra Summit and After,* IPCS Topical Series I (New Delhi: Institute of Peace and Conflict Studies, 2001), p. 37.

25. P. R. Chari, "Indo-Pak Summitry—Learning from the Past," in P. R. Chari et al., eds., *India and Pakistan,* p. 7.

26. Khursheed Mahmud Kasuri, "If India Fears Infiltration, They Should Talk."

27. P. R. Chari, "Stray Thoughts on the Agra Summit," in P. R. Chari et al., eds., *India and Pakistan,* p. 22.

28. Shujaat Bukhari, "PM Extends 'Hand of Friendship' to Pakistan," *Hindu,* 19 April 2003.

29. Government of India, Ministry of External Affairs, *Annual Report* (1 January 2003–31 March 2004), p. 28.

30. "India to Appoint High Commissioner, Restore Air Links to Pakistan," *Hindu,* 3 May 2003.

31. "Delhi-Lahore Bus Service Resumes," *Hindu,* 12 July 2003.

32. Amit Baruah, "India Proposes a Dozen Steps to Break the Ice with Pak," *Hindu,* 23 October 2003.

33. B. Muralidhar Reddy, "Pak Bans Renamed Militant Groups," *Hindu,* 16 November 2003; and B. Muralidhar Reddy, "Pak Offers Cease-fire Along LoC," *Hindu,* 24 November 2003.

34. Amit Baruah, "India Offers Cease-fire in Siachen," *Hindu,* 25 November 2003.

35. A chart displaying the proposals, responses, and counterproposals and their status in April 2004 may be seen in P. R. Chari, "Conventional CBMs and Arms Control," in Pervaiz Iqbal Cheema and Imtiaz H. Bokhari, *Arms Race and Nuclear Developments in South Asia* (Islamabad: Asia Printers, 2004), pp. 189–190.

36. The text of the India-Pakistan Joint Press Statement, Islamabad, 6 January 2004, may be seen in *Peace and Conflict* (IPCS Publication) 7, no. 2, p. 58.

37. B. Muralidhar Reddy, "India, Pakistan Outline Road Map for Dialogue," *Hindu,* 19 February 2004.

38. India-Pakistan Joint Press Statement, Islamabad, 18 February 2004, and Joint Statement agreed to by the foreign secretaries of India and Pakistan. Complete texts may be seen in *Peace and Conflict* 7, no. 3 (March 2004), p. 47; and *Peace and Conflict* 7, no. 7 (July 2004), pp. 36–37.

39. "India's 72 Proposals to Pakistan," *Times of India,* 3 September 2004.

40. "Fifth Point Along LoC Opened," *Dawn,* 17 November 2005.

41. "Only Realistic Way Is to Keep Dialogue On: Aziz," *Daily Times* (Islamabad), 24 October 2004.

42. B. Muralidhar Reddy, "Aziz Hopeful of Progress in Gas Pipeline Talks," *Hindu,* 25 October 2004.

43. "Bad Governance Has Not Led to Terrorism: Farooq," *Tribune,* 27 May 2002.

44. Ayaz Amir, "The Middle Path to Peace," *Dawn,* reproduced in *Indian Express,* 14 May 2004.

45. Since the NDA government came to power in 1998, there have been five persons who have tried their luck in Kashmir—R. K. Mishra (Track II), K. C. Pant (official negotiator), A. S. Dulat (Track II), Arun Jaitley (official points man), and Ram Jethmalani (Track II). See box item "Kashmir's Interlocutors," *Indian Express,* 22 April 2003. Now N. N. Vohra is the official negotiator, but Wajahat Habibullah has been unofficially deployed to bring on board recalcitrant elements among the Kashmiri politicians.

46. This has been extensively described in C. Dasgupta, *War and Diplomacy in Kashmir, 1947–1948* (New Delhi: Sage, 2002).

47. For an insider view of the Sandys-Harriman mission, see Y. D. Gundevia, *Outside the Archives* (Hyderabad: Sangam Books, 1984), pp. 249–254. A determined effort was made by the United States and the United Kingdom to prod India and Pakistan to reach a settlement of the Kashmir dispute by holding out blandishments and threats.

48. The arguments refuting the fetish of bilateralism have been elaborated in P. R. Chari, "Towards a New Paradigm for National Security," in P. R. Chari, ed., *Perspectives on National Security in South Asia: In Search of a New Paradigm* (New Delhi: Manohar, 1999), pp. 259–261.

49. Council on Foreign Relations, *New Priorities in South Asia: U.S. Policy Toward India, Pakistan, and Afghanistan,* Chairman's Report on an Independent Task Force Co-sponsored by the Council on Foreign Relations and the Asia Society (New York: Council on Foreign Relations, 2003), pp. 7–8.

50. Bruce Riedel, *American Diplomacy and the 1999 Kargil Summit at Blair House,* Policy Paper Series, Center for the Advanced Study of India, University of Pennsylvania, 2002, http://www.sas.upenn.edu/casi/reports/RiedelPaper051302htm. Riedel was present at the meeting.

51. These incidents are described in V. K. Sood and Pravin Sawhney, *Operation Parakram: The War Unfinished* (New Delhi: Sage, 2003), pp. 79–83.

52. Text of the Clinton-Sharif statement (Washington, 4 July 1999) may be seen in *The Hindu,* 6 July 1999.

53. "Musharraf's Four-point Formula on Kashmir," *India News Online,* 3 December 2001.

54. This objection was raised by Amanullah Khan, chairman of the Jammu and Kashmir Liberation Front (JKLF). Staff Report, "Fresh Options on Kashmir Being Considered: JKLF," *Daily News,* 19 January 2003.

55. This was apparently stated in an interview to an Indian newspaper. See editorial, "General Musharraf's Eminently Sensible Roadmap on Kashmir," *Daily Times,* 15 October 2004.

56. Mariana Baabar, "Demilitarisation in the Interest of India-Pakistan," *News,* 3 November 2005.

57. "Neighbour's Balochistan Remarks Intriguing Gen.," *Indian Express,* 31 December 2005.

9

Islamabad's New Approach to Kashmir

Hasan-Askari Rizvi

Kashmir, the most contentious issue between Pakistan and India, has remained intractable since 1947, although several attempts have been made at the bilateral and multilateral levels to resolve it. This has caused serious strains in Indo-Pak relations to the extent that they view each other as the major adversary and have been unable to evolve normal bilateral relations as neighbors. Both India and Pakistan link Kashmir with their state-identities. India interprets its rule over the Muslim-majority state of Jammu and Kashmir as evidence of its secular credentials. Pakistan describes Kashmir as integral to its Islamic identity and an unrealized aspect of the process that led to Pakistan's independence. Such a linkage, between Kashmir and the state identities of the two countries, is a major obstacle to evolving a mutually acceptable solution of the Kashmir problem.

The trouble in Indo-Pak relations may be traced back to the preindependence period, when the Indian National Congress Party and the Muslim League advocated two diametrically opposed notions of nationalism, i.e., one nation vs. two nations, and the conflicts in the process of partition in 1947. The negative sentiments caused by these developments were reinforced by the Kashmir problem and its lack of resolution.

In Pakistan, Kashmir is viewed as the primary cause of the problems in Indo-Pak relations. There is a general consensus in political circles that an amicable resolution of the Kashmir problem will contribute significantly to improving bilateral relations. Other problems in the two countries' relations are viewed as less salient and more amenable to solution than the Kashmir problem.

This chapter presents an analytical review of Pakistan's traditional position, which emphasizes that the people of Kashmir should be allowed to decide their political future in a plebiscite as set out in the United Nations resolutions of 1948–1949. It also examines the strategies adopted by Islamabad for pursuing this objective and deals with the rationale and sources of Pakistan's Kashmir policy. There follows a discussion of the nature and dynamics of the changes in Pakistan's options and strategies on Kashmir since September 2001. Pakistan is now willing to look beyond the implementation of UN resolutions and explore any possible option on Kashmir that is acceptable to India, Pakistan, and the people of Kashmir. This is a major flexibility in Pakistan's position on Kashmir, and it has engendered the hope that if India also showed flexibility in its traditional position, it might evolve a mutually acceptable solution. The chapter examines the factors that caused such a shift in Pakistan's position, and then outlines the broad categories of nonofficial proposals for resolution of the Kashmir dispute and Pakistan's strategies to deal with these proposals.

Pakistan's Traditional Policy on Kashmir

Pakistan's traditional case on the Kashmir dispute is based on the resolutions adopted by the United Nations Commission on India and Pakistan (UNCIP) in August 1948 and January 1949 and subsequently endorsed by the UN Security Council. These called for holding a plebiscite in Jammu and Kashmir (J&K) to determine whether the people wanted to join Pakistan or India.[1]

The UN Security Council remained actively engaged with the Kashmir problem for the next ten years, but these resolutions could not be implemented for a number of reasons. India and Pakistan did not agree on the modalities for holding the UN-proposed plebiscite in J&K. The UN sent several missions to India and Pakistan with proposals for the implementation of its resolutions on Kashmir. However, no mutually acceptable formula for holding a plebiscite could be agreed upon by the contending parties. Another major reason for inaction on the UN resolutions was that the Kashmir problem got entangled with the Cold War between the United States and the Soviet Union. Pakistan joined the US-sponsored regional security arrangements in 1954–1955 to obtain military equipment and weapons from the US for strengthening its security, primarily against India.[2] Meanwhile, India obtained the endorsement of Kashmir's accession to India by the Indian-administered Jammu and Kashmir (IJK) assembly, enabling it to argue that Kashmir was an integral part of India.[3] As the US aligned itself with Pakistan, the Soviet Union moved closer to India and, in 1955, the Soviet leadership accepted India's position on Kashmir.[4] The Soviet Union used two vetoes in the UN Security Council, in 1957 and 1962, to stall the draft resolutions on Kashmir.

The inability to obtain a solution to the Kashmir problem through the UN led Pakistan's policymakers to seek other methods to achieve that goal. One such option was bilateralism, which had been used in a limited way in the past. An opportunity to make use of this option developed in the aftermath of the Sino-Indian border conflict of October 1962, when the US and the United Kingdom persuaded India and Pakistan to initiate a bilateral dialogue on Kashmir in view of the regional situation due to this conflict. Pakistan's and India's foreign ministers (Zulfiqar Ali Bhutto and Sardar Swaran Singh) held six rounds of talks during December 1962 and May 1963. The dialogue was inconclusive because of a wide discrepancy in the perspectives of the two countries.[5] Pakistan demanded the implementation of the UN resolutions, while India maintained that Kashmir was a part of its integral territory by virtue of the instrument of accession signed between the ruler of Kashmir and the Indian government in October 1947.

In 1965, perturbed by what they perceived as India's efforts to integrate IJK in the Indian Union, Pakistan adopted military methods to secure a favorable solution of the Kashmir dispute. Its first military encounter with India, conducted in April 1965, was restricted to the Rann of Kutch, an area located between Pakistan's province of Sindh and India's state of Gujarat. In August Pakistan secretly dispatched an undeclared number of army and paramilitary personnel and some trained volunteers across the cease-fire line into IJK in order to engage in subversion and take on India's security forces. The underlying assumption was that as their activities built pressure on the Indian authorities in IJK, the people of IJK would rise up against them. This gamble did not evoke the desired uprising, escalating instead into the first full-fledged war between India and Pakistan (6–23 September 1965). The war proved inconclusive and both sides continued to maintain control of their respective parts of Kashmir. The Soviet-mediated Indo-Pak peace agreement, signed at Tashkent in January 1966, affirmed "their obligation under the [UN] charter not to have recourse to force and to settle their disputes through peaceful means."[6] The Kashmir issue remained stalemated, although Pakistan raised it at the global level from time to time, asking the UN to implement its resolutions on Kashmir by holding a plebiscite there. Pakistan's military debacle in the 1971 Indo-Pak war and the breakup of Pakistan clearly demonstrated that Pakistan's military option did not help its position on Kashmir.[7] This also adversely affected Pakistan's ability to pursue the diplomatic option on Kashmir.

The Simla Agreement (2 July 1972), which initiated the normalization of relations between India and Pakistan after the 1971 war, also did not offer any specific solution of the Kashmir dispute. It merely outlined a method for resolving this and other problems by emphasizing that the two sides would resolve their differences "by peaceful means through bilateral negotiations or by any other peaceful means mutually agreed upon between them." Kashmir is mentioned in the Simla Agreement in two places. Article 4 (ii) reads: "In Jammu and Kashmir, the line of control resulting from the ceasefire of December 17, 1971 shall be respected by both sides without prejudice to the recognized position of either side. Neither side shall seek to alter it unilaterally, irrespective of mutual differences and legal interpretations. Both sides further undertake to refrain from threat or the use of force in violation of this line." Article 6 suggests that the representatives of both governments will meet to discuss, among other things, "a final settlement of Jammu and Kashmir."[8]

This was the first time that Pakistan made a definite commitment to pursue the Kashmir issue at the bilateral level. India interpreted this to mean that Indo-Pak issues could be discussed only at the bilateral level. Pakistan, however, rejected this interpretation and argued that if a solution was not evolved through bilateral means, it could seek other recognized methods of peaceful resolution of disputes, although the preference would be for the bilateral approach. While addressing the National Assembly soon after returning from Simla, Zulfiqar Ali Bhutto, then president of Pakistan, argued that if bilateral negotiations failed, Pakistan could approach the UN for settlement of the Kashmir problem.[9] Since then Pakistan has continued to assert that it can pursue all the internationally recognized means of amicable settlement of disputes if the Kashmir problem is not settled at the bilateral level.

Kashmir was pushed to the periphery of Indo-Pak relations during 1972–1989 as Pakistan had to cope with the negative diplomatic and economic fallout of the 1971 Indo-Pak war and the country's dismemberment. The two sides, however, addressed the humanitarian problems caused by the war and also withdrew their troops across the international boundaries to their prewar positions. Bilateral relations improved as they revived diplomatic relations and initiated limited economic interaction and trade. During these years, Pakistan continued to raise the Kashmir issue in the annual session of the UN General Assembly and at other international forums, such as the Organization of Islamic Conferences and the Non-Aligned Movement (since 1979). However, it did not pursue any specific military or diplomatic strategies in support of its official position.

Kashmir returned to the main foreign policy agenda of Pakistan in late 1989, after the outbreak of insurgency in IJK. The insurgency attracted support from two major sources in Pakistan. First, Pakistan- and Afghanistan-based militant Islamic groups that actively participated in the resistance against the Soviet troops, often described as the Afghan war veterans, quickly became involved in the Kashmir movement. After the withdrawal of Soviet troops from Afghanistan in February 1989, they were looking for a new Islamic cause, which they found next door in IJK. Second, Pakistan's army and intelligence authorities, especially the military's Inter-Services

Intelligence (ISI), took advantage of the Afghan veterans' enthusiasm for Islamic causes, facilitating their involvement in Kashmir through provision of weapons and briefings for military activity in IJK. They also helped some Pakistan-based Islamic extremist groups, such as the Lashkar-e-Taiba, Jaish-e-Mohammad, and Jamaat-e-Islami volunteers, to engage in armed activities in IJK against the Indian and Kashmir state authorities. This low-cost strategy allowed Pakistan to keep the Indian army, the paramilitary forces, and police and intelligence agencies under pressure through the armed and violent activities of these Islamic groups, who were inspired by the Afghanistan experience and viewed the Kashmir struggle as an Islamic-ideological engagement. The Pakistani army and the ISI made funds available to the Pakistan-based Islamic groups engaged in IJK, as well as offering training facilities and providing some weaponry. Pakistan thus used the militant Islamic groups as an instrument of foreign policy. Due to state patronage, these groups proliferated in the 1990s and remained actively engaged in IJK till 2003.[10] Though Pakistan's security agencies have been discouraging them since 2003–2004 from entering IJK, some of them still manage to cross over to the Indian side.

Pakistan's support of these militant Islamic groups in their participation in the insurgency in IJK increased tensions in Indo-Pak relations. The Indian government refused to recognize the domestic roots of the insurgency and described the insurgency as foreign-sponsored terrorism.[11] It lobbied unsuccessfully with the US in 1992–1993 to have Pakistan declared a terrorist state that allowed its territory to be used by militant Islamic groups engaged in violence in IJK. Pakistan accused the Indian military and other security agencies of excessive use of force against ordinary people in Kashmir on the pretext of combating terrorism.

Several official and unofficial attempts were made in the 1990s to defuse tensions between Pakistan and India and improve their relations, but these attempts did not materialize, mainly because of the ongoing civil strife in IJK. What made Kashmir an intractable problem was India's and Pakistan's unwillingness to show any flexibility in their traditional positions, which equated Kashmir with their national identities and ideologies. India continued to claim that Kashmir was an integral part by virtue of the instrument of accession. Pakistan disputed the legitimacy of the instrument of accession and demanded that the people of Kashmir be given the right to determine their political future as laid down in the relevant UN resolutions of August 1948 and January 1949.

Against the backdrop of troubled relations with India, especially because of the Kashmir problem, the assignment of the highest priority to external defense contributed to strengthening the position of the military in Pakistan. Weak political institutions and processes inherited at the time of independence in 1947 further declined as the state focused on security against external threats and the advancement of its cause in Kashmir. The military shaped up as a major actor in policymaking on security and foreign affairs and, in October 1958, assumed power by overthrowing the civilian government. Since then the military has overthrown civilian/constitutional governments in March 1969, July 1977, and October 1999. This has enabled the military to have a firm grip on foreign and security policies, especially Pakistan's Kashmir policy and its relations with India. It has maintained a strident approach to Kashmir and India. The civilian governments, whenever these were in office, allowed the military to manage the India and Kashmir policies. The attempts by Benazir Bhutto in 1989 and Nawaz Sharif in 1999 to defuse tension with India did not succeed because the military top brass were not on board.

Sources of Pakistan's Kashmir Policy

Pakistan articulates the Kashmir issue with reference to its national identity and describes it as integral to the process that led to the establishment of Pakistan. The underlying assumption of Pakistan's demand was that the adjacent Muslim-majority areas would constitute Pakistan; Kashmir was a predominantly Muslim area, and thus it should have joined Pakistan. The ruler of Jammu and Kashmir, Maharaja Hari Singh, was opposed by the major Muslim groups in Jammu and Kashmir, and he agreed to sign the instrument of accession on 27 October 1947 so as to get Indian military support, hoping to save his rule in the face of the revolt against him in parts of Kashmir.

Another Pakistani argument is that India took the Kashmir problem to the UN Security Council and accepted the UN resolutions for holding a plebiscite in Kashmir to determine if the people of Kashmir wanted to join India or Pakistan; but, later, India backed out of this commitment. India should, Pakistan argues, honor its commitment.

In addition to the issues of national identity and the historical process, Pakistan's official circles argue that the state of J&K, as it stood in August 1947, had more natural territorial and economic links with Pakistan than with India. Pakistan relies on three rivers—the Indus, Jhelum, and Chenab—flowing from Kashmir, for agriculture. If India were to control the whole of Kashmir, it would exercise control over the lifeline of Pakistan's economy, namely agriculture. Though the Indus Waters Treaty (1960) provided a framework for sharing water between India and Pakistan, serious differences between Pakistan and India on the latter's decision to construct three dams (Wullar, Baglihar, and Kishan Ganga) in Kashmir raise the specter of serious water shortages in Pakistan's lean water period.[12]

Another factor influencing Pakistan's Kashmir policy is the role of Pakistanis of Kashmiri background. They occupy important positions in the bureaucracy, the military, and civil society, including political parties. They are the major supporters of the right of the people of Kashmir to decide their political future, and they use their political clout, as detailed above, to pressure the government of Pakistan to continue supporting this right. It may also be mentioned here that Kashmir and the right of self-determination for its people figure prominently in the programs of the major political parties, including the Pakistan People's Party (PPP), the Pakistan Muslim League (PML), and the Muttahida Majilis-e-Amal (MMA). The political leaders, with or without Kashmiri background, raise this issue time and again. The English-language as well as the vernacular press is vocal in supporting the Kashmir cause, although some favor a solution through dialogue, while others have expressed reservations as to whether the dialogue process can resolve Indo-Pak problems.

Therefore, one can argue that it is not merely the military and the bureaucracy that support the Kashmir cause; most political parties, the media, and civil society groups support the right of the people of Kashmir to decide their political future. The differences exist concerning strategies for resolving the Kashmir problem. Should Pakistan continue the policy of confrontation with India? How far has the role of Pakistan-based militant Islamic groups helped the Kashmir cause? Should Pakistan stick to the UN resolutions on Kashmir or make an effort to find a solution that is acceptable to India and Pakistan? Of late, this last view is gaining support. However, it is also argued that the representatives of the Kashmiri people should also be involved at some stage of the dialogue for evolving a mutually acceptable solution to the Kashmir issue.

In the late 1980s and the early 1990s, various civil society groups in Pakistan and India began active engagement with each other and explored the alternate approaches to Kashmir and other Indo-Pak problems. Pakistan's official circles stayed away from this unofficial interaction, but they did not attempt to stop it. This debate crystallized by the turn of the century, and the civil society groups that were engaged in dialogue with their Indian counterparts no longer insisted on the traditional Pakistani perspective on Kashmir, although they did not categorically discard it. These groups talked of a peaceful solution of the Kashmir problem that was mutually acceptable to India and Pakistan and took into account the wishes of the people of Kashmir. These civil society groups argued that efforts should be made to improve India-Pakistan relations without waiting for the settlement of the Kashmir problem. The political parties stayed away from the peace initiative by the civil society groups. However, their activists participated in the civil society process in their individual capacity and kept the party leadership informed of what was happening with reference to Indo-Pak relations at the nonofficial level.

It is interesting to note that the support for seeking an alternate solution of the Kashmir problem developed in the period when Pakistan's military and intelligence agencies and the militant Islamic groups were actively involved in the insurgency in IJK. The civil society groups did not buy the explanation of official circles and supporters of Islamic militancy that this was a low-cost strategy to pressure India without risking a head-on collision between the militaries of two countries. This argument weakened as the rise of Islamic militancy led to increased sectarian-Islamic violence in Pakistan. The killings by various sectarian groups caused much resentment at the societal level and enabled civil society groups and individuals to advocate a changed strategy toward Kashmir and India. The Islamic militancy option also ran into difficulties after the terrorist attacks in the US in September 2001.

Toward a Change in Kashmir Policy

It was before the inconclusive July 2001 summit between Indian prime minister Atal Bihari Vajpayee and Pakistani President General Pervez Musharraf at Agra that Pakistan gave clear signals of a shift in its traditional position on Kashmir, without changing its policy of support to Islamic militancy in Kashmir. Pakistan argued that it would accept any solution to the Kashmir problem that was acceptable to the people of Kashmir. This was a clear indication that Pakistan would not insist on the UN resolutions for the settlement of the Kashmir problem. After the failure of the Agra summit, Pakistan reverted to its traditional position on Kashmir. However, it periodically reiterated that it would accept any solution provided it was acceptable to the people of Kashmir.

Pakistan encountered strong diplomatic pressure against its policy of supporting Islamic militancy in Kashmir after the US and other Western countries embarked on a global effort to combat terrorism in the post–September 2001 period. It faced additional international pressure after the terrorist attacks on the Indian parliament on 13 December 2001. Though Pakistan condemned the attack, India accused Pakistan-based Islamic extremist groups for the incident and held Pakistan responsible for their action.

Pakistan faced a paradox. On the one hand, it was a player in the international coalition for combating terrorism. On the other hand, it supported militant Islamic groups engaged in armed conflict in IJK. Balancing these policies became increasingly difficult as the US and other major powers took exception to the use of violence for pursuing political agendas, especially attempts to change territorial divides. Initially, Pakistan defended its support to the Kashmir struggle by talking of a distinction between nationalist struggles and terrorism, claiming that the people engaged in the struggle for their national rights and freedom could not be labeled terrorists.

The terrorist attacks on the Indian parliament, however, escalated tensions between India and Pakistan. By the end of December 2001, India broke off bilateral interaction with Pakistan, including suspending air, rail, and road links, and bilateral trade was virtually discontinued. Diplomatic relations were downgraded with Pakistan and its High Commission (embassy) in New Delhi was asked to cut back its staff by 50 percent. Pakistan responded by imposing similar restrictions on the Indian High Commission in Islamabad. India also moved its troops in combat formation to the India-Pakistan border to build military pressure on Pakistan.[13] Pakistan followed suit. Some reports indicated that India considered the possibility of launching military action across the Line of Control (LoC) in Azad Jammu and Kashmir (AJK) to destroy the alleged terrorist training camps.[14]

Tensions between Pakistan and India eased when India decided in October 2002 to gradually withdraw its troops from the border positions. Pakistan also withdrew its troops from the advance positions on the border. However, the two sides continued to trade charges and countercharges and engaged in bitter polemical exchanges at the bilateral and multilateral levels.

The beginning of the change for the better in Indo-Pak relations was Indian prime minister Vajpayee's statement in Srinagar on 18 April 2003 that suggested the resumption of a dialogue with Pakistan for improvement of relations. The Pakistani prime minister, Mir Zafarullah Khan Jamali, welcomed the statement and expressed his government's desire to improve relations with India. Later, speaking in the lower house of the Indian parliament, Vajpayee talked of "a decisive and conclusive step" toward peace with Pakistan.[15]

Flexibility and Dialogue

Three major developments in 2003–2004 broke the impasse between Pakistan and India and set the stage for a dialogue on contentious issues. First, Pakistan's prime minister Zafarullah Jamali offered a cease-fire on the LoC in Kashmir, which India accepted. The cease-fire was implemented on 26 November 2003.

Second, General Pervez Musharraf, in a televised interview on 18 December 2003, offered to give up Pakistan's traditional policy of insistence on the implementation of the UN resolutions on Kashmir provided that India also show flexibility in its traditional stance. He also suggested that both should negotiate for evolving an acceptable resolution of the Kashmir problem.[16]

Musharraf offered a four-step proposal for evolving an acceptable solution: (1) Pakistan and India should start a dialogue. (2) They should accept that Kashmir is the central dispute. The dialogue should be composite, covering all issues, including Kashmir. (3) They should eliminate the options that are not acceptable to Pakistan, India, and Kashmiris. (4) They should adopt a solution of the Kashmir problem that is mutually acceptable to India and Pakistan.[17] Subsequently, he argued that the solutions should be acceptable to Kashmiris as well.

Third, Prime Minister Vajpayee attended the Twelfth South Asian Association for Regional Cooperation (SAARC) Summit Conference, held in Islamabad on 4–6 January 2004, and met with President Musharraf on the sidelines of the conference. This meeting produced a joint statement on 6 January that established the basis of a composite dialogue between the two countries for "peaceful settlement of all bilateral issues, including Jammu and Kashmir, to the satisfaction of both sides." Pakistan agreed that it would not allow any territory under its control to be used for supporting "terrorism in any manner." The two leaders expressed the hope that the positive trends in their relations set by the confidence building measures (CBMs) would be consolidated in the future.[18]

The underlying motivations of the joint statement were flexibility and pragmatism on the part of the two leaders. It set in motion a process that, if pursued to its logical conclusion with consistency, could prove to be a turning point in Indo-Pak relations, hitherto marked by distrust and hostility.

The normalization of relations between India and Pakistan continued despite the change of government in New Delhi in May 2004. India's new prime minister, Dr. Manmohan Singh, continued with the policy of improving relations with Pakistan initiated by the previous government. Manmohan Singh and Pervez Musharraf met in New York on 24 September 2004 and reaffirmed their determination to work for a peaceful resolution of their problems and improvement of bilateral relations. They did not criticize each other's policies in their addresses to the UN General Assembly in September 2004. Rather, they expressed their strong desire to pursue bilateral dialogue on contentious issues, including the Kashmir issue, in a "sincere and purposeful manner."

Three features of the Manmohan-Musharraf meeting are likely to influence the nature and direction of the Indo-Pak dialogue in the future. First, they agreed to continue with the ongoing dialogue process and reinforce it with the current and new CBMs. Second, they addressed the issue of Kashmir and agreed to explore all possible options for its peaceful and negotiated settlement. Third, the two leaders discussed the proposed gas pipeline from Iran to India via Pakistan against the backdrop of their expanding trade and economic relations. They agreed that this project "could benefit both India and Pakistan."[19] These sentiments were reinforced during the visit of Pakistani prime minister Shaukat Aziz to New

Delhi on 23–24 November and the dialogue between their senior officials in 2005.

The diplomatic moves in 2004 have determined the strategic direction of the composite dialogue for dealing with contentious issues. This is coupled with the expansion of the scope of the CBMs and initiation of new measures to reinforce the positive trends in their relations at the official, semiofficial, and nonofficial levels. The liberalization of the visa policy has enabled Indians and Pakistanis to visit each other's country.

Several factors have contributed to the change in Pakistan's policy toward Kashmir and India. First, Pakistan was unable to obtain international support for its position on the role of Pakistan-based extremist Islamic groups in IJK in the aftermath of the terrorists attacks in the US (September 2001) and on the Indian parliament in December 2001. Pakistan gradually pulled back from these groups in 2003–2004.

Second, Pakistan reviewed its policy on Islamic militancy after being confronted with the blowback effects of Islamic militancy in Afghanistan and Kashmir. Islamic extremism threatened the fabric of Pakistan's politics and society, because the armed Islamic extremists used their newly acquired power to settle scores with those who did not share their perspectives on Islam. Islamic-sectarian violence and killings and strong pressure on religious minorities threatened internal political order, peace, and stability. The extremist Islamic groups, angered by Pakistan's support for the US war against terrorism in Afghanistan, also made two attempts on the life of Pervez Musharraf in December 2003. These developments, especially the attempt by the extremist Islamic groups to take on the army, led the army senior commander to review their relations with militant Islamic groups.

Third, Pakistan's participation in the global coalition against terrorism allowed the lifting of US economic sanctions, enabling it to receive economic assistance from the US, the EU countries, and international financial institutions. This helped Pakistan cope with the economic predicament it faced in 2001 and thus contributed to the longevity of the army-dominated Musharraf regime. This was accompanied by a realization among the army leadership that combating Islamic extremism and terrorism, as well as improvement of relations with India, strengthens Pakistan's diplomatic positions and helps it to obtain economic and technological assistance as well as military hardware. The international economic and diplomatic support contributes to improving Pakistan's economy, which in turns sustains the primacy of the military in Pakistani politics and society.

In the past, the military pursued confrontation with India to sustain its enhanced role in Pakistan. It also restrained civilian governments if they attempted improvement of relations with India without taking the military into confidence. Now, the military leadership themselves favor improvement of relations with India because this contributes to improving

Pakistani's economy. The top brass have come to the conclusion that if Pakistan's economy improves at a pace to cope with internal economic pressure, they can continue to play a commanding role in the political system.

The change in the disposition of the military (especially the army) leadership is the major contributing factor toward Pakistan's changed position on bilateral relations with India and the Kashmir dispute. However, the army top brass wants improvement of relations to go along with the resolution of major Indo-Pak problems, especially the Kashmir dispute. They emphasize time and again that the ongoing CBMs cannot be a substitute for problem solving.

Opposition to the peace process comes mainly from the Islamic parties, including the MMA, and militant Islamic groups and their supporters. The government, however, is determined to pursue the policy of friendship with India and enjoys the support of the mainstream political parties on this issue. But if contentious issues are not resolved and there is no significant movement in the direction of solution of the Kashmir problem, the Pakistani government will find it difficult to pursue this policy. Islamabad can either slow down the CBMs or quietly allow the militant Islamic groups to revive low-key activities in IJK without formally abandoning the peace process with India.

Options on Kashmir

The current flexibility in the disposition of Pakistan has engendered the hope that India and Pakistan will agree on a workable resolution of the Kashmir problem. This calls for exploring possible options to evolve a solution acceptable to India, Pakistan, and the people of Kashmir. Various academic, journalist, diplomatic, and peace groups have evolved proposals for a peaceful resolution of the Kashmir problem.[20] These can be divided into the following major categories.

1. Partition proposals. These offer various criteria for division of the state of Jammu and Kashmir as it existed on 14 August 1947 on the basis of religion, linguistic and ethnic identities, and territorial adjustments. A well-known proposal is the Chenab Formula, which envisages the division of Kashmir along the river Chenab.
2. Recognition of the LoC as the international border, with mutually acceptable minor territorial adjustments. India appears to be inclined toward this solution; Pakistan and the Kashmiri separatists do not favor it. A variation of this proposal emphasizes the softening of the LoC by allowing easy movement of people, goods, and services across it. The inauguration of a bus service between

Muzaffarabad and Srinagar in April 2005 is viewed as the first step to soften the LoC.

The earthquake in Kashmir on 8 October 2005 neither brought the Kashmir issue near resolution nor pushed it back. However, there were two significant developments. First, the number of crossing points on the LoC increased from one to five. Because of the cumbersome procedure for obtaining permission to travel, this did not raise the number of travelers across the LoC. Only one or two crossing points were used for traveling. Second, India provided relief goods (i.e., tents, blankets, medicine, and food items) to the earthquake victims in AJK. Pakistan also dispatched relief goods for IJK through the crossing points on the LoC.

A delegation of the Hurriyat Conference traveled via the Srinagar-Muzaffarabad bus in June 2005 to meet their counterparts in AJK. Another Hurriyat delegation visited AJK in the first week of January 2006, but they had to travel by air from Delhi to Lahore because they did not get permission from the Indian government for traveling by bus across the LoC.

3. A district- or region-based (rather than whole-state) plebiscite to opt for accession either to India or to Pakistan.

4. A semi-independent or autonomous federal Kashmir, with guarantees for the widest possible internal autonomy. External security would be looked after by India and Pakistan under an international arrangement; they would be responsible for the security of their respective borders with China. Such an arrangement would guarantee the flow of Kashmiri river water to Pakistan.

5. Application of conflict management models such as the Aland Island, the Trieste, and the Andorra cases, and the Northern Ireland agreement. None of these models fully applies to Kashmir, but some useful lessons can be drawn.[21]

6. The handing over of the whole of Kashmir, or the Kashmir Valley and adjacent areas, to the UN Trusteeship Council for a specified period of time. At the expiration of this period a UN-managed vote would decide the political future of the areas and people placed under the trusteeship system.

7. Independence for the whole of Kashmir or a part thereof. (Some proposals combine partition and independence.) The Pakistani government and most political groups are not favorably disposed toward an independent and sovereign Kashmir comprising both parts of Kashmir and the Northern Areas.

8. On 25 October 2004, President Pervez Musharraf offered a proposal that divided the whole state of Jammu and Kashmir into seven zones, which would first be demilitarized; their future status would

then be determined through a dialogue. Two of the zones are currently under Pakistani control: AJK and the Northern Areas. Five zones are currently under Indian control: Jammu, Doda and Rojari, the Kashmir Valley, Kargil, and Ladakh. In November 2005, Pakistan floated the idea of demilitarization and self-rule for Kashmir without outlining its details.

9. A combination of the above proposals.

Some of the proposals offer a detailed plan, while others represent a set of ideas and suggestions. India and Pakistan can explore these proposals at the official or nonofficial level for evolving a framework for the resolution of the Kashmir problem.

The government of Pakistan is favorably disposed toward discussing all proposals and ideas on the future of Kashmir, first excluding those that are not acceptable to India and Pakistan. This may be followed by a detailed review of the rest of the proposals to understand their implications for India and Pakistan. The parties can evolve a new formula for settling the Kashmir problem by drawing on the available proposals. The underlying consideration should be to adopt a proposal that offers a win-win situation to India and Pakistan and is also acceptable to the major groups in Kashmir. Such a solution may be evolved through an intense dialogue phased over time.

Pakistan favors a dialogue for evolving an acceptable solution to the Kashmir problem that would be managed by India and Pakistan at the bilateral level. Direct involvement of other states should be avoided, although these states can extend blessings from the sidelines or help the two sides if the dialogue is deadlocked for some reason. Pakistan advocates the inclusion of Kashmiris in the dialogue process, but it has not offered any working formula to do that. The most difficult issue is to decide who will represent the Kashmiris. Addressing this issue in AJK may be less problematic, because the AJK government and most Kashmiri political parties support the government of Pakistan on the peaceful resolution of the Kashmir problem. But the issue is complex in IJK, given the diversity of the regions and a functioning government and state assembly whose legitimacy is questioned by some political groups, such as the All Parties Hurriyat Conference.

Concluding Observations

Pakistan's policymakers have traditionally assigned a high priority to external security, primarily due to the troubled relations with India and the non-resolution of the Kashmir problem. This has enabled the military to make major claims on scarce national resources, imposing prohibitive social and economic costs on the people and also strengthening the role of the military in Pakistan's politics and society.

Pakistan emphasized the centrality of the resolution of the Kashmir problem to improvement in Indo-Pak relations and insisted on the implementation of the UN resolutions on Kashmir. Though the Kashmir policy enjoyed widespread support in Pakistan, there was divergence on pursuing of confrontation with India and making relations with India dependent on the resolution of the Kashmir problem.

Since 2001, Pakistan has been expressing a willingness to set the UN resolutions aside and seek a solution of the Kashmir problem that is acceptable to India as well as to the people of Kashmir. Such flexibility improves the prospects of resolving the Kashmir problem, provided India is also willing to move away from its traditional position of describing Kashmir as an integral part of its territory. Several factors have contributed to Pakistan's changed position on Kashmir. The principal factor is the realization in the military, especially the army leadership, that accommodation with India, which involves the resolution of the Kashmir problem, helps to improve Pakistan's economy, and this in turn contributes to sustaining the military's commanding role in Pakistan's domestic context.

The ongoing unofficial and civil society interaction and CBMs should continue between Pakistan and India so that the major sectors of their societies, especially the business and trading community, the media, and academia, develop close interaction. These groups can initiate dialogue for exploring different options for the resolution of all bilateral problems, including Kashmir. Such a dialogue will help the two governments to initiate the official dialogue. Civil society groups can also keep their respective governments under pressure to continue engagement even if temporary problems arise in their relations. However, there is a strong feeling in Pakistan that the goodwill between India and Pakistan cannot be consolidated if the CBMs and increased interaction between the people of the two countries are not accompanied by a resolution of their bilateral problems.

Notes

1. The complete text of UNCIP resolutions of 13 August 1948 and 5 January 1949 can be found at http://www.un.org/documents/scres.htm. For details also see the chapter by Waheguru Pal Singh Sidhu, in this volume, and Lars Blinkenberg, *India-Pakistan: The History of Unsolved Conflicts*, vol. 1 (Odense, Denmark: Odense University Press, 1998), pp. 106–119; Alastair Lamb, *Kashmir: A Disputed Legacy, 1846–1990* (Karachi: Oxford University Press, 1993), pp. 168–170; S. M. Burke, *Pakistan's Foreign Policy: An Historical Analysis* (Karachi: Oxford University Press, 1973), pp. 32–34.

2. Pakistan joined the following defense arrangements in 1954–1955: US-Pakistan Mutual Defense Assistance Agreement, May 1954; the Southeast Asian

Treaty Organization (SEATO) in September 1954; the Baghdad Pact, later renamed the Central Treaty Organization (CENTO), in September 1955.

3. Initially India accepted the UN resolutions for determining the political future of Kashmir. The expectation in India's official circles was that Sheikh Muhammad Abdullah, prime minister of Kashmir in 1947–1953, would obtain a favorable response for India in the plebiscite. However, relations between Abdullah and the Indian government deteriorated in 1953, and Abdullah was removed from office and arrested by the Indian government. This development contributed to India's decision to back out of its commitment to hold the plebiscite. Meanwhile a new Kashmir Assembly was elected that subsequently endorsed Kashmir's accession to India.

4. For details, see Robert J. McMahon, *The Cold War on the Periphery: The United States, India and Pakistan* (New York: Columbia University Press, 1994), pp. 123–231, and William J. Barnds, *India, Pakistan and the Great Powers* (New York: Praeger, 1972), pp. 38–43.

5. For an analysis of the India-Pakistan talks, 1962–1963, see Timothy W. Crawford, "Kennedy and Kashmir, 1962–1963: The Perils of Pivotal Peacemaking in South Asia," *India Review* 1, no. 3 (July 2002), pp. 1–38.

6. S. M. Burke, *Pakistan's Foreign Policy*, p. 352.

7. For an overview of the major developments on Kashmir up to 1971, see Gowher Rizvi, "India, Pakistan and the Kashmir Problem," in K. M. Yusuf, ed., *Perspectives on Kashmir* (Islamabad: Pakistan Forum, 1994), pp. 19–70.

8. For the text of the Simla Agreement, see *Joint Communiqués, January 1968–December 1973* (Islamabad: Government of Pakistan, Ministry of Foreign Affairs, n.d.), pp. 204–207. Also available at http://www.jammu-kashmir.com/documents/simla.html.

9. Hasan-Askarı Rizvi, *Pakistan and the Geostrategic Environment: A Study of Foreign Policy* (London: Macmillan Press, 1993), pp. 26–27.

10. For an informed review of the dynamics and role of the Pakistan-based Islamic-extremist groups, see Amir Mir, *The True Face of Jehadis* (Lahore: Mashal Books, 2004), and Muhammad Amir Rana, *A to Z of Jihadi Organizations in Pakistan* (English edition of the book first published in Urdu in 2002) (Lahore: Mashal Books, 2004).

11. Robert G. Wirsing, *India, Pakistan and the Kashmir Dispute* (New Delhi: Rupa, 1994), p. 115.

12. Pakistan argues that the construction of these dams violates the Indus Waters Treaty, but India rejects this allegation and claims that the Indus Waters Treaty allowed India to build these dams because it was not diverting water.

13. For the escalation of tension between India and Pakistan in December 2001, see Celia W. Dugger, "Suicide Raid in New Delhi: Attackers Among 12 Dead," *New York Times*, 14 December 2001; Celia W. Dugger, "India Seeks International Support to Force Pakistan to Crack Down on Militants," *New York Times*, 20 December 2001.

14. Celia W. Dugger, "India Weighs Using Troops in Kashmir," *New York Times*, 23 December 2001; Rajiv Chandrasekaran, "Pakistan, India Mass Troops," *Washington Post*, 24 December 2001.

15. Wahid Hussein, Result Bailey, and Joanna Slater, "Despite Warming, Kashmir Remains a Divisive Issue," *Wall Street Journal*, 5 May 2003.

16. President Musharraf said, "We are for United Nations Security Council resolutions [on Kashmir]. However, now we have left that aside. . . . If we want to resolve this issue both sides need to talk with flexibility, coming beyond [the] stated

positions, meeting half way somewhere. We are prepared to rise to the occasion; India has to be flexible also." *Nation* (Lahore), 19 December 2003; *Dawn* (Karachi), 19 December 2003. While speaking at a dinner hosted in honor of visiting president of Kazakhstan Nursultan Nazarbayev on 8 December 2003, President Pervez Musharraf said, "To attain durable peace in South Asia, the Kashmir dispute must be resolved in a spirit of sincerity and flexibility. We are prepared to engage in a comprehensive dialogue with India." *Daily Times* (Lahore), 9 December 2003.

17. See Pervez Musharraf's statement in Washington, D.C. *News* (Lahore), 21 January 2002. He made similar statements in 2004.

18. For the full text of the joint statement, see *Daily Times*, 7 January 2004. See also Amy Waldman, "Indians in Deal with Pakistan for Peace Talks," *New York Times*, 7 January 2004.

19. Ibid.

20. For a review of various nonofficial proposals for the settlement of the Kashmir problems, see Rifaat Hussain, "Available Solutions and Proposals for Resolving the Kashmir Dispute," *National Development and Security* (Rawalpindi) 12, no. 3 (Spring 2004), pp. 1–32; Faisal Yousaf, *Kashmir: An Array of Options* (Islamabad: Kashmir Institute of International Relations, 2004); and Hasan-Askari Rizvi, "Peaceful Resolution of the Kashmir Dispute," *Strategic Studies* (Islamabad) 12, nos. 1 & 2 (Autumn–Winter 1994), pp. 119–132.

21. For an overview of the conflict resolution models, see Robert L. Butterworth, ed., *Managing Interstate Conflict, 1945–74* (Pittsburgh: University of Pittsburgh Press, 1976), pp. 1–84; Joel Krieger, ed., *The Oxford Companion to Politics of the World* (New York: Oxford University Press, 1993), pp. 28–29; Stephen Goodspeed, *The Nature and Function of International Organization* (New York: Oxford University Press, 1967), p. 52; Shireen M. Mazari, "Conflict Resolution Models and Kashmir," *News*, 15 September 2004; Kuldip Nayar, "Kashmir: A Way Out," *Hindustan Times*, 15 July 1991. For the Good Friday Agreement on Northern Ireland, see the website of the Northern Ireland Office of the British government.

PART 2
International Dimensions

10

Kashmir in the International System

Amitav Acharya and Arabinda Acharya

Notwithstanding the importance of the Kashmir issue, the sources and implications of the conflict remain seriously underresearched in the wider literature on international relations. At the same time, academic perspectives on the causes and implications of the dispute differ.[1] One of the important contributions of the literature on international relations theories is that they help identify the general conditions that shape the situations of war and peace in the international system. The Cold War literature on regional conflicts was largely nontheoretical, but one could detect two underlying approaches to regional conflicts in the Third World. One, popular in the West, viewed them from the prism of superpower rivalry. From this perspective, regional conflicts were mainly a sideshow to, and a reflection of, the Cold War competition between the US and the Soviet Union. Another perspective, developed by scholars from the Third World as well as the West, focused on the territorial and demographic predicament of the postcolonial states, especially the lack of fit between the territorial boundaries and ethnic composition of new "nation-states."[2] Neither approach paid attention to ideational elements behind conflict formations, especially issues of national and group identity and their impact on the conflict. More recently, scholars have examined the Kashmir conflict in terms of contested national identities. These insights represent important advances over traditional and mainstream international relations theories, such as realism and liberalism.

This chapter examines the application of international relations theory to the study of regional conflicts and cooperation in the context of the Indo-Pak dispute over Kashmir. The aim of the chapter is not to offer a detailed examination of the dispute and the prospects for its resolution. Rather, it selectively captures how the Kashmir conflict might look from an international relations theoretical perspective. The objective here is to identify the salient arguments embedded in the literature, which tend to get missed in the context of the Kashmir conflict if a less disciplined approach is applied. This is also pertinent to understanding the sources of the conflict and the prospects for its management and resolution, especially as, given the multidimensionality of the conflict, none of the approaches discussed here individually can explain it in its entirety.

Sources of the Conflict

In general, international relations theory offers three different lenses for understanding and explaining sources of international conflict. The first, realism, holds states to be the primary actors in international politics engaged in an unending struggle for power and relative gain, thereby making conflict and war inevitable. Much of the realist view of conflict was developed during the Cold War and offered an overarching framework, which saw superpower intervention as the central dynamic shaping the emergence and trajectory of regional conflicts across continents. In this sense, regional conflicts such as Kashmir reflected the international power rivalry, often as a safety valve for the underlying tensions between the superpowers, which could not be released in the central strategic balance or on the European continent because of the danger of uncontrolled escalation. The superpowers manipulated regional conflicts through security alliances, arms sales, arms aid, economic and technical assistance, and related means. In South Asia, for example, the US sought to enlist Pakistan in its web of alliances against the Soviet Union, which was interpreted by India as dragging the South Asian region into the Cold War rivalry.[3] Islamabad provided eager assistance to balance the larger powers' superior position in the region.[4] An enduring and protracted conflict involving Kashmir considerably undermined India's strategic significance. It also influenced the Western perception about India. Islamabad's success in bringing in extraregional powers, its capacity to create crises and wars and keep the Kashmir issue on the boil, effectively weakened India's power position in the global system.[5]

Later variants of realism, especially what is known as neorealism, tend to view the rise and decline of regional conflicts as primarily a function of the distribution of power. For example, neorealist scholars such as Kenneth Waltz and John Mearsheimer have argued that bipolar international systems tend to be more peaceful compared to multipolar ones.[6] The proponents of this view seek to validate the argument by the fact that World War II was not followed by any major armed conflagration on the world scale. During this period, armed hostilities among the nations were rather localized and less intense. However, the bipolar international system of the Cold War did not prevent three major wars between India and Pakistan involving Kashmir. And a structural realist perspective would predict that the end of bipolarity would lead to major escalation of regional conflicts such as Kashmir, but the Kashmir conflict has seen both escalation (Kargil) and de-escalation (recent peace moves). Hence, factors other than the presence or disappearance of bipolarity must be taken into consideration.

Traditionally, realism has paid far less attention to internal conflicts than to the international variety. It tends to ignore domestic political systems and ethnic and cultural identities that underpin regional conflicts in the Third World. A modified realist view would see the Kashmir conflict as being driven by the regional power rivalry between India and Pakistan. This would see the dispute as a manifestation of Indian hegemonism and Pakistan's efforts to resist it, as classical balance of power theory would dictate. From Islamabad's perspective, so long as India retains its designs of hegemony over South Asia, preeminence in Asia, and a great power role in the world, Pakistan would remain an obstacle to it.[7] The power rivalry is aggravated by the interplay of religious ideologies and national interests between India and Pakistan. Hence the Kashmir dispute serves as the defining element of a "regional security complex" (to use Barry Buzan's term), with a measure of autonomy from global power rivalries.

Security complexes are defined by a high degree of security interdependence, such that the security of one actor cannot be realistically explained except in terms of the security of other actors in the complex. While it captures one aspect of the Kashmir dispute, security complex theory does not offer any concrete indicators for measuring security interdependence. Nor does it clearly establish the relative importance of an interdependence of rivalry vis-à-vis an interdependence of cooperation. The security complex theory is a structural theory, which in its original and parsimonious formulation, at least, neglects the role of individual actors and domestic politics, as well as that of ideational factors, including competing ideas and identities, as sources of conflict. For example, in the context of Kashmir, such a view ignores the Kashmiri nationalist claim to independence both from India and Pakistan, based on distinct Kashmiri identity (the Kashmiriyat) and the right of self-determination.[8] This limits its utility in capturing and analyzing the Kashmir dispute. It is therefore difficult to explain the Kashmir conflict with systemic forces, including the changes in global power configurations.

A second theoretical perspective on international relations, liberalism, is more concerned with explaining the conditions for peace than the causes of war. But the absence of the conditions it identifies as conducive to peace may be seen as clues to the persistence of conflict. Liberalism has three variants, focusing on domestic politics, economic interdependence, and international institutions. In the context of Kashmir, it has been argued that domestic political constraints have trapped both India and Pakistan into a scenario where the Kashmir issue has become the respective countries' nationalist discourse that "Pakistan is incomplete without Kashmir" or that "Kashmir is the crown-symbol of Indian secularism." Kashmir and insurgency provide both countries with excuses for colossal conventional military and nuclear buildups. Even as Pakistan continues to grapple with democratic stabilization, there has always been a tendency on the part of Pakistan's ruling class to define the liberation of Kashmir as a test for political survival and legitimacy. The military in Pakistan has developed a strong vested interest in keeping the Kashmir issue alive as a way of maintaining its hold over power. The Kashmir conflict has been routinely used as a national rallying point, as an issue to distract the Pakistani public from concerns of social inequality, sectarian conflict, and absence of social progress.[9] The weakness in Pakistan's civil and political structures, its weak and corrupt civilian bureaucracy, and its feudal structures have prevented democratic consolidation despite periodic transitions from authoritarian rule. The low level of civic and political development in Pakistan has fueled, and is compounded by, an Islamic radicalism that began to increasingly permeate the Pakistani society, polity, and military in the 1980s. This was influenced by the Shia revolution in Iran and the penetration of the mujahidin into the *madrassas* of Pakistan during and in the aftermath of the Soviet invasion of Afghanistan. Lack of strong civilian control of the military has empowered intelligence agencies, which have provided training and supervised the prosecution of a low-intensity conflict against India in Kashmir. However, the Kashmir dispute does not automatically validate the liberal arguments on the nature of domestic polity and institutions as catalysts for conflict or peace. The Kargil conflict took place when Pakistan was under a democratically elected government. Conversely, the continued momentum and the pace of the revived peace overtures in 2004 from Pakistan have been possible because of Musharraf, who heads a military regime.

Liberalism as a theory of international relations identifies low levels of economic interdependence and the absence of international institutions providing dispute settlement mechanisms as factors conducive to conflict between states. The absence of close economic links between Pakistan and India and the low level of intraregional trade in general mean the absence of a major constraint on the use of force by either side to secure a final solution of the Kashmir conflict. The potential of the South Asian Association for Regional Cooperation (SAARC) in fostering economic integration has been stymied by the India-Pakistan disputes. SAARC has had no role in alleviating regional insecurities (Article 10 of the SAARC Declaration excludes "bilateral and contentious issues . . . from the deliberations") due to the lack of congruence of regime security concerns. The lack of congruence is further reflected in the absence of a regional consensus on the role of the regional preeminent power—India. Any potential role for SAARC in undertaking regional mediation efforts over the Kashmir issue has been repeatedly torpedoed by India and Pakistan.

A constructivist account of the Kashmir dispute captures the crucial issue of contested national identities as a source of the dispute and a factor affecting conflict resolution. One important aspect of this literature, which seeks to explain international relations based on culture and identity, needs to be noted at the outset. Constructivism does not present culture as a benign force in international relations. Culture and identity can promote conflict as well as cooperation, but the central point is that they must be taken into account if one is to develop an adequate understanding of international conflicts and their resolution.

From this perspective, the roots of the identity-dissonance that sustains the Kashmir conflict can be traced back to the partition of India based on the two-nation theory, which led to the development of different nationalisms that are now engaged in a contest of validation in the region.[10] On the one hand is India's civic and secular nationalism, founded on the principles of political pluralism, democratic governance, the federal structure of the Indian state, constitutionalism, and a democratic political culture that has been accommodative of diverse ethnic, linguistic, regional, and religious groups. It is important to bear in mind that this secular nationalism, conceived by its founders, such as Mahatma Gandhi and Jawaharlal Nehru, has aspired to erode the communal basis of politics. In recent years, however, it has been seriously challenged by a resurgent Hindu nationalism that believes in Hinduism as the dominant religion with which the ethnic and religious minorities of the country would have to seek accommodation and which takes the Indian Muslims to be disloyal to the Indian nation. But the contestation between the official secular nationalism and Hindu chauvinistic nationalism has not dampened the consensus that Kashmir constitutes the integral aspect of the Indian polity. Moreover, the Indian elite sees the Kashmir issue as a crucial test of its national cohesion. It fears that the secession of Kashmir would create a domino effect elsewhere, triggering violent regional, political, religious, and ethnolinguistic secessionist trends that would undermine the foundations of India's diverse liberal democratic polity and pluralism. This has been an issue that Indian leaders have found difficult to rationalize. As Nehru himself inquired, why only two nations of Hindus and Muslims? Why not nations of Sikhs, Christians, and Buddhists, even if some of these religious groups are separated by geography, race, and language?[11] "For if nationality is based on religion there are many nations in India."[12]

India's secular nationalism contrasts with a Pakistani national identity rooted in the two-nation theory. This affirms Pakistan's mission as the homeland of Muslims in South Asia. Its religious nationalism is premised on a pan-Islamic polity that would encompass the diverse ethnic, denominational, linguistic, and regional groups in its social mosaic. As a Muslim-majority state, Kashmir's integration with Pakistan would be essential to the completeness of Pakistan,[13] and has since been seen by the Pakistani elite as unfinished business of the partition. The idea of Pakistan as the homeland of the Muslims in South Asia suffered a major setback in 1947, when Kashmir acceded to India in the face of Pakistani incursion into the Kashmir Valley. Another setback, occurring in 1971, was the revolt by and loss of East Pakistan with the help of Indian intervention. Despite these blows to Pakistan's identity as the regional Muslim homeland, Pakistan continues to reject the Kashmiri nationalism that would be the basis of a Kashmiri state independent from both India and Pakistan. Indeed, Pakistan is not supportive of an independent Kashmir, believing that the choice, if ever a plebiscite takes place, would be between accession to Pakistan and that to India.

Between the Indian and Pakistani nationalisms lies an indigenous Kashmiri nationalism relying on a distinct articulation of the region's shared ethnic, linguistic, and regional characteristics. The Kashmiri identity, referred to as Kashmiriyat, has given Kashmiri nationalism a nonreligious orientation, its specificity derived from the fusion and assimilation of varied faiths and cultures. "The land, the climate, the geography shaped the evolution of their particular ethnic profile. A common language bound them closer into a distinct cultural grouping."[14] The object of Kashmiri nationalism is independence from both Pakistan and India. Except for Islamic militant groups, there is not much demand for accession to Pakistan among the Kashmiris. While the discourse on Kashmiri nationalism has sought to advance the argument that Kashmir's accession to India has been a major factor in stabilizing relations between the Hindus and the Muslims,[15] the potential for the rise of Hindu communalism has nonetheless made Kashmiris apprehensive about their future in India. Hindu communalism itself also suffers from internal contradictions, with the identification of the Jammu Hindus, the Dogra Hindus, and the Pandits with India.[16] Another challenge is the Tibetan Buddhist presence in Ladakh, which is more Tibetan than Kashmiri. The Kashmir Valley contains an ethnic mix reproducing the contestations between Indian and Pakistani nationalisms. The Soviet withdrawal from Afghanistan, followed by the influx of the jihadis into Kashmir, created the possibility of a militant Islamic nationalism replacing the ethnic nationalist agenda of Kashmiri self-determination of the earlier period. But it has also led to the emergence of a new ethnic nationalism of Kashmiris disaffected both by India's role and by the activities of Islamic militants based in Pakistan, which have exploited the

Kashmiri uprising in IJK for their own ends, rather than for the creation of a sovereign Kashmir state. In this sense, and given the ethnic mix of Kashmir and religious contestations within Pakistan, one cannot be entirely sure whether what we are witnessing in Kashmir is more of a clash between civilizations or within a civilization.

The competing identities of states and groups involved in the Kashmir dispute matter not only in capturing the complex roots of the conflict, but also in shaping the prospects for conflict resolution. They suggest limitations to approaches that conceptualize the Kashmir dispute as a conventional interstate territorial conflict, aggravated by outside intervention, whether it was the Cold War rivalry between the US and the (then) Soviet Union, or Chinese support for Pakistan now. In addition, approaches that do not take into consideration the domestic political configurations of both India and Pakistan are unlikely to make headway in moving the dispute toward durable resolution. While the international community does have a role in conflict resolution, this has to take into consideration the fact that the main factors affecting conflict resolution may be internal to both India and Pakistan, as well as to the Kashmir region itself.

Prospects for Stability and Conflict Resolution

Realists foresee no permanent escape from the "security dilemma" that states find themselves to be locked in. Their best hope is not peace, but the maintenance of stability through power balancing. Realists would argue that the best hope for Kashmir would be the maintenance of a stable balance of physical power between India and Pakistan. The competitive acquisition of nuclear weapons by India and Pakistan in 1998 serves as a test for the realist position that the balance of power (in this instance a balance of terror) would sustain peace between the two nuclear rivals. Nuclear deterrence encourages de-escalation and strategic restraint. Pakistan's nuclear capability nullifies India's traditional edge in conventional arms and perhaps deters a preemptive strike by India on Pakistani-held Kashmir to stamp out terrorist training camps. Realists would also argue that the risks of accidental nuclear conflict could be reduced through the negotiation and implementation of crisis stability measures (nuclear risk reduction measures), as well as arms control and confidence and security building measures initiatives. But one fundamental weakness of this position is that nuclear deterrence does not necessarily discourage limited wars. Under the shadow of the nuclear weapons, adversaries could undertake a range of minor ventures and proxy wars with impunity as surrogates for direct conflict.[17] One example of this dynamic was the 1999 Kargil episode. As the Kargil Review Committee noted, South Asian nuclear deterrence reduced the risks of major conventional wars only up to a given threshold, the margin of which was exploited by Pakistan.[18] Similarly, as Michael Krepon has noted, "Pakistan's support for separatism and militancy in Kashmir has notably coincided with its acquisition of covert nuclear capabilities."[19] Such instances, which also include the military mobilization by India and Pakistan following December 2001 terrorist attacks against the Indian parliament, could test strategic stability severely.

India's quest for great power status may also be conducive to the resolution of the Kashmir dispute. This would lead one to expect that India, as an emerging great power in international relations, with an eye on permanent membership on the UN Security Council, and with its new emphasis on economic growth and integration into the global economy, will want to step out of the South Asia tinderbox. India's emerging economic profile notwithstanding, the Indo-Pak imbroglio continues to keep New Delhi's wider strategic role circumscribed as India's net military power remains the sum of its own capabilities minus those of Pakistan (which are directed largely toward the diminution of New Delhi).[20] Stability in the Indo-Pak relations would allow India to devote more attention and resources to pursuing its economic and strategic interests in the Indian Ocean and Southeast Asia. India's "look east" policy, which calls for closer diplomatic-economic-strategic partnerships in the Asia-Pacific region, cannot be pursued meaningfully so long as it remains locked in a persisting confrontation with Pakistan. This will create new incentives for India to show greater flexibility on the Kashmir issue and accept international mediation in the dispute.

Liberal approaches would focus first and foremost on developing Indo-Pak economic interdependence, either bilaterally or through regional mechanisms. Economic cooperation at the regional level has the potential to galvanize nations to come together, accelerate the pace of development, and share the dividends. The bonds of togetherness born out of economic mutuality can in turn resolve intraregional tensions.[21] Trade and geo-economics have the potential to replace Cold War–era security preoccupations. Pakistan's strategic interests in Kashmir, for example, are driven partly by geo-economics, along with strategic and religious considerations; Kashmir contains the headwaters of the rivers running into West Punjab, Pakistan's main agricultural province, which is greatly dependent on irrigation for its prosperity.[22] Major General Akbar Khan, who planned the 1947 invasion of Kashmir, noted how vital, from the economic point of view, Kashmir is for Pakistan. "Our agricultural economy was dependent particularly upon rivers coming out of Kashmir . . . what then would be our position if Kashmir was to be in Indian hands?"[23]

Another area of economic interdependency concerns the energy sector. India is a rapidly growing energy market, with the ability to absorb new sources of supply as they materialize in the region. Pakistan could be a potential transit route for energy from Iran and Central Asia. This would require major capital investment and the construction of one or more new pipelines, a project that requires a degree of political stability within Pakistan and peace in India-Pakistan relations. According to some estimates, Pakistan could gain $600 to $800 million per year in transit fees.[24] It would also be able to use the pipelines to fulfill its own energy needs. India would benefit from diversified sources of pipeline gas and lower dependence on more expensive liquid natural gas.[25]

Though there are significant economic complementarities between India and Pakistan, they have not been exploited fully due to the political disposition of the two countries. In 2003–2004, India exported only $303.7 million worth of goods to Pakistan, out of $67.54 billion in total exports. India's imports from Pakistan were only $60.74 million in 2003–2004.[26] During this period, bilateral trade between India and Pakistan was on the order of $345 million, whereas India's exports alone to Bangladesh and Sri Lanka were $1.65 billion and $1.324 billion respectively.[27] Islamabad does not extend normal GATT/WTO rights or Most Favored Nation (MFN) status to India. Pakistan has a list of 600 items that can be legally imported from India. India granted MFN treatment to Pakistan in 1995–1996 and has no list of permitted or forbidden products.[28] Informal India-Pakistan trade is much larger, estimated at $1 to $2 billion annually,[29] involving such goods as chemicals, medicines, videotapes, cosmetics, and viscose fiber. These goods find their way either through third markets, such as Dubai and Singapore, or through smuggling. Legalizing and further developing this trade, which the Federation of Indian Chamber of Commerce (FICCI) estimates to be something like $3 to $4 billion annually,[30] could have a stabilizing effect on India-Pakistan relations and ultimately create opportunities for negotiating a settlement to the Kashmir dispute.

Liberal-institutionalists would suggest that concerns arising out of interdependence could be mitigated through institutionalized cooperation.[31] According to this view, nations concede "political advantages" to one another with the expectation of "receiving proportionate advantages in return."[32] Institutions change the incentive for states to cheat; they also reduce transaction costs, link issues, increase the amount of information available to participants in cooperative arrangements, and make commitments more credible.[33] A number of studies have established the impact of institutions, that "clear causal links unambiguously demonstrate that treaty rules independently influenced behavior,"[34] and that involvement of international organizations in "sanctions" strongly correlates with high levels of cooperation.[35] In South Asia, even though the SAARC is devoid of a security mandate, it could nonetheless provide a useful framework for functional cooperation that could create an improved climate for peace between India and Pakistan. Such progress could come through moving forward on the South Asia Preferential Trade Agreement (SAPTA).

Some may argue that interdependence or institutions alone will not suffice as conditions for peace in South Asia in the absence of genuine democratization in Pakistan. Realists also argue that democratization by itself is no guarantee of peace in the short term. Critics of the democratic peace theory have argued that newly democratizing states are often neither liberal nor peaceful.[36] Experience shows that democratization can fuel virulent nationalism and aggravate the danger of war. In fact, the earliest phases of democratization have triggered some of the world's bloodiest nationalist struggles, often leading up to armed violence, in a number of regions beginning to experiment with electoral democracy.[37] In the past, democratic governments in Pakistan have not necessarily brought about improved India-Pakistan relations. This is partly because, elections notwithstanding, the military has managed to cast a shadow over elected governments in Pakistan and influenced their policy on Kashmir. On the other hand, as the recent peace initiatives suggest, the military regime under President Musharraf is at the forefront in pushing for a lasting solution to the Kashmir problem. It is noteworthy that Musharraf has managed to keep the tempo going even as India underwent major political changes following general elections in 2004.

The involvement of both India and Pakistan in regional and international persuasion and socialization—mechanisms emphasized by constructivist theories of international relations—thus could create viable conditions for achieving lasting peace in Kashmir. Socialization is different from mediation and arbitration, which are more political and legal mechanisms, although the former can create more conducive conditions for the latter. The international community's early role in the Kashmir dispute stressed the facilitation of self-determination for Kashmir. The UN constituted the UN Commission on India and Pakistan (UNCIP) in July 1948 to assess the material conditions for the conduct of a UN-administered plebiscite. This was, however, overtaken by the deployment of Pakistani and Indian armed forces in the area. The United States, the United Kingdom, the Soviet Union, and the European Union have on a number of occasions shown interest in mediating on the Kashmir issue. But India has objected to such focused outside mediation, emphasizing that Kashmir is a bilateral dispute between India and Pakistan and must be dealt with bilaterally, without outside mediation. But bilateralism alone will not create sufficient domestic legitimacy for either side to sustain any solution that might be acceptable to the governments of the two countries. This is because of the sensitivity of the issue in both countries' domestic context. For Pakistan, the regime would find it extremely difficult to sell any proposal on Kashmir short of its secession from India and integration with Pakistan. Radical groups have castigated Musharraf's ongoing Kashmir peace overtures as betrayal and have questioned his legitimacy for going around the UNSC resolutions on Kashmir. As Musharraf himself admitted, "We cannot do anything against the wishes of the people of Pakistan. We need to develop a consensus with the people of Pakistan. The issue is very contentious."[38] From an Indian perspective, additional territorial concessions to Pakistan would also be too difficult to concede. It is in this context that Prime Minister Manmohan Singh ruled out further concessions on the LoC during his meetings with the visiting Pakistani president in April 2005.

Against this backdrop, and given the continued weakness of SAARC and its avoidance of security issues, one avenue for greater socialization between India and Pakistan would come from their common membership in wider Asian regional groupings (aside from the development of "second track" mechanisms and processes at the South Asian and wider Asia levels). The ASEAN Regional Forum (ARF) is the only multilateral security organization in the Asia-Pacific region. For the first time, India and Pakistan are members of the same regional security organization. Outside mediation in the Kashmir dispute remains a distant possibility so long as India champions strict adherence to the doctrine of noninterference in the internal affairs of states. But attitudes toward the doctrine are changing. Although the ARF is supposed to keep contentious bilateral issues such as Kashmir out of its agenda, common membership in a regional security organization will have a calming effect on India-Pakistan bilateral relations and offer an avenue through which the regional community could encourage restraint on the parties when conflict appears imminent.

Another helpful and complementary development initiative could be to persuade India and Pakistan to participate in a multilateral framework involving the US, China, and Russia, and possibly the European Union and Japan (or some combination thereof, although the US and China, as well as Russia, would have to be involved). Such a multilateral framework would ensure greater crisis stability in the subcontinent. China's close relations with Pakistan give it a measure of influence over Pakistan's decision to escalate the Kashmir dispute. Russia has a certain amount of goodwill with India, which is a major buyer of Russian weapons. Moreover, thanks to September 11, the US now enjoys close relations with both India and Pakistan (as well as closer understanding with China). This gives Washington an unprecedented ability not only to pull India and Pakistan back from the brink in the event of a crisis, but also to persuade them to more actively seek a lasting peaceful resolution of the conflict. This could be the basis of a system of at least five-party talks (with Japan and the EU serving as associate members if their full membership is not feasible) involving India, Pakistan, Russia, China, and the US. The aim of such talks would be to complement India-Pakistan bilateral negotiations, both by offering a stamp of international legitimacy and by facilitating the flow of resources that would be needed to ensure viable post-conflict peace and reconstruction in the Kashmir area. India might see this as unwelcome "outside" mediation in the Kashmir dispute. But a five-party framework involving India and Pakistan, which complements rather than substitutes for their bilateral efforts, does not have to be meddlesome. It could help promote a peaceful resolution of the conflict by offering strategic reassurance to both India and Pakistan that they could protect their core interests and derive security gains from a resolution of the Kashmir conflict, including an end to cross-border terrorism threatening India, and a role for Pakistan (through either partial or joint control over a postconflict Kashmir) that would satisfy its core interests in the dispute. The multilateral framework could ensure adequate local political and administrative autonomy for the Kashmiris through a system of democratic governance and international guarantees that would recognize and respect their ethnonational identity without necessarily creating a sovereign state. While a multilateral solution may sound unrealistic, it is perhaps no more so than alternatives advanced by the various parties.

Conclusion

Unlike realism or other rationalist perspectives on international relations, social constructivism argues that the interests and identities of states are not exogenous to the process of their mutual interaction. This is an important point in understanding the Kashmir conflict and prospects for its solution. The conflict defies simple definition and an easy solution. It is difficult to put the conflict in overreaching nationalist terms alone, or to define it as a competition over territory. Nor can it be explained solely in terms of the two-nation theory, referencing only the religious considerations that were the basis of the partition of the subcontinent in 1947.

This chapter has offered a broader perspective in defining the conflict, incorporating ideational variables, such as culture and identity, in addition to strategic and institutionalist considerations. Viewing Kashmir through this lens is useful not just in identifying its underlying causes, but also in seeking a lasting settlement. Cooperative multilateral arrangements and initiatives can do much to shed the rigidity of the two sides on the issue. Musharraf's suggestion that the two countries develop a consensus through debate and discussions before their leadership can determine what kind of solution is possible among India, Pakistan, and the people of Kashmir represented an acknowledgement that any solution to the conflict is not to be based on a predetermined formula, or on proposals unilaterally advanced by either side reflecting its narrow national interests.[39] Seeking the right formula for peace in Kashmir is not exogenous to the diplomatic, political, economic, and ultimately social interaction among India, Pakistan, and the Kashmiris.

Notes

1. Raju C. G. Thomas, "Reflections on the Kashmir Problem," in Raju G. C. Thomas, ed., *Perspectives on Kashmir: The Roots of Conflict in South Asia* (Boulder: Westview Press, 1992), p. 4.

2. See Mohammed Ayoob, *The Third World Security Predicament: State Making, Regional Conflict and the International System* (Boulder: Lynne Rienner, 1995).

3. S. Gopal, *Jawaharlal Nehru: A Biography*, vol. 2 (New Delhi: Oxford University Press, 1975), p. 184.

4. Baldev Raj Nair and T. V. Paul, *India in the World Order: Searching for Major Power Status* (Cambridge: Cambridge University Press, 2003), p. 74.

5. Ibid., p. 83.

6. Amitav Acharya, "Beyond Anarchy: Third World Instability and International Order After the Cold War," in Stephanie Neumann, ed., *International Relations Theory and the Third World* (New York: St. Martin's Press, 1997), pp. 159–211.

7. Baldev Raj Nair and T. V. Paul, *India in the World Order,* pp. 85–86.

8. Raju C. G. Thomas, "Reflections on the Kashmir Problem," pp. 4–5.

9. Sumit Ganguly, ed., *India as an Emerging Power* (London and Portland, OR: Frank Cass, 2003), p. 39.

10. See Ashutosh Varshney, "Three Compromised Nationalisms: Why Kashmir Has Been a Problem," in Raju G. C. Thomas, ed., *Perspectives on Kashmir: The Roots of Conflict in South Asia* (Boulder: Westview Press, 1992).

11. Raju Thomas, "Reflections on the Kashmir Problem," p. 22.

12. Jawaharlal Nehru, *The Discovery of India*, Robert I. Crane, ed. (New York: Anchor Books, 1960), pp. 313–314.

13. Zulfiqar A. Bhutto, *The Myth of Independence* (Lahore: Oxford University Press, 1969).

14. Riyaz Punjabi, "Kashmir: The Bruised Identity," in Raju G. C. Thomas, ed., *Perspectives on Kashmir,* pp. 136–137.

15. Sheikh Abdullah, Opening Address to the Jammu and Kashmir Constituent Assembly, 5 November 1951.

16. Ashutosh Varshney, "Three Compromised Nationalisms," p. 189.

17. Glenn Snyder, *Deterrence and Defence* (Princeton: Princeton University Press, 1961), p. 226; Michael Krepon, *The Stability-Instability Paradox, Misperceptions, and Escalation Control in South Asia* (Washington DC: The Henry L. Stimson Center, May 2003), p. 2.

18. *The Kargil Review Committee Report: From Surprise to Reckoning* (New Delhi: Sage, 2000), p. 22.

19. Michael Krepon, *The Stability-Instability Paradox,* p. 3.

20. Stephen P. Cohen, *India: Emerging Power* (Washington, DC: Brookings Institution Press, 2001), p. 198.

21. Arabinda Acharya, "Promoting Human Security in South Asia Through Multilateral Cooperation," in Dipankar Banerjee, ed., *SAARC in the 21st Century: Towards a Cooperative Future* (New Delhi: India Research Press, 2002), p. 177.

22. Lieutenant General Sir James Wilson, "Jammu and Kashmir Problem: The Truth—Part 1," *Journal of the United Services Institution of India*, vol. 127, no. 528 (April–June 1997), p. 253.

23. Major General Akbar Khan, *Readers in Kashmir* (Delhi: Army Publishers, 1970), p. 10.

24. "The Indo-Pak Trade Equation," *Rediff.com*, 19 June 2003, http://in.rediff.com/money/2003/jun/19spec2.htm (accessed 6 May 2005).

25. Kavita Sangani and Teresita Schaffer, "India-Pakistan Trade: Creating Constituencies for Peace," *South Asia Monitor* (Center for Strategic and International Studies, Washington, DC), no. 56, 3 March 2003, http://www.csis.org/saprog/sam/sam56.pdf (accessed 6 May 2005).

26. "Annual Report 2003–2004: Appendices," *Ministry of Commerce and Industry, Department of Commerce (India)*, http://commerce.nic.in/annual2004-05/englishhtml/appendices.htm (accessed 6 May 2005).

27. "Indo-Pak Bilateral Trade to Touch US$10 Billion by 2010," *Hindustan Times*, 5 January 2005.

28. Kavita Sangani and Teresita Schaffer, "India-Pakistan Trade."

29. "Neighbourly Trade or a Lot of Gas?" *The Pioneer*, 2 February 2005, http://meaindia.nic.in/opinion/2005/02/28op01.htm (accessed 6 June 2005).

30. "The Indo-Pak Trade Equation," *Rediff.com*.

31. Robert Keohane, "The Diplomacy of Structural Change: Multilateral Institutions and State Strategies," in Helga Haftendorn and Christin Tuschhoff, eds., *America and Europe in an Era of Change* (Boulder: Westview Press, 1999), p. 53.

32. Joseph M. Grieco, *Cooperation Among Nations* (Ithaca: Cornell University Press, 1990), p. 47.

33. Robert O. Keohane, *After Hegemony* (Princeton: Princeton University Press, 1984), pp. 89–92; Robert O. Keohane and Lisa L. Martin, "The Promise of Institutionalist Theory," *International Security* 20, no. 1 (Summer 1995), p. 42.

34. See Ronald B. Mitchell, *Intentional Oil Pollution at Sea: Environmental Policy and Treaty Compliance* (Cambridge, MA: MIT Press, 1994), and Anne-Marie Burley and Walter Mattli, "Europe Before the Court: A Political Theory of Legal Integration," *International Organization* 47, no. 1 (Winter 1993), pp. 41–46.

35. See Lisa L. Martin, *Coercive Cooperation: Explaining Multilateral Economic Sanctions* (Princeton: Princeton University Press, 1992).

36. See Fareed Zakaria, "The Rise of Illiberal Democracy," *Foreign Affairs* 76, no. 6 (1997), pp. 22–43.

37. Edward D. Mansfield and Jack Snyder, "Democratic Transitions, Institutional Strength and War," *International Organization* 56, no. 2 (Spring 2002), p. 297.

38. Cited in "Kashmir Is Not Integral Part of India," *Pakistan News*, 14 October 2003.

39. "Musharraf's Three-phased Formula for Resolving Kashmir Issue," *Hindu*, 18 April 2005.

11

The International Community and Kashmir: Mission Impossible?

Waheguru Pal Singh Sidhu

Since the end of the Cold War, Kashmir has remained in a constant state of turmoil. It was the locale of at least three major "nuclear" crises (in 1989–1990, in 1999, and in 2001–2002) between Indian and Pakistan. In all three instances the international community, especially the United Nations, was ineffective, despite the efforts of UN Secretary General Kofi Annan to use his good offices to ease tensions during the 2001–2002 crisis. However, other key international actors, particularly the United States, responded to and facilitated in resolving these crises. Although these Kashmir-related crises are likely to remain confined to South Asia, several factors, including humanitarian concerns, the role of the diaspora, and the fear of a nuclear exchange, will compel the international community to try to remain engaged.

However, despite these strategic and normative factors, the international community has not been very effective in dealing with Kashmir. This is due partly to the difficulties in operationalizing humanitarian norms and partly to the changing character of the UN-centered international community, Washington's preoccupation with its "war on terror," and the rise of India as a global power. Therefore, the engagement of the international community is likely to remain sporadic, episodic, and confined to crisis management; a more intrusive mediation (of the type evident in the Middle East) is unlikely in South Asia. This perspective challenges conventional thinking on the subject, which at one extreme argues that India, as the regional hegemon, will never allow external intervention of any kind, and at the other extreme asserts that a renewed UN peacekeeping operation is the only way to end the conflict.

This chapter begins with a historical overview of the engagement of the

UN-centered international community with Kashmir from 1948 to 1972. It will then note the primary reasons behind the disengagement of the world from Kashmir between 1972 and 1990. The next section will examine the three Kashmir crises since 1990 and note the role and effectiveness of key states in resolving these crises. The final section will seek to explain the sporadic nature of the international community's engagement with Kashmir from 1990 onward and suggest ways in which this engagement could be made both consistent and effective.

Historical Background

Kashmir, along with the Korean peninsula and the Palestinian question, was among the first crises to confront the newly established UN-centered international community in the post–World War II period. Today, nearly sixty years after the creation of the UN, these three crises have not only endured through the Cold War but pose some of the greatest challenges to the international community.

Kashmir was first brought to the attention of the UN in January 1948 by India's first prime minister, Jawaharlal Nehru, and remained on the agenda of the world body until 1971.[1] In taking the matter of the October 1947 incursion by tribesmen from Pakistan to the UN, Nehru assumed that the UN Security Council would simply brand Pakistan as the aggressor and ask it to withdraw. Instead the UNSC adopted Resolution 39, which established the UN Commission for India and Pakistan (UNCIP).[2] UNSC Resolution 47 of April 1948 enlarged UNCIP to include observers to stop the fighting that had broken out between Indian and Pakistani troops, and also to supervise the cease-fire, which went into effect on 1 January 1949.[3] Various resolutions adopted by the UNCIP in 1948–1949 sought, among other issues, to address the long-term question of the political future of Kashmir. In July 1949, India and Pakistan negotiated in Karachi and established the cease-fire line (CFL), which was to be observed by the enlarged UNCIP. The CFL effectively split Kashmir into Indian-administered Jammu and Kashmir (IJK) and Pakistan-administered Azad Jammu and Kashmir (AJK). On 30 March 1951, following the termination of UNCIP, the UNSC passed Resolution 91 establishing the UN Military Observer Group in India and Pakistan (UNMOGIP) to monitor the CFL.[4] Its basic mandate was and remains "to observe and report, investigate complaints of cease-fire violations and submit its findings to each party and the [UN] Secretary General."[5] UNMOGIP continues to operate even today and has the dubious distinction of being the longest-running but, perhaps, most feckless operation in the UN's history.[6]

In 1950 the UN Security Council also appointed Australian jurist Sir Owen Dixon as its special representative with the onerous brief of finding a settlement to the Kashmir issue that would be acceptable to both India and Pakistan. The eventual Dixon Plan, which offered two options, both involving partition, is the closest that anyone or any plan has come to finding an acceptable solution for Kashmir.[7] The first option called for "a plan for taking the plebiscite by sections or areas and the allocation of each section or area according to the result of the vote therein," while the second option called for

> a plan by which it was conceded that some areas were certain to vote for accession to Pakistan, some for accession to India, and by which, without taking a vote therein, they should be allotted accordingly and the plebiscite should be confined only to the uncertain area, which . . . appeared to be the Valley of Kashmir and perhaps some adjacent country.[8]

However, despite their best efforts, the UN could not bring the two sides to even explore the partition option. Although the Dixon Plan was abandoned, the UN continued its mediation efforts all through the 1950s and the early 1960s, but to no avail. This was the last serious effort on the part of the UN to seek a solution to the Kashmir imbroglio. From the mid-1960s, efforts at reaching a settlement were sought either through bilateral negotiations or through third parties operating outside the UN.

The outbreak of hostilities in Kashmir along the CFL in 1965 halted any mediation efforts and reflected the limited influence of the UNSC in preventing conflict. It also revealed the key role of the two superpowers in managing conflict on the subcontinent. For instance, in a rare moment of superpower unity during the Cold War, a joint arms embargo was imposed by Washington and Moscow on India and Pakistan, which, among other outcomes, eventually compelled the two warring parties to heed the UN's call for a cease-fire; this took place on 23 September.[9] Indeed, war was terminated following Moscow's mediation and the Tashkent Agreement of January 1966.

Similarly, in the 1971 war—primarily fought over the Bangladesh issue—it was the disunity between Washington and Moscow and their support for their respective allies, Pakistan and India, that was primarily responsible for keeping the UN out. Indeed, UNSC efforts at passing a resolution to halt the fighting were thwarted by a Soviet veto, and the matter was referred to the UN General Assembly. The only UNSC resolution (307) passed during this war was on 21 December 1971, five days after India's unilateral cease-fire.[10] Although Kashmir was not the center of this conflict or the resolution, this was the last UNSC resolution that dealt with Kashmir.

Although the UN is, clearly, not a monolithic actor and has at least three distinct components—the UNSC, the Secretariat, and the UN General Assembly—in the context of Kashmir this distinction is not appreciated in India, Pakistan, or Kashmir. In fact, for most Indians, Pakistanis, and

Kashmiris, the UN is a unitary actor represented only by the UNSC. One possible explanation for this misperception is that it was the UNSC that initially took the lead on the Kashmir issue by passing a series of resolutions that determined the subsequent role and scope of the UN's involvement in Kashmir.

It is difficult to ascertain precisely why the UN failed in its efforts to resolve the Kashmir crisis. However, there are several plausible explanations that might shed some light on this issue. First, between the late 1940s and the early 1960s the UN was a new and relatively weak actor on the world stage; its institutions and process were still in formation, and perhaps it did not have the necessary wherewithal—both in personnel and institutionally—to address crises of the complexity of Kashmir, the Middle East, and the Korean peninsula. Second, with Nehru (who was of Kashmiri stock himself) at the helm in New Delhi until 1964, and with his pioneering role in setting up and leading the Non-Aligned Movement, it would have been difficult for the UN or any group of countries to muscle India into accepting a solution that Nehru disapproved of. Nehru's thinking and firm resolve were probably also based on Indian public and political opinion, which would not have gone along with major concessions on Kashmir. Similarly, Pakistan, which joined the Baghdad Pact, the Central Treaty Organization in 1954, and the South East Asian Treaty Organization, also became closely tied with one of the superpowers and was led by a series of military dictators during the same period; it too could not be convinced to accept solutions that Islamabad considered unpalatable. The period after 1965 was, perhaps, the only time that the UN might have played a significant part, but it was upstaged by Moscow, which took a leading role in mediating between Islamabad and New Delhi, thus sidelining the UN.

1971 and Beyond

In twenty-three years (between 1948 and 1971) the UNSC passed as many as twenty-three resolutions dealing with Kashmir, and through the Dixon Plan it came closest to resolving this long-standing conflict. Yet since 1971, not only has the UNSC not passed a single resolution on Kashmir, but the entire issue appears to have completely slipped off the UN agenda. How did this dramatic shift come about?

There are at least three possible explanations. First, following the 1971 Indo-Pak war leading to the creation of Bangladesh, both countries signed the Simla Agreement in July 1972, which not only stated that the Kashmir issue would be resolved by bilateral means, but also clearly demarcated the Line of Control (LoC), making it a virtual border.[11] The Simla Agreement categorically states that "the two countries are resolved to settle their differences by peaceful means through bilateral negotiations or by any other peaceful means mutually agreed upon between them" and that "the line of control resulting from the cease-fire of 17 December 1971, shall be respected by both sides without prejudice to the recognised position of either side."[12] Indeed, the LoC, which runs for about 740 kilometres from Sangam (near Jammu) to point NJ 9842, short of the Siachen Glacier, was demarcated using a six-point grid reference under the Simla Agreement, making it almost as well delineated as a formal border.[13] The bilateral clause was stipulated at the behest of India, which as the victorious power felt that such an arrangement would allow it to negotiate the future of Kashmir from a position of strength. The same clause was probably accepted by a defeated Pakistan because it felt that rather than not having any option to negotiate, it might be better to at least be able to negotiate bilaterally. Significantly, the United States and other major powers also welcomed the agreement, which in effect took them off the hook on the Kashmir issue.

Since then, India argued that following the establishment of the LoC, the UN mandate for UNMOGIP had lapsed. Pakistan, however, disagreed and insisted on the continuation of the observer mission to monitor the LoC, which, Islamabad asserted, was an updated version of the original 1949 CFL. Consequently, while Pakistan has diligently continued to report Indian violations along the LoC, India has not lodged a single complaint with UNMOGIP since 1972.[14] Consequently, UNMOGIP, which can only be disbanded or terminated by a decision of the UNSC, is likely to continue in ineffectual perpetuity until there is a consensus on Kashmir within the Security Council.

Second, following the 1971 war, India emerged as the undisputed power in South Asia and, although still a weak state, it was relatively the strongest state on the subcontinent. India's 1974 nuclear test, although conducted for a complex set of reasons, also contributed to this sense of strength and confidence. In contrast, Pakistan suffered a humiliating defeat and, following the emergence of Bangladesh, was also bifurcated and lost a substantial part of its territory and military power. Simultaneously Moscow's support for India increased, making any prospect of the Kashmir issue being successfully referred to the UNSC a near impossibility. In addition, the rapprochement between Beijing and New Delhi, which began in the late 1970s and evolved into a slow détente in the 1980s, provided a tacit endorsement by China of India's dominant position in the subcontinent. In contrast, while China now emerged as Pakistan's closest ally, Beijing's position on Kashmir became more equivocal. Consequently, India was able to block efforts by Pakistan to internationalize Kashmir in general and to prevent it from being put on the UN's agenda in particular.

Third, from 1971 until the start of the *tahrik* (the movement for independence) in 1989, Kashmir remained relatively quiet. Indeed, during this period IJK became increasingly integrated into the Indian polity, while AJK similarly became part of Pakistan's polity. Although Kashmiri leaders, such as Sheikh Abdullah, continued to insist on autonomy, they no longer challenged the 1947 accession of Kashmir by the then maharaja, Hari Singh, to India.[15] Ironically, it was the increasing integration of IJK politics with the national Indian politics that led the ruling Congress party to pressure the IJK political leadership for the sake of narrow party political gains. This in turn detracted from the special status that IJK had acquired, and the "unfree" (sic) elections of March 1987 set the stage for the *tahrik* and the next confrontation.[16]

Three Post–Cold War Crises

The end of the Cold War witnessed the emergence of three nuclear crises over Kashmir.[17] With the UN virtually shut out from Kashmir, the international community increasingly relied on the world's emerging hyperpower to maintain the fragile peace. While the United States, along with a couple of key allies, did manage to do this—sometimes only just—it kept the rest of the international actors out as well. Indeed, in allowing the United States to be the key, and sometimes the only, actor dealing with Kashmir, the international community inadvertently let itself be sidelined or, worse, dictated to by Washington.

The 1990 Crisis

The 1990 crisis developed soon after Pakistan conducted its biggest military exercise, *Zarb-i-Momin*, in late 1989. New Delhi perceived this exercise as a cover to support the militancy in Kashmir as, in its wake, a new insurgency movement erupted in IJK. While the roots of this *tahrik* clearly lay in IJK, many of the militants were allegedly operating out of camps in Pakistan. In fact, according to one assessment, the Pakistani government "began to take a more active role in support of the Kashmiri protests. Training camps of various kinds multiplied. . . . There were more people and material going across the border from Pakistan to Kashmir."[18] India, while accusing Pakistan of training and supporting the militants, rushed reinforcements to the Kashmir Valley and threatened to carry out "hot-pursuits" across the border into Pakistan to strike the alleged training camps. Pakistan considered this a hostile act, and at the height of this tension, Islamabad is reported to have threatened to weaponize its nuclear capability to counter any Indian attack.

As the tension built up, the two superpowers, in perhaps one of the earliest instances of post–Cold War cooperation, issued démarches to the two prime ministers, to convey their governments' concerns regarding the tension as well as possible suggestions to defuse the crisis.[19] This led to a couple of high-level meetings, including one between India's foreign minister I. K. Gujral and his Pakistani counterpart, Sahabzada Yakub Khan, who met on 25 April 1990 in New York on the sidelines of the special session of the UN devoted to international economic cooperation. Although the meeting was far from cordial (it was described as "frank" and "businesslike"), both sides agreed that tension should be reduced and confrontation avoided. For this purpose, they agreed that

1. The directors general of military operations of India and Pakistan should remain in touch with each other.
2. Both sides should exercise restraint.
3. Channels of communications should be kept open at all levels.[20]

Even as the crisis continued and the war of words escalated between Islamabad and New Delhi, India and Pakistan established a back channel of communication with each other through the US embassies in their capitals. Indeed, Ambassador William Clark in New Delhi and Ambassador Robert Oakley in Islamabad played a critical role in defusing the crisis. Almost a month later, US President George H. W. Bush, in close coordination with Moscow, sent Deputy National Security Adviser Robert Gates to visit India and Pakistan. Gates arrived in Islamabad on 20 May 1990, met President Ghulam Ishaq Khan, and made the following points: Washington had wargamed every possible Indo-Pak confrontation and Pakistan was the loser every time; in the event of a war, Islamabad should not expect any support from Washington; and Pakistan must refrain from supporting terrorism in IJK.[21] Gates's message to the Indian leaders was the same: India must avoid provocation, for, although India would win a war, the long-term costs would exceed any short-term benefits.[22] Although the so-called Gates mission is widely considered to have brought the 1990 crisis to an end, there are indications that the crisis was on the way to a resolution even before his visit.

The Kargil Confrontation

In May 1999, intruders were spotted on the Indian side of the LoC in the Kargil region of IJK. The resulting confrontation differed markedly from previous crises in many respects.[23] This was the first major crisis after both India and Pakistan had tested several nuclear devices and declared themselves to be nuclear weapon states in May 1998. Unlike past incidents (when each may have harbored some doubt about the nuclear weapons capability of the other), in this instance both sides were well aware of the presence of nuclear weapons in each other's arsenal. In fact, according to one account, India is reported to have prepared at least half a dozen nuclear weapons for delivery during the course of the conflict,[24] and Pakistan too is reported to have moved its missiles into launch positions.[25] Second, in the South Asian context, this was the first time since 1984 (when India launched a preemptive assault to occupy the Siachen Glacier area) that one side had occupied a disputed territory. Thus the Pakistani action of crossing the LoC in the Kargil area of IJK signalled a major breakout and challenged the relative stability that had been established under the nonweaponized deterrence relationship between the two antagonists since the early 1980s. Finally, Kargil was different because it was the longest, and perhaps bloodiest, military confrontation between the two countries, and (also unlike the others) it did not end with a bilaterally negotiated peace treaty. To a large extent the crisis was resolved at the behest of a third party, the United States.

Interestingly, unlike past crises, during the early part of the Kargil crisis, Indian prime minister Atal Bihari Vajpayec remained in contact with his Pakistani counterpart, Nawaz Sharif, over the telephone.[26] The two sides also communicated through a back channel, which had reportedly been established soon after the Lahore Declaration in February 1999 to discuss a number of bilateral issues, including Kashmir.[27] This back channel was apparently shut down around 29 June when Islamabad publicly distanced itself from one of the key interlocutors.

However, the back channel notwithstanding, there is no doubt that the role played by the international community was vital in resolving the crisis, especially during the latter half. International pressure on Pakistan to withdraw its troops from the Indian side of the LoC, led primarily by the United States, was evident in US President Bill Clinton's telephone admonitions to Sharif, the G-8 communiqué, China's neutrality rather than support for Islamabad, and the visit of General Anthony Zinni, commander in chief of the US Central Command to Islamabad for a one-to-one meeting with Pakistan's (then) Army Chief General Pervez Musharraf. This forced an increasingly isolated Pakistan to look for a way out, which came in the form of a meeting between Sharif and Clinton in Washington on 4 July 1999.[28] In the joint statement at the end of this meeting it was agreed that Pakistan would unilaterally withdraw its troops and take steps "for the restoration of the LoC in accordance with the Simla Agreement."[29] The last of the Pakistani troops withdrew from Indian territory on 26 July 1999, bringing the longest Indo-Pak military confrontation to an end. Thus, even the *Kargil Review Committee Report*, submitted to the Indian parliament on 24 February 2000, grudgingly acknowledges that the "US sponsored withdrawal of the intruders from the Indian side of the LOC probably came as a welcome face saving device for the Pakistani establishment."[30]

The 2001–2002 Crisis

A new crisis erupted when New Delhi launched Operation Parakram (Valor) in December 2001 following attacks by terrorist groups, reportedly operating from Pakistan, on the legislative assembly in Srinagar (the capital of IJK) on 1 October 2001 and on the Indian parliament on 13 December 2001.[31] India mobilized its conventional strike forces to hit alleged training camps in the Pakistan-controlled part of Kashmir and warned of a "limited war." Speaking on 3 January 2002, India's prime minister Vajpayee issued what can only be described as a nuclear threat when he declared that "no weapon would be spared in self-defence. Whatever weapon was available it would be used no matter how it wounded the enemy."[32] Within days of this statement India test-fired the nuclear-capable Agni-I missile. This missile test was clearly an attempt to intimidate Pakistan. Subsequently Pakistan's president Musharraf too issued a nuclear threat, in April 2002, and test-fired three ballistic missiles—the Ghauri, Ghaznavi, and Abdali—in late May 2002.[33] Pakistan's vice chief of Army Staff Mohammad Yusuf Khan, who witnessed the tests, warned that India should realize that "we mean business. They must remember that Pakistan is a nuclear state."[34] Soon after the missile tests, on 1 June 2002, the Pakistani ambassador to the United Nations, Munir Akram, cautioned that Pakistan could resort to the use of nuclear weapons even in a conventional conflict if it considered its losses to be unacceptable.[35] The nuclear brinkmanship was further compounded by the two sides withdrawing their diplomats, closing down official channels of communication, and not allowing any back channel of communication (as there had been during the Kargil crisis).

In January 2002, UN Secretary General Kofi Annan's efforts to try to resolve the crisis directly were thwarted by New Delhi's refusal to allow him to visit India. The motives behind New Delhi's refusal lay in the post-1972 aversion to having the UN involved in Kashmir and the underlying posture that Kashmir is a bilateral issue to be resolved between India and Pakistan. Consequently, Annan's visit was confined to Pakistan, and despite asserting on Pakistani soil that the old UN resolutions on Kashmir are "not enforceable in a mandatory sweep," Annan was unable to placate India's phobia.[36]

In this scenario it was left to some key countries, notably the United States and Great Britain, to try to mediate. The first attempt, through hectic shuttle diplomacy in January 2002 by US Secretary of State Colin Powell, was accepted by India and Pakistan and did help to reduce the tensions significantly. However, as tensions rose again in May–June 2002, several countries sought to convey their alarm by issuing a travel advisory on 1 June 2002, asking their nationals to withdraw from both India and Pakistan. Simultaneously, diplomatic efforts included a visit by US Deputy Secretary of State Richard Armitage to Pakistan and India in early June. After Armitage's trip Powell gave a guarantee to India of President Musharraf's commitment to stop cross-border infiltration. Only then did New Delhi finally call off its planned attack on Pakistan. This was the last military episode of Operation Parakram, although the troops were finally withdrawn on 16 October 2002, following the successful conclusion of elections in IJK.

Mission Impossible?

While the definition of the international community has evolved since the early days of the Cold War, and will continue to evolve even in the post–Cold War world dominated by a single hyperpower and a weakened UN, there is no doubt that the international community, however defined, has played and will continue to play a critical role in trying to address the Kashmir conflict, even if it does not manage to resolve the issue once and for all. Even a cursory glance at the above-mentioned crises clearly indicates the important role played by other states and organizations. The only change has been the nature and intensity of the engagement. This is amply demonstrated in the three Kashmir crises since 1990, where the United States invariably led the international response.

There are, of course, several strategic and normative reasons behind the efforts of the international community to remain engaged with Kashmir. At the strategic level, Kashmir, which is located at the crossroads of Central Asia, China, Pakistan, Afghanistan, and India, is a vital piece of real estate in the geopolitical relations among these countries. The geostrategic stakes in this region have been raised further following Washington's war on terror and the presence of US troops in the region. Kashmir also still has the potential to spark a major conflict, possibly even a nuclear exchange, between India and Pakistan. Moreover, after the 1986 Chernobyl nuclear reactor accident in Ukraine, there is a growing realization that any nuclear fallout, however limited, still has the potential of affecting regions well beyond the immediate area of the nuclear incident. Thus, the outcome of even a limited nuclear exchange in South Asia is unlikely to remain confined to the subregion and is likely to affect other regions, including the all-important oil supply sea routes to and from the Persian Gulf.

In the post–Cold War era, Kashmir has also attracted international attention because of the indigenous insurgency in IJK, which began in 1989. The insurgency attracted two types of support from the outside. First, Kashmiris who had settled in the United Kingdom, the United States, and Canada extended political and financial support to the political movement in IJK. They relied on their linkages with the political circles in the adopted country to mobilize support for their perspectives on Kashmir, especially its political future.[37] Second, the Pakistan-based militant Islamic groups, most of whom had been engaged in the struggle in Afghanistan against the Soviet military, turned their attention toward Kashmir after the withdrawal of Soviet troops from Afghanistan in February 1989.[38]

The Kashmiri insurgency also appears to be inspired by a number of post–Cold War international developments, including the fall of the Berlin Wall (1989), the emergence of independent Muslim states in Central Asia (1991–1992), and the emphasis on democracy, human rights, and self-determination in the post–Cold War period. Indeed, human rights groups were drawn to Kashmir following complaints of human rights violations, killings, detention without trial, and harassment of ordinary people. Both the militant groups and Indian security forces (military, paramilitary forces, police, and intelligence agencies) have been accused of use of excessive violence and threats against noncombatants; this not only raised humanitarian concerns but was also echoed in *The Responsibility to Protect*, a report prepared by the International Commission on Intervention and State Sovereignty.

This humanitarian urge was also evident in the prompt and impressive international response following the deadly earthquake in Kashmir on 8 October 2005, which displaced 3.5 million people. The relief for the earthquake victims came not only from the traditional humanitarian organizations and agencies but also from nonhumanitarian organizations such as the North Atlantic Treaty Organization. This action, coming in the wake of unprecedented response to the Asian tsunami, underlines the international community's commitment to reacting to humanitarian crises in almost every part of the world.

At the normative level, there are several reasons for the international community to remain actively engaged with Kashmir. First, as a logical corollary to the recently articulated norm of the responsibility to protect, it could be argued that there is also an emerging norm of the responsibility to prevent war, especially nuclear war. Second, in the post–Cold War world, maintaining the sanctity of borders—however disputed—has also emerged as a critical international norm.[39] Third, there is also a desire to engage with weak or failing states, especially if there is a possibility that these states will become inadvertent havens for armed nonstate groups.[40] Finally, in the wake of the events of September 2001 there is also a new impetus to deal with the threats posed by armed nonstate groups, especially those that have the potential of acquiring nuclear, chemical, biological, or radiological weapons.[41] However, operationalizing these norms and acting on these concerns remain a challenge for the international community.

While Washington has often offered its services for mediation purposes and Islamabad has expressed its willingness to entertain such an arrangement, India is unlikely to agree on a formal role for the United States.

Although India has previously acquiesced to letting the United States play a limited role as a conduit to convey messages to Pakistan and vice versa (during the 1990 crisis) and in resolving an ongoing crisis (during the 1999 Kargil confrontation), it is reluctant to allow any third party to mediate between Islamabad and New Delhi on core issues, such as nuclear risk reduction measures and maintaining peace and tranquillity along the LoC. This became evident in the run-up to and during the visit of President Clinton to India in March 2000.[42]

Given this Indian attitude, the United States could alternatively conduct separate bilateral interactions with both Islamabad and New Delhi to convince them to take unilateral steps to ensure peace and stability in the region. This is clearly the approach that Washington has followed: Senior US officials have been negotiating separately with their Indian and Pakistani counterparts since the two countries conducted nuclear tests in May 1998. Although the bulk of these negotiations have dealt with bilateral relations between Washington and Islamabad, and Washington and New Delhi, and with concerns regarding the further proliferation of nuclear weapon capability, some segments of them have also addressed the issue of keeping peace between India and Pakistan, particularly in Kashmir. Clearly, despite its protestations to the contrary, New Delhi has not been averse to letting Washington play the role of conveying the Indian perspective to Islamabad, especially when it is not speaking directly to the Pakistani establishment.

This attitude was apparent during the course of Clinton's visit to South Asia in March 2000. Initially, when it was announced that Clinton would also be touching down in Islamabad for a few hours at the end of his India visit, the Indian government tried its best to dissuade him and the US administration from planning to have him do so. However, once Clinton was in New Delhi, the Indian government was not disinclined to let the US president raise certain issues on India's behalf with Pakistan's military leadership during his stopover in Islamabad. In a particularly telling incident Vajpayee publicly asked Clinton to discuss the issue of cross-border terrorism in Kashmir when the latter was in Islamabad, a message that Clinton promised to (and did subsequently) carry.[43] Although this change was prompted by the brutal massacre of thirty-six Sikhs in Kashmir at the start of Clinton's visit to India, there is little doubt that, following the visit, New Delhi has endorsed Washington's role in ensuring the absence of violence and respect for the LoC, particularly in Kashmir.

In return, India has also tacitly accepted the right of Washington to convey Islamabad's concerns to New Delhi and acknowledge some sort of facilitating role in prompting the two estranged neighbors to negotiate. This became evident in the course of the 2001–2002 crisis, when New Delhi was at the receiving end of Washington's concerns.

However, an exclusively Washington-led engagement is problematic for at least three reasons. First, a long-term resolution of the Kashmir issue requires a sustained and virtually open-ended engagement and the stamina to persevere through the cycle of ups and downs that comes with it. However, given Washington's preoccupation, in its so-called war on terror, with Afghanistan, Iraq, and the Middle East, it is likely to have a limited attention span regarding Kashmir. Any administration is likely to involve itself in a dispute between other nations reluctantly, and only if it feels that its own strategic interests are at stake. This was certainly the case in 2001–2002 when US troops were located in Pakistan as well as in Afghanistan and there was a realization that any dust-up between Islamabad and New Delhi would invariably affect the US military presence in the region.

Second, there is concern that as the United States becomes increasingly committed in the Middle East and other crises, it might not have the capacity to become involved in a future South Asian emergency. As a corollary, there is also concern among some scholars that if India and Pakistan come to expect an inevitable US facilitation every time there is a crisis, they are unlikely either to try to build a stable strategic regime or to work to resolve the Kashmir issue bilaterally.

Third, there are also strategic concerns, on the part of other members of the international community who aspire to reestablish a multipolar world, that a US-only role in Kashmir invariably means that the rest of the world will be held hostage to US biases and contradictions. This in turn is likely to further consolidate the unipolar moment rather than strengthen the cause of multilateralism and the revival of a multipolar world.

Conclusion

In the first twenty-three years of the present Kashmir crisis, the UN played a pivotal role and came the closest to fostering a permanent settlement. However, since 1972 the UN has been completely sidelined and is unlikely to be a key player in the future resolution of this issue. Since 1972, and particularly since 1990, the international response to Kashmir has invariably remained distracted, episodic, and largely unipolar. However, the involvement of the US-led international community is likely to remain confined to crisis management; a more intrusive mediation (of the type evident in the Middle East) is unlikely in South Asia. This is partly on account of the preoccupation of the unipolar, US-led international community with other crises (such as Iraq and the Middle East) and partly due to the reluctance of India (especially a rising India) to allow international involvement beyond a certain point. This scenario is likely to continue unless other key international actors, such as the European Union, also become engaged in efforts to resolve this long-standing conflict. In doing so they could choose from several options: to support any bilateral process of resolution through political, diplomatic, and economic means; to establish a quasi-multilateral process (such as the Quartet in the Middle East) to facilitate India and Pakistan in seeking solutions; and, perhaps the most ambitious option, to try to revive either the regional or the UN-centered multilateral process. While the first option is clearly preferred, it needs to be effectively sustained. Until then, Kashmir will remain the gauntlet that taunts the international community.

Notes

1. The first UN Security Council resolution on Kashmir was passed on 17 January 1948 and can be found at http://ods-dds-ny.un.org/doc/RESOLUTION/ GEN/NR0/047/63/IMG/NR004763.pdf?OpenElement.
2. The text of Resolution 39 of 17 January 1948 is available at http://ods-dds-ny.un.org/doc/RESOLUTION/GEN/NR0/047/63/IMG/ NR004763.pdf?OpenElement.
3. The text of Resolution 47 of the 21 April 1948 UN Security Council resolution establishing UNCIP is available at http://ods-dds-ny.un.org/doc/ RESOLUTION/GEN/NR0/047/72/IMG/NR004772.pdf?OpenElement.
4. The text of Resolution 91 of the 30 March 1951 UN Security Council resolution creating UNMOGIP is available at http://ods-dds-ny.un.org/doc/ RESOLUTION/GEN/NR0/072/10/IMG/NR007210.pdf?OpenElement.
5. See http://www.un.org/Depts/DPKO/Missions/unmogip/unmogipB.htm for the mandate of UNMOGIP.
6. For the current status, strength, and other facts and figures, see http://www.un.org/Depts/dpko/missions/unmogip/facts.html.
7. For the gist of the Dixon Plan see Paul Bowers, "Kashmir," *House of Commons Research Paper 04/28*, 30 March 2004, pp. 15–17, http://www. parliament.uk/commons/lib/research/rp2004/rp04-028.pdf. See also A. G. Noorani, "The Dixon Plan," *Frontline*, 12–25 October 2002.
8. S/1791, "The Dixon Report," 15 September 1950, paragraph 54, reproduced in P. Lakhanpal, *Essential Documents and Notes on Kashmir Dispute*, 2nd ed. (New Delhi: International Books, 1965).
9. The UNSC passed five resolutions between 4 September and 5 November 1965 before the cease-fire finally held.
10. The text of Resolution 307 of 21 December 1971 noting the cease-fire and cessation of hostilities is available at http://ods-dds-ny.un.org/doc/RESOLUTION/ GEN/NR0/261/67/IMG/NR026167.pdf?OpenElement. Since then, there has not been a single resolution on the Kashmir issue.
11. The text of the July 1972 Simla Agreement is available at http://www. jammu-kashmir.com/documents/simla.html.
12. Ibid.
13. For a brief history of the demarcation, see Lt. Gen. (Dr.) M. L. Chibber, "Line of Control in Jammu & Kashmir—A Part of Simla Agreement," at http://www.vijayinkargil.org/perspectives/LoC.html.

14. See chapters by P. R. Chari and Hasan-Askari Rizvi in this volume for the domestic underpinnings of India's and Pakistan's Kashmir policies.

15. Verghese Koithara, *Crafting Peace in Kashmir: Through a Realist Lens* (New Delhi: Sage, 2004), p. 60.

16. Ibid., p. 62.

17. See the chapter by Sir John Thomson in this volume for details of the nuclear dimensions of the Kashmir dispute.

18. Michael Krepon and M. Faruqee, eds., "Conflict Prevention and Confidence Building Measures in South Asia: The 1990 Crisis," *Occasional Paper No. 17* (Washington, DC: Henry L. Stimson Center, April 1994), p. 6. This is a transcript of a meeting convened by the Stimson Center to discuss the 1990 crisis. Among the participants were the former US ambassadors to India and Pakistan and South Asian diplomats and military personnel.

19. "Turning Down the Heat," *India Today*, 15 May 1990, p. 22.

20. Press statement issued by the High Commission of India, Islamabad, 6 May 1990.

21. Seymour Hersh, "On the Nuclear Edge," *The New Yorker*, 29 March 1993, pp. 67–68; Krepon and Faruqee, "Conflict Prevention and Confidence Building Measures," pp. 8–9; and J. Burns, "US Urges Pakistan to Settle Feud with India over Kashmir," *New York Times*, 21 May 1990.

22. Devin Hagerty, "Nuclear Deterrence in South Asia: The 1990 Indo-Pakistani Crisis," *International Security*, Winter 1995/1996, p. 101.

23. For details of the Kargil conflict, see Waheguru Pal Singh Sidhu, "In the Shadow of Kargil: Keeping Peace in Nuclear South Asia," in Adekeye Adebajo and Chandra Sriram, eds., *Managing Armed Conflict in the 21st Century*, special issue of *International Peacekeeping* 7, no. 4 (Winter 2000), pp. 189–206. See also Shaukat Qadir, "An Analysis of the Kargil Conflict 1999," *RUSI Journal*, April 2002, pp. 24–30.

24. Raj Chengappa, *Weapons of Peace* (New Delhi: HarperCollins, 2000), p. 437. This, however, has been denied by Indian officials.

25. Bruce Riedel, *American Diplomacy and the 1999 Kargil Summit at Blair House*, Policy Paper Series (Center for the Advanced Study of India, University of Pennsylvania, 2002).

26. See "Dial-A-PM," *India Today*, 28 June 1999, and "Kargil Calendar," *India Today*, 26 July 1999.

27. Vajpayee and Sharif signed the Lahore Declaration on 21 February 1999 following a high-profile bus trip made by Vajpayee from Delhi to Lahore. The declaration called for the "resolution of all outstanding issues, including Jammu and Kashmir." This was the first time that India had agreed to put Kashmir on the agenda. Along with the declaration, the Indian and Pakistani foreign secretaries also signed a memorandum of understanding. This too called for a resolution of Jammu and Kashmir in addition to measures to reduce the risk of accidental or unauthorized use of nuclear weapons, and expressed the need to implement "existing Confidence Building Measures" and upgrade communication links between the two directors-general of military operation. See http://www.meadev.gov.in/lahore.htm.

28. W. P. S. Sidhu, "The U.S. and Kargil," *Hindu*, 15 July 1999.

29. The text of the joint Clinton-Sharif statement is available at http://www.economictimes.com/kargil/update72.htm.

30. See *Kargil Review Committee Report*, p. 82, presented to the parliament of India on 24 February 2000.

31. V. P. Malik, "Lessons from Army Deployment: Coercive Diplomacy and

Defence Credibility," *Tribune*, 16 December 2002, and Shishir Gupta, "When India Came Close to War," *India Today*, 23 December 2002, pp. 27–29.

32. T. Jayaraman, "Nuclear Crisis in South Asia," *Frontline*, 21 June 2002.

33. T. Jayaraman, "Nuclear Crisis in South Asia" and "N-Deterrent Gave India Second Thoughts: Musharraf," *Times of India*, 18 June 2002.

34. Lt. General Kamal Matinuddin, "India-Pakistan Standoff," *Regional Studies* 21, no. 3 (Summer 2003).

35. T. Jayaraman, "Nuclear Crisis in South Asia."

36. "Stepping Up International Pressure on Pakistan," *Hindu*, 19 December 2001; B. Murlidhar Reddy, "Annan Drops India Visit," *Hindu*, 24 January 2002.

37. See, for instance, Paul Bowers, "Kashmir," http://www.parliament.uk/commons/lib/research/rp2004/rp04-028.pdf, and the Kashmir Forum, http://www.house.gov/pitts/initiatives/kashmir/020718kf-fairemarks.htm.

38. I am grateful to Hasan-Askari Rizvi for providing this perspective and linking the *tahrik* with other international issues.

39. See Shireen M. Mazari, "Regional Security Concerns: A View from Pakistan," in Dipankar Banerjee and Gert W. Kueck, eds., *South Asia and the War on Terrorism: Analysing the Implications of 11 September* (New Delhi: India Research Press, 2003), pp. 78–80.

40. There are two motives behind this norm: First, there is increasing realization that failing or failed states provide the ideal breeding ground for transnational nonstate terrorists. It is this phenomenon that made Afghanistan the ideal home for Al-Qaida. Second, the international community, represented by the state-centric United Nations, is ill equipped to deal with nonstate actors. Therefore, the only way for the international community to deal effectively with the phenomenon of nonstate actors operating out of failing or failed states is to strengthen these states to ensure that they do not inadvertently become safe havens for transnational terrorist outfits. See, for example, "Investing in Prevention: An International Strategy to Manage Risks of Instability and Improve Crisis Response," Prime Minister's Strategy Unit (United Kingdom), February 2005, http://www.strategy.gov.uk/downloads/work_areas/countries_at_risk/report/index.htm.

41. This was evident in the strongly worded UN Security Council Resolution 1373, passed on 28 September 2001—the same day that the Nobel peace committee awarded the prize jointly to the UN and Secretary General Kofi Annan. The resolution reaffirmed not only the "inherent right of individual or collective self-defense," but also the "need to combat by all means, in accordance with the Charter of the United Nations, threats to international peace and security caused by terrorist acts." The trend was also apparent in the setting up of the ad hoc UN Security Council Counter-Terrorism Committee. Subsequently UNSC Resolution 1456, passed on 20 January 2003, called on all states to take urgent action to prevent and suppress all active and passive support of terrorism.

42. "US Willing for Mediation on Kashmir If Asked: Clinton," *News*, 17 February 2000. In fact, after the visit of President Clinton to the region, particularly Islamabad, in late March 2000, even the US appears to have retreated from its offer to mediate. See Amit Baruah, "U.S. Will Not Mediate on Kashmir, Says Clinton," *Hindu*, 26 March 2000. Interestingly, even Pakistan appears to have given up on direct mediation by the US. See "Kashmir Ruining Economy: Pakistan May Forgo Mediation Option, Says CE," *Dawn*, 31 March 2000.

43. See *Remarks by the President and Prime Minister Vajpayee of India in Joint Press Statement*, Hyderabad House, New Delhi, press release of the White House Press Secretary, 21 March 2000.

12

Kashmir: "The Most Dangerous Place in the World"?

John Thomson

This chapter deals with the interaction among three issues, each important in itself and more so in combination: Kashmir, the Indo-Pak nuclear rivalry, and global nuclear proliferation. Between the first and the second and also between the second and the third the connections are obvious, but until India and Pakistan tested nuclear weapons in May 1998, there was little or no connection between Kashmir and nuclear proliferation. Now there is. The resulting three-way interaction involves such questions as how the nuclear rivalry affects Kashmir, and also how Kashmir affects the rivalry. Similarly, how does the rivalry (in which Kashmir is subsumed) impact the global proliferation problem and how does that in turn influence the other two issues?

Each of the three issues has its own complicated history. That of Kashmir is contained in the other chapters in this volume. On the earlier history of the nuclear rivalry, an extensive literature led by George Perkovich's *India's Nuclear Bomb* makes it unnecessary to delve into the long gestation of the two forces, though something must be said about their separate motivations. Their asymmetry has already affected the nature of the confrontation and will influence the two sides' force planning, their political as well as their military strategy, and their responses to the international community's concerns about proliferation, all matters that will be discussed below. So too with the crises of 1999 and 2001–2002. Nuclear proliferation is the subject of a huge literature beyond the scope of this study. It is, however, obvious that influential countries, notably the US, who feel threatened by its two main manifestations—nuclear terrorism and the rise of new nuclear weapons states—have been deeply concerned by the South Asian tests of 1998 trumpeting the arrival of two new nuclear arsenals, the first since the Non-Proliferation Treaty (NPT) came into force in 1970.

The new nuclear situation in South Asia engages the attention of the great powers in three separate but interconnected ways. Following the revelation of A. Q. Khan's black market sales,[1] all of them are concerned about terrorist, especially Islamic extremist, access to nuclear materials and know-how. Equally, they are concerned that other states will, like India and Pakistan, pursue secret programs to develop nuclear weapons, that such states may be helped by the black market network, and that under these pressures the whole nonproliferation regime may unravel. Finally, the great powers are concerned at the possible use (which they tend to rank relatively high) of nuclear weapons in South Asia and, irrespective of that, at the influence that two new nuclear arsenals may have on the balance of power in Asia.

Some of the discussion below of these nuclear issues may be thought to break new ground. However that may be, the interaction between them and the well-worn issues of Kashmir and the Indo-Pak confrontation are undeniably important and evidently require new thinking.

This chapter suggests that having come in 2001–2002 to the brink of a war with nuclear dimensions, India and Pakistan are each beginning to adjust their priorities. Old military strategies are perceived as too dangerous and old political positions as parochial and thus unsuited to defending national interests and exploiting opportunities in the new, rapidly developing Asia. Kashmir is not ceasing to matter, but it is losing its unique importance as the touchstone for Indo-Pak relations and for the standing of the two countries in the modern world. Both have other fish to fry. Kashmir is not helping India become a great power or Pakistan a modern one.

"The Most Dangerous Place in the World": Myth or Reality?[2]

After two wars, innumerable skirmishes, a surprise incursion, major hostile military maneuvers, and a prolonged insurgency, no one can doubt that the Kashmir dispute causes serious conflict. Nor can there be any guarantee that it will not again lead to war or to military adventures involving nuclear deployment and possibly the use of a nuclear weapon.

Most Western analysts hold that another Indo-Pak military confrontation is a serious possibility, and, in that context, the risk that a nuclear weapon will be used is significant. Indeed, most believe this risk is higher in South Asia than elsewhere. This body of opinion does not necessarily claim that the presence of nuclear weapons makes conflict more likely, maybe the reverse. But if conflict occurs, nuclear weapons add enormously to the risks of catastrophe.

To cite a recent example of the Western school, the experts at the Carnegie Endowment for International Peace judged in early 2005 that "avoiding nuclear war in South Asia will require political breakthroughs in Indian-Pakistani relations and Sino-Indian relations, and domestic reform in Pakistan."[3]

Against this, the dominant line of thinking in South Asia, supported by minority Western opinion, holds that a nuclear balance makes confrontation less serious and is a deterrent to all-out war. This school draws sometimes on claims that South Asians are inherently peace-loving and in any case can be trusted to behave in a mature way. The main argument, however, is derived from the success of mutual deterrence between NATO and the Warsaw Pact during the Cold War. What worked to keep the peace between the two superpowers will also work, it is claimed, between India and Pakistan. Both countries are comfortable in discounting Western apprehensions. Both have a stated policy of credible minimum deterrence—though that was not the policy actually pursued by either the US or the Soviet Union.

The first school holds that neither the Kashmir situation nor the nuclear balance is stable, while the second claims that the nuclear balance is not only stable but also lends stability to the disturbed relationship between the two countries and hence discourages instability in Kashmir. The two schools tend to concentrate on different questions. The South Asians ask: in the event of a crisis, will we behave responsibly? and reply yes, while the Westerners evaluate the probabilities of a military crisis with the potential to go nuclear and rate them relatively highly. Essentially, these were the opposing views at the time of the nuclear tests in 1998. Events since then, especially the Kargil adventure in 1999 and the crisis of 2001–2002, have caused some reconsideration. Nevertheless, neither side has moved far, and the two schools continue to assess differently the degree of risk involved in having two new nuclear arsenals.[4] Since both schools are tinged by nationalism—the first by Western fears, especially after September 11, and by a claim to understand better than others the risks of cold war; the second by the rejection of double standards and by a natural wish to deny they have embarked on risky policies—it is perhaps permissible for historians to note the facts and avoid judgment. But this will not do for policymakers. Success or failure in the future, and even peace or war, hinges upon the judgments involved. For this purpose, the safest conclusion in 2005 is Michael Krepon's: "It is unsettling to note that none of the key elements of nuclear risk reduction (with the possible exception of good fortune) are now present in South Asia."[5] At the heart of this unsettled situation is the dispute over Kashmir.

What is the Kashmir dispute, and is it intractable? The dispute (in which Kashmiris tend unhelpfully to be relegated to a subordinate position) is between two countries both claiming that it affects the very essence of their nationhood. On this basis, it involves considerations beyond Kashmir, and may well be intractable. However, if the dispute is restated to be a question of how to divide (or if the Kashmiris had their way, reunite) the old princely state and its population, it no longer looks intractable, only difficult. Concessions on territory can be balanced against concessions relating to people.[6]

How do the two nuclear arsenals relate to the dispute? They are relevant in a direct military way only if the two rivals threaten war or go to war. This is a possibility. However, nuclear weapons have no utility within Kashmir. They are too extreme as an answer to infiltration; evidently they do not deter it; and the insurgents cannot use them, even if they could get them, without blowing up their own cause. It is just possible to imagine the use of a radiological "dirty bomb" against an Indian army base, but the notion is far-fetched. If such a bomb is to be used, it would be more effective to do as the Chechens did with their demonstration device left in a Moscow park and give evidence of a similar capability in New Delhi or Mumbai.[7]

Well, then, are the nuclear arsenals irrelevant? No. They are highly valued by both sides, but for different reasons. The Indian nuclear program was driven largely by the ambition of Indian scientists to prove themselves of world class (which they did) and by a political ambition to claim a place at the world's "top table." The armed forces were barely involved: The objectives were civil, not military, though there was an element after the 1962 war of "keeping up" with China. By contrast, the Pakistani program was almost wholly military both in its concepts and in its products. (Pakistan still has a tiny nuclear program for the production of electricity, whereas India's is substantial.) The bomb was intended to keep pace with India, to deter India from using its superior conventional forces, and, if necessary, to use as a war-fighting weapon. It is under the control of the military, and "first use" is explicitly foreseen. Though the motivations are asymmetrical, the nuclear arsenals have become integral to the strategies of the two countries. So in this sense they are crucial to the confrontation over Kashmir, but they were not directly caused by Kashmir and, as we have seen, have no value there.

Nevertheless, Kashmir has been at the root of the nuclear confrontation between India and Pakistan. A highly experienced US diplomat puts it this way: Kashmir is still "the key problem between New Delhi and Islamabad," and the US sees the Kashmir dispute "primarily as a tinder box that could be the flashpoint of a nuclear conflagration."[8]

This is true in two ways that play into each other. First, successive Pakistani governments have chosen (with a large measure of public support) to identify Pakistani interests and even the character of the state with their claim to Kashmir. A government that resigned this claim, or that was comprehensively defeated in war with India, could not survive. Moreover, its fall could trigger grave internal instabilities. So the "ultimate weapon" appears necessary.

Second, in the dispute, India is content with the status quo while Pakistan is the *demandeur* requiring change. But as time passes, India gets stronger and Pakistan relatively weaker. The Indian defense budget, though a smaller percentage of the total budget than Pakistan's, eclipses the latter; the military imbalance on the ground, in the air, and at sea is becoming more pronounced; and India's industrial base is much larger than Pakistan's. Since Pakistan wants change, it is obliged to follow inherently risky policies, and as its relative position weakens, the policies get more risky. Thus, the Kashmir dispute is the cause of high risk.

Only in their nuclear arsenals are the two countries approximately equal. So Pakistan is bound to place a high value on its nuclear weapons and to view them as a crucial lever to produce change. Pakistan also sees these weapons as the ultimate defense against military catastrophe. Surely (so Pakistani leaders tend to reason) the Indians will prefer to make a concession or *in extremis* will refrain from pressing their military advantage rather than risk a nuclear explosion above their soil.

But perhaps, in the event, the Indians will not be deterred, will not find the Pakistani threat credible, or will misunderstand Pakistani intentions. So there is both a prospect that nuclear arsenals will be brought into play and a possibility that they will not produce the result intended. "There appears to have been considerable confusion and ambiguity in New Delhi and Islamabad in sending, as well as receiving, critical signals during the 2001–2002 border confrontation."[9] Thus, there is a potentially unstable situation involving nuclear arsenals.

This is not mere theory. Events since 1998 have shown the instability is actual. Kargil (1999) and the confrontations of 2001–2002 were true nuclear crises in the sense that Berlin in 1961 and Cuba in 1962 were nuclear crises. As with those famous episodes, there were varying views and assessments on both sides carrying with them serious perils of misunderstanding and miscalculation.

In the Kargil case, the Pakistanis relied on the threat of escalation to oblige the Indians to fight conventionally in very adverse circumstances. The threat worked but the Pakistanis lost, because the force of the Indian conventional attack combined crucially with the unexpected strength of political intervention by President Clinton.

In the confrontation of 2001–2002 the Indian mobilization went to the limit, short of actual hostilities, in testing Pakistani resolution. But since Pakistan held firm, the Indians were left with a choice between an ineffective pinprick (e.g., bombing terrorist training camps) and a major conventional thrust bearing a considerable risk that it would escalate to a nuclear level. With American help, the Indians achieved some minor concessions, e.g., the temporary arrest by the Pakistani authorities of some terrorist group leaders, but that was a small return for a huge mobilization. The threat of escalation prevailed, and the Indian forces stood down in October 2002.[10]

What are the lessons? The existence of the two nuclear arsenals did not prevent risky action by both sides. In the Kargil case, the nuclear umbrella encouraged the Pakistanis to make a hostile move, which had always been open to them but was taken only after the parties declared themselves nuclear weapon states. Yet when the Indians responded, the Pakistani air force was not sent across the Line of Control (LoC). In both cases the Indians were, up to a point, deterred by the threat of escalation, yet in the first instance they won and in the second they did not lose. Politics, including American interventions, proved as powerful as weaponry.

In Indian and Pakistani strategic thinking, the role played by suppositions about the US is unlike anything in the Cold War. It has been well observed that "the regional rivals have found a new use for nuclear weapons since they went nuclear officially in 1998. Both countries have engaged in a creative expansion of nuclear strategy *to invite outside intervention* [the emphasis is in the original] in their conflict over Kashmir."[11] In using implied nuclear threats against the other to entice the US to intervene on their side, the two rivals are playing to the fear, well publicized by Americans themselves, of a South Asian war leading to a nuclear exchange. So far the US has obliged, but on its own terms, and neither side has got exactly what it expected. The history of US relations with South Asia does not suggest that either Indians or Pakistanis are particularly acute about reading American intentions or reactions. Nor are the Americans necessarily going to make the right calls or make them in time. So, here is another potential element of instability in the nuclear environment.

Nor does that close the account on unpredictabilities. A further element current in South Asia but absent from the Cold War is the extent of indigenous terrorism, especially with a religious base. South Asia has a lot of terrorism with various objectives and now a lot of nuclear materials. Terror does not need nuclear weapons, but beware: Terrorists of whatever stripe do not have to have nuclear weapons in their own hands to promote a crisis with a nuclear dimension.

Would the removal of a major uncertainty, namely a resolution of the Kashmir dispute and an end to terrorism, make an important difference? Probably, yes. If Kashmir ceased to be the touchstone of relations between the two rivals, the governments might not have much to quarrel about and the peoples might find a good deal in common. Eventually, the two countries might even cooperate in a "Monroe Doctrine" for the subcontinent. But that is for the distant future. In mid-2005 uncertainties still dominate, and so it is too soon to dismiss the probability of at least one more risky crisis with a nuclear dimension.

Is it then true that Kashmir, as President Clinton said in March 2000, is "the most dangerous place in the world"? Few if any experts would have come to that conclusion during the Cold War or even during most of the 1990s. North Korea, Iraq, Palestine, and the former Yugoslavia all would have taken precedence. But suddenly the statement became true in 1998, with the flaunting of the hitherto concealed nuclear arsenals. The crisis over Kargil and the consequences of the attack on the Indian parliament seemed to confirm it. True, the rivals did not actually go to war, and nuclear weapons probably had a good bit to do with that. But Westerners at least were more impressed by the huge risks both sides were prepared to take; stopping short of suicide was not seen as an encouraging sign. Without further revelations, the best answer to Clinton's dictum is that from 1998 to at least 2002 it was not a myth.

What Comes Next?

Is the dictum still true? From the standpoint of mid-2005, what expectations should we have?

Indian prime minister Manmohan Singh has indicated more readiness to negotiate the future of Kashmir both with Pakistan and with the Kashmiris themselves than Delhi has ever previously shown. The only non-negotiable issue, he stated, was the Line of Control; though some might say that in apparently dropping the old claim to all of Kashmir, he was actually making a concession. President Pervez Musharraf took, if anything, a still bolder step (relatively speaking) in admitting that the UN resolutions no longer applied, thus implying that Pakistan would not insist on a plebiscite and could settle for a divided Kashmir. Improved relations between the general public in both countries may even be ahead of those between governments. If the two leaders remain in power, practical agreements are conceivable beyond the 2005 symbolic opening of a bus service linking the two Kashmirs. But the Indian government is a precarious coalition, and at least two attempts to assassinate Musharraf have failed only by seconds. So though there is hope, fragility and uncertainty are still in the forefront.

In Kashmir itself, the cease-fire begun in 2003 is still officially in force, but in practice violence has decreased rather than stopped. The relatively forthcoming attitudes of both sides remain vulnerable to terrorist atrocities, and there are people—mainly non-Kashmiris—who would like, for their own ends, to provoke instability and a return to intransigence. Another Kargil adventure obviously involving the Pakistani army seems unlikely, but another provocation like the high-visibility attack on the Indian parliament remains in the cards. However, neither side will forget the severity of the crisis that followed. It is generally believed that nuclear weapons were put on high alert.[12]

While the nuclear confrontation has made some military and political authorities more cautious, nuclear prowess has made others more cocky and inclined to hectoring. An acute observer noted in December 2001, "There is a growing belief in New Delhi that the time has come to call Pakistan's nuclear bluff. If it does not, India places itself in a permanent vulnerability to cross-border terrorism from Pakistan."[13] Those sentiments are less in evidence in 2005, but they are submerged, not abolished. Conventional preemptive attacks have been mentioned.[14] On the Pakistani side no one any longer talks of launching a war deliberately, but there is still a tough readiness to take risks in order to stand up to India, to maintain claims to Kashmir, and to engage international support.

Tough talk combined with nuclear weapons and a tendency toward adventurism alarmed the US (and others) and caused Washington to abandon its traditional hands-off policy asserting that Kashmir should be settled in direct negotiations between the two parties. With the admitted advent of nuclear weapons and the ebullient talk that celebrated the tests in 1998, Washington decided intervention was necessary to contain risks and, if possible, to bring closure to the disputes. The high points of otherwise low-key American pressure came in the crises of 1999 and 2001–2002. Paradoxically, US intervention worked to the disadvantage of Pakistan, which had long solicited it, and to the benefit of India, which had with equal persistence rejected it. US intervention is still at work: Musharraf has thrown in his lot with Washington and has been savaged over Kashmir and Indo-Pak relations, while Delhi, also seeking friendship with Washington, has become open to US influence. The belief that the US is essentially on their side accounts for some of the Indian cockiness.

For such reasons as these, toughness between the two rivals in mid-2005 is likely to lead less to hostilities or to the breaking off of diplomatic talks than to bolstering the military, including nuclear arsenals. The probability of an arms race has been challenged on the ground that the process might be so slow as hardly to constitute a "race," but there can be walking races as well as running races. Leaving semantics aside, it is hard to deny that the two countries are in a competitive mode. Indians customarily dispute that they should be twinned or hyphenated with Pakistan, and in some senses that is maintainable, but hardly in relation to nuclear weapons. Pakistan says it does not aim to match India weapon for weapon, but its doctrine of credible minimum deterrence obliges it to look at worst-case scenarios (because it is allowing itself no room for mistakes) and to make sure that India does not steal a nuclear march, such as buying an American missile defense system. Such a move would intensify arms racing.[15]

With its huge scientific establishment, its greater resources, and, inevitably, an eye on China, India is under multiple temptations to expand and improve its nuclear arsenal. If nothing intervenes, expansion and/or improvement are almost inevitable. India has the same minimum credible deterrence doctrine as Pakistan, so Indian experts too will look at worst cases, and will do so in relation not just to one potential opponent, but to two. The rate at which expansion and improvement occur will vary, no doubt, over the decades. We need not suppose that the South Asian rivals will duplicate the kind of mindless, dangerous competition that led the two superpowers to pile up tens of thousands of bombs and warheads. Presumably, they will be much more circumspect. Yet we cannot dismiss the fact that every nuclear power so far has felt obliged to create arsenals far larger and more sophisticated than those commonly credited to India and Pakistan in 2005.[16] Nor can we forget the conventional arms race in which the two rivals have been involved for sixty years. But arms racing does not necessarily lead to conflict, and there are signs that the high level of tension since 1998 is moderating.

A Turning Point?

The crisis of 2001–2002, seen retrospectively, may be judged a turning point of sorts. In strategic thinking the lesson could be drawn that with current force-structures there exists no natural firebreak to hold back escalation once large-scale fighting begins and, hence, no profit and much danger in large-scale provocations and conflicts. Presumably, both countries judge that the prospect of serious conflict will draw in the US and possibly other great powers, for instance China. The resulting pressures are likely to reduce freedom of action in all South Asian capitals. Islamabad already may be recognizing that an unusually favorable combination of circumstances— nuclear parity with India, a privileged position in Washington, continued insurgency in Kashmir, the ability to create military initiatives as at Kargil and to support cross-border terrorism, a better than usual economic situation—has led to no victories in the Kashmir struggle. This being so, it may seem better to focus the national interest on goals that are more achievable and more profitable. New Delhi, for its part, may have learned that it cannot cow Pakistan and that the Kashmir issue, inevitably involving Siamese twinning with the opponent, makes India a parochial power, not a natural companion for the great powers.

In mid-2005, it is premature to expect a comprehensive settlement of the Kashmir dispute. Progress may be made while the present leaders remain in power, yet a settlement may elude them. But there are signs— hopeful but not conclusive—that in Islamabad, and even more so in Delhi, the Kashmir issue is in decline. That is not to say that anyone who used to care has ceased to do so: It is still an issue that can destroy governments and disrupt the peace. But Kashmir is slipping down the scale of priorities. For the middle classes, especially in India, enhancing the standard of living is more important, and for the elites the prestige of great power status is the main objective.

To understand what is happening, we need to recognize the revised setting in which the Indo-Pak dispute is being played out. For one thing, the demand for energy is rising sharply, producing both competition and cooperation. Though Pakistan and India may collaborate in a gas pipeline from Iran, they will be competitors for energy supplies from the Middle East and possibly Central Asia. At the same time, India and China are scrambling, usually competitively, sometimes cooperatively, to gain energy resources in Iran, Central Asia, Africa, and Latin America. Already in 2004, China's oil imports rose by 33 percent and India's by 11 percent. By 2010, India expects to move up from the world's sixth largest energy consumer to the fourth.[17] All three countries—and Japan—are likely to give very high priorities to energy imports and to the development of nuclear power.

The nuclear power that matters may be more civil than military, but since the two emerge from the same technology, the proliferation of nuclear technology and the necessary industrial plant are likely to become an even more central issue than they are already. The tensions over controlling the nuclear development of North Korea and Iran may be the first of several such crises. The positions of India and Pakistan (and Israel) pose an acute problem. On the one hand, given that they possess full fuel cycles (including enrichment plants), to leave them outside the international nonproliferation regime would deny them the imports they need to create electricity from nuclear reactors, and thus could lead them to the black market and to illicit sales as well as purchases. On the other hand, including them in the regime, on a par with the forty or so states that could have made nuclear weapons but have not, seems to reward those who "broke the rules" at the expense of those who did not. This could contribute to the unraveling of the whole regime and could encourage further states to start on the military nuclear path. The latest US policy seems to be running both risks simultaneously, the first with Pakistan, the second with India.

President Bush has taken the bull by the horns and, apparently without consultation, has done a deal with India (in July 2005) that on the face of it is hard to reconcile with the nonproliferation regime—and indeed with his own public statements about the need to hold the line and not reward those who break rules. Whether Congress will give him the necessary legislative support, and whether the Nuclear Suppliers Group can be brought to acquiesce in a privileged position for India, remain to be seen. As it stands at the beginning of 2006, the Bush–Manmohan Singh agreement places no effective limits on the size or nature of the Indian nuclear force; it actually assists it by allowing the Indians to use all their indigenously produced fissile material for weapons while facilitating the separate production of whatever fuel the Indians need for electricity production—a win-win situation for India and a no-win one for Pakistan. The latter is, however, allowed to buy nuclear weapons–capable F-16s. The consequences of the agreement are likely to play out over many years. Bush would hardly have taken so radical and risky a step without more inducements than the expectation of a favorable market for US business. The explanation probably lies in his view of the emerging balance of power in Asia.

Bush believes in the reality of a strategic competition between China on the one hand and the US supported by Japan on the other. Given that he is uncertain of Russian support, he particularly wants India as an ally, and the Indians are delighted at last to have the friendship of the world's only superpower. Where does this leave Pakistan? Will Washington provide sufficient inducements for Islamabad not to cleave in its traditional way to Beijing? If the two South Asian rivals find themselves on opposite sides of a tense balance of power struggle, it can hardly fail to be reflected in their Kashmir policies. But if they are on the same side—or if the capitals concerned have the wisdom to avoid an old-fashioned power competition—Kashmir should benefit.

Conclusions

Willy-nilly, Kashmiris are caught up in a grid of interlocking tensions that have little or nothing to do with them and about which they can do nothing effective except to avoid making the situation worse. The nuclear weapons tests of 1998 introduced into the Indo-Pak relationship a new element that made their rivalry more intense and more dangerous, as the Kargil adventure and the crises of 2001–2002 demonstrated. When the peak was passed in May 2002, it was seen that while the old verities—for example, India cannot lose in Kashmir; both capitals put their own interests ahead of Kashmiri interests—remained valid, they were changing under the impact of the nuclear dimension. The risks of severe conflict outweighed the possible advantages: There was no secure stopping point on the ladder of escalation. The great powers, especially the US, were deeply concerned and ready in their own interests to intervene. US intervention worked both in reducing the perils of nuclear deployment and in overcoming Indian resentment. Should a Kashmir settlement be achieved, it will owe much to US influence.

Nevertheless, that is not the only and perhaps in the long run not the most effective route to a settlement. By a process slower and more subtle than formal negotiation, redefinition by both sides of their respective national interests is reducing the significance of Kashmir. India concentrates on the general acceptance of its claim to be a great power and seeks international support for permanent membership on the Security Council, for acceptance by the Nuclear Suppliers Group, and such. With the way ahead obvious, if not easy, India is likely to learn that economic prowess matters more than nuclear weapons. Facing tougher and murkier prospects, Pakistan needs, first, a national determination to develop into the first truly modern and prosperous Islamic state; and second, successes on the road to this objective. When New Delhi perceives this to be in its own interest and acts accordingly, the world will know India has achieved maturity. Meanwhile, to counter terrorism and to contain nuclear proliferation, the international community needs to help Pakistan, and that depends upon the Pakistanis themselves taking the essential decisions.

Both countries must beware of finding themselves on opposite sides of an Asian balance of power struggle. And they need to cooperate in curbing nuclear risks and in limiting the siren song of excessive nationalism. All this is easier to do as rivalry and endeavor focused on Kashmir fade in the light of new objectives. The happiness of the Kashmiri people may yet be served by new approaches and new voices in Srinagar, New Delhi, and Islamabad. It will be a fortunate day for them when neither capital cares passionately about their land.

Notes

1. The metallurgist A. Q. Khan, hailed in Pakistan as "the father of the bomb," turns out to have fathered nuclear weapons developments in Iran, Libya, and North Korea (all of which he has admitted) and probably elsewhere. He operated undetected for many years through an extensive international network, most of which remains in place. Immediately after his confession, Khan was pardoned by President Pervez Musharraf and has not been available to Western intelligence agencies. Except in Pakistan, it is widely assumed that he received official help in his profitable black market activities.

2. Remarks made by President Clinton while preparing for his visit to South Asia in 2000. Jonathan Karp and Glenn Burkins, "Clinton to Face Diplomatic Challenges During His Visit to India: Pakistan Relations, Arms Control Rank High on His List," *Wall Street Journal*, 17 March 2000.

3. George Perkovich, Jessica T. Mathews, Joseph Cirincione, Rose Gottemoeller, and Jon B. Wolfsthal, *Universal Compliance: A Strategy for Nuclear Security* (Washington, DC: Carnegie Endowment for International Peace, 2005), p. 159. See Michael R. Kraig, "The Political and Strategic Imperatives of Nuclear Deterrence in South Asia," *India Review* 2, no. 1 (2003), p. 39.

4. Michael Krepon presents the best description of the opposing views of the deterrence optimists and pessimists in Michael Krepon, Rodney W. Jones, and Ziad Haider, eds., *Escalation Control and the Nuclear Option in South Asia*, Chapter 1

(Washington, DC: The Henry L. Stimson Center, 2004). See also his contribution, "The Stability-Instability Paradox: Misperceptions and Escalation Control" (Chapter 10) in Rafiq Dossani and Henry S. Rowen, eds., *Prospects for Peace in South Asia* (Stanford: Stanford University Press, 2005). Other contributions in both the above edited volumes are also relevant. For international opinion in 1998, see *Disarmament Diplomacy*, nos. 25 and 27. See also Michael Quinlan in *Survival* 42, no. 4 (Winter 2000–2001), and United States Institute of Peace Special Report 129, January 2005. Kenneth Waltz (the leading Western advocate of the view that a nuclear standoff increases safety) and Scott D. Sagan argue the issue in their book, *The Spread of Nuclear Weapons: A Debate Renewed* (New York: W. W. Norton, 2003). For the official Indian view, see Jaswant Singh's statement in George Perkovich, *India's Nuclear Bomb: The Impact on Global Proliferation* (Berkeley: University of California Press, first published 1999; 2001 edition with afterword), p. 484. Kanti Bajpai's P.C. Lal Memorial Lecture, New Delhi 2000, brought up to date at a conference at Stanford University, 4 and 5 January 2002, is in India the classical academic analysis. At the same conference, Hasan-Askari Rizvi's paper dealt succinctly with Pakistan's strategic culture. See also Kraig, "The Political and Strategic Imperatives"; Bharat Karnad, *Nuclear Weapons and Indian Security* (Delhi: Macmillan, 2002); and Zia Mian, A. H. Nayyar, and M. V. Ramana, "Making Weapons, Talking Peace: Resolving the Dilemma of Nuclear Negotiations," *Economic and Political Weekly*, 17 July 2004.

5. In Dossani and Rowen, eds., *Prospects for Peace in South Asia*, p. 269.

6. Hasan-Askari Rizvi in Chapter 9 of this volume recommends a shift in focus from "state identities to human beings." See also Husain Haqqani and Ashley J. Tellis, *India and Pakistan: Is Peace Real This Time?* (Washington, DC: Carnegie Endowment for International Peace, 2004), p. 21.

7. Pran Krishan Pahwa, "The Nuclear Dimension," in Rear Admiral Raja Menon, ed., *Weapons of Mass Destruction: Options for India* (New Delhi: Sage, 2004), pp. 22, 27, 28.

8. Howard B. Schaffer, "U.S. Interests in South Asia," in Dassani and Rowen, eds., *Prospects for Peace in South Asia*, p. 336.

9. Rahul Roy-Chaudhury, "Nuclear Doctrine, Declaratory Policy, and Escalation Control," in Krepon et al., eds., *Escalation Control*, p. 117.

10. This crisis awaits further research. Meanwhile, see Krepon in Dossani and Rowen, eds., *Prospects for Peace in South Asia*, especially pp. 278–279, and Waheguru Pal Singh Sidhu, "Terrible Tuesday and Terrorism in South Asia," *South Asian Survey* 10, no. 2 (2003).

11. Rajesh M. Bustky, "Coercive Diplomacy in a Nuclear Environment: The December 13 Crisis," in Dossani and Rowen, eds., *Prospects for Peace in South Asia*, p. 311.

12. The evidence so far is not conclusive and confusion about the terminological definitions of successive operations in the preparation of missiles adds to the uncertainty, but it strains credulity to suppose that no steps were taken to prepare missiles or aircraft. See the chapters by Feroz Hassan Khan, "Nuclear Signaling, Missiles and Escalation Control in South Asia," and Rahul Roy-Chaudhury in Krepon et al., eds., *Escalation Control*.

13. C. Raja Mohan, quoted in Rajesh Basrur, "Coercive Diplomacy in a Nuclear Environment: The December 13 Crisis," in Dossani and Rowen, eds., *Prospects for Peace in South Asia*, p. 305.

14. Rodney W. Jones, "Nuclear Stability and Escalation Control in South Asia: Structural Factors," in Krepon et al., eds., *Escalation Control*, especially pp. 35–44.

15. See, for example, Basrur in Dossani and Rowen, eds., *Prospects for Peace in South Asia*, p. 324.

16. The International Institute for Strategic Studies, in *The Military Balance 2004–2005* (London: Taylor and Francis, 2004), conservatively credits both India and Pakistan with forty-plus operational warheads aligned to an in-service delivery system.

17. *South Asian Monitor*, no. 80, 2005 (Washington, DC: Center for Strategic and International Studies); Pramit Mitra in *Yale Global*, 14 March 2005, http://yaleedu/article.print?id-5419; Keith Bradsher, "Two Big Appetites Take Seat at the One Table," *New York Times*, 18 February 2005; Edward Luce and Farhan Bokhari, "India Offers Pakistan Pipeline Talks," *Financial Times,* 11 February 2005.

PART 3
Toward Settlement

13

Settling the Kashmir Conflict: The Internal Dimension

Iffat Idris

Any attempt to resolve the Kashmir conflict has to start with the under-standing that it comprises two distinct but interrelated conflicts, rather than a single one. The first is the international dispute between India and Pakistan, dating back to partition, over territorial control of Jammu and Kashmir. The second considerably postdates partition and is essentially an internal conflict between Muslims in Indian-administered Jammu and Kashmir (IJK) and the government in New Delhi.[1] In addition to these overt conflicts, there have been problems over autonomy, political freedom, and economic development between Islamabad and Azad Jammu and Kashmir (AJK).

Most of the focus in attempts to resolve the Kashmir dispute has been on the first aspect: the conflict between India and Pakistan. This was per-haps to be expected, given that this conflict has so frequently led to war in the subcontinent, but it is equally important to resolve the to date neglected internal conflict between Kashmiri Muslims and the Indian government in IJK, and to address the grievances of Kashmiris in AJK. Only a holistic approach will yield long-term results.

This chapter focuses on how to resolve the armed conflict in IJK and how to address the grievances of Kashmiris in IJK and AJK. The deliberate stress on internal peace processes is justified for a number of reasons.

First, if measured in terms of loss of life, physical and emotional injury, and economic hardships, Kashmiris are suffering far more as a result of internal grievances than they are because of the failure to resolve the wider issue of who controls Jammu and Kashmir: India or Pakistan. The latter dis-pute has also caused much suffering (divided families, travel restrictions, loss of life due to cross-border shelling, etc.), but today its impact is felt less directly than that of the internal conflict. If these internal issues can be addressed, a marked improvement can be seen in the lives of ordinary Kashmiris.

It should also be noted that such internal issues as human rights abuses, regional autonomy, and economic development can be resolved (to a considerable extent) even in the absence of international resolution; should conflict continue between Kashmiri Muslims and the Indian government, however, it will be extremely difficult for India and Pakistan to resolve their dispute.

Failure to resolve the internal conflict, especially in IJK, carries the constant danger of escalation into a full-scale war between India and Pakistan. The Kargil conflict stemmed from the internal conflict. So too did the 2001 attack on the Lok Sabha, the lower house of the Indian parliament in New Delhi; that attack led to a massive troop deployment along the Indo-Pak international border and, for some months, the threat of another Indo-Pak war. Any subsequent resolution of the international conflict—possibly leading to a changed status for Jammu and Kashmir—could still be implemented. Resolution of internal issues would not prevent that.

Finally, as this chapter will show, the current situation (post–September 11) offers considerable potential for the resolution of internal issues, especially in IJK. The global rejection of all forms of nonstate-actor violence has made Kashmiri Muslims more inclined to compromise on their demand for secession from India.

Arguments can be and have been put forward for the international dispute between India and Pakistan over the territorial control of Jammu and Kashmir to be resolved first, and internal issues addressed later. This chapter will not detail the history of efforts at resolution of the Indo-Pak dispute; suffice it to say that the record of failure, and the subsequent suffering of the Kashmiri people, clearly point to the need for a different approach.

The Northern Ireland experience provides a useful model.[2] There are clear similarities between the Northern Ireland conflict and that in IJK. Both involve minority and majority religious communities with totally polarized aspirations for their homeland; in both, conflict between militant groups and state troops is waged in civilian areas; resolution of both entails overcoming multiple obstacles. To date, the Northern Ireland peace process has not delved into the long-term issue of the future of the province—that is, whether this future should involve continued membership in the United Kingdom or secession to Ireland. That difficult issue was deliberately put on hold in the 1998 Good Friday Agreement, while comparatively easier issues of restoring peace and building relationships between divided communities were to be tackled first. This approach successfully ended large-scale conflict in Northern Ireland, brought all parties to the negotiating table, and improved the lives of ordinary people in the province (providing security, attracting investment, and creating jobs). Some problems have persisted, of course, in securing the decommissioning of armed groups[3] and in activating the devolved governance framework. Nonetheless, there is reason to be hopeful that building trust through this approach will make the issue of Northern Ireland's future, whenever it is addressed, easier to resolve.

In the same way, the issue of Kashmir's final status—accession to India or Pakistan, independence, or something in between—is an extremely difficult one for India, Pakistan, and the Kashmiri people to resolve. Any final status settlement will certainly involve massive compromises and concessions on long and deeply held positions. But movement ahead on resolving internal issues and improving the lives of ordinary Kashmiris should not be held hostage to progress on the international dispute. As with Northern Ireland, progress on resolution of internal Kashmiri issues carries the clear potential to make the international Indo-Pak dispute easier to resolve.

What Has Hindered Resolution of Internal Issues?

Kashmiri grievances against India (in the case of IJK) and Pakistan (in the case of AJK) are long-standing and cover the gamut of issues from human rights abuse, to denial of political freedom and autonomy, to lack of economic development. They are described elsewhere in this volume.[4] A number of efforts have been made to address these internal issues by the respective governments on both sides of the Line of Control (LoC), albeit with varying success. These "internal peace processes" are reviewed below.

Indian Jammu and Kashmir

The root causes of the conflict in IJK have been attributed to Kashmiri resentment fueled by cynical misgovernance in IJK (culminating in the 1987 elections rigging), a combination of increased education levels but a lack of good jobs, and external influences such as the Afghan jihad.[5] But the clash between the Indian government and the Kashmiri people over self-determination has served as the central overt issue in their ongoing conflict. India has consistently refused to acknowledge the Kashmiri right of self-determination to be expressed through a plebiscite on secession or accession. New Delhi's contention is that ratification of the 26 October 1947 instrument of accession by the Jammu and Kashmir Assembly was equivalent to the plebiscite promised by India's governor-general Mountbatten to the Kashmiri people as a condition of accepting that accession.[6] For New Delhi, Jammu and Kashmir is a "permanent and integral part" of the Indian union.[7] On other issues, however, and with an interest in defusing the conflict, India has shown some flexibility. In addition, Kashmiri political and civil society organizations have initiated on-the-ground processes to allow for local interests to be voiced. For example, Kashmiri Muslim political groups have formed umbrella organizations to enable Kashmiri Muslims to speak with one voice, while civil society organizations (CSOs) have applied pressure on New Delhi to address Kashmiri grievances (notably over human rights abuses) and on militants to give up violence.

Regional (state) autonomy and devolution. IJK's relationship with the center and its internal administrative setup have been a constant source of tension between New Delhi and Srinagar, and between different communities within IJK.

With regard to regional (state) autonomy, this was supposedly guaranteed by Article 370 of the Indian constitution.[8] In practice, successive central and state governments conspired to undermine this and integrate IJK with the rest of India,[9] leading to resentment among Kashmiri Muslims. The State Autonomy Committee was one of a number of initiatives to look into the issue of autonomy for IJK. Its 1999 report recommended the "restoration of autonomy to Jammu and Kashmir"—leaving only defense, external affairs, and communications with the central government.[10] The report was approved through a resolution by the state assembly but rejected by the BJP government in New Delhi.

The BJP has long called for the abrogation of Article 370; it sees all talk of state autonomy as "anti-national."[11] It and other politicians in New Delhi fear that autonomy for IJK could "set a precedent" that would be followed by other states. If IJK is granted special powers, the argument goes, what is to stop other states from demanding the same? Proponents of this viewpoint fail to take into account the special history of Jammu and Kashmir and its unique position as India's only Muslim-majority state. The accession of Jammu and Kashmir to India has always been controversial; judged according to the principles on which the Indian subcontinent was partitioned, the state could as easily have gone to Pakistan. The fact that Jammu and Kashmir is India's only Muslim-majority state could be used as justification to allow *its* secession but not that of others demanding the same right. (Note, though, that this argument works both ways: India must keep at least one Muslim-majority state to negate the perception that it is a "Hindu" country, and to protect its official secularism.)

The second major source of opposition to IJK's autonomy is members of non-Muslim groups within the state, including the Pandits, Jammu Hindus, and Ladakh Buddhists. Members of these minority groups have expressed fears of Muslim majority rule, seeing their groups' protection as lying within central control of IJK and/or devolution (see below).[12] Ironically, regional autonomy is also opposed by some hardcore Kashmiri separatists, who see it as a ploy by India to persuade Kashmiris to give up their demand for secession.[13]

The problem is that, while central control has been seen as crucial by non-Muslim communities in the state, large numbers of Kashmiri Muslims hold regional autonomy as nonnegotiable. One way in which the government of India has attempted to resolve this dilemma is by "devolution": dividing IJK into smaller administrative units and thereby freeing non-Muslim minorities of Muslim control. Devolution is strongly supported by the BJP and other Hindu parties.[14]

In May 1995 the Narasimha Rao government passed the Ladakh Autonomous Hill Council Act (LAHC), creating autonomous councils in Leh and Kargil, along with an interdistrict council to promote coordination and communal harmony. In 1996 the National Conference government of Farooq Abdullah set up the Regional Autonomy Commission. The reconstituted commission prepared a report recommending the abolition of the LAHC and the division of IJK into multiple provinces. Opposition from New Delhi scuppered this proposal.[15]

Devolution is a controversial issue within IJK. The creation of the LAHC, for example, at least partially fulfilled the aspirations of Ladakh Buddhists, who had long felt overshadowed by Kashmir Valley control, but angered Kashmiri Muslims. The latter condemned it as "amounting to Kashmir's territorial disintegration." Kashmiri Muslims oppose splitting the state on historic grounds: They want the pre-1947 Jammu and Kashmir to be preserved as a united entity. They also see division of IJK as an attempt to dilute their numerical majority. Opposition is not universal. There *are* Kashmiri Muslims willing to countenance devolution, but only if it takes place within the wider context of autonomy for IJK from the center.[16]

Following the 2002 election of the People's Democratic Party (PDP)–Congress government in IJK and the induction in 2004 of a Congress-led government in New Delhi, a change is apparent in Indian attitudes to regional autonomy. The Singh government announced its commitment "to respecting the letter and spirit of Article 370 of the Constitution that accords a special status to Jammu and Kashmir."[17] Addressing a news conference in November 2004, Prime Minister Singh declared: "We have made it clear . . . as far as regional autonomy is concerned [the] sky is the limit."[18] To date, however, there has been no substantive move to restore Article 370 autonomy, e.g., reversing the administrative integration of the IJK with the rest of India.

Restoration of regional autonomy could go a long way to defusing the conflict in IJK. It would be a significant concession by the Indian government to Kashmiri Muslim demands and could help persuade them to drop their call for complete secession. In order to ensure that minority communities in IJK do not feel threatened, however, autonomy would have to be accompanied by decentralization within IJK.

Normalization through elections. A few years into the Kashmir insurgency, it was clear that New Delhi's policy of applying more and more force to crush the separatist movement was not proving effective. Indeed, it was proving countereffective by fueling Kashmiri anger at India and thus support for militancy. New Delhi was also concerned about its international image. Years of central (i.e., governor's) rule in IJK belied the impression it was trying to put across that the Kashmir conflict was an imported one, with few indigenous roots, and that it was not a major problem.

As part of an alternative approach, the Indian government tried to promote "normalization" in the Kashmir Valley by restoring elected government. This was initially planned in 1993, but administrative problems and threats from militant groups led to repeated postponements.[19] The Indian government tried to encourage the electoral process by releasing several Kashmiri leaders in May 1994, including Yasin Malik, Shabbir Shah, Abdul Ghani Lone, and Syed Ali Shah Geelani. This did not have the desired effect: All announced they would boycott elections because they were taking place within the framework of the Indian constitution, so that they did not give Kashmiris the option to decide their own future. (In October a further 276 political prisoners were freed, a signal of the Indian government's determination to continue the "goodwill approach," even if it was not yielding results.)

National elections for the Lok Sabha, the Indian lower house, were held in May 1996, including in IJK. While it is impossible to get precise voter turnout figures, the general assessment of observers and the media was that turnout was extremely low and that the Indian authorities used extreme tactics to try to generate a higher turnout. There were numerous reports of voters being forced to the polling stations at gunpoint.[20] The 1996 electoral exercise did little for India's credibility on Kashmir in the international community, and did even less to restore Kashmiri Muslim confidence in Indian rule. In September 1996, elections were held for the state assembly. These were also largely boycotted by Kashmiris. However, subsequent elections, described below, have been more successful.

The failure of India's early attempts at normalization through elections can be attributed to a number of factors: strong opposition (accompanied by threats of violence) from Kashmiri militant groups, a boycott by Kashmiri political groups, the perception among Kashmiri Muslims that voting implied acceptance of Indian rule (something most greatly resented), and the poor security environment that made election arrangements difficult. All these combined to render what was presented as an exercise in democratic participation ineffective and meaningless.

Cease-fires and dialogue. The first decade of conflict in IJK saw both sides—India and Kashmiri militants—determined to battle it out. The period was marked by a complete absence of dialogue between the two sides. But a dramatic change came in July 2000 with the announcement of a cease-fire by the Kashmiri militant group, Hizbul Mujahidin (HM). Accepted by Prime Minister Vajpayee's government, the cease-fire was soon (3 August 2000) followed by talks in Srinagar between the militant group and the Indian government. This was a major departure from India's traditional position that it would only talk to elected representatives of the Kashmiris, a condition that ruled out talks with both militants and the separatist All Parties Hurriyat Conference (APHC). However, the talks collapsed when the Indian government refused to include Pakistan, as demanded by HM, and the cease-fire was called off on 8 August 2000. Two days later HM claimed responsibility for a car bomb outside the State Bank of India building in Srinagar that took more than a dozen lives.

In November 2000 the Vajpayee government took the initiative in announcing a suspension of combat operations against militant groups in IJK for the duration of Ramadan. That cease-fire was extended twice, but hopes that it would jump-start a political process were dashed by the APHC's rejection of talks.[21] It wanted Pakistan included in talks as well (a condition unacceptable to India), claiming that without Islamabad, "Such a process of talking will end up nowhere."[22] Vajpayee called off the suspension in May 2001. Foreign Minister Jaswant Singh explained that the decision was made because "militant groups in the region had not cooperated and had continued with their campaign of violence."[23]

Both cease-fire and dialogue initiatives have been impeded by divisions among Kashmiri militant and political groups. Hizbul Mujahidin's cease-fire announcement in 2000 drew strong criticism from other militant groups in IJK, who actually intensified their attacks.[24] Indeed, ninety-three people, including a group of Hindu pilgrims and their mostly Muslim porters, were massacred across IJK within a twenty-four-hour period during the cease-fire.[25] Similarly, the eventual agreement of some in the APHC to talk to the Indian government—even though Pakistan was not included—led to a split within the organization. The APHC now has two factions: one that is pro-talks, led by Mirwaiz Umar Farooq and Maulana Abbas Ansari, and the other strongly opposed, led by Syed Ali Shah Geelani. The two have still not been reconciled.

Despite these obstacles, some sort of dialogue process between New Delhi and Kashmiri separatists (at least the strictly political groups) was sustained in the years following the collapsed cease-fire. Vajpayee's special representative N. N. Vohra held talks with Kashmiri political leaders, and direct talks between the APHC and the Indian government took place for the first time in January 2004. N. N. Vohra was retained in the same capacity by the Congress-led national government elected in May 2004.

Efforts to end conflict and promote dialogue have been helped by several militants abandoning the armed struggle. Yasin Malik, Shabbir Shah, and Firdous Syed[26] are among the most famous ex-fighters, all of whom have opted for dialogue and political struggle instead of the gun. Indian governments have shown some willingness to engage with these ex-combatants but have so far not made any significant concessions to them, for example, addressing their demands for human rights abuses to be curbed and looked into. India's use of some former militants as informants and even as counterinsurgents has proved detrimental to promotion of peace in IJK. Groups like Ikhwan-al-Muslimoon, headed by Kukka Parrey, have been implicated in attacks, including assassinations of human rights activists and journalists, as well as in cases of intimidation, abduction, and extortion.[27] Pro-India counterinsurgents operate outside the law and add to the overall level of violence in the state.

Human rights abuses. For many Kashmiri Muslims the biggest hesitation in accepting Indian rule is their anger at human rights abuses perpetrated by Indian forces. This is a very real and justifiable grievance. Human rights abuses, while not precisely chronicled, have occurred on a massive scale in IJK.[28] A disturbing feature of this abuse has been official legitimization and condoning of these incidents, and failure to take action. This is seen, for example, in "abuse-enabling" legislation such as the Prevention of Terrorism Act (POTA), promulgated in 2002,[29] and in the dearth of punishments meted out to those responsible for human rights violations.[30]

In recent years, however, New Delhi has shown some willingness at least to acknowledge the problem. That has led to forward movement within IJK. Chief Minister Mufti Sayeed's 2002 Common Minimum Program, which outlined the agenda of the PDP-Congress coalition government in IJK, specifically included measures to improve the human rights situation in the Kashmir Valley.[31] Unfortunately, matching rhetoric with action proved harder. An initial pledge to investigate abuses committed by the notorious Special Operations Group (SOG), for example, was abandoned. The SOG was simply disbanded without investigating past crimes. Similarly, the government announced a compensation package for abuse victims and their families, but there have been reports of discrimination between Muslims and non-Muslims when it comes to actually paying out.[32]

The new Congress-led government in New Delhi made a commitment to repeal POTA, acknowledging that it "has been grossly misused in the past two years."[33] This eventually happened in September–October 2004 through the POTA (Repeal) Ordinance. Commentators on the Indian right raised concerns about the consequent creation of a "policy vacuum" in dealing with terrorism—especially financing. In response, the UPA (United Progressive Alliance) government introduced new legislation to amend other legal frameworks, notably the Unlawful Activities (Prevention) Act and the Foreign Exchange Management Act. This has led skeptics on the Indian left and in IJK to express concern about whether the repeal of POTA would really make a difference, given the augmentation of other frameworks, and that cases from before the repeal remained subject to POTA.

Civil society movements. There have also been efforts by Kashmiris outside government to tackle the massive suffering caused by human rights abuses. The Association of Parents of Disappeared Persons was formed in 1994 by lawyer Parvez Imroze and a mother whose sixteen-year-old son "disappeared." In the decade since its formation the APDP has acquired a reputation in the human rights field, but it has made relatively little impact in terms of actually curbing abuse and getting justice for victims and their families.

The APDP is an example of civil society organizations within IJK: ordinary Kashmiris—distinct from political activists and leaders and from separatists—banding together to express their views. Unfortunately, such civil society movements have been held back, on the one hand, by threats and punitive actions by the militants and, on the other, by restrictions imposed by the Indian authorities (including on funding for NGOs).[34] India has even stopped civil society meetings to discuss the Kashmir issue that were held outside Kashmir. For example, a planned meeting for February 2002 of Kashmiri civil society groups in Nepal, funded by Germany, was called off after Indian pressure on both Nepal and Germany.[35] A two-part meeting was later (December 2004) organized in Kathmandu by Pugwash; the first closed-door part was a civil society meeting for journalists and NGO leaders, while the second included separatist leaders and former Indian and Pakistani officials.[36]

Other civil society initiatives have been to build bridges among different communities within IJK and evolve shared Kashmiri positions. Former militant Firdous Syed founded the Kashmir Foundation for Peace and Development Studies, dedicated to building a climate of peace and reconciliation between Muslim and Hindu communities in IJK. In 2004, Yasin Malik launched a signature campaign for Kashmiri inclusion in the Indo-Pak dialogue process. The campaign received well over 1.5 million signatures from Kashmiris from all communities, and the results of the effort were put on public display in New Delhi.

Overall, though, such "reconciliation" initiatives have had limited success in bringing different Kashmiri communities together. This is perhaps to be expected, given strong Kashmiri Muslim resentment against India and equally strong Pandit resentment against Muslims, whom they hold respon-

sible for uprooting them from their homes in the Kashmir Valley. The fact
that Pandit refugees have continued to live in appalling conditions in camps
in Jammu and other parts of the state has sustained their feelings of bitterness and anger toward Muslims. Polarization of different religious communities in IJK was also fuelled by the rise of political Hinduism in India in
the late 1980s and 1990s. Indeed, the plight of Hindu Pandits and their suffering at the hands of Kashmiri Muslims appeared in one of the election slogans used by the BJP.[37]

Economic revival. It is widely recognized that conflict and extremism can
be fueled by socioeconomic deprivation.[38] Conversely, giving people
opportunities and jobs, along with improving their living conditions, gives
them a stake in society and reduces the attraction of extremism and militancy. The poor socioeconomic conditions of most Kashmiris have added to
their frustration,[39] and thus have been a factor in pushing them to support
militancy. Conflict has made matters worse by wiping out one of the major
sources of revenue in IJK, namely tourism. Indian governments in the past
have spent millions on security in IJK but very little on economic development.[40]

Soon after coming to power in late 2002, Chief Minister Mufti Sayeed
said that IJK needs "our own version of the Marshall Plan."[41] In November
2004 the Indian government unveiled a new strategy to achieve peace in
IJK; its central pillar was accelerated economic development. During Prime
Minister Singh's visit to IJK that month, he announced a $5 billion develop-
ment package for the state over the next four years, which would include
power projects, investment in education, and an upgrade of the airport.
These initiatives can make a big difference, but only if they are implemented and ordinary Kashmiris feel the benefits. The Indian government has yet
to fulfill its pledges on investment in IJK, while corruption within the state
remains a problem.

Kashmiri pragmatism. War-weariness on the part of Kashmiri Muslims
living in IJK has fostered a marked willingness to compromise with India.
Many Kashmiris, looking at the changed global environment after
September 11 and international opprobrium for any form of nonstate-actor
violence, are pragmatic about the chances of achieving their goal of secession from India. Common sense dictates that, if they have not been able to
win this through the twelve years of armed struggle before September 11,
they certainly will not be able to do so afterward.

The change in Kashmiri Muslim thinking was reflected in their participation in the 2002 elections. In marked contrast to the 1996 elections,
turnout in some areas was significant.[42] The result was also significant: success for Mufti Sayeed's People's Democratic Party. Unlike the discredited

National Conference (NC), the PDP advocates greater regional autonomy from IJK but, unlike the APHC, accepts that IJK is part of India.

Some analysts have interpreted the vote for the PDP as a sign of Kashmiri pragmatism and willingness to give up their long-standing demand for self-determination and secession from India. Others, however, saw it as pragmatism of a different kind: Even in the struggle for a "free" Kashmir, IJK needs an efficient administration capable of providing electricity, water, roads, education, healthcare, etc. The vote for the PDP was a vote against the corrupt, inefficient NC and for a (presumably) better-run IJK. The truth probably lies somewhere in between. In January–February 2005, Kashmiris also participated in municipal elections, held in IJK after almost thirty years: Turnout was as high as 70 percent in some areas, with over 20 percent in Srinagar, 34 percent in Anantnag, and 55 percent in Pulwama.[43] Again, this could be seen either as a demand for administrative improvement or as a sign of Kashmiri acceptance of Indian rule—or both.

In sum, attempts to resolve the internal conflict in IJK between Kashmiri Muslims and India were for years held up by the latter's determination to crush Kashmiri separatism solely through force. A rethinking in later years led to the recognition that alternative approaches needed to be taken: dialogue with Kashmiri groups, restoration of elected governments, facing up to human rights abuses, and promoting economic development. India's mixed record on implementation of these various initiatives suggests either a lack of sincerity on the part of New Delhi (that it was going through the motions rather than genuinely attempting to address Kashmiri Muslims' grievances) or a difficulty in carrying through its pledges. In recent years, however, that record has greatly improved, and successive Indian governments seem committed to winning over Kashmiri Muslims. These efforts have been encouraged by a new willingness on the part of a growing number of Kashmiri Muslims to compromise on their demand for secession from India. As yet, though, words have not wholly been matched by actions.

Azad Jammu and Kashmir and the Northern Areas

The people of Azad Jammu and Kashmir and the Northern Areas do not seem to have reached the same level of disillusionment and resentment toward Pakistan as seen in IJK toward India. There has been no anti-Pakistan insurgency or conflict in the region, and none of the massive human rights abuses seen across the LoC. Nonetheless, there are serious issues and resentment felt by people in AJK toward Pakistan.

To date, very little has been done to address these. Pakistan has successfully used the conflict in IJK to push aside such "uncomfortable" issues in AJK and the Northern Areas as political freedom, autonomy, and economic development. The result is that very little has changed on the ground for ordinary Kashmiris. Political processes in the province remain dominated by affiliates of central parties: the Muslim Conference and PPP. Pro-independence parties remain restricted. Similarly, electoral processes continue to be manipulated in favor of allies of the central government, as seen in the 2001 election of the Muslim Conference. The prevalence of local politicians willing to "sell out" for personal gain, combined with restrictive controls from the center, continues to effectively suppress free political expression in AJK.

Among ordinary people in AJK, the conflict in IJK has had opposite effects. Some feel compelled *not* to speak out against Islamabad, seeing this as a betrayal in the face of common enemy India. Others have been inspired to clamor for the same right of self-determination being demanded by Kashmiri Muslims in IJK. While the latter are a significant and growing force, Pakistan has successfully managed to suppress them and prevent them from making political headway.

No attempt has been made by Pakistan to address constitutional issues with regard to AJK and the Northern Areas. As far as Pakistan is concerned, the Northern Areas are a permanent part of the country. AJK continues to enjoy independence on paper, but little in practice.

On the economic front, there have been numerous pledges from the center for greater investment and development in the state, but little has been done in practice.[44] The fact that the Azad Jammu and Kashmir government is dominated by a small clique of generally corrupt political leaders (e.g., Sardar Abdul Qayyum Khan and his son, Raja Mumtaz Rathore, Barrister Sultan Mehmood) has not encouraged reform and good governance.

In sum, while grievances of AJK and Northern Areas Kashmiris toward Pakistan are comparable to those of Kashmiri Muslims in IJK toward India, much less has been done by the central government to address them.

Additional Pro-Peace Initiatives

Two significant developments have taken place with respect to internal peace processes in IJK and AJK in recent years. These include a reduction in Pakistan's support for Kashmiri separatist groups and increased contact between Kashmiris across the LoC.

Pakistan was forced to curb its support for Kashmiri militant groups (support it had never officially acknowledged) as a consequence of the September 11 attacks in the United States. India successfully latched on to the "war on terror" launched by the Bush administration and made very effective use of the December 2001 attack on the Lok Sabha in New Delhi to portray the conflict in IJK as one of "Pakistan-sponsored terrorism." Faced with a hostile global environment, President Pervez Musharraf had no choice but to announce in January 2002 that Pakistan would be making greater efforts to curb movement of militants across the LoC.[45] Musharraf banned some Kashmiri outfits operating within Pakistan and launched a general crackdown on extremist, armed religious groups in the country.[46]

While the domestic impact of that crackdown is debatable (sectarian attacks continue to take place in Pakistani cities), it did have an impact in IJK. Speaking in March 2002, Prime Minister Vajpayee conceded that "changes in Pakistan have had a favourable impact on the situation in Jammu and Kashmir."[47] In April 2003, at a rally in Srinagar, Prime Minister Atal Bihari Vajpayee offered the "hand of friendship" to Pakistan. A further reduction in violence followed the November 2003 announcement by Pakistan of a cease-fire across the LoC, a fact acknowledged even by India.[48] In January 2004, Pakistan and India launched what has, to date, been an extremely positive peace process. This and continued international opprobrium for any kind of nonstate-actor violence make it highly unlikely that Islamabad will revive its support for Kashmiri militant groups. The weakening of Kashmiri militant groups has further consequences: It makes it even harder for Kashmiri Muslims in IJK to win secession from India by force, and hence makes them more inclined to engage in dialogue with New Delhi and agree to settlements that fall short of secession. The attacks of September 11 have thus, ironically, promoted the chances of peace in IJK, although on terms more acceptable to New Delhi.

The first Muzaffarabad-Srinagar bus service was launched on 7 April 2005. An outcome of the wider peace process between India and Pakistan, the service considerably facilitated contact between Kashmiris in AJK with those in IJK. Partition in 1947 and the subsequent Indo-Pak wars led to many Kashmiri families being divided from each other on different sides of the LoC. Kashmiris marrying across the LoC often found themselves cut off from their families of origin, thanks to the huge difficulties in travelling to the other side. This division and the inability to meet family and friends have been a source of suffering for these divided Kashmiri families. The Muzaffarabad-Srinagar bus service, with its relatively easy travel permit procedures, offers a chance for long-divided families to meet up.

Given its goal of uniting loved ones across the LoC, it is perhaps not surprising that the bus service has been welcomed by Kashmiris in both AJK and IJK. The only source of opposition has come from some extremist militant groups in IJK[49] and hard-line politicians like Syed Ali Geelani, who see the service as acceptance of the division of Kashmir and thus as a betrayal of the Kashmiri cause. Passengers, particularly from IJK, were threatened with death if they travelled on the bus, and one day before the service was to be launched, militants carried out a daring attack on the center housing passengers. Some people did abandon their travel plans because of the militants' threats but, to date, the service has proved very popular with ordinary Kashmiris, and thousands are applying to use it. The Kashmir bus service offered hope for divided families, and in the wider context of the Indian-Pakistani peace process, it helped create an environment of goodwill and trust. Plans were subsequently proposed by both New Delhi and Islamabad to increase such travel links across the LoC.

Augmenting and Sustaining the Current Process

As described above, a number of initiatives have taken place, mostly in IJK, to address the grievances of Kashmiri Muslims. Success has been greater in some areas than others, but the potential for improving the lives of Kashmiris in IJK and AJK remains. Realizing this potential will require action by the Indian and Pakistani governments, by Kashmiris on both sides of the LoC, *and* by the international community.

The initiatives that have been or are being undertaken to date and their impact (success or failure in terms of promoting peace) highlight key areas that have to be addressed in future initiatives: the importance of tackling human rights abuses; of allowing political freedom and the emergence of representative Kashmiri voices on both sides of the LoC, as the next logical step, of promoting dialogue among all parties; of providing jobs and economic development to the peoples of IJK and AJK; and of continuing the current peace process between India and Pakistan (ensuring Kashmiri participation). These factors might vary somewhat in the degree of priority—human rights abuses clearly come first—but all are important for resolving the Kashmir problem.

While the onus to ensure the above is on all parties, their specific responsibilities will vary depending on their role.

Actions to Be Taken by New Delhi

The Indian government is perhaps in the best position to bring about change in IJK and to promote peace there as well as across the LoC. The right policies and signals from New Delhi could persuade Kashmiri Muslims to give up their demands for secession. As seen, successive governments have launched positive initiatives—elections, dialogue with Kashmiri groups, economic development, etc.—which are a definite move in the right direction. New Delhi needs to sustain these initiatives and implement them more fully.

In particular, it needs to be more vigorous in tackling human rights abuses: repealing repressive legislation, conducting genuine investigations of past abuses, taking punitive action against the guilty parties, and allowing human rights organizations to operate in the state. These measures will only win Kashmiri hearts and minds if they are accompanied by a change in the "face of India" in IJK: an overall reduction in the military presence there, and replacement of the notorious paramilitary and other forces by new forces with clean, unbloodied hands. Improving human rights is one ingredient in the prescription to improve the lives of ordinary Kashmiris; another is fulfilling its pledges on economic investment—developing the state's infrastructure, promoting economic growth, and creating jobs. A third is restoring Article 370 autonomy (or at least a measure of this) and genuine political freedom in the state.

Dispute resolution can only come about through dialogue with *all* Kashmiri groups (denying access to the negotiating table encourages militancy and the resort to violence), with Pakistan, and, by fostering civil society movements, among different communities in IJK. Note that in addressing the grievances of Kashmiri Muslims in IJK, the Indian government must also address those of non-Muslim minorities.

Actions to Be Taken by Islamabad

If India is in the best position to promote change in Kashmir, Pakistan is not far behind. As discussed above, Pakistan has already been able to achieve a reduction in violence in the region. For long-term peace, the Pakistani government must continue the policies of no support for Kashmiri militants and of curbing infiltration across the LoC. And it must continue the dialogue process with India. Islamabad has similar responsibilities with regard to AJK as New Delhi does to IJK. It has to reduce its control of the state, promote political freedom, and allow AJK governments to run their own affairs. Again, as with India and IJK, these moves must be accompanied by economic investment, development, and good governance. In the longer term, Pakistan needs to address the constitutional status of AJK and the Northern Areas and to ensure that any arrangement reflects the wishes of residents.

Actions to Be Taken by Kashmiris

Kashmiris are without doubt the biggest victims in the Kashmir dispute. While India and Pakistan can do much to relieve their suffering, the Kashmiris can also do much to help themselves.

In IJK specifically, Kashmiri Muslims have to give up militancy. In the post–September 11 environment it is an approach that will never work; indeed, it will only damage their cause, and it brings about the most suffering to their own people. The second major responsibility for Kashmiris on both sides of the LoC is to work for the emergence of representative political groups to speak on their behalf—in AJK with Islamabad, in IJK with

New Delhi. Kashmiri political leaders have to resolve their internal differences and evolve a common platform. That is a precondition for effective dialogue with Islamabad and New Delhi, particularly on the future status of Jammu and Kashmir. In the case of IJK, particular effort must be made to promote dialogue and reconciliation among various communities and groups.

Kashmiris should encourage the current Indo-Pak peace process and take advantage of the new opportunities for cross-LoC contact (for example, the bus service). The large Kashmiri diaspora in Britain, the United States, and other countries can also play a role by cutting off support for militant groups, promoting dialogue processes, and funding development in AJK and IJK.

Actions to Be Taken by the International Community

While the onus for carrying forward internal peace processes rests with India, Pakistan, and the Kashmiris, the international community can play a significant role. It can pressure Islamabad and New Delhi to address the grievances of Kashmiris in their respective parts of Kashmir; it can provide financial and other support for development initiatives in AJK and IJK; and it can offer support to carry forward the dialogue between India and Pakistan and among Kashmiris.

Conclusion

This chapter has highlighted the importance of resolving internal issues in AJK and IJK among Kashmiris and between the Pakistani and Indian governments respectively. It has explained the benefits in terms of reduced suffering for Kashmiris and improved chances for resolution of the "international" Kashmir dispute between India and Pakistan in taking this approach.

The chapter has also shown the efforts made in recent years to address these issues. As indicated, they have been far more substantive (at least in terms of effort) on the IJK side than on the AJK side. But a key weakness in these efforts has been lack of implementation—that is, a failure to translate laudable rhetoric into concrete action. Despite the relative lack of success to date, there remains considerable potential for internal peace processes to make progress and for there to be a marked improvement in the situation of ordinary Kashmiris on both sides of the LoC. In order to realize this potential, there is a need for actions to be taken by a range of diverse actors: the Indian and Pakistani governments, Kashmiris in AJK, Kashmiri Muslims and non-Muslims in IJK, the international community, and so on.

Is the potential for peace and resolution of internal issues likely to be realized? Optimism is encouraged by the ongoing peace process between India and Pakistan, by the growing signs of pragmatism among Kashmiri Muslims in IJK (especially after September 11), and by the growing realization on the part of IJK and central Indian governments that they need to address long-standing grievances of the Kashmiris. Various other factors, however, urge caution. These include continued resistance to peace initiatives by hard-liners on both sides of the LoC and in India and Pakistan; the record of past peace processes between India and Pakistan that have ended in failure; the failure by Islamabad to acknowledge, let alone address, grievances of Kashmiris on its side of the LoC; and the difficulties inherent in trying to get coordinated action from diverse, multiple actors. Weighing up these factors, one can only conclude that the potential for resolution of internal issues in AJK and IJK definitely exists, but its realization is by no means certain.

A final and very relevant question concerns the extent to which progress on internal issues in AJK and IJK is dependent on progress in the international peace process between India and Pakistan. The latter is clearly having a positive effect on the former, particularly in IJK, where the reduction in conflict has paved the way for Indian and state governments to address Kashmiri grievances. But will the opposite occur if India and Pakistan resume hostilities? Given that Pakistan will still be under immense international pressure not to support militant groups, even if the peace process collapses, Islamabad is unlikely to resume backing Kashmiri militants. The conflict in IJK will therefore remain at its current relatively low level. Furthermore, many of the actions that the Indian and state governments need to take in IJK to promote peace are quite independent of Pakistan: addressing human rights abuses, promoting economic development, allowing political freedom, and so on. These actions can be taken irrespective of the state of Indo-Pak relations. The same is even more true of Pakistan and AJK: The steps it must take there have nothing (at least as far as immediate steps such as political freedom are concerned) to do with India.

Ultimately, however, peace in the region will depend on resolution of *all* Kashmir disputes: internal and international. Progress on the former will undoubtedly help the latter. That is why it is so important to continue the struggle for peace *on all fronts.*

Notes

1. While the reasons for the internal conflict in IJK relate primarily to Kashmir's Muslim population, other communities have been greatly impacted and drawn into the conflict. It should also be noted that "Kashmiri Muslim" refers to the religious identity of those fighting against Indian rule: It does not imply that they form a single, unified entity.

2. See Roger McGinty, "The Irish Peace Process: Background Briefing," 1998, http://cain.ulst.ac.uk/events/peace/bac.htm; Michael Cox, Adrian Guelke, and Fiona Stephen, eds., *A Farewell to Arms? From "Long War" to Long Peace in Northern Ireland* (Manchester: Manchester University Press, 2000); C. Gilligan and J. Tonge, eds., *Peace or War? Understanding the Peace Process in Northern Ireland* (Ashgate: Aldershot, 1997).

3. This issue would appear to have been resolved by the IRA's 28 July 2005 statement, in which it ordered a formal end to the armed campaign, told volunteers to use exclusively peaceful means, and authorized a representative to engage with the Independent International Commission on Decommissioning to complete the process to put its arms verifiably beyond use.

4. For discussions of these grievances, see the chapters by Kaur and Asif in the present volume.

5. See, for example, Sumit Ganguly, *The Crisis in Kashmir: Portents of War, Hopes of Peace* (Cambridge: Cambridge University Press, 1997).

6. "[I]t is my government's wish that, as soon as law and order have been restored in Kashmir, and her soil cleared of the invader, the question of accession should be settled by reference to the people." Governor-General Mountbatten, 27 October 1947, India Office Library Records, L/P&S/13/1854B, pp. 497–498. That pledge was reiterated by Gopalaswami Ayangar on 17 October 1949: "[T]he Government of India . . . have committed themselves to the position that an opportunity would be given to the people of the state to decide for themselves whether they will remain with the Republic or wish to go out of it." Cited in M. J. Akbar, *Kashmir: Behind the Vale* (New Delhi: Viking, 1991), p. 136.

7. PM Atal Bihari Vajpayee's New Year's Eve message on 31 December 2002 called on Pakistan to accept that the state of Jammu and Kashmir was an integral part of India and would always remain so; see BBC News Online, http://bbc.co.uk/2/hi/south_asia/2617253.stm. Vajpayee's successor as PM, Manmohan Singh, reiterated the same point: "India will not accept any further partition of the country on religious lines. I also do not have the mandate for allowing the redrawing of boundaries." "India Seeks 'Borderless' Kashmir," BBC News Online, http://news.bbc.co.uk/2/hi/south_asia/4594061.stm.

8. Article 370 gave Jammu and Kashmir a special status and limited the powers of the federal government to three areas: defense, external affairs, and communications; everything else would be decided by the J&K government. See Alastair Lamb, *Kashmir: A Disputed Legacy, 1846–1990* (Karachi: Oxford University Press, 1991), pp. 190–192.

9. For example, in May 1954 the Lok Sabha was empowered to legislate on a wider range of subjects than those listed in Article 370; in 1958 the Indian Administrative Service and police were authorized to function in the state. See Iffat Malik, *Kashmir: Ethnic Conflict, International Dispute* (Karachi: Oxford University Press, 2002), pp. 108–110.

10. Praveen Swami, "The Long Haul," *Frontline* 19, no. 16 (3–16 August 2002).

11. Ibid. It should be noted, however, that in order to form a coalition government (the NDA), it had to give up this demand.

12. The Kashmiri Pandits Convention at Jammu in December 1991 adopted a resolution calling for "Establishment of a 'Homeland' for the Kashmiri Hindus in the Kashmir Valley, comprising the regions of the Valley to the East and North of the River Jhelum. . . . The 'Homeland' be placed under the Central administration with a Union Territory status, so that it evolves its own economic and political infrastruc-

ture." D. P. Kumar, *Kashmir: Return to Democracy* (New Delhi: Cosmo, 1996), pp. 80–81.

13. E.g., "Syed Ali Gillani, the Kashmiri leader whose views are closest to the mood in Kashmir and Islamabad, has rejected the autonomy option, vowing to 'oppose it tooth and nail.' . . . This proposal . . . is also unacceptable to the major militant Kashmiri groups whose participation is vital to any solution." *Nation*, 27 November 2004.

14. Swami, "The Long Haul."

15. New Delhi feared that the creation of provinces along communal lines would encourage the formation of a Muslim state within IJK. For details see Swami, "The Long Haul."

16. Notably, the National Conference subscribes to this view. See the chapter by Kaur in this volume.

17. International Crisis Group, *India/Pakistan Relations and Kashmir: Steps Towards Peace*, ICG Asia Report No. 79, Brussels and Islamabad, 24 June 2004, p. 7.

18. "India Suggests Greater Autonomy for Kashmir," *Washington Post*, 25 November 2004.

19. Militant opposition to elections was manifested, for example, in the assassination of Wali Mohammed Yatoo, a National Conference leader and former speaker of the state assembly in March 1994, and the attempted assassination of Farooq Abdullah and Rajesh Pilot during a visit to IJK in the same month.

20. "Throughout Kashmir Valley, systematic use of intimidation and vote-rigging was carried out by Indian authorities. . . . Everywhere . . . the story was the same: Indian soldiers and police forced the Kashmiris to vote. It was a fraud of careless transparency and brutality." Tim McGirk, "Kashmiris Vote at the Point of Indian Guns," *Independent*, 24 May 1996. See also "Indian Guns Force Kashmir Voters to the Ballot Box," *Times*, 24 May 1996, and "Spoiled Ballot?" *The Economist*, 11 November 1996.

21. The BJP government first appointed Planning Commission Chairman K. C. Pant as its mediator with the Kashmiris in April 2001. Pant tried to persuade Kashmiri groups to come to the negotiating table but failed to overcome their objections. He was replaced by N. N. Vohra in 2003.

22. APHC Chairman Abdul Ghani Bhat, "Kashmiri Separatists Snub Peace Offer," BBC News Online, http://news.bbc.co.uk/2/hi/south_asia/1298464.stm.

23. BBC News Online, http://news.bbc.co.uk/2/hi/south_asia/1347431.stm.

24. "Kashmir Truce Inflames Rival Rebel Groups," *Guardian*, 31 July 2000.

25. "93 Dead in Kashmir Massacres," *Guardian*, 3 August 2000.

26. "After the first few years of militancy, by 1992–93 or so, I had come to realise the futility and destructiveness of armed struggle as a means to achieve our ends in Kashmir. I had also seen through Pakistan's game, which was to exploit us for its own ends. Once clear about both these issues I decided to come overground. . . . For me the gun was out forever." Firdous Syed, "Sharing Dreams," symposium, "Frameworks for Peace," December 2000, http://www.india-seminar.com/2000/496.htm.

27. International Crisis Group, "Kashmir: The View from Srinagar," ICG Asia Report No. 41, 21 November 2002, Brussels.

28. See, for example, Patricia Gossman, *The Human Rights Crisis in Kashmir* (New York: Human Rights Watch, 1993); and Sir William Goldhart et al., *Human Rights in Kashmir* (Geneva: International Commission of Jurists, 1995).

29. Other controversial legislation includes the Jammu and Kashmir Public

Safety Act of 1978, which allows detainees to be held for up to two years without trial; the Jammu and Kashmir Disturbed Areas Act of 1990, which allows relatively low-ranking security personnel to shoot anyone suspected of disturbing public order; and the Armed Forces Special Powers Act, which effectively gives the security forces a free hand to use force.

30. The National Human Rights Commission (NHRC) was set up in 1993 to address domestic and international concerns about human rights violations. In 1997 a State Human Rights Commission (SHRC) was set up in IJK, specifically to examine human rights issues in the state. Neither the NHRC nor the SHRC has the authority to investigate allegations of abuse by the army and paramilitary forces. These are investigated by the security forces themselves. This is a far from effective process, as noted by the *Indian Express*: "It has been noted that poor investigation and the often deliberate destruction of evidence have allowed many who are guilty of massacres, torture and rape to get away unscathed, or very lightly even when they are brought to book." "Blot on the BSF," *Indian Express*, 23 April 2002.

31. For the full text of the Common Minimum Program, see the official website of the Jammu and Kashmir government, http://jammukashmir.nic.in/govt/welcome.html.

32. See Parvez Imroze, "India's Civil Society Has Failed Kashmiri Society," *Communalism Combat*, 10th Anniversary Issue, August–September 2003.

33. ICG, *Steps Towards Peace*, p. 7.

34. Any NGO that receives foreign funding must register under the Foreign Contribution (Regulation) Act 1976, originally passed to block money coming in from extremist Islamic groups and to curtail the activities of Christian missionaries. Registration under the FCRA is a lengthy and costly process and limits NGOs to receiving funds in a single account—something that becomes problematic for NGOs with geographically spread-out operations. FCRA also covers payments for visits abroad.

35. The Conference on Strengthening Peace Initiatives in Kashmir was called off after the Nepali government cancelled visas of participants and the German government withdrew funding—both under pressure from New Delhi.

36. Participants considered the December 2004 meeting effective. Some Kashmiris considered the Indians too heavy-handed in denying travel permission to some separatist leaders. Details of the meeting have been available on the Pugwash website, http://www.pugwash.org.

37. In 1991–1992 the BJP launched its *Ekta Yatra* (Unity March). Starting in Kanyakumar, at the southernmost tip of India, the plan was to end the march on Republic Day (26 January) with the raising of the Indian tricolor in Lal Chowk, Srinagar. The cry throughout the 1,400 km journey was *"Chalo Kashmir! Karpom Kashmir!"* (Forward to Kashmir! Save Kashmir!). Specifically with reference to BJP support for Kashmiri Pandits, Rita Manchanda writes that the BJP and its ally the RSS have "by politically appropriating the issue of Kashmiri Hindu refugees transformed an agitation against the central government into one of Muslim fundamentalists against a Hindu state." "Playing with Fire," *Far Eastern Economic Review*, 26 September 1990, p. 34.

38. See, for example, Joan Nelson, "Poverty, Inequality and Conflict in Developing Countries," http://www.rbf.org/pdf/poverty.pdf, and Rasheed Draman, "Poverty and Conflict in Africa: Explaining a Complex Relationship," http://www.parlcent.ca/povertyreduction/seminar1_e.pdf.

39. In the 1980s Kashmiris actually enjoyed a better standard of living than their parents and grandparents, but the rise in living standards was exceeded by the

rise in expectations brought on by increased literacy and education levels and greater awareness of developments outside IJK. Growing numbers of graduates found there were no suitable jobs for them—a situation exacerbated by the blatant discrimination in government employment favoring Hindus—and they were not prepared to do the kinds of manual labor jobs their parents and grandparents had done. See Iffat Malik, *Kashmir*, pp. 164–166, for elaboration.

40. G. M. Sadiq once complained to Indira Gandhi: "If I were to tell you that the law and order situation requires one more division of the army, you would send it, without the blink of an eye, but if I ask you to set up two factories you will tell me twenty reasons why it cannot be done." Cited in Victoria Schofield, *Kashmir in the Crossfire* (London: I. B. Tauris, 1996), p. 208. See Malik, *Kashmir,* pp. 161–164, for elaboration of India's economic policy toward IJK.

41. Speech at the 50th National Development Council Meeting, New Delhi, 21 December 2002, cited in ICG, "Steps Towards Peace," p. 13.

42. Official figures put the turnout at 46 percent, from a total of 5.6 million eligible voters. "Kashmir Assembly Elections," BBC News Online, http://news.bbc.co.uk/2/hi/south_asia/2249016.stm.

43. "Civic Polls: Reassertion of Democratic Process," *Daily Excelsior,* 18 February 2005.

44. See Roger Ballard, "Kashmir Crisis: View from Mirpur," *Economic and Political Weekly*, 2–9 March 1991. Ballard notes that "the level of expenditure on rural development . . . has long been a good deal lower in Azad Kashmir than in the rest of Pakistan." The only major investment by Islamabad was on the Mangla Dam, which provided benefits to Pakistan rather than to AJK, where it caused considerable uprooting and resentment.

45. In a speech on 12 January 2002, President Musharraf declared: "No organizations will be able to carry out terrorism under the pretext of Kashmir. . . . whoever is involved with such acts will be dealt with strongly whether they are from inside or outside of the country." "Musharraf Declares War on Extremism," BBC News Online, 12 January 2002, http://news.bbc.co.uk/2/hi/south_asia/1756865.stm.

46. The two groups banned in January 2002 were Lashkar-e-Taiba and Jaish-e-Mohammad. In November 2003 the Musharraf government banned a further three groups, one of them the renamed Jaish-e-Mohammad.

47. "Vajpayee Says Kashmir 'Improved,'" BBC News Online, 18 March 2002, http://news.bbc.co.uk/2/hi/south_asia/1879326.stm.

48. "Big Drop in Kashmir Violence," BBC News Online, 29 December 2003, http://news.bbc.co.uk/2/hi/south_asia/3353871.stm.

49. Notably, the Muttahida Jihad Council, comprising eleven armed groups, announced that it would not oppose the bus service on the grounds that it would "benefit the ordinary people of held Kashmir." "Kashmir's Council Backs Bus Service," *Dawn,* 17 March 2005.

14

Kashmir:
From Persistence to Progress?

Cyrus Samii

The peace process between India and Pakistan since January 2004 has piqued hopes for resolving the Kashmir conflict. Such a resolution would be a dramatic accomplishment indeed. As the chapters in this volume detail, J&K has been a continual bone of contention, the object of three wars, and a theater of engagement in a fourth war between the two countries.[1] Decades of heavy-handed and corrupt rule by New Delhi and state politicians spawned a violent separatist struggle in India-administered Jammu and Kashmir (IJK) in 1989. The uprising has been fueled by the heightened political awareness of a new generation of Kashmiris[2] and the material support from Pakistan. The insurgency has dragged on, fragmenting politically and becoming increasingly consumed by "jihadist" violence. The bombings, clashes with Indian military and paramilitary forces, and other violence claimed at least forty thousand lives by 2005.[3]

Drawing on the views presented in this volume, this conclusion chapter will examine three themes relevant to resolving the conflict: (1) the contours of the post–January 2004 opportunity that has arisen for resolving the conflict; (2) the sources of the conflict's intractability that would have to be addressed to realize this opportunity; and (3) the elements of a workable framework for creating a positive dynamic, including steps that could be taken by the international community. Rather than addressing the causes of the *onset* of conflict, the approach here will be to address the causes of the conflict's *persistence*. This is most appropriate for the Kashmir case, because the dynamics as of 2005 are quite distinct from those of 1989–1990. The conflict itself has brought about important societal transformations in IJK,[4] and Pakistan and India have been affected by important changes domestically and internationally.[5]

225

An Opportunity at Hand?

The Indo-Pak peace process was formally restarted in the form of a "composite dialogue" through a joint press statement issued at the end of the January 2004 SAARC summit in Islamabad. In the statement, Indian prime minister Atal Bihari Vajpayee and Pakistani president Pervez Musharraf expressed confidence "that the resumption of the composite dialogue will lead to peaceful settlement of all bilateral issues, including Jammu and Kashmir, to the satisfaction of both sides."[6] The Islamabad declaration came after seven years of sporadic attempts at peace interspersed with bouts of turmoil, and there was good reason for skepticism about the chances for resolving the Kashmir conflict.[7]

But by mid-2005, some tangible developments provided grounds for optimism. India and Pakistan sustained cooperation by maintaining a November 2003- declared cease-fire along the LoC, reopening cross-LoC transport links, and moving further than ever toward ending their long-standing and costly military standoff on the Siachen Glacier in J&K. As a result, Kashmiris were given new opportunities to restore cross-LoC ties and rehabilitate shell-fire-damaged areas along the LoC in IJK and in Pakistan-administered Azad Jammu and Kashmir (AJK).[8] Violence remained a regular occurrence within Muslim-majority areas of IJK, but compared with the previous years, events in 2005 were in line with a diminishing trend in violence since 2001.[9] Levels of infiltration by militants coming across the LoC into IJK also dropped significantly.[10] The most striking display of the new cooperative spirit was the 7 April 2005 start of a regular bus service connecting IJK's summer capital, Srinagar, to AJK's capital, Muzaffarabad.[11]

Bilateral Progress

Domestic political volatility in India and Pakistan has made past peace processes between them fragile. Progress in addressing the Kashmir conflict has suffered as a result. But the process begun in January 2004 was thrown off course neither by an election and government change in India nor by a legitimacy crisis in Pakistan. For New Delhi, the Congress-led United Progressive Alliance (UPA) government, elected into office in May 2004, continued the composite dialogue with Pakistan without delay and with vigor, suggesting that normalization with Pakistan suits interests across the Indian political spectrum.[12] Even if developments between New Delhi and IJK have not moved as quickly, a willingness to work cooperatively with Islamabad has provided a foundation for progress in addressing the Kashmir conflict.[13]

In the past, Pakistani political leaders have used rhetorical or genuine confrontation with India to overcome legitimacy crises at home.[14] There are reasons to be hopeful that this dynamic is no longer relevant. In a domestic row that followed President Musharraf's decision to renege on a commitment to resign his army post in late 2004, he did not abandon the peace process. Rather, if there was any link between the two developments, it seemed to be that Musharraf profited from the public's sense that the peace process could be delivered *only if* he were to retain his position at the helm of the army. The Musharraf government's energetic pursuit of the peace process with India seems to be on the basis of lessons learned and deep, long-term interests. The acquisition of nuclear weapons—covertly by the late 1980s and overtly as of May 1998—may have shored up Pakistan's confidence vis-à-vis India and nullified the logic of confrontation stemming from resentment toward India's regional hegemony.[15] The inability to win any concessions from India in the Kargil episode, an outcome consolidated by US diplomatic intervention, may have taught Pakistan's military and foreign policy establishment the limits of their ability to exploit the nuclear "balance of terror" to their advantage. Pakistani leaders, including in the military, may realize that poor relations with India cost Pakistan more economically and in terms of international reputation than the conflict costs India. India's economy and international position have risen respectably, while Pakistan has fallen behind on both counts. The continuation of these trends would erode Musharraf's reputation as an effective leader—a sore price indeed for a man looking to secure his legacy.

These underlying developments gave rise to the successful April 2005 summit between Musharraf and Indian prime minister Manmohan Singh. At the end of the summit, the two leaders issued a statement describing the peace process as "irreversible."[16] In remarks delivered during the course of the summit, Musharraf declared that India and Pakistan had arrived at the defining moment in the peace process and that the time had come to consider settlement options.[17] Leaders of the political opposition in India, including former prime minister Atal Bihari Vajpayee, criticized the UPA's strategy in the peace process, but they did not protest the goals.[18] Skillful diplomatic spadework laid the foundation for the successful summit, distinguishing it from past failures like the 2001 Agra summit.[19]

Positive Dynamics in IJK and AJK

These tangible developments and improvements in Indo-Pak relations came about as major Kashmiri protagonists began to show new enthusiasm for working toward peace. Within IJK, moderate leaders in the All Parties Hurriyat Conference (APHC), the most prominent separatist political body, have sought to engage with Islamabad and New Delhi and have carried out campaigns to forge a Kashmiri consensus. In the wake of the April 2005 Indo-Pak summit, an APHC delegation made a June 2005 trip to the

Pakistani side of the LoC to meet Pakistani and AJK-based Kashmiri leaders. The trip opened a new chapter, because the APHC had for a long time set such a meeting in Pakistan as a precondition for entering into dialogue with New Delhi. In meetings with activists and political leaders, members of the delegation countenanced, if not actively promoted, discussion of settlement options that would not involve significant territorial transfers between India and Pakistan or full reunification and independence for J&K.[20] The trip came amid appeals by some of its membership to be brought into the peace process. Members of the moderate APHC faction, including the current chairman, Mirwaiz Umar Farooq, have made increasingly vocal appeals for Kashmiri involvement in a settlement process. The Jammu and Kashmir Liberation Front (JKLF) leader and one-time armed militant Yasin Malik had recently concluded a grassroots signature campaign calling for Kashmiris to be included in any peace talks.

These APHC members' willingness to negotiate has come after a partial revival of democratic politics in IJK.[21] In 2002, IJK state assembly elections ushered in a People's Democratic Party (PDP)–Congress Party governing coalition, as power was democratically transferred away from the National Conference party. Turnout was low in Srinagar and in other parts of the Kashmir Valley, the areas where alienation with New Delhi runs the highest. Reports of intimidation by Indian and paramilitary forces as well as by militants added to the perception that the election was not truly free.[22] But a silver lining was visible. The elections allowed everyone in the state to witness the democratic change in leadership. The IJK state and Indian union government's fair recording of the low turnout figures ironically demonstrated some degree of credibility in the elections process. In January and February 2005, municipal elections were held in IJK after a twenty-seven-year lapse. These municipal elections saw remarkably high turnout in many regions, even where separatist sentiments have run high.[23] A majority of Kashmiris seemed to place pragmatism above separatist dogma. In civil society too, as Kaur details in her chapter, democratic space has been preserved despite the violence, with professional, student, and religious associations having continually held elections throughout the past fifteen years. The 2002 and 2005 outcomes may represent a creeping advance in restoring the credibility of democracy in IJK. Such a restoration would help to push to the background the legacy of electoral connivances by New Delhi and corrupted IJK politicians.[24] Electoral gains by the PDP have forced the separatist leaders, including in the APHC, to address Kashmiris' day-to-day concerns more directly.

Finally, in AJK as well there are some hopeful signs. Sardar Qayyum Khan, former AJK prime minister and a prominent political figure, has stated that in his estimation, the time for violent militancy has ended, and that a "soft LoC" might serve as the basis for a solution.[25] Syed Salahuddin, the supreme leader of the prominent Kashmiri militant group Hizbul Mujahidin, based in AJK, has in the past hinted at willingness to engage in a political process, even if his remarks following the April 2005 summit and June 2005 APHC delegation visit were far from conciliatory.[26] But after the July 2005 London terrorist attacks, international pressure rose to new levels on the Pakistani government to dismantle the militant networks operating out of AJK. Finally, in addition to the June 2005 delegation visit, occasional meetings among prominent political and civil society leaders from IJK, AJK, India, and Pakistan have helped to achieve some cross-LoC political coordination.[27] Nonetheless, Srinagar-Muzaffarabad relations may be the most underdeveloped of the diplomatic axes relevant to a settlement.

Sources of Intractability

It may be banal to speak of history as a sequence of opportunities seized or not seized and challenges met or not met. But such is the nature of the moment that has arisen since January 2004. The opportunity that has come about could easily fade if the sources of the Kashmir conflict's intractability are not addressed.

The chapters in this volume have helped to illuminate a number of problems that have contributed to the conflict's persistence. This persistence is manifested in the heightened risk of escalation in the Indo-Pak dispute and the low-intensity war in IJK since 1989. Some of the problems have to do with the type of attention paid to the issue, while other problems derive from Kashmiri leaders' inability to organize to advance collective Kashmiri interests in the peace process. However, even if proper attention is paid and Kashmiris can effectively organize, mistrust and fear still create formidable obstacles to lasting peace. The following section will elaborate on the relevant dynamics.

War as the Only Means

For both India and Pakistan, political engagement has been either desultory or weak and has provided little strategic guidance. New Delhi has not formed a coherent strategy for winning over a critical mass of separatists, relying instead on forcefully suppressing their mobilization. As Chari points out in his chapter, governments in New Delhi have shown little patience for proper political dialogue, frequently changing interlocutors and demanding impossibly immediate results from them in negotiations with separatist leaders. The reason for this approach, it seems, is that Indian strategists are captive to views that downplay Kashmiris as agents in the conflict. Official, amateur, and mainstream media analyses regularly take the Kashmir conflict to be a Pakistan-driven proxy war first and foremost, and such analyses tend to disregard the uniqueness of IJK's terms of association with the Indian union.[28] They also downplay how governments in New Delhi and IJK eroded IJK's special political status through means that violate both the spirit of IJK's terms of accession and any norms of democracy or proper judicial review.[29] The issue of restoring IJK's special status is often confused (perhaps intentionally) with the debate over the legitimacy of India's and Pakistan's competing claims to the whole of J&K.[30]

Civilian and military leaders in Pakistan have often not seen eye to eye on strategies for dealing with Kashmir, with the military usually winning out. The most spectacular episode remains the Kargil conflict, which forced the collapse of the 1999 peace process. The reasoning for the military's dominance over Kashmir policy may have to do with the benefits that the military has derived from the persistence of the Kashmir conflict. Indeed, the Pakistani military could be said to have actually *depended* on the persistence of the conflict. As the major element of tension vis-à-vis India, the conflict can justify the military's absorption of about a quarter of the central government budget as well as its control of other parts of the foreign policy.[31] Also, in a manner that mirrors the situation for IJK, AJK's autonomy was provided for at the time of partition. But, as Asif describes in her chapter, throughout the postpartition period, Pakistani governments have directly controlled AJK's political and economic affairs, suppressed political mobilization by pro-independence groups, and appeared unwilling to entertain any complaints about their heavy-handedness in AJK.

That a coercion-intensive, military-driven approach has been inadequate for addressing the Kashmir conflict is clear. The Indian deployment to IJK has been among the largest operational deployments of military forces since World War II, with deployment strengths of at least 250,000–500,000 army and paramilitary forces since 1990.[32] But despite the attrition of many militant leaders, Indian armed forces have not been able to defeat the militants. Neither in AJK has Pakistan silenced pro-independence parties, even if they have not turned to arms against the state. Finally, whether explicitly backed by Pakistan or not, neither can the militants claim any major successes aside from their ability to simply survive.

Kashmiri Political Fragmentation

Kashmiri separatist leaders unanimously state that there can be no end to the conflict until Kashmiris are given a seat at the negotiating table along with New Delhi and Islamabad. But the occupant of that "seat" remains to be determined. As Kaur's chapter in this volume illustrates, politics in the Kashmir Valley and other Muslim-majority areas in IJK is marked by gamesmanship, fleeting alliances of convenience, and personality politics.

Institutionalized means for aggregating collective Kashmiri political interests have been elusive.

This fragmentation has partly resulted from interference by New Delhi and Islamabad, as each has sought to secure its own strategic interests within IJK. By colluding with Farooq Abdullah to use politically motivated detentions and intimidation to guarantee a favorable outcome in 1987 IJK state elections, the Rajiv Gandhi–led government in New Delhi alienated a generation of Kashmiris from democratic politics. The temporary suspension of democracy in the state in January 1990 and the subsequent horrors committed during the New Delhi–directed governor's rule further deepened the alienation.[33] Even if New Delhi's political approach became more sophisticated by 1991, Kashmiris' attempts to reconstitute themselves politically continued to be blocked. New Delhi's absolute intolerance for separatist political mobilization manifested itself through questionable detentions, custodial executions, and torture. Paramilitary units, including brutal irregular outfits composed of "turned" militants, have been among the agents of New Delhi's coercion.[34] Up to the June 2005 APHC delegation visit to Pakistan, governments in New Delhi have restricted the movement of Kashmiri separatist leaders in IJK and internationally.

Pakistani support for militants in IJK has also obstructed the Kashmiri political organization. Such support has aimed at preventing a critical mass of political groups in IJK from reaching a "separate peace" with New Delhi. Militants have been supported in operations to assassinate and intimidate political figures to prevent them from moving toward such a settlement. In the run-up to the 2002 elections, moderate APHC member Abdul Ghani Lone was assassinated, robbing IJK of a venerated broker between hard-liners and moderates.[35] Other less prominent political actors have suffered the brunt of such coercion. The 2005 municipal elections produced a humiliating spectacle in which many victorious candidates, targeted by militants' threats, resigned before taking up their seats and publicly apologized for participating in the elections.[36] In addition, Pakistani support has aimed at weakening independence-oriented militants and empowering militants favoring accession to Pakistan. The withdrawal of Pakistani support to the independence-minded JKLF in the mid-1990s and the subsequent support to the Pakistan-leaning Hizbul Mujahidin were evidence of this.[37]

Opinion research in IJK has demonstrated that a large majority of Kashmiris prefer independence as a final status objective over either further integration with India or accession to Pakistan. A large majority of respondents also favor negotiation as the sole means for achieving a settlement.[38] Thus, Pakistani-supported militancy has obstructed the organization of political will *on the basis of the majority interests within IJK*. The result is dissociation between the political aspirations of most Kashmiris and the insurgency ostensibly being fought on their behalf. These circumstances also explain why strategists in Pakistan, presumably associated with the Inter-Services Intelligence Agency (ISI), would support the militancy. Since Pakistan cannot rely on a critical mass of people in IJK to do its bidding, it is left only with the option of empowering a minority to impose a pro-Pakistan line.

Aside from interference by New Delhi and Islamabad, Kashmiri political coordination has also been undermined by local-level political gamesmanship, leading to the collapse of institutions for aggregating Kashmiri interests. Herein lies the root of what might be called the "Kashmiri ownership" problem. Since the outbreak of the uprising in 1989, politics among Kashmiris has undergone a steady process of "de-institutionalization."[39] By the 1990s, a reputation for corrupt opportunism finally caught up with the once paramount National Conference (NC), reducing it to a mere shell. Marginal Kashmiri political actors had come to the fore by that time, including the parties of the Muslim United Front (MUF), which convened to run candidates against the NC in the 1987 elections. Having been thwarted in their electoral bids, many from the MUF joined in the 1989 uprising either as part of the JKLF-led militancy or as separatist activists. The unity of purpose would not last. Feeling the squeeze from Indian counterinsurgency forces and Pakistan's intensified support to select pro-Pakistan militants, a number of former MUF leaders organized in 1993 to pursue a political strategy through the APHC. Other groups, with Pakistan's support, continued with the militancy; the most prominent has been the Hizbul Mujahidin.

But the political actors of the APHC were, and continue to be, severely constrained in their ability to forward collective Kashmiri interests. The APHC parties, for example, are tied to their long-nonnegotiable separatist demands. In seeking to engage with the peace process, APHC leaders run the risk of losing face and acquiring politically costly reputations as "opportunists." In addition, the APHC has always functioned as more of a forum than a unitary political force.[40] The current factionalization of the APHC is evidence of this lack of unity of purpose.[41] Finally, the APHC does not seem to have commanded the allegiance of a broad enough segment of the population to serve as the sole representative of Muslims in IJK and AJK, with the PDP and National Conference having attracted significant numbers of votes in the 2002 and 2005 elections.[42] This is in addition to the strong opposition the APHC faces from non-Muslims in Jammu and Ladakh. The APHC is not alone in suffering from such limits to political effectiveness. The Islamic-nationalist Hizbul Mujahidin and more jihadist and transnational groups associated with Lashkar-e-Taiba and Jaish-e-Mohammad function more like loose, horizontally structured networks than coherent political organizations. The JKLF has been split since Amanullah Khan's

AJK-based faction parted ways with Yasin Malik's IJK-based faction after Malik renounced violence in the mid-1990s.[43]

Kashmiri political fragmentation is a fundamental obstacle to negotiations necessary to bring about a political resolution. New Delhi and Islamabad are tempted to evade genuine negotiations and seek advantage by playing Kashmiri factions off of each other. New Delhi and Islamabad also have reasons to be skeptical about whether any moderate Kashmiri leaders could implement an agreement over threats from militants or accusations of "opportunism" by political rivals. Such dynamics of fragmentation are common to protracted conflicts.[44]

Layered Commitment Problems

Even if Kashmiris manage to organize politically and New Delhi and Islamabad give proper political attention to the conflict, mistrust and fear could still block cooperation. Layered "commitment problems" are one manifestation of such mistrust. A commitment problem is one in which a party to a proposed agreement cannot credibly commit that he or she will not renege on the agreement at some point in the future. Such commitment problems constrain parties from being able to reach cooperative agreements to manage their relations.[45] The commitment problem logic clearly prevails in the case of IJK. Because of the legacy of cynical Indian misrule in IJK, weak judicial checks on government, and the rise of a chauvinistic Hindu nationalism, Kashmiris have reason to doubt that the Indian government can credibly commit to a reasonable political agreement.[46] In 1999–2000, the National Conference–led IJK state government submitted to the National Democratic Alliance (NDA) government in New Delhi proposals for restoring many of IJK's autonomy provisions.[47] The NDA not only rejected the proposals but hinted that it would not uphold a promise by past Indian governments to consider restoring "maximum autonomy" for IJK.[48] The response only affirmed Kashmiri suspicions about New Delhi's unwillingness to compromise in good faith. Even if negotiations on autonomy are opened, can any current Indian government credibly promise that a less accommodating future government *will not* come to power and undo IJK's autonomy?

The mistrust and resulting commitment problems also descend to the regional and district levels along communal lines. Communal identity is closely correlated with autonomy preference in IJK, with Muslims typically preferring more autonomy and Hindus and Buddhists preferring less.[49] Hindus in Jammu and Buddhists in Ladakh have expressed doubt whether their interests would be protected in a more autonomous IJK, which would be dominated by Kashmiri Muslims.[50] This is exacerbated by perceptions that Islamism is on the rise among Muslims in IJK.[51] Can a current

Kashmiri leadership guarantee to the Hindus and Buddhists in IJK that Islamists *will not* play an increasingly powerful role and impose their agenda in an autonomous IJK? Such concerns have driven Hindus and Buddhists in Jammu and Ladakh to push for more regional autonomy vis-à-vis the IJK state government and to have New Delhi serve as their guarantor. The reverse holds with respect to Muslims vis-à-vis Hindus in Jammu. Hindus dominate Jammu regional politics with their slight majority, and Muslim-dominant districts in Jammu remain relatively underdeveloped.[52] In exchange for Jammu Muslims' support for increasing Jammu's autonomy, can the Hindu leaders in the region credibly promise that they will then work to provide more development opportunities to Muslims in the region? Can they promise that Jammu Muslims *will not* suffer as chauvinistic Hindu nationalism surges in Jammu?

These commitment problems make it impossible to find a workable political compromise at the New Delhi–IJK level and within IJK. Without such a compromise, legitimate public administration and the rule of law are impeded. The tensions inherent in these commitment problems lead actors to seek and seize windows of opportunity not to strike cooperative deals, but to make unilateral gains.

Fearing the Wrong Precedent

Another constraint on New Delhi's ability to find a negotiated settlement with the Kashmiri separatists is fear among Indians, whether disingenuous or not, that any appeasing moves toward IJK's independence would set the wrong precedent.[53] According to this view, militancy and terrorism would be seen as having won for separatists in IJK an exceptional concession by the Indian union. This precedent could unleash centrifugal forces, perhaps stiffening the separatist resolve in other parts of the union. The fear is especially associated with the separatist conflicts simmering in India's northeastern provinces of Nagaland and Assam. More immediately, any national party in India that makes a deal to enhance IJK's autonomy risks being branded as "too soft on terrorism." In an opposite way, any Kashmiri party that takes New Delhi's hand risks being branded "opportunistic."

Similar concerns hold for the leadership in Islamabad. Nationally, it may be true that the loss of East Pakistan/Bangladesh in the 1971 Indo-Pak war undercut Pakistan's claims to the validity of the two-nation theory, upon which the 1947 partition of the subcontinent was based. But two-nation ideology nonetheless continues to serve as a basis for legitimizing Pakistan as a Muslim state and defending against other "subnationalisms."[54] The revival of Baloch and Sindh nationalism poses some risk to Pakistan's integrity. If Islamabad were to submit to a Kashmir settlement that seemed to involve many concessions, the resulting reputation for softness could serve as fuel for such revived nationalisms. Politically, however, the Musharraf government may be less constrained by being branded as weak than as ineffective. This actually serves the process of resolving the conflict.

Militants as Unrestrained Agents in the Conflict

The violence committed by militants in IJK, and the Indian military and paramilitary forces' responses to militant provocation, introduce mayhem and suffering into the lives of millions in IJK and trap the people of India and Pakistan under the shadow of war. Militancy constricts the space in which a peace process can move forward. Militants' attacks against politicians or activists engaging in any peace process make it too risky for a critical mass of Kashmiris to come together and push the process forward. Overreaching responses by the Indian military and paramilitary forces erode the trust and goodwill needed to elicit cooperation from peace-seeking Kashmiris and other Muslims in IJK. Continued militant attacks raise suspicions within New Delhi about Pakistan's intentions given its tacit, if not overt, support to the militants.

These dramatic results are achieved despite the militants' relatively small numbers. As discussed by Kaur, Chandran, and Zeb in their chapters, the militants' numbers are estimated at between two and four thousand, with the pool of recruits (mostly based in AJK and Pakistan) estimated to be in the tens of thousands, and the moral support base in IJK, AJK, and Pakistan estimated in the hundreds of thousands.[55] With these numbers, militants launch about 1,500 attacks in IJK per year amid the massive deployments of Indian troops and paramilitary forces tasked to root them out.

For the militancy within IJK, these numbers have some important implications. First, given the immense numerical imbalance relative to Indian military and paramilitary forces, the motivation driving the average militant must be fierce—likely much stronger than the motivation driving the average soldier or paramilitary operative. As Kaur notes, militant leaders have claimed that with two thousand fighters they can keep the hundreds of thousands of Indian army and paramilitary forces engaged at a high tempo. Second, the persistence of the militancy despite this numerical imbalance is a testament to its robustness for meeting recruitment, financial, weapons-dispensing, logistics, and other material needs. Third, one should search for motivations and opportunities sustaining militancy at the microlevel and one should not necessarily rule out fringe behaviors as part of what sustains that militancy. Personal loss may stimulate a desire for revenge; adolescent anomie may stimulate an attraction to combative ideology. Any of these micromotivations may fuel the militancy.

If the shadowy activities of carrying out attacks, trafficking guns, running training camps, or gathering and conveying militancy-related intelligence can somehow be lucrative relative to other options, then those who do well out of militancy have an interest in finding ways to perpetuate it, and they will do so as long as the circumstances permit.[56] Many analyses of the conflict and circumstances in IJK, AJK, and Pakistan suggest that economic logic is indeed at work, particularly for Pakistan-based jihadist organizations.[57] This economic logic is sustained by the lack of alternative livelihood opportunities in Pakistan, AJK, and IJK. Insofar as the conflict inhibits the emergence of such alternatives, it contributes to its own perpetuation. In these conflict-distorted economies, external funding by Islamist networks and diaspora groups is also prominent in fueling the war economy. An important part of the process of ending the militancy—and thus allowing space for a settlement—would be providing alternative livelihoods for would-be militants both in IJK and on the Pakistani side of the LoC.[58]

In addition to the economics of the militancy, there is the psychological dimension. If militancy or waging jihad satisfies psychological needs of retribution or "keeping up the fight," quenches a "spiritual addiction," or bestows honor (perhaps through martyrdom), then broad political processes are unlikely to fully contain violence associated with militancy. Close examination of the lives and experiences of individual militants has revealed the significance of such psychological factors.[59] An implication here is that a political process alone may be insufficient to contain the militancy. In the short run, such militancy can only be contained by physical protective and preventive measures by police and soldiers. In the long run, local and national government, perhaps in collaboration with NGOs, will have to implement education, reconciliation, and other local-level processes to foster a temperament more conducive to peace. Such programs could be among the building blocks of a peace framework, discussed further below.

This characterization of militants as uncontrollable agents should not be carried too far. As Suba Chandran and Rizwan Zeb detail in their chapters, the militant groups vary significantly in their composition and political aims. In forming strategies for disarming or co-opting militants, New Delhi must be sensitive to these differences and distinguish between those who will only act as "spoilers" and those who can be drawn into the peace process. Islamabad must find ways to rein in the semiautonomous networks within Pakistan that indoctrinate, mobilize, finance, and arm the militants. Only then can confidence be sustained to push ahead in the peace process in the face of sporadic militant attacks.

Militancy as a Strategic Crutch in the Conflict

The militants may not be acting with the same ultimate objectives as the Pakistani leadership or the majority of Kashmiris, but the persistence of the militancy is at least partially attributable to its strategic utility to Pakistani strategists and separatists in IJK. As discussed above, pro-Pakistan militants have been Pakistan's most reliable political lever in IJK. Strategically, Pakistani support (whether tacit or explicit) helps to convince Indian strategists that Indian forces cannot impose a military solution on the Kashmir conflict. In these terms, the persistence of the militancy-induced violence in IJK can be reduced to an interaction between strategists in New Delhi and Islamabad. In considering cutting off support to the militants, Islamabad may be uncertain of New Delhi's commitment to reciprocate. Islamabad may fear that New Delhi will launch an effort to end the militancy and reach a separate peace exclusive of Islamabad. New Delhi faces a similar situation vis-à-vis Islamabad insofar as New Delhi may fear that a troop withdrawal will not be met reciprocally by Islamabad. Islamabad could support allies in IJK to use the window provided by the Indian withdrawal. With either tacit or explicit support from Islamabad, pro-Pakistan militants could use the window to expand their areas of control. New Delhi would ultimately lose ground and become more dependent on Islamabad in bringing about a settlement.

At the bilateral level, support for militancy is a way for Pakistan to balance against India's conventional military superiority. Here, too, Indo-Pak strategic logic locks in Islamabad's dependence on the militants. The security dilemma induced by the Pakistani search for strategic balance contributes to Indian strategists' continuing efforts to develop forward and offense-premised military doctrine vis-à-vis Pakistan.[60] This Indian response reinforces Pakistani strategists' interests in maintaining options for asymmetrical escalation in Kashmir. The mistrust between the Indian and Pakistani leaderships gives the militants leverage over the peace process. To the extent that militant groups in IJK feel they could be losers, they may sabotage the process with terror tactics, playing on suspicions in India about Pakistan's intentions.[61]

Even if the leadership in Pakistan wants to dismantle the militancy network, it is not clear that it could do so entirely. Many of the groups have sources of financial sustenance that are independent of the government. Such sources include ties to foreign Islamic organizations, as well as independent commercial ventures and fundraising within IJK, AJK, and Pakistan. Religious schools that support jihad are mostly funded privately and few of them register with the state, indicating a good degree of independence.[62] Also, Pakistan's security and legal apparatuses are in poor condition—underequipped, poorly managed, suffering from corruption and infiltration, and subject to intimidation by militant groups.[63] Finally, political leaders from all sides of the political spectrum are challenging President Musharraf's legitimacy, putting him in a weak position to muster the political support necessary to take on the militants and Islamists who support them.

Among Muslims in IJK, particularly in the Kashmir Valley, polls and anecdotal reports show ambivalence toward the militancy.[64] Active support may not appear to be widespread, but based on comparisons to insurgencies elsewhere, the number of active supporters needed to sustain the militancy is quite small.[65] In the Kashmiri press, attacks on soft civilian targets are generally condemned, although militant attacks against security forces are not. Such quietude is noteworthy, given that the expressed interests of the militants run counter to majority sentiments among Muslims in IJK; neither is accession to Pakistan a majority interest, nor does Islamist jihadism correspond to the types of Sufi and secular values that predominate among Muslims in IJK.[66] As with Islamabad, tacit support for militancy can be understood as a strategic crutch. An end to violence, the thinking goes, would lead New Delhi to believe that it has won, without the need to deliver any concessions.[67] Indian forces' clampdowns on peaceful modes of separatist protest make Kashmiris less willing to express disapproval of militancy. Given the investment of lives and agony in the fight for *azadi*, it may be emotionally unbearable for many Muslims in IJK to give up with nothing tangible to show at the end.

Toward a Peace Framework

The opportunities and sources of intractability described above set the terms for future steps in the peace process. Steps can be taken to consolidate already achieved gains in the peace process, particularly those associated with restoring cross-LoC ties. These actions should aim to enhance ownership by the people of IJK and AJK in bringing about normalcy to their lives. By doing so, a positive dynamic could be developed in IJK and AJK. This positive dynamic will open space to address the problems posed by Kashmiri political fragmentation, layered commitment problems in IJK, fears of setting the wrong precedent, continued militancy-related violence in IJK, and strategic dependence on militancy.

Consolidating Gains Across the LoC

A transformative development in the peace process since 2004 has been India's and Pakistan's acceptance of the concept of a "soft border" between IJK and AJK. This notion has also been received positively by moderate political leaders in AJK and IJK.[68] The initiation of the Srinagar-Muzaffarabad bus service, followed by proposals to open additional routes, has been the primary manifestation of this concept.

Realization of the soft border concept would directly benefit the people of IJK and AJK. The reopened routes could allow for the revitalization of a large, "natural" zone of commercial and social exchange in the region, linking the Kashmir Valley to Pakistani markets, transport routes, and, ultimately, ports.[69] The cross-LoC initiatives would complement cross-border cooperation projects in the works to link Indian and Pakistani Punjab.

In realizing the soft border, new arrangements would be necessary to manage the increased cross-LoC traffic flow as well as cross-LoC social exchanges. Cross-border commercial regimes would need to be developed and implemented, and family reunification programs could be coordinated through offices on either side of the LoC. A positive political dynamic could be generated if the people of IJK and AJK have a high degree of decision-making autonomy in launching and managing cross-LoC initiatives. As Kaur points out in her chapter, one criticism of the Srinagar-Muzaffarabad bus service launch was that officials in AJK and IJK had little say in how the program was carried out. Despite the welcomed reopening of the route, it generated resentment, particularly in the Kashmir Valley, because of the heavy-handedness of New Delhi and Islamabad. The governance crisis in IJK poses a challenge in enhancing local ownership in IJK, but increased cross-LoC exchange has the potential to bring large benefits to the average person in IJK, and the political risks for New Delhi are few in establishing such practical arrangements. Creativity and pragmatism should be able to overcome the problems posed by the governance crisis.

To ease political tensions in the long run, the soft-border arrangements will have to be matched by the restoration of at least some of the autonomy provisions for both IJK and AJK. For IJK, proposals exist for redressing the constitutional erosion and economic dependency that have undermined IJK's autonomy within the Indian union. These include the proposals of the State Autonomy Committee (2000, discussed above) and the Delhi Policy Group (1998). These proposals should be given serious consideration. Such redress should be based on the recognition that IJK's accession to the Indian union was always conditional and that changes to this status have followed neither due democratic processes nor norms of proper judicial review. The importance of symbolic gestures, like restoring the original IJK state government nomenclature, should not be underestimated.[70] Similarly for Pakistani governments, by restoring AJK's autonomy in parallel with IJK, Pakistan would help to create a sense of wholeness for the people of J&K and build political support for dismantling the militant infrastructure in AJK.[71]

Addressing the Sources of Intractability

Addressing the sources of the conflict's intractability is necessary to build a foundation for durable peace, but the depth and political nature of these problems make them resistant to any mechanical solutions. Sometimes what is necessary is a fundamental change in preferences or perceptions, perhaps as a result of a shock, a long period of interaction and learning, or assiduous persuasion. It is simply up to the Kashmiris to find a way to use their own political resources to overcome their political fragmentation. Part of this process would be dialogues across numerous axes (IJK-AJK, region-to-region, district-to-district, Hindu-Muslim-Buddhist) and at numerous levels (official, civil society, and mass public). Of course, New Delhi and Islamabad should revise their policies to be sure that they are not undermining this process. Such revision would be predicated on their formulation of coherent political approaches to address the demands of separatists and independence seekers in IJK and AJK. In addition, when official government representation is tainted to the extent that it is in IJK and AJK, civil society engagement is essential to ensure that the true interests of the people are represented in the peace process.

New Delhi and Islamabad will have to come to terms with the legitimacy of separatist and independence demands. An attitude shift would also be required for New Delhi and Islamabad to move beyond their concerns about "setting the wrong precedent." A view that has prevailed in these capitals is that fighting separatism demonstrates the central government's *resolve* and deters centrifugal forces in the periphery. This view would have to be exchanged for one recognizing that restoring autonomy demonstrates the central government's *fairness*, thus removing the periphery's fears about the central government's excessive centripetal tendencies. To some extent, such a perceptual shift is already under way in India and Pakistan as part of the trends toward more decentralized federalism.[72] Another view that has prevailed is that claims to J&K are essential to national integrity. This view would have to be exchanged for one respecting the strict autonomy conditions through which IJK and AJK came into association with India and Pakistan, respectively. Such attitudinal changes in New Delhi and Islamabad, if credibly conveyed, could remove suspicions in IJK and AJK, lowering the number of people supporting militancy.[73]

Third-party arrangements can play a crucial role in helping to overcome a strategic impasse. In a domestic context, third-party arrangements can be established through checks-and-balances institutions. The commitment problem between New Delhi and IJK results in part from a lack of robust constitutional checks on the central government. This lack of checks and balances allowed for the erosion of IJK's special constitutional provisions in the 1950s and 1960s and New Delhi's subsequent heavy-handedness in IJK. In AJK, a similar lack of checks and balances has allowed AJK's quasi-sovereign status to be thoroughly undermined, although the result has not been an insurgency. At least on the IJK–New Delhi axis, checks-and-balances institutions would have to be fashioned to guarantee any restored autonomy provisions. Such institutions may also be necessary to deal with communal tensions at the district level within IJK.

At the international level, third-party arrangements could conceivably play a role in helping India and Pakistan overcome their strategic impasse. As discussed above, India and Pakistan face a withdrawal dilemma with respect to Indian troop presence in IJK and Pakistan's tacit and explicit support to militants operating in IJK. Such a dilemma, in which each side is unwilling to risk being "suckered" by the other, is a common problem contributing to the protraction of armed conflicts.[74] Solutions include the establishment of trust among the protagonists, a change in one or both protagonists' preferences such that a commitment to withdraw becomes credible, the intercession of a third-party guarantor, or, most preferably, some combination of all three. The first process is occurring through the composite dialogue, and as discussed above, Islamabad faces pressures that have likely shifted strategic preferences. The question remains whether India and Pakistan would accept a third-party withdrawal verification mechanism, perhaps a revised UNMOGIP (UN Military Observer Group in India and Pakistan) mandate or an ad hoc arrangement. Limits on international intervention in Kashmir have historically had to do with New Delhi's insistence that the 1972 Simla Agreement between India and Pakistan obliged both parties to deal with the issue bilaterally. However, India has not always held bilateralism to be sacrosanct in dealing with Pakistan.[75] It would seem that when it is well conceived and pragmatic, New Delhi has appreciated facilitation by international third parties.

The material incentives contributing to the militancy are part of a larger set of economic distortions associated with the conflict, affecting the economy in IJK in particular.[76] In IJK, despite massive state debt, the private economy has been bolstered by services and industries supporting the massive troop presence.[77] Troop withdrawal will bring about the contraction of such "khaki industries," introducing new economic hardships. Alternative livelihoods will have to be created to dampen the effects of this contraction. Creating alternative livelihoods, combined with rehabilitation and reintegration of ex-militants, victims, and their families, means that peace will carry a heavy price tag.[78] Part of this expense should be paid through direct assistance from the Indian government or members of the international community. Sustainable economic growth should also be promoted. The reopening of cross-LoC trade should promote such economic growth in the region, but this should be complemented with investments, especially in agriculture and horticulture, tourism, timber, and hydroelectric production.[79] Offers of increased development assistance, of the kind currently provided through the World Bank and Asian Development Bank, could help to ensure that the peace dividend is ample. A larger peace dividend should lure more people into the peace process in IJK and AJK.

Conclusion

This chapter has reflected the guarded optimism of most chapters in this volume. Indeed, as discussed above, good reason exists to believe that an extraordinary opportunity has arisen since the January 2004 Islamabad summit to make progress in addressing the Kashmir conflict. Of course, conflict resolution processes tend to go through stages that include creation of a space for cooperation, work toward a settlement, implementation of the settlement, and active monitoring and consolidation of the settlement. Despite the positive developments since the Islamabad summit, the disputants in IJK, AJK, India, and Pakistan are still working on the first stage and just planning for the second. Even if conditions have combined to create an extraordinary opportunity, the road to peace is likely to be long and the process complex.

Notes

1. J&K was the object of contention in the Indo-Pak wars of 1947–1949 and 1965 and the Kargil conflict (1999, a "war" insofar as battle deaths exceeded 1,000). J&K was a theater of engagement in the third Indo-Pak war (1971).

2. On heightened political awareness among the postpartition generation of Kashmiris in IJK, see Edward W. Desmond, "Himalayan Ulster," *The New York Review of Books* 40, no. 5 (4 March 1993), and Sumit Ganguly, *The Crisis in Kashmir: Portents of War, Hopes of Peace* (Cambridge: Cambridge University Press, 1997).

3. The Indian Ministry of Home Affairs counts about 40,000 deaths from 1990 to 2005. See Government of India, Ministry of Home Affairs, *Annual Report 2004–2005*, Annexure II, p. 164. Kashmiri separatists protest this figure, sometimes claiming that the death toll of civilians alone is 80,000–100,000. Press reports in mid-2005 estimated a total of over 66,000, mostly civilians. See, e.g., Ashok Sharma, "India, Pakistan Vow to Keep Kashmir Truce," *Associated Press*, 8 August 2005.

4. Kaur discusses these transformations in detail in her chapter in this volume.

5. On these domestic and international changes, see chapters in this volume by Chari, Rizvi, and Idris.

6. "India-Pakistan Joint Press Statement," Islamabad, Ministry of External Affairs (New Delhi), 6 January 2004, http://164.100.17.21/speech/2004/01/06ss01. htm.

7. This skepticism is captured well in Christine Fair, *India and Pakistan Engagement: Prospects for Breakthrough or Breakdown*, United States Institute of Peace Special Report, January 2005, and Praveen Swami, *Quickstep or Kadam*

Taal? The Elusive Search for Peace in Jammu and Kashmir, United States Institute of Peace Special Report, March 2005.

8. Before the cease-fire on the LoC, "a typical month might mean [artillery] exchanges of over 400,000 rounds." Charles Sanctuary, "Contentious Line of Control," BBC News Online, 4 January 2002, http://news.bbc.co.uk/2/hi/south_asia/377916.stm. Akhtar's chapter in this volume illustrates the significance of the cease-fire for communities along the LoC.

9. This diminishing trend is recorded in the Indian Ministry of Home Affairs' *Annual Report 2004–2005*. Home Ministry figures show a diminution from a peak of twelve violent incidents per day in 2001 down to five per day in 2005. While the Home Ministry's counts should be read with skepticism, the trend is probably close to the reality.

10. Indian Home Minister Shivraj Patil stated during questioning in the Rajya Sabha on 11 May 2005 that the infiltration levels had dropped 61 percent since 2002, from an average of about eleven per day to four or five per day. The drop is likely due to the post–September 11 Pakistani domestic clampdown on militant groups, Indian border forces' construction of a security fence along the LoC, and the cessation (due to the cease-fire) of Pakistan's use of shelling as cover for militant infiltration.

11. The bus service had been on the table for many years, but only in late 2004 could New Delhi and Islamabad move beyond differences over travel documents. In the week prior to the 7 April launch, jihadist militants threatened to kill the passengers, and then on 6 April burned down the passenger holding facility in Srinagar. Ten of the twenty-nine would-be passengers traveling on the Srinagar-to-Muzaffarabad trip withdrew because of the threats. Somini Sengupta, "Arson Attack Tries to Foil Start of India-Pakistan Bus Service," *New York Times*, 7 April 2005. Islamabad joined New Delhi in condemning the terrorist attacks, the first time in memory (and probably ever) that New Delhi and Islamabad delivered such a blunt *joint* message against terrorism.

12. See Chari's chapter in this volume for more details.

13. This does not contradict Idris's central argument in her chapter. It simply suggests that positive developments in Indo-Pak relations should have positive implications for IJK–New Delhi relations.

14. Hard-line rhetoric toward India was part of General Muhammad Zia-ul-Haq's early strategy for legitimizing his rule following the 1977 coup, until his attention shifted to Afghanistan. During parliamentary rule from 1988 to 1999, the political opposition of the day would regularly seek political gain by attacking government efforts toward normalization with India. International Crisis Group, *Kashmir: The View from Islamabad*, ICG Asia Report No. 68, 4 December 2003 (online).

15. Jean-Luc Racine, "The Indian Syndrome: Between Kashmir and the Nuclear Predicament," in Christophe Jaffrelot, ed., *Pakistan: Nationalism Without a Nation?* (London: Zed Books, 2002).

16. "India-Pakistan Joint Press Statement," New Delhi, Ministry of External Affairs (New Delhi), 18 April 2005, http://164.100.17.21/speech/2005/04/18js01.htm.

17. According to Musharraf, the April summit had brought India and Pakistan to the fourth and final step of his proposed "four-point" resolution formula of high-level talks, mutual acknowledgment of the dispute, ruling out of unacceptable options, and discussion of an actual settlement. Refer to P. R. Chari's chapter in this volume for more on Musharraf's formula.

18. "Peace Process Has Taken Worrying Turn: Vajpayee," *Asian Age*, 16 June 2005.

19. See P. R. Chari's chapter in this volume for the causes of the Agra summit failure.

20. The exception in the delegation was Yasin Malik, leader of the IJK faction of the Jammu and Kashmir Liberation Front (JKLF), who continued to demand independence for J&K. Geelani and others from his faction in the APHC, who endorse accession to Pakistan, were not in the delegation. Feeling abandoned by Islamabad, Geelani remained a staunch critic of the peace process. However, it should be clarified that Musharraf had not made any official statements as of the June 2005 trip, suggesting Pakistan's acceptance of a "modified status quo" settlement.

21. In their chapters in this volume, Kaur and Idris are more skeptical about attempts to deepen democracy in IJK.

22. "Assembly Elections: Under the Shadow of Fear [summary of 2002 election report by Institute of Social Sciences, New Delhi]," *Economic and Political Weekly*, 26 October 2002, and "Kashmir Assembly Election: How Free and Fair? [summary of 2002 election report by Jammu and Kashmir Coalition for Civil Society]," *Economic and Political Weekly*, 11 January 2003.

23. Kanchan Lakshman, "Jammu and Kashmir Get Grassroots Democracy After 27 Years," *South Asia Tribune*, 4 February 2005 (online); Ashutosh Misra, "The Changing Definition of Kashmir," *Indian Express*, 13 April 2005 (online).

24. This troubling legacy began in 1953 when Indian prime minister Jawaharlal Nehru ordered the imprisonment of IJK state prime minister Sheikh Mohammed Abdullah and backed Bakshi Ghulam Mohammad, a rival of the sheikh in the National Conference party, as a replacement. It continued through the unseemly alliance of Indian prime minister Rajiv Gandhi and IJK chief minister Farooq Abdullah, which was forged to ensure Farooq's victory in the 1987 state assembly election. Sumantra Bose, *Kashmir: Roots of Conflict, Paths to Peace* (Cambridge, MA: Harvard University Press, 2003), pp. 44–101.

25. "Qayyum Rejects Independent Kashmir," *Asian Age*, 23 July 2004 (online).

26. Salahuddin (then known as Mohammad Yusuf Shah) ran as a Muslim United Front candidate for a legislative seat in the 1987 IJK state legislative assembly elections. He was arrested during the course of the elections and was reportedly tortured and humiliated during nine months in prison. Mohammad Shehzad, "For Dialogue and Armed Struggle, Together: Interview with Syed Salahuddin, Hizbul Mujahideen Leader," *Frontline* 20, no. 11 (24 May–6 June 2003) (online edition).

27. Such intra-Kashmiri dialogue meetings have taken place in April 2002 in Dubai, in November 2004 in Kathmandu, and in July 2005 in Srinagar.

28. For introspective assessments of the shortcomings of mainstream analyses within India, see Tavleen Singh, "Kashmir: A View from India," *Logos Journal*, no. 4.1, Winter 2005 (online); Tavleen Singh, *Kashmir: Tragedy of Errors* (New Delhi: Viking, 1995); and Teresa Joseph, "Kashmir, Human Rights and the Indian Press," *Contemporary South Asia* 9, no. 1 (2000).

29. As Kaur discusses in her chapter in this volume, Article 370 of the Indian constitution provided for IJK's special autonomy. But between 1954 and 1972, IJK's special autonomy was eroded through a series of questionable measures by New Delhi and pliant IJK state governments and rulings of the Supreme Court of India. For details, see A. G. Noorani, "Article 370: Law and Politics," *Frontline* 17, no. 19 (16–29 September 2000) (online edition).

30. The current New Delhi–appointed IJK state governor, S. K. Sinha, put forward this curious formulation in a April 2005 speech: "There is much talk of India denying self determination to the people of J and K when the fact is that Pakistan, by failing to withdraw its forces from J and K did not allow a plebiscite to be held as required by the United Nations resolutions." Sinha did, however, offer forward-looking proposals for resolution. S. K. Sinha, "Jammu and Kashmir: Past, Present and Future," *Journal of the United Service Institution of India* 135, no. 560 (April–June 2005).

31. Husain Haqqani, "Pakistan's Endgame in Kashmir," *India Review* 2, no. 3 (July 2003).

32. The Indian military has not offered precise figures. These estimates reflect what often appear in press accounts.

33. For an account of this period, see Desmond, "Himalayan Ulster."

34. Abuses in IJK have been documented in Human Rights Watch (HRW), *India's Secret Army in Kashmir: New Patterns of Abuse Emerge in the Conflict,* May 1996; HRW, *Behind the Kashmir Conflict: Abuses by Indian Security Forces and Militant Groups Continue,* July 1999; Amnesty International (AI), *India: Punitive Use of Preventive Detention Legislation in Jammu and Kashmir,* ASA 20/10/00 (May 2000); AI, *India: A Trail of Unlawful Killings in Jammu and Kashmir: Chithisinghpora and Its Aftermath,* ASA 20/24/00 (June 2000); AI, *India: Impunity Must End in Jammu and Kashmir,* ASA 20/023/2001 (April 2001); and Prabhu Ghate, "Kashmir: The Dirty War," *Economic and Political Weekly,* 26 January 2002 (online version).

35. Rekha Chowdhary, "Kashmir: Lone's Liberal Legacy," *Economic and Political Weekly,* 22 June 2002 (online version), and Lawrence Lifschutz, "Death in Kashmir: Perils of 'Self-determination,'" *Economic and Political Weekly,* 3 August 2002 (online version).

36. Muzamil Jameel, "Valley Winners Say Sorry to Militants," *Indian Express,* 15 February 2005 (online edition).

37. A. G. Norrani, "Contours of Militancy," *Frontline* 17, no. 20 (30 September–13 October 2000) (online version).

38. Shankar Raghuraman, "Only 3% Kashmiris Want to Be with Pak," *Times of India,* 17 April 2005 (online version); "79% Say Solve Kashmir First," *Outlook India,* 25 August 2003 (online version); Padmanand Jha, "Till Freedom Come: Where Errors Reign, Kalashnikovs Bloom," *Outlook India,* 8 October 1995 (online version). These findings are consistent with a poll of 400 Kashmir Valley inhabitants conducted by Mehraj Hajni in autumn 2004 for the International Peace Academy's project, *Kashmir: New Voices, New Approaches.*

39. Reeta Chodhari Tremblay, "Kashmir: The Valley's Political Dynamics," *Contemporary South Asia* 4, no. 1 (March 1995).

40. Rekha Chowdhary, "Kashmir: Elections 2002: Implications for Politics of Separatism," *Economic and Political Weekly,* 4 January 2003 (online version).

41. See Kaur's chapter in this volume for details on the split.

42. Kaur's chapter illustrates the likely limits to the APHC's support base in IJK. In AJK, both mainstream and separatist political leaders have rejected the APHC's leadership. In 2002, when the APHC sought to hold elections to constitute a leadership to negotiate with New Delhi, AJK-based JKLF faction leader Amanullah Khan declared the process "defective" and "unacceptable" and called the APHC unrepresentative of the people of J&K. Amanullah's attitude was likely reflective of his bitter rivalry with IJK-based Yasin Malik. "Amanullah Khan Objects to Hurriyat," *Hindu,* 16 February 2002 (online). On mainstream leaders in IJK reject-

ing the APHC, see "PoK's PM: Hurriyat Decision on Kashmir Can't Be Accepted," *Press Trust of India*, 27 June 2005 (wire report).

43. Victoria Schofield, *Kashmir in Conflict: India, Pakistan and the Unending War* (London: I. B. Tauris, 2003), pp. 174–175.

44. I. William Zartman, *Elusive Peace: Negotiating an End to Civil Wars* (Washington, DC: Brookings Institution, 1995), pp. 340–341, and Charles King, *Ending Civil Wars* (Oxford: Oxford University Press, 1997), pp. 33–35, 44–47.

45. On problems of credible commitment in civil wars, see James D. Fearon, "Why Do Some Civil Wars Last So Much Longer Than Others?" *Journal of Peace Research* 41, no. 3 (May 2004).

46. A similar argument is put forward in Nirvikar Singh, "Cultural Conflict in India: Punjab and Kashmir," in Beverly Crawford and Ronnie D. Lipschutz, eds., *The Myth of "Ethnic Conflict": Politics, Economics, and "Cultural" Violence* (Berkeley: University of California Press, 1998).

47. The State Autonomy Commission, convened in 1996, presented its final report to the state assembly in June 2000. See the 8–21 July 2000 issue of *Frontline* (vol. 17, no. 14) for discussions of proposals and the initial response in New Delhi.

48. Praveen Swami, "The Long Haul," *Frontline* 19, no. 16 (3–16 August 2002). Schofield cites her own interview with then–IJK governor G. C. Saxena to suggest that New Delhi's response was actually more nuanced. See Schofield, *Kashmir in Conflict*, p. 230. Nonetheless, what matters for the sake of the analysis was that Kashmiris perceived that New Delhi had rejected restoring autonomy.

49. The reasons have to do with a historical correlation between class privilege and communal identity in J&K. Muslims have been the more deprived class historically, despite being the majority. See Bose, *Kashmir*; Ganguly, *The Crisis in Kashmir*; and Pankaj Mishra, "The Birth of a Nation," *The New York Review of Books* 47, no. 15 (October 2000).

50. Rekha Chowdhary, "Debating Autonomy," *Seminar: Frameworks for Peace*, no. 296, December 2000 (online); Balraj Puri, "The Autonomy Debate," *Frontline* 17, no. 6 (18–31 March 2000). The June 2000 debate in the IJK state assembly over the State Autonomy Commission was especially rancorous. See Schofield, *Kashmir in Conflict*, pp. 229–230.

51. Yoginder Sikand, "The Changing Course of the Kashmiri Struggle: From National Liberation to Islamist Jihad?" *Muslim World* 91, no. 2 (Spring 2001).

52. During partition and up to the start of the uprising in 1989–1990, Hindu-Muslim relations had been more contentious and violent in Jammu than in the Kashmir Valley. The backwardness of the Muslim-dominant districts in Jammu contributes to intercommunal mistrust about whether the Hindu leadership will protect Muslim interests. On the need to address cleavages between Hindus and Muslims in Jammu, see Yoginder Sikand, "Hindu-Muslim Relations in Jammu: Alternative Ways of Understanding," *Qalandar*, no. 30, March 2005 (online).

53. Prominent Indian strategic commentators such as K. P. S. Gill tend to argue from this position. See K. P. S. Gill, "J&K: Forward to the Past?" *South Asia Intelligence Review* 1, no. 15 (28 October 2002) (online).

54. Haqqani, "Pakistan's Endgame in Kashmir."

55. See also Praveen Swami, "Terrorism in Jammu and Kashmir in Theory and Practice," *India Review* 2, no. 3 (July 2003), and Jessica Stern, "Pakistan's Jihad Culture," *Foreign Affairs* 79, no. 6 (November/December 2000).

56. On economic incentives in armed conflict, see Paul Collier, "Doing Well out of War," and David Keen, "Incentives and Disincentives for Violence," both in

Mats Berdal and David Malone, eds., *Greed and Grievance: Economic Agendas in Civil War* (Boulder: Lynne Rienner Publishers, 2000).

57. Surinder Oberoi, "Kashmir Is Bleeding," *Bulletin of the Atomic Scientist* 53, no. 2 (March/April 1997); Stern, "Pakistan's Jihad Culture"; Siddhartha Prakash, "The Political Economy of Kashmir Since 1947," *Contemporary South Asia* 9, no. 3 (November 2000); Eqbal Ahmad, "The Roots of Violence in Pakistani Society," in Zia Mian and Iftikar Ahmad, eds., *Making Enemies, Creating Conflict: Pakistan's Crisis of State and Society* (Lahore: Mashal, 1997).

58. However, a challenge is to ensure that militancy is not *rewarded*, in which case perverse incentives are created for falsely presenting oneself as a militant to reap the rewards offered in disarmament, demobilization, and reintegration (DDR) programs.

59. Bose, *Kashmir*, pp. 102–107; Firdous Syed, "Sharing Dreams," *Seminar: Frameworks for Peace*, no. 296, December 2000 (online); Stern, "Pakistan's Jihad Culture."

60. The Indian army has been working to operationalize the so-called Cold Start doctrine, which would allow for quicker forward mobilization vis-à-vis Pakistan. Subhash Kapila, "India's New 'Cold Start' War Doctrine Strategically Reviewed," *South Asia Analysis Group,* Paper no. 991, 4 May 2005 (online).

61. On such dynamics, see Andrew Kydd and Barbara F. Walter, "Sabotaging the Peace: The Politics of Extremist Violence," *International Organization* 56, no. 2 (Spring 2002).

62. Stern, "Pakistan's Jihad Culture."

63. Fair, "India and Pakistan Engagement."

64. Raghuraman, "Only 3% Kashmiris Want to Be with Pak"; A. G. Noorani, "Contours of Militancy"; see also Kaur's chapter in this volume.

65. At a panel discussion on Kashmir in January 2005 hosted by the International Peace Academy and Institute for Defense and Strategic Studies in Singapore, experts on insurgency in South Asia and Islamic militancy stated that active support from less than 5 percent of the population would be sufficient to sustain the militancy in IJK. In her chapter in this volume, Kaur quotes a militant leader who claims that only 2,000 militants are needed at any given time to keep the Indian army and paramilitary forces engaged at a high tempo.

66. Sikand, "The Changing Course of the Kashmiri Struggle."

67. Noorani, "Contours of Militancy."

68. Siddharth Varadarajan, "'Soft Border' Emerges as Common Vocabulary," *Hindu*, 15 April 2005 (online).

69. Geography dictates that the ports most easily accessible from the Kashmir Valley by land are in Pakistan, not India.

70. Amitabh Mattoo, "India's 'Potential' Endgame in Kashmir," *India Review* 2, no. 3 (July 2003).

71. Verghese Koithara, *Crafting Peace in Kashmir: Through a Realist Lens* (New Delhi: Sage, 2004), p. 290.

72. Amitabh Mattoo, "India's 'Potential' Endgame."

73. Malini Parthasarathy, "Winning the Battle over Kashmir," *Hindu*, 5 August 2002 (online); Ayesha Jalal, "Kashmir Scars: A Terrible Beauty Is Torn," *The New Republic*, 23 July 1990.

74. For an application to civil wars, see Barbara F. Walter, *Committing to Peace: The Successful Settlement of Civil Wars* (Princeton: Princeton University Press, 2001). The logic extends readily to interstate wars.

75. See Chari's and Sidhu's chapters in this volume for details.

76. See Kaur's chapter in this volume.

77. See also Oberoi, "Kashmir Is Bleeding."

78. Suri's chapter in this volume helps to clarify the scale of the economic, medical, and psychological programs needed to rehabilitate those who have been victims or participants in the militancy in IJK.

79. Wahajat Habibullah, "The Political Economy of the Kashmir Conflict," United States Institute of Peace Special Report, June 2004.

APPENDIX

Chronology of the Kashmir Conflict

1846

- On 16 March the Dogra ruler Raja Gulab Singh of Jammu and the British East India Company signed the Treaty of Amritsar, which transferred the Kashmir Valley to Gulab Singh for a sum of Rs 7,500,000. The Dogra acquisition of the valley led to the creation of the state of Jammu and Kashmir and marked the beginning of its modern history.

1905

- *Mirwaiz* (religious leader) Maulvi Rasool Shah set up an educational institution, the *Anjumum-i-Nusrat-ul Islam,* in Jammu and Kashmir to provide schooling for poor Muslims and fund those who wished to study abroad. The institution also served as a platform for articulating Muslim demands for social reform to the government.

1922

- The Young Men's Muslim Association was formed with the aim of improving the conditions of the Muslim community.

1931

- The first organized protest against Dogra rule was carried out on 13 July. Approximately twenty-two Muslim demonstrators were killed by state police. Subsequently known in Kashmiri history as "Mar-

tyrs Day," 13 July was seen as marking the formal beginning of a struggle against the maharaja's rule.
- A commission of inquiry headed by a senior British official, B. Glancy, was set up in November to look into Muslim grievances.

1932

- On 22 March the Glancy Commission submitted a report confirming the existence of the grievances of the state's subjects and suggested recommendations providing for adequate representation of Muslims in the state's services. The maharaja accepted these recommendations but delayed implementation, leading to another agitation in 1934.
- Jammu and Kashmir's first political party, the All Jammu and Kashmir Muslim Conference, was established on 17 October with Sheikh Abdullah as its president and Ghulam Abbas as its general secretary.

1934

- Based on the recommendations of the Glancy Commission, Maharaja Hari Singh promulgated a constitution for the Jammu and Kashmir state providing a legislative assembly for the people. Under this constitution, elections were held on 3 September and the legislative assembly was duly inaugurated on 17 October.

1935

- The government of India and the Jammu and Kashmir government signed the Gilgit lease on 26 March. According to the lease, the Gilgit Wazarat area, north of the Indus, and its dependencies were leased to the British for a period of sixty years.

1939

- Sheikh Abdullah dissolved the All Jammu and Kashmir Muslim Conference in June and formed the Jammu and Kashmir National Conference.

1941

- Some members of the National Conference (Chaudri Ghulam Abbas, Mirwaiz Yusuf Shah, among others) broke away from the party and revived the All Jammu and Kashmir Muslim Conference.

1946

- The National Conference launched the "Quit Kashmir" movement from May to June, demanding abrogation of the Treaty of Amritsar and restoration of sovereignty to the people of Kashmir. The state was placed under martial law and Sheikh Abdullah was arrested.

1947

- Fresh elections to the Jammu and Kashmir legislative assembly were held in January, which were boycotted by the National Conference. The Muslim Conference took part in the elections and won the largest elected representation in the assembly.
- The Indian subcontinent became independent from British rule and was partitioned into two states, Pakistan and India, on 14 and 15 August respectively. Rulers of the princely states, which included the state of Jammu and Kashmir, were given the option to accede to either country. In an effort to remain independent, the maharaja proposed to enter into standstill agreements with both India and Pakistan on 12 August. This was accepted by Pakistan on 16 August.
- By September demonstrations and protests in Poonch against the maharaja turned into a full-scale secessionist movement from the state. With alleged military support from Pakistan, the Poonch rebellion escalated rapidly.
- From 22 to 24 October the rebels gained control over substantial parts of Poonch and rapidly advanced toward Srinagar. They formally announced their independence from the maharaja, declared the territory under their control as the state of *Azad* (or free) Kashmir, and set up a provisional government under the aegis of the Muslim Conference.
- In return for military assistance, the maharaja signed an instrument of accession to India on October 26. Sheikh Abdullah was sworn in as prime minister of Indian Jammu and Kashmir (IJK) on 31 October to head an emergency administration.
- In November a full-scale war broke out between India and Pakistan.

1948

- India lodged a complaint under Article 35 of the UN charter on 1 January, charging Pakistan with aggression in Kashmir.
- On 17 January the UN Security Council passed its first resolution on Kashmir. Text of the resolution is available at http://www.un.org/documents/scres.htm.
- The UNSC adopted Resolution 39 on 20 January, setting up the three-member UN Commission for India and Pakistan (UNCIP).

Text of the resolution is available at http://www.un.org/documents/sc/res/1948/scres48.htm.

- On 21 April UNSC passed Resolution 47, increasing the UNCIP membership from three to five members. It further stated that the "question of the accession of Jammu and Kashmir to India and Pakistan should be decided through the democratic method of a free and impartial plebiscite." The text of this resolution is available at http://www.un.org/documents/sc/res/1948/scres48.htm.

- UNSC passed Resolution 51 on 3 June, reaffirming its earlier resolutions. The text of the resolution is available at http://www.un.org/documents/sc/res/1948/scres48.htm.

- On 13 August UNCIP proposed a cease-fire agreement between India and Pakistan calling for the withdrawal of tribesmen and other Pakistani nationals and Indian forces from the state of Jammu and Kashmir.

- In Pakistan, the Ministry of Kashmir Affairs and Northern Areas was set up to serve as a "coordinating link" between the government of Azad Jammu and Kashmir (AJK) and Pakistan.

1949

- A cease-fire was put into effect between Indian and Pakistani troops in Kashmir on 1 January. The cease-fire left India in control of most of the valley, as well as Jammu and Ladakh, while Pakistan gained control of Azad Kashmir and the Northern Areas.

- UNCIP passed a resolution on 5 January reaffirming the 21 April 1948 UNSC resolution that called for a "free and impartial plebiscite" in Jammu and Kashmir. India and Pakistan accepted the principle enshrined in the resolution but failed to arrive at a truce agreement due to differences in interpretation of the procedure for and extent of demilitarization of the state of Jammu and Kashmir.

- On 27 July India and Pakistan signed the Karachi Agreement defining a cease-fire line in the state of Jammu and Kashmir to mark the effective limit of the sovereignties of the two states. An agreement was also concluded between the provisional Muslim Conference government in AJK and Islamabad allotting control of defense, foreign policy, negotiations with UNCIP, and the affairs of the Northern Areas to Pakistan.

- Article 306A was added to the Indian constitution on 17 October, affirming that New Delhi's jurisdiction in IJK would remain limited to the three subjects specified in the instrument of accession: defense, foreign affairs, and communications. (Article 306A became part of the Indian constitution in 1950 as Article 370.)

- In December UNSC President General A. G. L. McNaughton endeavored to mediate directly between the Indian and Pakistani delegations at the UN and presented a series of proposals known as the McNaughton proposals.

1950

- In April the UNSC appointed Sir Owen Dixon as the UN representative in place of UNCIP to find a solution to the India-Pakistan dispute over Kashmir. The gist of the Dixon Plan presented to the UN on 15 September can be found at http://www.parliament.uk/commons/lib/research/rp2004/rp04-028.pdf.
- On 28 December an ordinance titled the Rules of Business of the Azad Kashmir Government, 1950, was enacted to serve as the basic law for AJK.

1951

- Following the termination of UNCIP, the UNSC passed Resolution 91 on 30 March, establishing the UN Military Observer Group in India and Pakistan (UNMOGIP) to monitor the cease-fire line. The complete text of the resolution can be found at http://www.un.org/documents/sc/res/1951/scres51.htm.
- From August to September the first postindependence elections were held in IJK. The National Conference won all forty-five legislative assembly seats unopposed.
- The interim constitution of IJK came into force on 20 November.

1952

- The Dogras' hereditary position as rulers of Kashmir was formally abolished in June and replaced by a constitutional head of state, the *Sadar-i-Riyasat*, to be elected by the constitutional (later legislative) assembly for a period of five years.
- On 24 July the Delhi Agreement was signed between the Indian government and representatives of IJK. According to the terms of the agreement, Jammu and Kashmir was declared a part of India while retaining a substantial degree of autonomy.

1953

- India-Pakistan talks over Kashmir under the chairmanship of Frank D. Graham, the UN representative for Kashmir, opened in Geneva on 4 February.

- The first prime ministerial meetings between India and Pakistan took place in Karachi in July. (Further meetings between the prime ministers of India and Pakistan followed: in New Delhi in August 1953 and May 1955, and in Karachi in September 1960. None of these meetings produced any concrete results on the Kashmir dispute.)
- On 7 August Sheikh Abdullah was removed from office and arrested. Bakshi Ghulam Mohammad was sworn in as IJK's new prime minister.

1954

- Under the leadership of Bakshi Ghulam Mohammad, the democratically elected Constituent Assembly of the state of Jammu and Kashmir ratified the state's accession to India on 23 January. A presidential order approved the extension of the center's jurisdiction in Jammu and Kashmir from the original three subjects to others in the union list.

1957

- IJK's new constitution came into effect in January.
- The UNSC passed a resolution on 24 January reiterating its resolutions on Kashmir that called for a final settlement "in accordance with the will of the people expressed through the democratic method of a free and impartial plebiscite conducted under the auspices of the UN."

1960

- India and Pakistan signed the Indus Waters Treaty on 19 September to resolve a dispute regarding the utilization of irrigation water from the Indus Basin. The treaty was signed under the auspices of the World Bank and allocated the waters of the Eastern Rivers (the Sutlej, the Beas, and the Ravi) to India and those of the Western Rivers (Indus, the Jhelum, and the Chenab) largely to Pakistan. An abridged text of the treaty is available at http://www.stimson.org/southasia/?sn=sa20020116300.
- Direct ministerial talks between India and Pakistan were held in December.

1962

- India and China fought a war on account of a border dispute in the Ladakh region. At the end of the war, China occupied 37,555 sq km at Aksai-chin and Demochok in Ladakh.

1963

- In March Pakistan and China signed a boundary agreement on "delimitation" of the boundary between Pakistan's Northern Areas and China's Xinjiang province. Under this agreement, Pakistan ceded a sizeable chunk of territory in this region to China.
- Reports that a sacred relic of the Prophet Muhammad was stolen from the Hazratbal Shrine near Srinagar stirred protests in Srinagar and Pakistan in December.

1964

- On 3 January the "missing" relic was mysteriously returned to the Hazratbal Shrine. However, tensions ran high in Srinagar throughout January.

1965

- In January, the working committee of the National Conference announced that the party would dissolve itself and merge into India's ruling Congress Party. On 10 January, the Congress Party's working committee unanimously accepted the merger offer. Subsequently, Articles 356 and 357 of the Indian constitution became applicable in IJK, allowing the governor to declare president's rule in the event of a "constitutional breakdown," without consulting the state legislature.
- India and Pakistan engaged in a series of clashes in the Rann of Kutch in April 1965. Under British mediation a cease-fire was declared on 30 June.
- In August Pakistan undertook Operation Gibraltar, sending in armed infiltrators across the cease-fire line into IJK. India retaliated and war broke out between India and Pakistan on 5 September.
- As the US placed an arms embargo on both sides, the UNSC brokered a cease-fire that came into effect on 23 September, ending the war. (The UNSC passed five resolutions between 4 September and 5 November 1965 before the cease-fire finally held.)

1966

- Under Russian mediation, Indian Prime Minister Lal Bahadur Shastri and Pakistani President Ayub Khan met at Tashkent and resumed talks on Kashmir in January. They signed the Tashkent Agreement on 10 January, agreeing to withdraw their armies to their pre-1965 positions and to restore normal mutual relations. Text of the Tashkent Agreement can be found at http://www.acdis.unic. edu/homepage.docs/Links.doc/Treaty.docs/tashkent.html.

1970

- The 1970 AJK Government Act was promulgated, introducing a presidential form of government in AJK.

1971

- Indo-Pak relations deteriorated as India intervened in the civil war in East Pakistan between the Pakistani army and East Pakistani rebels who were demanding greater autonomy. On 17 December Pakistani forces in Dhaka surrendered unconditionally to Indian forces, ending the third Indo-Pak war after just fourteen days. The 1971 war resulted in the breakup of Pakistan and the emergence of Bangladesh as an independent country on 6 December 1971. Kashmir saw limited conflict.
- On 21 December UNSC passed a resolution noting the cease-fire and the cessation of hostilities between India and Pakistan. The text of the resolution can be found at http://www.un.org/documents/sc/ res/1971/scres71.htm.

1972

- On 2 July India and Pakistan signed the Simla Agreement, according to which both agreed to settle disputes through bilateral talks and negotiations. The pact also talked of upholding the cease-fire line, renamed the Line of Control (LoC). Text of the agreement can be found at http://www.stimson.org/southasia/?sn=sa20020114201.

1974

- A parliamentary form of government was introduced in AJK under its first constitution, which was called the Interim Constitution Act of 1974. The constitution also led to the creation of the AJK Council in Islamabad.
- India conducted its first nuclear test at Pokhran in Rajasthan on 18 May.
- Pakistani Prime Minister Zulfiqar Ali Bhutto took steps to integrate AJK into Pakistan by giving Gilgit agency representation in Pakistan's national assembly.

1975

- Prime Minister Indira Gandhi and Sheikh Abdullah signed the Kashmir Accord (24–25 February) through which IJK was made a "Constituent Unit" of India with the Indian parliament reaffirming its right to legislate on any matter concerning the territory of the state. Article 370 was retained but functioned in name only.

1977

- The pro-independence Jammu and Kashmir Liberation Front (JKLF) was formed in the United Kingdom on 5 May. Its founding members included Amanullah Khan, Yasin Malik, and Maqbool Ahmed Butt.

1984

- On 11 February Maqbool Ahmed Butt, cofounder of JKLF, was hanged in Tihar jail in India on charges of killing an Indian embassy official in London.
- India launched a preemptive assault to occupy the Siachen Glacier, an area where the LoC was undefined. Since 1984, India and Pakistan have been fighting a low-key "war" for control of the glacier.

1985

- The South Asian Association for Regional Cooperation (SAARC) was set up on 8 December with the aim of serving as a platform for "the peoples of South Asia" and accelerating the process of economic and social development in its member states: Bangladesh, Bhutan, India, Maldives, Nepal, Pakistan, and Sri Lanka.

1986

- From 20 to 25 February unprecedented Hindu-Muslim communal violence broke out in the Kashmir Valley.
- On 7 March IJK's chief minister G. M. Shah was dismissed and governor's rule was imposed.

1987

- India launched Operation Brasstacks, its largest military exercise, in December. The exercise alarmed the Pakistani military, which moved its southern reserve into combat-ready formation near the border in Punjab. US mediation is believed to have helped defuse the crisis.

- On 23 March an anti–National Conference alliance, the Muslim United Front (MUF), was formed in IJK.
- State elections were held in IJK. Amid massive charges of rigging, they led to a victory for the National Conference–Congress alliance and a defeat for the MUF.

1988

- In December India and Pakistan signed the Non-Attack Agreement, consenting to "refrain from undertaking, encouraging or participating in, directly or indirectly, any action aimed at causing destruction of, or damage to, any nuclear installation or facility in the other country." This agreement was ratified and implemented in 1992.

1989

- Rajiv Gandhi and Benazir Bhutto signed an agreement to establish hotlines between prime ministers of India and Pakistan.
- Throughout late 1988 and 1989, JKLF and other pro-independence parties carried out a series of attacks on government buildings and state officials in IJK. Strikes and "black days" were observed throughout the Kashmir Valley on 15 August 1988 (India's Independence Day), 26 January 1989 (India's Republic Day in 1950), and 11 February 1989 (the fifth anniversary of the death of JKLF cofounder Mohammad Maqbool Butt).

1990

- By January the simmering rebellion of 1988–1989 erupted into mass resistance to Indian rule in the Kashmir Valley.
- On 30 March Ashfaq Wani, a prominent leader of the JKLF, was killed by Indian security forces in Srinagar.
- In May the *mirwaiz* (religious leader) of the northern Kashmir Valley, Maulvi Farooq, was killed in his Srinagar home by gunmen said to be from the Hizbul Mujahidin (HM). Umar Farooq, his sixteen-year-old son, was installed as the new *mirwaiz* of Kashmir.
- First round of foreign secretary–level Indo-Pak talks were held in Pakistan in July.
- From July to September, the Kashmir Valley was brought under martial law as the Indian government enacted an Armed Forces

Special Powers Act and a Disturbed Areas Act to back up existing IJK emergency regulations.

- Second round of Indo-Pak talks were held at New Delhi from 9 to 10 August.
- Third round of Indo-Pak talks were held from 18 to 20 December.

1991

- India and Pakistan signed an Agreement on Advance Notice of Military Exercises, Maneuvers and Troop Movements.

1992

- The Muzaffarabad high court ruled that Gilgit, Skardu, and Hunza were integral to AJK and that their administration be handed over to the AJK government.
- India and Pakistan agreed to implement measures to prevent air-space violations and to permit overflights and landing by military aircraft.

1993

- With alleged support from Pakistan, the Hizbul Mujahidin (HM), a pro-Pakistan militant group, emerged as the dominant guerrilla group in the armed struggle in IJK.
- On 9 March the All Parties Hurriyat Conference (APHC), an alliance of twenty-three political, religious, and social organizations, was set up to further the cause of Kashmiri self-determination.

1994

- In mid-1994 Yasin Malik was freed after four years in prison. He declared an indefinite JKLF cease-fire in IJK.

1995

- Yasin Malik formed his own breakaway faction of JKLF.

1996

- On 16 February the Indian government imposed a ban on the JKLF under the Unlawful Activities (Prevention) Act.
- On 18 September a ban was imposed on Harkat-ul-Ansar (HuA) and

Hizbul Mujahidin (HM) under Section 3(IIIA) of the J&K Criminal Law Amendment Act.

- Elections were held in September in IJK to constitute a new legislative assembly. The National Conference won a two-thirds majority in the eighty-seven-member legislature. Farooq Abdullah became IJK's chief minister.

1997

- A series of secretary-level talks were held between India and Pakistan (on 30 March in New Delhi, from 19 to 23 June in Islamabad, and from 15 to 18 September in New Delhi). On 23 June the foreign secretaries of the two countries agreed to a "composite dialogue" to discuss at the level of foreign secretaries issues of peace and security, Jammu and Kashmir, Siachen, the Wullar barrage and Tulbul navigation projects, Sir Creek, economic and commercial cooperation, and the promotion of friendly exchanges.

1998

- On 11 and 13 May India conducted three nuclear tests at Pokhran in Rajasthan.
- On 28 and 30 May Pakistan reciprocated by conducting nuclear tests in the Chagai district, Baluchistan.
- On 4 June a joint communiqué on India and Pakistan's nuclear tests was issued by the Five Permanent Members of the UN Security Council (P5) in Geneva. They condemned the nuclear tests and urged both countries to address "the root causes of the tension" between them, "including Kashmir."
- On 6 June the UNSC passed Resolution 1172 endorsing the joint communiqué of the P5 and encouraging both India and Pakistan to "find mutually acceptable solutions that address the root cause of tensions, including Kashmir." Text of the resolution is available at http://www.un.org/Docs/scres/1998/scres98.htm.
- On 12 June the G-8 (Group of Eight) foreign ministers also issued a communiqué that endorsed UNSC Resolution 1172 and urged India and Pakistan "to resume without delay a direct dialogue that addresses the root causes of the tension, including Kashmir."

1999

- On 20 February Indian Prime Minister Atal Bihari Vajpayee crossed over the Pakistani border on the inaugural run of the Delhi-Lahore bus service to meet Pakistani Prime Minister Nawaz Sharif at Lahore. On 21 February they signed the Lahore Declaration, committing the two nations to peacefully resolving all disputes, including Kashmir. Text of the Lahore Declaration can be found at http://www.usip.org/library/pa/ip/ip_lahore19990221.html.

- A limited war broke out between India and Pakistan in May after Pakistani infiltrators were sighted on the Indian side of the LoC in the Kargil region.
- Following a meeting with US President Bill Clinton in Washington, Prime Minister Nawaz Sharif issued a statement on 4 July calling for the withdrawal of the Pakistani intruders. Pakistan withdrew from Kargil on 26 July.
- In August India shot down a Pakistani aircraft it claimed had entered its airspace, an allegation Pakistan denied.
- In December, a New Delhi–bound Indian Airlines aircraft was hijacked from Kathmandu to Kandahar by Harkat-ul-Ansar activists. After weeklong negotiations between the hijackers and the government of India, New Delhi agreed to release three well-known militants, Maulana Masood Azhar, Syed Umar Saeed Sheikh, and Mushtaq Ahmed Zargar, in exchange for the release of the hostages.
- The Pakistani supreme court ruled that the Northern Areas should be granted constitutional status and representation in the national legislature.

2000

- Hizbul Mujahidin declared a temporary cease-fire in July but revoked it after two weeks amid a sharp escalation of guerrilla violence in IJK.

2001

- From 14 to 16 July Pakistani President General Pervez Musharraf visited India at Prime Minister Vajpayee's invitation for summit-level talks. The two leaders met at Agra for a round of talks, which proved inconclusive.
- On 1 October suspected militants attacked the legislative assembly in Srinagar.
- The Indian parliament was attacked by armed suspected Lashkar-e-Taiba (LeT) militants on 13 December while the parliament was in session. Following the attack, India broke off bilateral interactions with Pakistan; severed air, road, and rail links; and suspended bilateral trade. Pakistan followed suit.

- India launched Operation Parakram (Might), mobilizing its conventional strike forces to hit alleged training camps in AJK and warning Pakistan of a "limited war."

2002

- In January Musharraf announced a crackdown on jihadi groups operating across the LoC from Pakistani territory. Among others, LeT and JeM were banned.
- Abdul Ghani Lone, the leader of the People's Conference (PC), a moderate party favoring self-determination, was assassinated in Srinagar in May by suspected pro-Pakistan extremists.
- State elections were held in IJK in May, resulting in a victory for the coalition of the Congress–People's Democratic Party (PDP) government.

2003

- In a speech in Srinagar on 18 April, Indian Prime Minister Vajpayee extended a "hand of friendship" to Pakistan and called for resumption of dialogue.
- On 26 November India and Pakistan agreed to implement a ceasefire along the LoC and on the Siachen Glacier.
- In an interview with the BBC on 18 December, Musharraf offered to give up Pakistan's traditional policy of insistence on the implementation of the UN resolutions on Kashmir.
- In December India and Pakistan approved plans for a track two dialogue among former senior army generals, diplomats, and intellectuals to discuss the reduction of defense budgets, nuclear restraint, stabilization, and trade ties.

2004

- By early January all transportation links (air, bus, and rail) were restored between India and Pakistan.
- Indian Prime Minister Vajpayee attended the Twelfth South Asian Association for Regional Cooperation (SAARC) Summit Conference held at Islamabad, Pakistan, from 4 to 6 January. He and General Musharraf met on the margins of the summit and agreed to resume the stalled diplomatic dialogue and to resolve peacefully all contentious issues, including Kashmir.
- On 6 January India and Pakistan issued a joint statement known as the Islamabad Declaration, calling for the resumption of a composite dialogue for "peaceful settlement of all bilateral issues, including

Jammu and Kashmir, to the satisfaction of both sides." Pakistan also agreed not to allow its territory to be used for supporting "terrorism in any manner." In addition, the two countries decided to establish a South Asia Free Trade Area (SAFTA) by 1 January 2006, promising to reduce intraregional import tariffs to between 0 and 5 percent.

- In January, talks were also held with Kashmiri separatists for the first time at the highest levels of the Indian government.
- A series of foreign secretary talks were held between India and Pakistan in February and June. From 19 to 20 June expert-level talks on nuclear confidence building measures (CBMs) were also held in Islamabad. In addition to upgrading the existing hotlines between their directors-general of military operations, India and Pakistan agreed to establish a hotline between their foreign secretaries to reduce nuclear risks and reconfirmed commitments made in Lahore (1999) to refrain from further nuclear tests.
- Pakistani President Musharraf and Indian Prime Minister Manmohan Singh met in New York on the sidelines of a UN General Assembly meeting on 24 September.
- In December prominent Kashmiris from IJK and AJK attended a conference organized by the Pugwash Conferences in Kathmandu, Nepal. For the first time leaders from both sides of the LoC held a meeting separate from both India and Pakistan. At the end of the meeting they issued a joint statement that called on India and Pakistan to work with Kashmiris for a settlement of the dispute.

2005

- On 7 April India and Pakistan initiated a bus service between Muzaffarabad (the capital of AJK) and Srinagar (the capital of IJK).
- At a summit meeting in New Delhi on 18 April, President Musharraf and Prime Minister Singh issued a joint statement reaffirming their commitment to the existing confidence building measures and the process of normalization between India and Pakistan. A list of new CBMs was also proposed, including additional bus services across the LoC in Kashmir, the movement of trucks across the LoC, the possible start of a Lahore-Amritsar bus service, and allowing divided Kashmiri families to meet at designated places along the LoC.
- On 2 June a nine-member delegation of the APHC (including Mirwaiz Umar Farooq and Yasin Malik) traveled to AJK and Pakistan by the Srinagar-Muzaffarabad bus service. During their two-week visit they met with prominent political leaders from Pakistan and AJK.
- On 5 September Indian Prime Minister Manmohan Singh held a meeting with members of the APHC. Although the talks proved

inconclusive, India agreed to cut troop levels within IJK, provided militant infiltration and violence ceased.

- During a four-day visit to Pakistan in October, India's foreign minister, Natwar Singh, signed two security cooperation accords during talks with his Pakistani counterpart, Khurshid Kasuri. The agreements signed on 3 October included a deal promising advance warning of ballistic missile tests and setting up a hotline between the coast guards of both countries.

- On 8 October a magnitude 7.6 earthquake struck Pakistan, India, and Afghanistan. The epicenter of the earthquake was located near Muzaffarabad, the capital of AJK. The earthquake caused widespread destruction in northern Pakistan and northern India. The worst-hit areas were AJK, Pakistan's North-West Frontier Province (NWFP), and western and southern parts of the Kashmir Valley in IJK. Most of the casualties resulting from the earthquake were in Pakistan, where the official death toll topped 84,000. In India, the estimated death toll was over 1,800. The earthquake rendered over 3 million people homeless.

- On 29 October India and Pakistan agreed to open five centers on the LoC to enable delivery of aid to quake victims and facilitate meeting of relatives from both sides of Kashmir. The proposed crossings are Nauseri-Tithwal, Chakoti-Uri, Hajipur-Uri, Rawalakot-Poonch, and Tattapani-Mendhar.

- The Thirteenth SAARC summit was held in Dhaka from 8 to 13 November. At the summit, Indian prime minister Manmohan Singh raised the issue of cross-border terrorist attacks in the IJK, adding that there would be no demilitarization or deployment of the army in IJK so long as cross-border terrorism continued. Pakistan's prime minister, Shaukat Aziz, meanwhile, said there was a "trust deficit" between the two countries. These exchanges contrasted sharply with the SAARC summit of January 2004, when Pakistani president Pervez Musharraf and then–prime minister of India Atal Bihari Vajpayee had agreed to launch the peace process.

2006

- On 2 January a three-member All Parties Hurriyat Conference (APHC) delegation led by Mirwaiz Umar Farooq arrived in Lahore, Pakistan. Other members of the delegation were Professor Abdul Ghani Butt and Balal Ghani Lone. Mirwaiz Umar Farooq stated that their visit to Pakistan and AJK was to show solidarity with the people affected by the 8 October earthquake. The APHC leaders also met with Musharraf and Prime Minister Aziz during their stay.

- Indian foreign secretary Shyam Saran and Pakistani counterpart, Riaz Mohammad Khan, met in Delhi for a third round of bilateral normalization dialogue from 16 to 18 January and agreed to sustain the peace process.
- On 17 February, India and Pakistan relaunched a cross-border train service, the Thar Express, after a period of forty-one years. The train connects Karachi in Pakistan to Jodhpur in India. (Munabao and Khakrophar serve as the last railway stations of India and Pakistan respectively.)
- A roundtable conference of Indian Kashmiri politicians and separatist leaders is convened by Indian prime minister Manmohan Singh in New Delhi on 25 February. The APHC rejects Singh's invitation and decides to stay away from the conference calling it "premature."
- On 24 March, Manmohan Singh flagged off the first bus linking Amritsar in India to Nankana Sahib in Pakistan. Speaking on the occasion, Singh offered a "treaty of peace, security and friendship" to Pakistan.

Acronyms and Abbreviations

AIKS	All India Kashmiri Samaj
AJK	Azad Jammu and Kashmir
APDP	Association of Parents of Disappeared Persons
APHC	All Parties Hurriyat Conference
ARF	ASEAN Regional Forum
BJP	Bharatiya Janata Party
BNF	Balwaristan National Front
BSF	Border Security Force
CBM	confidence building measure
CSOs	civil society organizations
GOC	General Officer Commanding
HELP	Human Effort for Love and Peace
HkA	Harkat-ul-Ansar
HM	Hizbul Mujahidin
HuM	Harkat-ul-Mujahidin
ICNA	Islamic Circle of North America
IDP	internally displaced persons
IDSS	Institute of Defence and Strategic Studies
IJK	Indian-administered Jammu and Kashmir
IPA	International Peace Academy
ISI	Inter-Services Intelligence
J&K	Jammu and Kashmir
JeM	Jaish-e-Mohammad
JKLF	Jammu and Kashmir Liberation Front
JKPP	Jammu Kashmir People's Party
KANA	Ministry of Kashmir Affairs and Northern Areas

KIIR	Kashmir Institute of Internal Relations
KSG	Kashmir Study Group
KWF	The Kashmir Women's Forum
LAHC	Ladakh Autonomous Hill Council Act
LeJ	Lashkar-e-Jabbar
LeT	Lashkar-e-Taiba
LoC	Line of Control
MC	Muslim Conference
MMA	Muttahida Majilis-e-Amal
MUF	Muslim United Front
NALC	Northern Areas Legislative Council
NC	National Conference
NCMC	National Crisis Management Cell
NDA	National Democratic Alliance
NGO	nongovernmental organization
NVDPP	Neelum Valley Disaster Preparedness Project
NVIDP	Neelum Valley Integrated Development Programme
PDP	People's Democratic Party
PML	Pakistan Muslim League
PoK	Pakistan-occupied Kashmir
POTA	Prevention of Terrorism Act
PPP	Pakistan People's Party
PRCS	Pakistan Red Crescent Society
ROKM	Relief Organization for Kashmiri Muslims
SAARC	South Asian Association for Regional Cooperation
SAFHR	South Asian Forum for Human Rights
SAFTA	South Asia Free Trade Area
SAPTA	South Asia Preferential Trade Agreement
SAW	Society for Advancement of Women
SIMI	Students' Islamic Movement of India, the
SOG	Special Operations Group
SSP	senior superintendent of police
UJC	United Jihad Council
UNCIP	United Nations Commission on India and Pakistan
UNMOGIP	UN Military Observer Group in India and Pakistan
UNSC	United Nations Security Council
UPA	United Progressive Alliance
VDC	Village Defense Committee
WISCOMP	Women in Security, Conflict Management, and Peace

Bibliography

Abdullah, Sheikh Mohammad. *Flames of the Chinar: An Autobiography.* Abridged, translated from Urdu, introduced by Khushwant Singh. New Delhi: Penguin India, 1995.

Adebajo, Adekeye, and Chandra Sriram, eds. *Managing Armed Conflict in the 21st Century.* Special issue, *International Peacekeeping* 7, no. 4 (Winter 2000).

Akbar, M. J. *India: The Siege Within.* Hammondsworth, Middlesex, UK: Penguin, 1985.

———. *Kashmir: Behind the Vale.* New Delhi: Viking, 1991.

Ali, Nasreen. "Diaspora and Nation: Displacement and the Politics of Kashmiri Identity in Britain." *Contemporary South Asia* 12, no. 4 (December 2003).

Amnesty International. *India: Punitive Use of Preventive Detention Legislation in Jammu and Kashmir.* ASA 20/10/00 (May 2000).

———. *A Trail of Unlawful Killings in Jammu and Kashmir: Chithisinghpora and Its Aftermath.* ASA 20/24/00 (June 2000).

———. *Impunity Must End in Jammu and Kashmir.* ASA 20/023/2001 (April 2001).

Arif, K. M. *Khaki Shadows: Pakistan 1947–1997.* Karachi: Oxford University Press, 2001.

Ayoob, Mohammed. "The Primacy of the Political: South Asian Regional Cooperation in Comparative Perspective." *Asian Survey* 25, no. 4 (April 1985).

———. *The Third World Security Predicament: State Making, Regional Conflict, and the International System.* Boulder: Lynne Rienner Publishers, 1995.

Azad, Maulana Abdul Kalam. *India Wins Freedom: An Autobiographical Narrative.* Bombay: Orient Longmans, 1959.

Banerjee, Dipankar, ed. *SAARC in the 21st Century: Towards a Cooperative Future.* New Delhi: India Research Press, 2002.

Banerjee, Dipankar, and Gert W. Kueck, eds. *South Asia and the War on Terrorism: Analysing the Implications of 11 September.* New Delhi: India Research Press, 2003.

Barnds, William J. *India, Pakistan and the Great Powers.* New York: Praeger, 1972.

Behera, Ajay Darshan. "The Supporting Structures for Pakistan's Proxy War in

Jammu & Kashmir." *Strategic Analysis* (Institute for Defence Studies and Analyses, New Delhi) 25, no. 3 (June 2001).

Behera, Navnita Chadha. *State, Identity and Violence: Jammu, Kashmir and Ladakh.* New Delhi: Manohar, 2000.

Berdal, Mats, and David Malone, eds. *Greed and Grievance: Economic Agendas in Civil War.* Boulder: Lynne Rienner Publishers, 2000.

Bhutto, Zulfiqar A. *The Myth of Independence.* Lahore: Oxford University Press, 1969.

Blinkenberg, Lars. *India-Pakistan: The History of Unsolved Conflicts.* Odense, Sweden: Odense University Press, 1998.

Bose, Sumantra. *Kashmir: Roots of Conflict, Paths to Peace.* Cambridge, MA: Harvard University Press, 2003.

Bukhari, Fayaz. "Dying Day by Day." *Himal* (Kathmandu). November 2002.

Burke, S. M. *Pakistan's Foreign Policy: An Historical Analysis.* Karachi: Oxford University Press, 1973.

Burley, Anne-Marie, and Walter Mattli. "Europe Before the Court: A Political Theory of Legal Integration," *International Organization* 47, no. 1 (Winter 1993).

Butalia, Urvashi. *The Other Side of the Silence: Voices from the Partition of India.* Durham, NC: Duke University Press, 2000.

Butalia, Urvashi, ed. *Speaking Peace: Women's Voices from Kashmir.* New Delhi: Kali for Women, 2002.

Cater, Charles K. *The Regionalization of Conflict and Intervention.* New York: International Peace Academy, May 2003.

Chandran, Suba. "Monitoring an Active Border: A Case for Neutral Observers." *Swords and Ploughshares* 25, no. 3 (Winter 2003–2004).

Chari, P. R., ed. *Perspectives on National Security in South Asia: In Search of a New Paradigm.* New Delhi: Manohar, 1999.

Chari, P. R., and Pervaiz Iqbal Cheema. *The Simla Agreement 1972: Its Wasted Promise.* New Delhi: Manohar, 2001.

Chari, P. R., Pervaiz Iqbal Cheema, and Stephen P. Cohen. *Perception, Politics and Security in South Asia: The Compound Crisis of 1990.* London: Routledge-Curzon, 2003.

Chari, P. R., Mallika Joseph, and Suba Chandran, eds. *India and Pakistan: The Agra Summit and After*, IPCS Topical Series I. New Delhi: Institute of Peace and Conflict Studies, 2001.

Cheema, Pervaiz Iqbal, and Imtiaz H. Bokhari. *Arms Race and Nuclear Developments in South Asia.* Islamabad: Asia Printers, 2004.

Chengappa, Raj. *Weapons of Peace.* New Delhi: HarperCollins, 2000.

Chopra, V. D., and M. Rasgotra, eds. *Genesis of Regional Conflicts: Kashmir, Afghanistan, West Asia, Cambodia, Chechnya.* New Delhi: Gyan Publishing House, 1995.

Choudhury, G. W. *Pakistan's Relations with India, 1947–1966.* London: Pall Mall, 1968.

Chowdhary, Rekha. "Debating Autonomy." *Seminar: Frameworks for Peace* (online), no. 296 (December 2000).

———. "Kashmir: Lone's Liberal Legacy." *Economic and Political Weekly* (Mumbai). 22 June 2002.

———. "Kashmir: Elections 2002: Implications for Politics of Separatism." *Economic and Political Weekly* (Mumbai). 4 January 2003.

Cohen, Stephen P. *India: Emerging Power.* Washington, DC: Brookings Institution Press, 2001.

———. *The Idea of Pakistan*. Washington, DC: Brookings Institution Press, 2004.

Council on Foreign Relations. *New Priorities in South Asia: U.S. Policy Toward India, Pakistan, and Afghanistan*. Chairman's Report on an Independent Task Force Co-sponsored by the Council on Foreign Relations and the Asia Society. New York: Council on Foreign Relations, 2003.

Cox, Michael, Adrian Guelke, and Fiona Stephen, eds. *A Farewell to Arms? From "Long War" to Long Peace in Northern Ireland*. Manchester: Manchester University Press, 2000.

Crawford, Beverly, and Ronnie D. Lipschutz, eds. *The Myth of "Ethnic Conflict": Politics, Economics, and "Cultural" Violence*. Berkeley: University of California Press, 1998.

Dabla, Bashir A. *Impact of Conflict Situation on Women and Children in Kashmir*. Srinagar: Save the Children Fund North West India, June 1999.

———. "Suicides in the Kashmir Valley." *New Hope Journal* (Kashmir Foundation for Hope and Peace, Srinagar) 2 (March–April 2001).

Dabla, Bashir A., Sandeep Nayak, and Khurshid-ul-Islam. *Gender Discrimination in the Kashmir Valley*. New Delhi: Gyan Publishing House, 2000.

Dasgupta, C. *War and Diplomacy in Kashmir, 1947–48*. New Delhi and Thousand Oaks, CA: Sage, 2002.

Desmond, Edward W. "Himalayan Ulster." *The New York Review of Books* 40, no. 5 (4 March 1993).

Dossani, Rafiq, and Henry S. Rowen, eds. *Prospects for Peace in South Asia*. Stanford: Stanford University Press, 2005.

Esposito, John L., and John O. Voll. *Islam and Democracy*. Karachi: Oxford University Press, 1996.

Fai, Ghulam Nabi. *"Kashmir: Past, Present and Future."* South Asian Journal (Lahore, online), January–March 2004.

Fair, Christine. *India and Pakistan Engagement: Prospects for Breakthrough or Breakdown*. United States Institute of Peace Special Report, January 2005.

Fearon, James D. "Why Do Some Civil Wars Last So Much Longer Than Others?" *Journal of Peace Research* 41, no. 3 (May 2004).

Fradkin, Hillel, Husain Haqqani, and Eric Brown, eds. *Current Trends in Islamist Ideology,* Volume 1. Washington, DC: Hudson Institute, 2005.

Ganguly, Sumit. *The Crisis in Kashmir: Portents of War, Hopes of Peace*. Cambridge: Cambridge University Press, 1997.

———. *Conflict Unending: India-Pakistan Tensions Since 1947*. New York: Columbia University Press, 2001.

Ganguly, Sumit, ed. *India as an Emerging Power*. London and Portland, OR: Frank Cass, 2003.

———. *The Kashmir Question: Retrospect and Prospect*. London and Portland, OR: Frank Cass, 2003.

Ghate, Prabhu. "Kashmir: The Dirty War." *Economic and Political Weekly* (Mumbai). 26 January 2002.

Gill, K. P. S. "J&K: Forward to the Past?" *South Asia Intelligence Review* (Institute for Conflict Management, New Delhi, online) 1, no. 15 (28 October 2002).

Gilligan, C., and J. Tonge, eds. *Peace or War? Understanding the Peace Process in Northern Ireland*. Ashgate, UK: Aldershot, 1997.

Goldhart, William, Dalmo de Abreu Dallari, Florence Butegwa, and Vitit Muntarbhorn. *Human Rights in Kashmir*. Geneva: International Commission of Jurists, 1995.

Gopal, S. *Jawaharlal Nehru: A Biography*. New Delhi: Oxford University Press, 1975.

Gossman, Patricia. *The Human Rights Crisis in Kashmir*. New York: Human Rights Watch, 1993.

Government of India, Ministry of Home Affairs. *Annual Report 2003–2004*.

———. *Annual Report 2004–2005*.

Grieco, Joseph M. *Cooperation Among Nations*. Ithaca: Cornell University Press, 1990.

Gundevia, Y. D. *Outside the Archives*. Hyderabad: Sangam Books, 1984.

Gupta, Amit, and Nazir Kamal. *Prospects of Conventional Arms Control in South Asia*. Albuquerque: Cooperative Monitoring Center, Sandia National Labs, 1998.

Gupta, Sisir. "The Indus Waters Treaty." *Foreign Affairs Reports* (New Delhi) 9, no. 12 (December 1960).

———. *Kashmir: A Study in India-Pakistan Relations*. London: Asia Publishing House, 1966.

Habibullah, Wahajat. *The Political Economy of the Kashmir Conflict*. United States Institute of Peace Special Report, June 2004.

Haftendorn, Helga, and Christin Tuschhoff, eds. *America and Europe in an Era of Change*. Boulder: Westview Press, 1999.

Hagerty, Devin. "Nuclear Deterrence in South Asia: The 1990 Indo-Pakistani Crisis." *International Security* (Winter 1995/1996).

Haider, Moinuddin. "Global Terrorism: Its Genesis, Implications, Remedial and Counter Measures." Paper prepared for seminar at the Institute of Regional Studies, Islamabad, June 2005.

Hans, Asha. "Women Across Borders in Kashmir: The Continuum of Violence." *Canadian Women's Studies* 19, no. 4 (Winter 2000).

Haqqani, Husain. "Pakistan's Endgame in Kashmir." *India Review* 2, no. 3 (July 2003).

Haqqani, Husain, and Ashley J. Tellis. *India and Pakistan: Is Peace Real This Time?* Washington, DC: Carnegie Endowment for International Peace, 2004.

Hasan, K. Sarwar, ed. *The Kashmir Question: Documents on the Foreign Policy of Pakistan*. Karachi: Pakistan Institute of International Affairs, 1966.

Hersh, Seymour. "On the Nuclear Edge." *The New Yorker* (29 March 1993).

Human Rights Commission of Pakistan. *State of Human Rights in Azad Jammu and Kashmir: Report of HRCP Fact-finding Mission*. Islamabad, July 2004.

Human Rights Watch Report. *India's Secret Army in Kashmir: New Patterns of Abuse Emerge in the Conflict*. Vol. 8, no. 4(c) (May 1996).

———. *Behind the Kashmir Conflict: Abuses by Indian Security Forces and Militant Groups Continue*. Vol. 7/99, C 1104 (July 1999).

Imroze, Parvez. "India's Civil Society Has Failed Kashmiri Society." *Communalism Combat* (Mumbai). August–September 2003.

Institute of Social Sciences. "Assembly Elections: Under the Shadow of Fear [summary of 2002 election report by Institute of Social Sciences, New Delhi]." *Economic and Political Weekly* (Mumbai). 26 October 2002.

International Crisis Group. *Kashmir: Confrontation and Miscalculation* (ICG Asia Report No. 35). Brussels and Islamabad, 11 July 2002.

———. *Kashmir: The View from Srinagar* (ICG Asia Report No. 41). Brussels and Islamabad, 21 November 2002.

———. *Kashmir: The View from Islamabad* (ICG Asia Report No. 68). Brussels and Islamabad, 4 December 2003.

———. *Kashmir: The View from New Delhi* (ICG Asia Report No. 69). Brussels and Islamabad, 4 December 2003.

————. *Kashmir: Learning from the Past* (ICG Asia Report No. 70). Brussels and Islamabad, 4 December 2003.

————. *India/Pakistan Relations and Kashmir: Steps Towards Peace* (ICG Asia Report No. 79). Brussels and Islamabad, 24 June 2004.

Jaffrelot, Christophe, ed. *Pakistan: Nationalism Without a Nation?* London: Zed Books, 2002; New Delhi: Manohar, 2002.

Jalal, Ayesha. "Kashmir Scars: A Terrible Beauty Is Torn." *The New Republic* (23 July 1990).

Jammu and Kashmir Coalition for Civil Society. "Kashmir Assembly Election: How Free and Fair? [summary of 2002 election report by Jammu and Kashmir Coalition for Civil Society]." *Economic and Political Weekly* (Mumbai). 11 January 2003.

Jamwal, N. S. "Terrorist Financing and Support Structures in Jammu and Kashmir." *Strategic Analysis* (Institute for Defence Studies and Analyses, New Delhi) 26, no. 1 (January–March 2002).

————. "Terrorists' Modus Operandi in Jammu and Kashmir." *Strategic Analysis* (Institute for Defence Studies and Analyses, New Delhi) 27, no. 3 (July–September 2003).

Jan, Sadaqat. "The POK Puppet Show." *Frontline* (New Delhi) 18, no. 16 (4–17 August 2001).

Jan, Tarik, and Ghulam Sarwar, eds. *Kashmir Problem: Challenge and Response.* Islamabad: Institute of Policy Studies, 1990.

Jayaraman, T. "Nuclear Crisis in South Asia." *Frontline* (New Delhi) 19, no. 12 (8–21 June 2002).

Jeelani, Aasia. "Turmoil and Trauma." *Voices Unheard: A Newsletter of Kashmiri Women's Initiative for Peace and Disarmament* (Srinagar). 2002.

Jha, Prem Shankar. *Kashmir 1947.* Delhi: Oxford University Press, 1996.

Joseph, Teresa. "Kashmir, Human Rights and the Indian Press." *Contemporary South Asia* 9, no. 1 (2000).

Joshi, Manoj. *The Lost Rebellion: Kashmir in the Nineties.* New Delhi: Penguin Books, 1999.

Kapila, Subhash. "India's New 'Cold Start' War Doctrine Strategically Reviewed." *South Asia Analysis Group.* Paper no. 991 (online), 4 May 2005.

Kargil Review Committee. *From Surprise to Reckoning: The Kargil Review Committee Report.* New Delhi and Thousand Oaks, CA: Sage, 2000.

Karnad, Bharat. *Nuclear Weapons and Indian Security.* Delhi: Macmillan, 2002.

Kartha, Tara. *Tools of Terror.* New Delhi: Knowledge World, 1999.

Kashmir Study Group. *Kashmir: A Way Forward.* Kashmir Study Group, February 2000.

Katakam, Anupama. "Terror in Mumbai." *Frontline* (New Delhi) 20, no. 7 (11 April 2003).

Kaul, Suvir, ed. *The Partitions of Memory: The Afterlife of the Division of India.* Bloomington: University of Indiana Press, 2001.

Keohane, Robert. *After Hegemony.* Princeton: Princeton University Press, 1984.

Khan, Akbar. *Raiders in Kashmir.* Delhi: Army Publishers, 1970.

King, Charles. *Ending Civil Wars.* Oxford: Oxford University Press, 1997.

Koithara, Verghese. *Crafting Peace in Kashmir: Through a Realist Lens.* New Delhi and Thousand Oaks, CA: Sage, 2004.

Korbel, Josef. *Danger in Kashmir.* Princeton: Princeton University Press, [1954] 1966.

Kraig, Michael Ryan. "The Political and Strategic Imperatives of Nuclear Deterrence in South Asia." *India Review* 2, no. 1 (2003).

Krepon, Michael. *The Stability-Instability Paradox, Misperceptions, and Escalation Control in South Asia.* Washington, DC: The Henry L. Stimson Center, May 2003.

Krepon, Michael, Jenny S. Denzin, and Michael Newbill, eds. *Declaratory Diplomacy: Rhetorical Initiatives and Confidence Building*, Report 27. Washington, DC: The Henry L. Stimson Center, May 1999.

Krepon, Michael, and M. Faruqee, eds. "Conflict Prevention and Confidence Building Measures in South Asia: The 1990 Crisis." Occasional Paper No. 17. Washington, DC: Henry L. Stimson Center, April 1994.

Krepon, Michael, and Chris Gagne. *Nuclear Risk Reduction in South Asia.* New Delhi: Vision Books, 2003.

Krepon, Michael, Rodney W. Jones, and Zaid Haider, eds. *Escalation Control and the Nuclear Option in South Asia.* Washington, DC: The Henry L. Stimson Center, 2004.

Krepon, Michael, and Amit Sevak, eds. *Crisis Prevention, Confidence Building, and Reconciliation in South Asia.* New Delhi: Manohar, 1996.

Kumar, D. P. *Kashmir: Return to Democracy.* New Delhi: Cosmo, 1996.

Kumaraswamy, P. R., ed. *Security Beyond Survival.* New Delhi and Thousand Oaks, CA: Sage, 2004.

Kydd, Andrew, and Barbara F. Walter. "Sabotaging the Peace: The Politics of Extremist Violence." *International Organization* 56, no. 2 (Spring 2002).

Lamb, Alastair. *Kashmir: A Disputed Legacy, 1846–1990.* Karachi: Oxford University Press, 1993.

Lifschutz, Lawrence. "Death in Kashmir: Perils of 'Self-determination.'" *Economic and Political Weekly* (Mumbai). 3 August 2002.

Malik, Iffat. *Kashmir: Ethnic Conflict, International Dispute.* Karachi: Oxford University Press, 2002.

Manchanda, Rita. "Playing with Fire." *Far Eastern Economic Review*, 26 September 1990.

———. "Kashmir's Worse-Off Half: Women Are the Silent Sufferers in the War over Kashmir." *Himal* (Kathmandu). May 1999.

Manchanda, Rita, ed. *Women, War, and Peace in South Asia: Beyond Victimhood to Agency.* New Delhi and Thousand Oaks, CA: Sage, 2001.

Manchanda, Rita, Bandita Sijapati, and Rebecca Gang. *Women Making Peace.* Kathmandu: South Asian Forum for Human Rights (SAFHR), 2002.

Martin, Lisa L. *Coercive Cooperation: Explaining Multilateral Economic Sanctions.* Princeton: Princeton University Press, 1992.

Matinuddin, Kamal. "India-Pakistan Standoff." *Regional Studies* (Institute of Regional Studies, Islamabad) 21, no. 3 (Summer 2003).

Mattoo, Amitabh. "India's 'Potential' Endgame in Kashmir." *India Review* 2, no. 3 (July 2003).

Mazari, Sher Khan. *A Journey to Disillusionment.* Karachi: Oxford University Press, 1999.

McGinty, Roger. *The Irish Peace Process: Background Briefing.* INCORE, University of Ulster, 20 April 1998.

McGrath, Allen. *The Destruction of Pakistan's Democracy.* Karachi: Oxford University Press, 1996.

McMahon, Robert J. *The Cold War on the Periphery: The United States, India and Pakistan.* New York: Columbia University Press, 1994.

Mehta, Jagat S. "The Indus Waters Treaty: A Case Study in the Resolution of an International River Basin Conflict." *National Resource Forum* (United Nations) 12, no. 1 (February 1988).

Menon, Rajan. "The New Great Game in Central Asia." *Survival* 45, no. 2 (2003).

Menon, Rajan, ed. *Weapons of Mass Destruction: Options for India*. New Delhi and Thousand Oaks, CA: Sage, 2004.

Menon, Ritu, and Kamila Bhasin. *Borders and Boundaries: Women in India's Partition*. New Brunswick, NJ: Rutgers University Press, 1998.

Mian, Zia, and Iftikar Ahmad, eds. *Making Enemies, Creating Conflict: Pakistan's Crisis of State and Society*. Lahore: Mashal, 1997.

Mir, Amir. *The True Face of Jehadis*. Lahore: Mashal, 2004.

Mishra, Pankaj. "The Birth of a Nation." *The New York Review of Books* 47, no. 15 (October 2000).

Mitchell, Ronald B. *Intentional Oil Pollution at Sea: Environmental Policy and Treaty Compliance*. Cambridge, MA: MIT Press, 1994.

Mohan, C. Raja. *Crossing the Rubicon: The Shaping of India's New Foreign Policy*. New Delhi: Viking, 2003.

Nair, Baldev Raj, and T. V. Paul. *India in the World Order: Searching for Major Power Status*. Cambridge: Cambridge University Press, 2003.

Nelson, Joan M. *Poverty, Inequality and Conflict in Developing Countries*. New York: Rockefeller Brothers Fund, 1998.

Neumann, Stephanie, ed. *International Relations Theory and the Third World*. New York: St. Martin's Press, 1997.

Noorani, A. G. "Article 370: Law and Politics." *Frontline* (New Delhi) 17, no. 19 (16–29 September 2000).

———. "Contours of Militancy." *Frontline* (New Delhi) 17, no. 20 (30 September–13 October 2000).

———. "The Dixon Plan." *Frontline* (New Delhi) 19, no. 21 (12–25 October 2002).

Oberoi, Surinder. "Kashmir Is Bleeding." *Bulletin of the Atomic Scientists* 53, no. 2 (March/April 1997).

Parker, Karen, and Ghulam Nabi Fai, eds. *Beyond the Blame Game: Finding Common Ground for Peace and Justice in Kashmir*. International Kashmir Peace Conference, Washington, DC, 2003.

Perkovich, George. *India's Nuclear Bomb: The Impact on Global Proliferation*. Berkeley and Los Angeles: University of California Press, 1999.

Perkovich, George, Jessica T. Mathews, Joseph Cirincione, Rose Gottemoeller, and Jon B. Wolfsthal. *Universal Compliance: A Strategy for Nuclear Security*. Washington, DC: Carnegie Endowment for International Peace, 2005.

Policzer, Pablo. "Neither Terrorists nor Freedom Fighters." Paper presented at the American Political Science Association Conference, Chicago, IL, 2–5 September 2004.

Prakash, Siddhartha. "The Political Economy of Kashmir Since 1947." *Contemporary South Asia* 9, no. 3 (November 2000).

Puri, Balraj. *Jammu and Kashmir: Triumph and Tragedy of Indian Federalisation*. New Delhi: Sterling, 1981.

———. "The Autonomy Debate." *Frontline* (New Delhi) 17, no. 6 (18–31 March 2000).

Qadir, Shaukat. "An Analysis of the Kargil Conflict 1999." *RUSI Journal* (April 2002).

Rana, Muhammad Amir. *Gateways to Terrorism*. London: New Millennium, 2003.

———. *A to Z of Jehadi Organizations in Pakistan*. Translated by Saba Ansari. Lahore: Mashal, 2004.

Rehman, Khalid, and Ershad Mehmood. *Kashmiri Refugees: Facts, Problems and Ways Out* (in Urdu). Islamabad: Institute of Policy Studies, 2003.

Riedel, Bruce. *American Diplomacy and the 1999 Kargil Summit at Blair House.* Policy Paper Series, Center for the Advanced Study of India, University of Pennsylvania, 2002.

Rizvi, Hasan-Askari. *Pakistan and the Geostrategic Environment: A Study of Foreign Policy.* London: Macmillan Press, 1993.

Rowen, Henry, and Rafiq Dossani, eds. *Peace and Security in South Asia.* Stanford: Stanford University Press, 2005.

Sahni, Sati. *Kashmir Underground.* New Delhi: Har-Anand, 1999.

Sangani, Kavita, and Teresita Schaffer. "India-Pakistan Trade: Creating Constituencies for Peace." *South Asia Monitor* (Center for Strategic and International Studies, Washington, DC) 56 (March 2003).

Sawhny, Karan R., ed. *Kashmir: How Far Can Vajpayee and Musharraf Go?* New Delhi: Peace Publications, 2001.

Schofield, Victoria. *Kashmir in the Crossfire.* London: I. B. Tauris, 1996.

———. *Kashmir in Conflict: India, Pakistan and the Unending War.* London: I. B. Tauris, 2003; New Delhi: Viva, 2003.

Shehzad, Mohammad. "For Dialogue and Armed Struggle, Together: Interview with Syed Salahuddin, Hizbul Mujahideen Leader." *Frontline* (New Delhi) 20, no. 11 (24 May–6 June 2003).

Sidhu, Waheguru Pal Singh. *Enhancing Indo-US Strategic Cooperation*, Adelphi Paper 313. Oxford: Oxford University Press, 1997.

Sikand, Yoginder. "The Changing Course of the Kashmiri Struggle: From National Liberation to Islamist Jihad?" *Muslim World* 91, no. 2 (Spring 2001).

———. "Hindu-Muslim Relations in Jammu: Alternative Ways of Understanding." *Qalandar* (online) no. 30 (March 2005).

Singh, Anita Inder. *The Origins of the Partition of India.* New Delhi: Oxford University Press, 1987.

Singh, Jasjit, ed. *Kargil 1999: Pakistan's Fourth War for Kashmir.* New Delhi: IDSA Knowledge World, 1999.

Singh, Tavleen. *Kashmir: Tragedy of Errors.* New Delhi: Viking, 1995.

———. "Kashmir: A View from India." *Logos Journal* (online) no. 4.1 (Winter 2005).

Sinha, S. K. "Jammu and Kashmir: Past, Present and Future [lecture to the United Service Institution of India, April 28, 2005]." *Journal of the United Service Institution of India* 135, no. 560 (April–June 2005).

Snyder, Glenn. *Deterrence and Defence.* Princeton: Princeton University Press, 1961.

Sood, V. K., and Pravin Sawhney. *Operation Parakram: The War Unfinished.* New Delhi and Thousand Oaks, CA: Sage, 2003.

Stedman, Stephen John. "Spoiler Problems in Peace Processes." *International Security* 22, no. 2 (Fall 1997).

Stern, Jessica. "Pakistan's Jihad Culture." *Foreign Affairs* 79, no. 6 (November/December 2000).

———. *Terror in the Name of God.* New York: Ecco, 2004.

Swami, Praveen. "A Beleaguered Force." *Frontline* (New Delhi) 16, no. 3 (January–12 February 1999).

———. "'Pro-Active' After Pokhran: A Perspective on Terrorism in J&K." *Faultlines* (Institute for Conflict Management, New Delhi, online) 1, no. 1 (May 1999).

Cyrus Samii was senior program officer for the International Peace Academy, New York, for the programs Kashmir: New Voices, New Approaches; International Presences in the Middle East Peace Process; and The Iraq Crisis and World Order, as well as for programs on regional organizations in peacekeeping. He is currently a doctoral candidate in political science at Columbia University, New York.

Waheguru Pal Singh Sidhu is currently a faculty member at the Geneva Centre for Security Policy, having previously served as senior associate with the International Peace Academy, New York, where he directed the project Kashmir: New Voices, New Approaches. His recent books include *The United Nations and Regional Security: Europe and Beyond* (coeditor with Michael Pugh) and *China and India: Cooperation or Conflict?* (coauthor with Jing-Dong Yuan).

Kavita Suri is special correspondent for *The Statesman* in Indian-administered Jammu and Kashmir. She was assistant director for a documentary film on Kashmiri Hindu refugees titled *And the World Remained Silent,* produced and directed by Ashok Pandit. She is presently a WISCOMP (Women in Security, Conflict Management, and Peace) fellow, researching the impact of terrorism on women's education in the Kashmir Valley, and she is also a doctoral candidate at Jammu University.

John Thomson was UK permanent representative at the United Nations in 1982–1987 and British high commissioner in India in 1977–1982. Before that he was undersecretary in charge of defense and disarmament, minister at NATO, chief of the assessments staff (seconded to the cabinet office), and head of policy planning. He has also served as director's visitor at the Institute for Advanced Study at Princeton, trustee of the Institute for Advanced Studies in the Humanities at Edinburgh, and senior fellow at the Lichtenstein Institute on Self-Determination at Princeton.

Rizwan Zeb is a research fellow at the Institute of Regional Studies, Islamabad, and visiting faculty at the Department of Defense and Strategic Studies at Quaid-i-Azam University, Islamabad. Recent publications include *Ghazi*, on the Special Service Group of the Pakistan Army, and (with Suba Chandran) *Indo-Pak Conflict: Ripe to Resolve?*

Index

About the Book

Uniquely representing all sides in the conflict over Kashmir, this innovative new book provides a forum for discussion not only of existing proposals for ending the conflict, but also of possible new paths toward settlement.

Contributors from India, Pakistan, and Kashmir explore the national and subnational dimensions of the ongoing hostilities, the role of the international community, and future prospects. The result is an informed overview of the present state of affairs—and a realistic examination of the potential for peaceful resolution.

Waheguru Pal Singh Sidhu is on the faculty of the Geneva Centre for Security Policy. He is coeditor of both *The United Nations and Regional Security: Europe and Beyond* and *China and India: Cooperation or Conflict?* **Bushra Asif** is a consultant with the Social Science Research Council (SSRC) in New York. **Cyrus Samii**, formerly senior program officer at the International Peace Academy, is a doctoral candidate in political science at Columbia University.